AF764648

THE

DIGEST OF JUSTINIAN

VOLUME II

THE DIGEST OF JUSTINIAN

TRANSLATED

BY

CHARLES HENRY MONRO, M.A.
FELLOW OF GONVILLE AND CAIUS COLLEGE CAMBRIDGE
BARRISTER AT LAW

VOLUME II

Cambridge
at the University Press
1909

CAMBRIDGE
UNIVERSITY PRESS

University Printing House, Cambridge CB2 8BS, United Kingdom

Cambridge University Press is part of the University of Cambridge.

It furthers the University's mission by disseminating knowledge in the pursuit of education, learning and research at the highest international levels of excellence.

www.cambridge.org
Information on this title: www.cambridge.org/9781107651012

First published 1909
First paperback edition 2014

A catalogue record for this publication is available from the British Library

ISBN 978-1-107-65101-2 Paperback

PREFATORY NOTE

AT the time of Mr C. H. Monro's lamented death 336 pages of this volume were already printed off, and there existed also a considerable amount of manuscript, on which he had been at work. This had not received his final revision, but it has been thought best to print it substantially as it stands, rectifying only a few obvious slips and omissions, too unimportant to call for indication. The parts of this volume not due to Mr Monro are the passages from D. 13. 7. 8. 4 to the end of the title, and from D. 14. 1. 1. 18 to the end of the volume.

I am sensible that the task of completing Mr Monro's volume ought to have fallen into better qualified hands. That my work is not worse than it is must be put down to the fact that I have had the advantage of Professor Reid's advice on many difficult passages. But as I have not ventured to impose on him the burden of revising the whole, the responsibility for all defects rests entirely on me. I can only hope that what is meant as an expression of gratitude may not discredit the memory to which it is dedicated.

W. W. BUCKLAND.

24 *March* 1909

CONTENTS.

VII.

VIII.

IX.

X.

XI.

XII.

XIII.

XIV.

XV.

ERRATUM.

p. 167 *read* TENTH BOOK.

I.

ON SETTLING BOUNDARIES.

DIGEST OF JUSTINIAN.

SEVENTH BOOK.

I.

On Usufruct and the Rights of the Usufructuary.

1 Paulus (*on Vitellius* 3) Usufruct is the right to enjoy the use and produce of another man's property without encroachment on the substance thereof.

2 Celsus (*Digest* 18) In fact, usufruct is a right over a material object, and, when the object is gone, the usufruct must needs go too.

3 Gaius (*Daily matters or golden things* 2) A usufruct can be created in any landed estate by way of legacy, the heir being ordered to convey the usufruct to the party; and he is held to convey it, if he takes the legatee on to the land or suffers him to enjoy the use and produce thereof. Even without a testament, however, if anyone wishes to create a usufruct, he can effect his object by means of pacts and stipulations. 1. A usufruct may exist[1] not only in lands and houses, but also in slaves, beasts of draught, and other kinds of property, 2. but in order to prevent the bare ownership becoming altogether valueless, in consequence of the usufruct being constantly outstanding, it has come to be held that the usufruct may be extinguished in certain definite ways and revert to the bare ownership. 3. Add that in whatever kind of way the usufruct is established or terminated, the bare *usus* can in practice be established or terminated in the same way.

4 Paulus (*on the Edict* 2) Usufruct is, in respect of many incidents, a portion of the ownership, and it is a distinguishable thing (*exstat*)[2], as it can be made to take effect either at once or from and after a day named.

5 Papinianus (*Questions* 7) A usufruct can from the very first be created with respect to an undivided share in a thing or a several share; it can also in both cases equally be lost by lapse

[1] For *constitit* read *consistit*. [2] Cf. Roby.

of the statutable period, and on the same principle be reduced in pursuance of the *lex Falcidia*; moreover, on the death of one who promised [to grant a usufruct], the burden of the obligation is divided according to the shares held in his inheritance, and if the usufruct has to be given in a landed estate which is owned in common, then, if one of the co-owners should be defendant in an action [brought to enforce the obligation], the conveyance which will have to be made will correspond with the share of the one so defending.

6 GAIUS (*on the provincial Edict* 7) A usufruct can be created in several different ways; for example, by way of legacy. On the other hand the bare ownership itself can be given by way of legacy, with reservation of the usufruct, so as to let such usufruct remain with the heir. 1. Moreover, a usufruct may be created on an action *familiæ erciscundæ* (for dividing an inheritance) or *communi dividundo* (partitioning common property), the judge making an order which gives the bare ownership to one party and a usufruct to the other. 2. People may acquire usufructs not only directly, but also through any persons whom they have under their *potestas.* Moreover, there is nothing to prevent my slave being appointed heir and thereupon the bare ownership being left by way of legacy with the reservation of the usufruct.

7 ULPIANUS (*on Sabinus* 17) When a usufruct is left by way of legacy, the whole produce of the property goes to the usufructuary. A usufruct may be bequeathed either in landed property or in something movable. 1. Where a usufruct is left in landed property, say a house, all returns from the property go to the usufructuary, as well as anything there may be coming from buildings, courtyards and whatever else is appurtenant to the house. Accordingly, the law is that the usufructuary can have an order authorizing him to take possession of an adjoining house on the ground of *damnum infectum* (anticipated damage), and that he will hold possession of the same as owner, if the other party persist in withholding security, and this without losing anything when the usufruct expires. On the same principle, so Labeo says, the owner of the property is not at liberty even to raise the height of the building without your [the usufructuary's] consent, just as, where the bequest is of the usufruct of a vacant space, a building cannot be erected on the spot; and this opinion I should say is correct. 2. Seeing then that the whole produce of the thing goes to the usufructuary, he can, in fact, so we read in Celsus (*Dig.* 18), be

compelled, by application to the judge, to repair the house; so far only, however, as to keep it wind- and water-tight; but if any part should have collapsed from age, neither party is bound to repair it, though, if the heir does repair it, he must allow the usufructuary to use it. Hereupon Celsus raises the question as to how far the usufructuary must keep it wind- and water-tight, assuming that he is not compellable to repair what has collapsed from age; and, in fact, [as he tells us,] he is chargeable with [only] a moderate amount of repair, seeing that, if he is legatee of the usufruct, he undertakes other burdens as well, such as *stipendium* and *tributum* (property taxes), or a personal allowance[1], or an alimentary provision charged by testament on the property. This we read in Marcellus (b. 13.) 3. Cassius too says (*Jus civile* 8) that, by application to the judge, a usufructuary may be compelled to repair, just as he is compelled to plant trees; and all this, so Aristo observes, is sound. What Neratius says (*Parchments* 4) is that the usufructuary cannot be prevented from repairing, just as he cannot be prevented from ploughing or cultivating; and not only may he execute necessary repairs, but he may make improvements of a luxurious description, such as plastering, ornamental flooring and the like; still he is not at liberty to enlarge the buildings or to remove anything that is of use,

8 THE SAME (*on the Edict* 40) even where he intends to put something better in the place; and this view is correct.

9 THE SAME (*on Sabinus* 17) Again, if there is a legacy of the usufruct of land, then, whatever springs on the land and whatever can be gathered on it is produce (*fructus*) and belongs to the legatee, provided always that he takes it in accordance with [what would be] the judgment of a fair arbitrator; in fact, Celsus himself declares (*Dig.* 18) that he may be compelled to cultivate properly. 1. And, if there are bees on the land, he has a right to the usufruct in these as well. 2. If the land contains stone quarries, and he desires to hew stone, or it has chalk-pits or sand-pits, according to Sabinus, he has a right to work all these as a careful proprietor would work them, and with this opinion I agree. 3. Even if these quarries were discovered subsequently to the bequest of the usufruct, what was bequeathed being the usufruct of the whole field, and not of portions of it, they still are included in the legacy. 4. Closely connected with the above is a point often

[1] *Salarium*: perhaps read *solarium*, ground-rent. M.

discussed as to cases of accession: and the rule adopted is that the rights of the usufructuary extend to alluvial ground. If however an island makes its appearance in a river over against some estate, Pegasus has it that no usufruct therein belongs to the usufructuary of the riparian land, though it is an accession to the bare ownership; it is, he says, so to speak, a special estate, the usufruct in which does not belong to you. There is something to be said for this view: where the increase is imperceptible, the usufruct itself is enlarged, but where the part added by accretion is plainly discernible by itself, it does not accrue so as to benefit the usufructuary. 5. Again, Cassius tells us (*Jus civile* 8) that profits derived from fowling and hunting go to the usufructuary, consequently those from fishing do so too. 6. The produce of a nursery bed, I should say, will go to the usufructuary, with liberty to him, that is, both to sell and to plant, but he is bound, with a view to the re-stocking of the land, to have the nursery bed ready and always renew it, as a sort of working plant for the land, so that it can be handed over to the owner when the usufruct expires. 7. Of [actual] working plant he has a right to the produce, but he is not at liberty to sell it; the fact is that if there is a bequest of a usufruct in land, and there is some field from which the owner was in the habit of getting stakes or osiers or reeds for purposes connected with the land a usufruct in which was bequeathed, I should say that the usufructuary can make use of the field; subject to this, that he must not sell anything out of it, unless, of course, it so happen that a usufruct was left him in the actual willow bed or the wood containing the stakes or in the bed of reeds; if that should be the case, he can sell: Trebatius himself says that the usufructuary can cut coppice and beds of reed to the extent to which it was generally done by the proprietor, and can sell, even where such proprietor himself was not in the habit of selling [what he cut] but of using it: the position of the usufructuary must be regarded with reference to the quantity that is taken, not to the nature of the use made of it.

10 POMPONIUS (*on Sabinus* 5) From coppice the usufructuary may take props and boughs from trees; from wood which is not coppice he can take what he wants for his vineyard, provided he does not impoverish the estate.

11 PAULUS (*the Digest of Alfenus epitomized* 2) But where the trees are of great size he is not allowed to fell them.

12 ULPIANUS (*on Sabinus* 17) Where trees are pulled up or thrown down by the force of the wind, the usufructuary, according to Labeo, can carry them away simply for his own use and for [the needs of] his house, but he must not use the timber for fuel, if he has some other source of supply for that purpose; and this I hold to be correct; otherwise it would follow that, if the whole estate should be visited by the above mishap, the usufructuary could carry off every single tree. Labeo holds however that he can cut down timber so far as is required for the repair of the house, in the same way, he adds, as he can burn lime or dig gravel or take anything whatever which is needed for buildings. 1. Where the legacy is of the usufruct of a ship, I should say that the ship may be sent on a voyage, even though there should be some danger of shipwreck, as the very object of having a ship is to send her to sea. 2. The usufructuary can either take the produce of the thing himself or assign the right to take it to someone else, or he can lease such right or sell it; a man who leases uses and so does a man who sells. Indeed, if he grants it to someone on *precarium* (at will), or gives it away, I should say that he uses it, and consequently retains the usufruct; this is stated in fact by Cassius and Pegasus, and it is approved of by Pomponius (Extracts from Sabinus 5). We may add that I do not retain the usufruct merely where I let it myself; even where someone lets it as a voluntary agent on my behalf, I still, according to Julianus (b. 35), retain it. Suppose, however, instead of my letting it, that such voluntary agent, in my absence and without my knowledge, enjoys the use and produce himself: I still retain the usufruct, in virtue of the fact that I have acquired an action on *negotia gesta*, and this is supported by Pomponius (b. 5). 3. On one point Pomponius is doubtful. Suppose a runaway slave in whom I have a usufruct stipulates for something on the ground of my property (*ex re mea*), or takes delivery of something: do I retain the usufruct [in the man] by this fact, on the principle that I am thereby using him? On the whole he accepts the view that I do. Very often, he says, a man may not be making use of slaves on the spot, but yet he retains a usufruct in them; for instance, where a slave is sick, or he is a child, and so cannot discharge any service, or where he is a man in extreme old age; there is no doubt that if you plough a field, and the field is so barren that it bears no crops, still you retain the usufruct. Julianus however (*Dig.* 35) says that, even without the runaway slave making any stipulation at all, the usufruct may still be retained; the owner, he says, retains possession

even when the slave has taken to flight, and exactly on the same principle a usufruct may be retained too. 4. He also discusses the following point: suppose someone [under these circumstances,] acquires possession of the slave, must we hold that, just as the slave ceases to be possessed by the bare owner, so too the usufruct is lost? To this he says, first of all, that it may be maintained that the usufruct is lost, but even granting this to be the case, it must still be held that whatever the slave may have stipulated for on the ground of the property of the usufructuary within the legal period goes[1] to the usufructuary. From this, he says, we may infer that, even if the slave is in the possession of someone else, still the usufruct is not lost, provided always the man actually stipulates for something on my behalf, and it makes very little difference whether he has got into the possession of the heir, or of someone to whom the inheritance was sold, or of someone who acquired the bare property by a legacy, or of a mere depredator; all that is required to enable the usufruct to be retained being a disposition of mind amounting to a desire to retain it, and some act or other done by the slave on behalf of the usufructuary. This opinion is not unsound. 5. Julianus (*Dig.* 35) discusses the following question. Suppose a thief plucks or cuts off ripe fruit on the tree; who can sue him in a *condictio* (personal action to recover it)? is it the owner of the land or the usufructuary? As to this, he holds that as fruit does not become the property of the usufructuary unless he gathers it, even though someone else should sever it from the ground, it rather follows that it is the bare owner who has a right to bring the *condictio*, but the usufructuary has the right of action for theft, because he had an interest in the fruit being left where it was. On the other hand, Marcellus is struck with the consideration that, if the usufructuary afterwards gets hold of the fruit in question, it will perhaps become his property; and, if it does, what other account can you give of the matter than the following: that the property in such fruit first passes to the owner, and then, when the usufructuary gets hold of it, it becomes his? The case would resemble that of a thing which is bequeathed on a condition, which is, for a time, the property of the heir, but, as soon as the condition is fulfilled, passes to the legatee. In fact, the truth is that the right of *condictio* belongs to the bare proprietor; but, when the ownership is in suspense, (to use Julianus's own language as applied to the case of young which are allowed to grow up and to a thing delivery of which has been

[1] del. *potest.* M.

taken by a slave in whom there is a usufruct, where he has not yet paid the price, but, however, has given security to the vendor,) it is correct to say that the right to bring a *condictio* is in suspense, †and that still more the ownership is in suspense†[1].

13 THE SAME (*on Sabinus* 18) If there is a legacy of the usufruct in anything, the bare owner can claim security in respect of the thing, this to be ordered on motion made to the judge (*officio judicis*); for, just as the usufructuary has a right to use and produce, so the bare owner has a right to be assured in respect of his ownership. This applies to every usufruct, as Julianus agrees (*Dig.* 38). On a legacy of a usufruct, the usufructuary ought not to be allowed to bring an action for it until he gives security that he will use and take the produce in such wise as to satisfy a reasonable arbitrator; and if there are several [heirs] at whose charge the usufruct is left, security should be given to every one separately. 1. Accordingly, when an action is brought in the matter of a usufruct, the judgment does not turn simply on what has been done already, but involves also directions as to the exercise of the right of usufruct for the future. 2. For cases of damage already done the usufructuary is answerable under the *lex Aquilia* as well, and he is liable to an Interdict *quod vi et clam*, so Julianus says; there being no doubt at all that a usufructuary is amenable to the proceedings mentioned and also to actions for theft, just like any other person who should have been guilty of any such offences in respect of another man's property. Moreover, to the question what is the use of the prætor holding out a special action when there was already a good right of action under the *lex Aquilia*, [Julianus] replied that whereas there were cases in which the action under the *lex Aquilia* was not available, for that reason a judge was assigned, so that the party might go by his decision; a man, for instance, who does not plough up the arable land, who does not plant fresh vines, or who allows watercourses to fall out of repair is not liable under the *lex Aquilia*. Similar rules apply to a man who has the *usus* simply. 3. If a dispute should arise between two usufructuaries, Julianus lays down (*Dig.* 38) that the fairest plan is that they should be allowed actions analogous to the *communi dividundo*, or else that they should give mutual undertakings by stipulation as to the way in which they will exercise their respective usufructs; why, asks Julianus, should the prætor allow them to proceed to the extremity of an armed conflict, when he is able to

[1] Meaning obscure and text doubtful. Some would omit the last clause. Cf. M.

bring them to terms by the exercise of his judicial authority? This opinion is upheld by Celsus himself (*Dig.* 20), and I agree that it is sound. 4. A usufructuary has no right to make the owner's position worse, but he is at liberty to make it better. [In the first place,] it may be that what was bequeathed was a usufruct in land, and then the usufructuary is not allowed to cut down fruit-trees or to destroy the mansion or to do anything that will injure the bare property. If the estate happened to be one that was used for purposes of luxury, and contained pleasure-grounds, alleys, or shady and agreeable walks under trees other than fruit-trees, he has no right to fell such trees in order to make, say, kitchen-gardens or anything else calculated to bring in profit. 5. Hereupon the question has been asked whether the usufructuary himself may open quarries or chalk-pits or gravel-pits; and I should say that he may go as far as this, provided it will not entail his taking with a view thereto some part of the arable land itself which is required [for other purposes]. Accordingly he can search for beds suitable either for quarrying or for mining operations similar thereto, so that he can either work such mines of gold, silver, sulphur, copper, iron, and other minerals as were opened by the owner, or he may open them himself, if this does not obstruct agricultural operations; and should it chance that there is more to be got by such workings than by the vineyards, plantations or olive groves which are there already, perhaps he will be allowed to cut these down, seeing that he is at liberty to improve the position of the bare owner. 6. Where however the works set on foot by the usufructuary poison the atmosphere of the farm (*agri*) or are likely to require large numbers of workmen, pickers, etc., so that the whole thing is more than the bare owner of the estate can put up with, the usufructuary cannot be held to be exercising his right in accordance with the view that would be held by an impartial arbitrator. We learn further that he cannot erect a building on the land, except such a one as is necessary in connexion with the gathering of produce. 7. [Secondly] the thing in which a usufruct was left may be a house, and then, as Nerva the son says, the usufructuary may even put in windows, and he can also add wall-paint, pictures, marble slabs, statuettes, or anything else that serves for ornament to a dwelling-house. But he will not be allowed to alter the shape of rooms, or throw them together, or divide them, or reverse the front or back doors, or throw open retired places, or alter the hall, or make a different arrangement of the pleasure-grounds; in short, what he can do is to improve what he finds without altering the character of the house. Moreover, according to Nerva, a legatee of the usufruct of a house is not at liberty to raise the height of the building, even if this should obstruct no lights, because the roof would be more exposed to disturbance ; and Labeo lays down the same rule as to the bare owner. Nerva adds that the usufructuary cannot block up windows. 8. Where, again, the usufruct is of a dwelling-house, the usufructuary cannot let out lodgings in it, or break the house up into separate apartments ; no doubt, he may let, but he must let the whole as one dwelling-house. Add that he must not set up a public bath there. With regard to the statement that he must not let out lodgings, this must be understood to mean what are commonly called *deversoria* (travellers' quarters), or *fullonica* (fullers' workshops). For my own part, I should say that, even where there is a bath in the house which is commonly available for the use of the owner's household and is placed in some retired part of the house or among agreeable apartments, he would not be acting rightly nor in accordance with what would be held by a reasonable arbitrator, if he were to proceed to let it out for public use, any more than if he were to let the house as a place to stall horses, or, where the house had a building available for a stable and coach-house, he were to let it as a bakery,

14 PAULUS (*on Sabinus* 3) even though he would make much less profit by the practice.

15 ULPIANUS (*on Sabinus* 18) If however he should affix any structure to the house he cannot afterwards take it down or detach it ; no doubt anything once detached he can claim at law as owner. 1. Further, where the usufruct[1] bequeathed is of slaves, he must not put them to a wrong use, he must deal with them in accordance with the characters of the respective slaves. If he sends a copying clerk into the country and makes him carry a hod of lime, turns an actor into a bath attendant or a concert singer into a hall porter, or takes a man from the wrestling ground and sets him to superintend the emptying[2] of privies, he will be held to be making a wrong use of the property of the bare owner. 2. He is bound further to furnish the slaves with food and clothing corresponding to their respective ranks and characters. 3. In fact, Labeo lays down the general rule that, in the case of movables of every kind, the usufructuary must keep within certain limits, so as not to spoil them by special roughness

[1] For *usus fructus* read *usu fructu*, cf. M.
[2] For *stercorandis* read *destercorandis*, cf. M.

or hard usage; indeed otherwise he can even be sued under the *lex Aquilia.* 4. And, if the usufruct bequeathed is in articles of clothing, the bequest not being in terms implying the usufruct of a quantity [but of specific things], the proper rule is that the usufructuary must so use the things as not to use them up; still he must not let them out, as a respectable man would not make that use of them. 5. Accordingly, if the usufruct bequeathed were of theatrical apparel or curtains or equipment of some other kind, he must not use anything anywhere but on the stage. Whether he may go so far as to let [such things] out is a point to consider, but I should say that he may, and even where the testator's own practice was to lend them and not to let them for hire, still I think the fructuary may let both theatrical and funeral attire. 6. The owner of the bare property has no right to interfere with the fructuary so long as the latter uses the thing in such a way as not to put him [the owner] in a worse position. In the case of some things, there is a doubt whether the proprietor would be acting within his rights if he forbad the other to use them, such as tuns, in the case, for instance, of a usufruct of land, and some hold that the use may be forbidden, even where the tuns are let into the ground, and they hold the same of vats, barrels, jars, and pitchers, also of window-panes, where the usufruct bequeathed is of a house. I should say however, unless there were an intention to the contrary, that the whole equipment of the land or the house is included. 7. The bare proprietor cannot subject the land to a servitude, nor is he at liberty to let a servitude be lost; no doubt, so Julianus tells us, he can acquire a servitude, even against the will of the fructuary. On the same principle, the fructuary cannot acquire a servitude for the land, but he can keep one up; and we may add that if any servitude should be lost by the fructuary's non-user, he will be liable on that account. The owner of the property cannot subject the land to a servitude even with the fructuary's consent,

16 PAULUS (*on Sabinus* 3) unless it be one by which the fructuary's position would be none the worse; for example, where the owner grants a servitude to a neighbour to the effect that he himself shall not have the right to raise his house.

17 ULPIANUS (*on Sabinus* 18) He may make the spot religious with the usufructuary's consent; this is held in deference to religion. Indeed in some cases the proprietor can make the ground religious even without such consent; suppose, for instance, he buries the body of the testator in it, there being no other equally convenient place for the interment. 1. It being assumed that the proprietor is not to put the fructuary in a worse position, the question is often asked whether the owner of a slave [in whom someone has a usufruct] can punish him. According to a note to Cassius by Aristo, he has an unrestricted right of punishment, provided he acts without malice [towards the usufructuary], although the usufructuary is not allowed to spoil the slave's capacity by calling upon him for unsuited or unaccustomed services, or to disfigure him with scars. 2. The owner however may very well surrender the slave for *noxa*, if he does it without malicious intent, as surrender for *noxa* does not by law put an end to usufruct any more than does acquisition of the ownership by use, where this takes place after the usufruct has been created. It is true that no action can be allowed for recovery of the usufruct, unless the amount at which the value of the matter in question in the noxal action is assessed is offered by the fructuary to the surrenderee. 3. Should anyone kill the slave, I never had any doubt that the fructuary may have an *utilis actio*, framed on the lines of the *lex Aquilia*.

18 PAULUS (*on Sabinus* 3) Where the usufruct bequeathed is of a field, fresh trees must be planted in the place of any that have died off, and the old ones will belong to the usufructuary.

19 POMPONIUS (*on Sabinus* 5) Proculus holds that [the usufruct in][1] a block of chambers can be bequeathed in such terms as to subject it to a servitude to exist in favour of some other block forming part of the inheritance, in some such words as these :—"If such a one promises my heir that nothing shall be done on his part so as to raise the height of such and such buildings, then I give and bequeath to him the usufruct of the said buildings": or as follows :—"I give and bequeath to such a one the usufruct of such a house so long as it shall not be built higher than as it now stands." 1. If, where trees are blown down by the wind, the proprietor does not take them away, the result being that a usufruct in the estate or a footway over it is enjoyed less commodiously, the usufructuary can sue him by the appropriate action.

20 ULPIANUS (*on Sabinus* 18) If a man makes a legacy as follows: "I give and bequeath the yearly produce of the Cornelian estate to Gaius Mævius," these words ought to be understood to amount to the same thing as a legacy of the usufruct in the estate.

[1] Cf. M.

21 THE SAME (*on Sabinus* 17) If the usufruct bequeathed is of a slave, then whatever the slave acquires by his own services or through the property of the fructuary belongs to the latter, whether the slave stipulates or takes delivery of possession. But, if the slave is appointed heir to some one or receives a legacy, Labeo makes a distinction turning on the question for whose sake it is that he is appointed heir or gets the legacy.

22 THE SAME (*on Sabinus* 18) Again, the question arises what ought to be done where a gift is made to a slave in whom someone has a usufruct. In any such case, if something was left or given to the slave with a view to the benefit of the fructuary, the slave acquires for the latter; if it was for the benefit of the bare proprietor, he acquires for such proprietor; if it was for the sake of the slave himself, he acquires for his owner, and the law does not consider the question how the donor or testator got his knowledge of the slave or to whom he is indebted for it. Moreover, if a slave in whom there is a usufruct has something given him by way of fulfilling a condition, and it is ascertained that the condition was inserted with a view to the benefit of the fructuary, the correct view is that what is given goes to the latter; it may be remembered that the rule is the same in the case of a *donatio mortis causa*.

23 THE SAME (*on Sabinus* 17) But just as the slave by stipulating acquires for the benefit of the fructuary, so too, according to Julianus (*Dig.* 30), he can by informal agreement acquire an *exceptio* for the fructuary. He says further that by taking a formal release he can procure a discharge for the fructuary. 1. And as we have already said that what is acquired by the slave's services goes to the fructuary, it should be understood that the slave may be compelled to work; in fact, according to a written opinion of Sabinus and a dictum of Cassius (*Jus civile* 8), the fructuary has a right to inflict moderate corporal punishment; only he must not put the slave to the torture nor scourge him severely.

24 PAULUS (*on Sabinus* 10) If a man, intending to make a gift to one who has the usufruct of a slave, makes a formal promise on the stipulation of the slave himself, he will contract an obligation towards the usufructuary; as it is a matter of ordinary usage that a slave in the position in question should be able to make a stipulation for the usufructuary.

25 ULPIANUS (*on Sabinus* 18) Moreover if a man stipulates for something for himself or Stichus, a slave held in usufruct [by someone else], intending thereby a gift to the usufructuary, the proper view to take is that if the money is paid to the slave, it will belong to the usufructuary. 1. Sometimes however the question for whom it is that a slave so held in usufruct acquires is in suspense; suppose, for instance, he [the slave] purchases a slave and takes delivery, without, so far, paying the purchase money, but only giving security to the vendor that it shall be paid, and, in the meantime, the question is asked who owns the slave [so purchased]. To this Julianus says (*Dig.* 35) that the ownership is in suspense, and the payment of the purchase money will determine who is owner; and that, if payment is made out of the monies of the fructuary, the slave had been his by relation back: and in fact the same holds where, to take another case, a slave [held in usufruct] makes a stipulation for the repayment of money which he is going to advance; here the advance itself will determine the question who gets the benefit of the stipulation. It is evident then from this that the ownership is in suspense until the price is paid. What however is to be said in a case where the price is only paid after the usufruct has come to an end? Julianus says (*Dig.* 35) that the essential question still is where the payment came from; but Marcellus and Mauricianus hold that, as soon as the usufruct is gone, the ownership [in the slave purchased] will appertain to the person who has the property [in the slave who made the purchase]; however the view of Julianus is the more indulgent. Should the price be paid out of the monies of both [proprietor and usufructuary], then, according to Julianus, the ownership will appertain to both, rateably, that is, according to the respective sums which they paid. Supposing, however, the slave pays out of the monies of both on one and the same occasion, for instance, he had to pay ten thousand as the price, and he paid ten [thousand] out of the monies of each, for which of the two does the slave really make the acquisition? [The answer is that,] if he pays by counting out the money, the question is who was owner of the coins paid first; as for those paid afterwards, he [, the other owner,] can sue to recover them as owner, or, if the money is already paid away by the recipient, it is a case for a *condictio* [to recover the amount]; but if the slave pays the whole sum [of twenty thousand] in a bag, he does not pass the property in anything to the recipient, and consequently he is not held so far to acquire for anyone the property

in the thing bought; as, where the slave pays more than the price, he does not pass the property in the money. 2. If the same slave lets out his own services and stipulates for a definite sum to be paid every year, this stipulation, so far as it relates to the years for which the usufruct lasts, will entitle the usufructuary, but, so far as it relates to the ensuing years, although at the outset it entitled the usufructuary, it passes to the bare owner, true as it is that, as a rule, when title under a stipulation is once acquired to any particular person, it does not pass to anyone else, unless it be to his heir or to someone by whom he is arrogated. On a similar principle, in a case in which the usufruct [in a slave] is bequeathed for every one of a number of years in succession, and the slave hires out his services with a stipulation such as above mentioned, with every loss of the usufruct by *capitis diminutio* and subsequent reacquisition of the same, the benefit of the stipulation will shift, and, after going to the heir, it will come back to the usufructuary. 3. It is a matter of question whether gain which is not allowed to go to the usufructuary must needs go to the bare proprietor. As to this, Julianus lays down (*Dig.* 35) that gain which will not go to the fructuary does in fact go to the bare proprietor. Lastly, he says that where a slave stipulates on the strength of the fructuary's property for the bare owner expressly or by his order, he acquires for such owner; but, on the other hand, if he stipulates for the fructuary, not on the strength of the fructuary's property nor yet in consideration of his own services, the stipulation is inoperative. 4. If a slave who is held by way of usufruct stipulates for a conveyance of the usufruct in himself, either without naming any particular person or on behalf of his bare proprietor expressly, he acquires for such proprietor, the case being like that of a slave owned by two persons in common, in which, if the slave stipulates on behalf of one of his owners for something which already belongs to such owner, the stipulation is void, because, when a man stipulates for his own property, it is a void act, but, if the slave stipulates on behalf of the other owner [for the same thing], he acquires the whole [for him]. 5. The same writer, Julianus, in the same book, has the following: if the usufructuary lets out the slave's services to the slave himself, this is null and void; as a matter of fact, he says, if a slave in whom I have a usufruct makes a stipulation with me founded on my property, this has no effect, any more than, if another man's slave who should be serving me in good faith did the same thing, he would acquire title for his owner. Similarly, he adds, even if the slave hires my property from me, the usufructuary, this will not bind me. In short, the general rule he lays down is this: where a slave [in whom I have a usufruct], by making a stipulation with another, would acquire for me, any stipulation which he makes with me for the same thing is inoperative; unless indeed, Julianus adds, he stipulates with me or hires from me expressly on his owner's behalf. 6. If you put the case of two fructuaries [of the same slave], and the slave makes a stipulation for something on the strength of the property of one of them, the question arises whether that one becomes entitled to the whole, or only to a share such as he has in the usufruct. It may be remembered indeed that the very same question is discussed in Scævola (Questions 2) with reference to the case of two *bona fide* possessors; what that author says is that it is commonly held and in fact stands to reason that, if the slave's stipulation is founded on the property of one of the two, then part is acquired for that one exclusively [of the other], and part for the owner; but, if the stipulation is made [on behalf of either] expressly, it does not admit of doubt, the name of the party being mentioned, that he acquires the whole. A similar result follows, he says, where the slave stipulates by the order of one of the two; as an order is taken to be equivalent to express mention. The same rule must be applied in the case of fructuaries too, so that, in any case in which what goes to the fructuary is less than the whole, it [that is, the rest,] will go to the bare proprietor; we have already shown that he [such proprietor] can acquire by a title founded on the property of the fructuary. 7. With regard to the statement made above that the fructuary can acquire [through the slave] by a title founded on his own property or on the slave's services, a point to consider is whether this applies only where the usufruct is created by way of legacy, or it holds equally where the title is founded on delivery or stipulation or any other ground. But the correct view is that of Pegasus, which in fact is followed by Julianus (b. 16), that the fructuary acquires in every case.

26 PAULUS (*on Sabinus* 3) If a slave held in usufruct lets out his services, and, before the expiration of the period of service agreed on, the usufruct comes to an end, the period runs on for the benefit of the bare proprietor. Moreover, where the slave at the outset stipulates for a fixed sum as the consideration for a fixed amount of service, if he [the usufructuary] suffers *capitis diminutio*, a similar result follows.

27 ULPIANUS (*on Sabinus* 18) If the testator left fruit on the tree already ripe, the fructuary will get them, if he found them still on the tree when the legacy vested; in fact even standing crops go to the fructuary. 1. Where the owner was in the habit of using shops for the sale of his wares or the transaction of business, then no doubt the fructuary will be at liberty to let them for the sale of wares, even though these should be of a different kind; all that has to be attended to is that the usufructuary do not destroy the character of the property nor make use of his usufruct in a manner which amounts to an insult or affects the proprietor's good name. 2. Where the usufruct bequeathed is that of a slave whom the testator used to employ, so to speak, for indeterminate services, if the usufructuary gives him some kind of schooling or teaches him an accomplishment, he can make use of the accomplishment or skill so acquired. 3. If anything is owing by way of a charge for drains or has to be paid for the channel of an aqueduct which crosses the land, this burden will fall on the fructuary; and if there is anything due by way of a contribution for keeping up the highway, I should say that the fructuary will have to bear this too; and, on the same principle, where anything has to be contributed out of the produce on the occasion of troops passing, or, again, has to be paid to the municipal authorities, all these dues will be chargeable to the fructuary; as a matter of fact, possessors of land are in the practice of assigning to the municipal authorities a fixed portion of their produce at a reduced valuation, as also of discharging taxation[1] due to the Treasury. 4. If the land has been subjected to any kind of servitude, the fructuary will be bound to allow it, and consequently, if there is an obligation to create a servitude existing in pursuance of a stipulation, I should say the rule is the same. 5. We may add this question: if a slave has been sold, but the purchaser is debarred under a penalty from putting him to certain specified uses, and then there is a bequest of a usufruct in the slave, is the usufructuary bound to attend to the same restrictions? My opinion is that he is so bound; otherwise he is not enjoying the usufruct in accordance with what would be held by an impartial arbitrator.

28 POMPONIUS (*on Sabinus* 5) A bequest can be made of the usufruct in old gold and silver coins which are habitually used as ornaments.

[1] For *fusiones* read *functiones*. Cf. Roby, 185.

29 ULPIANUS (*on Sabinus* 18) We are told by Celsus (*Dig.* 32) and Julianus (*Dig.* 61) that a man may make a bequest of a usufruct in the whole of his property, as long as this does not exceed in value three-fourths of the inheritance; and this is the better opinion.

30 PAULUS (*on Sabinus* 3) Where a man who has two houses bequeaths the usufruct in one of them, then, according to Marcellus, the heir is at liberty to raise the height of the other so as to interfere with the lights of the first, because, even where a house is darkened, it is still possible to live in it. The rule must be taken subject to this qualification that the house must not be darkened completely, there must be some moderate access of light retained such as will suffice for the needs of the occupiers.

31 THE SAME (*on Sabinus* 10) The expression "founded on the property of the fructuary" (*ex re fructuarii*) is held to apply to any gift or allowance which the fructuary may have made to the slave, or any profit that the latter may make in the course of managing the fructuary's affairs.

32 POMPONIUS (*on Sabinus* 33) Where a man makes delivery of a single house, which is the only one he has, or of a piece of land, he may reserve a servitude which is personal and not prædial, for example, *usus* or usufruct. However, if he reserves a right of pasturage or a right to live on the land, this too is a valid reservation, as there are many cases of forest tracts in which the profits are taken by pasturing cattle on them; and where what is reserved is a right to live on the land, whether such reservation is for a definite time or for the life of the party who makes it, this is held to amount to reserving the *usus*.

33 PAPINIANUS (*Questions* 17) If the usufruct is bequeathed to Titius and the bare property to Mævius, and Titius dies in the lifetime of the testator, nothing is left in the hands of the party named heir; indeed, this is laid down by Neratius himself. 1. It is agreed that in certain cases the usufruct in a thing does not receive the same treatment in law as the property[1]; thus where proceedings are taken to recover a portion of an estate or a portion of a usufruct,

[1] I read *proprietatis* for *partis*, the latter word standing alone in the MS: M. would read both words, and so did the Basilica. Cf. D. 44. 2. 14. 1. Assuming this last view to be correct, I should be inclined to read, or at least to understand, *partis* after *usumfructum*, and the meaning would be "the usufruct in a part does not receive the same treatment as the property in a part."

and thereupon, the suit being lost, an action is brought to recover a further portion which is derived from accrual, then, according to Julianus, in the action for the property, the *exceptio* of "judgment pronounced" is a good defence, but in that for the usufruct, it is not a good defence, because the additional portion of the land itself —say an alluvial strip—would accrue to the first portion, but the [additional portion of] usufruct would accrue to the person.

34 JULIANUS (*Digest* 35) Whenever a usufruct is bequeathed to two persons in terms importing that they are to enjoy the same in alternate years, then, if the bequest is made in the words "to Titius and Mævius," it may fairly be said that it is given for the first year to Titius and then to Mævius; but, if there are two legatees of the same name, and the words are as follows:— "I give the usufruct to the two Titii for alternate years," then, unless they come to an understanding as to which of them is to have it first, they will be in one another's way. If, however, Titius [in the case first mentioned,] should, in the course of one of his years of usufruct, acquire the ownership, then, for the time, he will not have what was bequeathed him (viz. the usufruct), though Mævius will have a right of usufruct every other year, and thereupon, if Titius should dispose of the ownership, he will have his usufruct, because, supposing the case were that a usufruct was bequeathed me on a suspensive condition, and, before the event happened, I acquired the ownership from the heir, but while the event was still pending, I disposed of such ownership to someone else, I should be allowed to enjoy the legacy. 1. If you bequeath the usufruct of a farm to your tenant [therein], he can bring an action to recover such usufruct, and he can sue your heir on the contract of lease, by doing which he will secure that he shall not have to pay any rent and that he will get back the cost he has incurred in the cultivation. 2. The question whether the testator bequeaths the usufruct of his entire property or of separate specific objects has, I should say, a practical bearing in the following way:—if a house is burnt down, the usufruct of the house, where specifically bequeathed, cannot be sued for; but where the bequest was of a usufruct in the whole property, there can be an action for a usufruct in the bare site: a man who bequeaths the usufruct of his property generally is held to bequeath the usufruct, not only of the things which are there in specific form, but in fact of his whole substance, and part of the substance of his property is the site in question.

35 THE SAME (*on Urseius Ferox* 1) If a usufruct has been bequeathed, but the person named heir delays making entry in order to defer the acquisition of the legacy, in the opinion of Sabinus this will have to be made good. 1. A bequest was made to me of the usufruct in a slave, it being added that on the termination of my usufruct he was to be free: after this I accepted from the heir an estimated equivalent of the usufruct in money: the slave, according to an opinion given by Sabinus, will not on that account be thereupon free, because when I have got something as an equivalent for the slave, I may be said to be enjoying the usufruct in him, and the contingent event on which he becomes free remains the same as before, so that he will acquire his freedom on the occurrence of my death or *capitis diminutio*.

36 AFRICANUS (*Questions* 5) A man first bequeathed the usufruct of a vacant plot of ground and then built a block of chambers thereon, after which the building collapsed or was burnt down in the testator's lifetime: the opinion given was that the usufruct could be claimed. On the other hand a corresponding conclusion would not hold, if the usufruct were bequeathed in the block itself, and thereupon first the place were made into a bare site and after that into a block again. It would be a similar case to this last if there were a bequest of the usufruct in bowls, which were thereupon reduced to a mass of metal and this again made into bowls; as, however true it might be that the original character of bowls was restored, still they would not be the same bowls as those in which usufruct was bequeathed. 1. I stipulated with Titius that he should give me the Cornelian estate, reserving the usufruct; after which Titius died; the question was asked what it was that his heir was bound to give me. Our authority answered that the real question was what was the intention in the reservation of the usufruct; if the real agreement was that a usufruct should be established simply in the person of someone or other, then the heir will only be bound to convey the bare ownership; but if it was that the usufruct should be reserved for the promisor alone, his heir would have to give ownership with immediate enjoyment. That this is the true state of the case appeared, he said, more plainly in the case of a legacy, as where an heir at whose charge the bare ownership is bequeathed with a reservation of usufruct dies before proceedings are taken on the testament, there is still less room for doubt that the heir of such heir will have to give the ownership with enjoyment. The construction is the same where the legacy is

made on a condition and the heir dies pending the fulfilment of the condition. 2. A usufruct in a slave was bequeathed to Titius ; and, at a time when the heir was already in default as to conveying the usufruct, the slave died ; the only possible conclusion is, so our authority says, that the obligation of the heir is measured by an amount representing the interest the legatee had in there being no default ; so that, in short, an estimate should be made of the value of the usufruct reckoned from the time [of default] to the day on which the slave died ; and this implies further that, if Titius died himself, then, in like manner, there would have to be an amount given to his heir which would represent the value of the usufruct from the time when default was first made down to the day of Titius's death.

37 THE SAME (*Questions* 7) The following question has been asked. I stipulated with you that you should give me a usufruct in something or other for the next ten years, but you failed to give it, by your own default, and so five years passed. How stands the law ? Again, suppose I stipulated with you that you should give me the services of your slave Stichus for the next ten years, and as before, five years passed. The answer made was that there was a good action for both usufruct and services for the time which you allowed to pass without the gift being made.

38 MARCIANUS (*Institutes* 3) There is no user on the part of the usufructuary where neither he himself uses nor anyone else uses on his account ; as, for instance, a person who bought [the usufruct] or hired it or took it as a gift, or who volunteered to act as agent to the usufructuary. There is, no doubt, this distinction to be made, that, if I sell a usufruct, then, even though the purchaser should make no use of the thing, I am regarded as still retaining the usufruct ;

39 GAIUS (*on the provincial Edict* 7) because a man who enjoys the purchase money is regarded as having [the usufruct] just as much as one who has the use and enjoyment of the actual thing :

40 MARCIANUS (*Institutes* 3) but, if I give the usufruct away, I no longer retain it, unless the donee uses the thing.

41 THE SAME (*Institutes* 7) It must be held on the whole that there can be a good bequest of a usufruct in a statue or a picture,

because even objects such as these can be turned to a certain use if put in a suitable place. 1. There are some estates of such a kind that they are rather a source of expense than of profit, still a usufruct can be left even in such estates.

42 FLORENTINUS (*Institutes* 11) If there should be a bequest of the use to one man and the produce (*fructus*) to another in respect of the same thing, the fructuary will get whatever remains after the just claims of the usuary are satisfied; but this will not prevent him from having some use too with a view to having produce. 1. It makes a practical difference whether you have a usufruct left you in the testator's property or in the money value thereof; if what is left is the usufruct in the property, you must deduct from such property any specific thing which is given you by a separate bequest, and you will have a usufruct in all the rest; but if what is bequeathed is the usufruct of the value in money, the valuation will comprise even the thing so separately bequeathed. The fact is that where a testator bequeaths the same thing over and over again, this does not enlarge the legacy, but, when a particular thing has been bequeathed, you can enlarge the legacy by bequeathing the estimated value of it as well.

43 ULPIANUS (*Rules* 7) A usufruct can be bequeathed even of a share in the testator's property, and, if it is not said expressly what share, it is taken to be half the property.

44 NERATIUS (*Parchments* 3) A usufructuary is not at liberty to put fresh plaster on walls which are at the time in a rough condition, because, granting that he would put the owner in a better position by improving the building, still he cannot do this in pursuance of any right that he has as usufructuary; it is one thing for him to maintain what he received, and another to set up something new[1].

45 GAIUS (*on the provincial Edict* 7) Just as the cost of a slave's board falls on the person who has a usufruct in him, so too cost incurred through his illness it is plain as a matter of common sense must fall on the same person.

46 PAULUS (*Extracts from Plautius* 9) In a testament a stranger is appointed heir, an emancipated son is passed over, and the ownership [in the whole estate] is bequeathed to the mother of the testator, with a reservation of the usufruct; in this case, if

[1] For *an* etc. read *aliud novum facere*. M.

the *bonorum possessio contra tabulas* is sued out, the full ownership must, in deference to filial duty, be given to the mother. 1. Where the testator orders that his heir shall repair a block of chambers in which he bequeaths the usufruct, the usufructuary can bring an action on the testament to compel the heir to execute the repairs.

47 POMPONIUS (*Extracts from Plautius* 5) Should the heir fail to execute them, and the usufructuary in consequence be unable to get the benefit of his usufruct, the latter's own heir will have a right of action accordingly; the damages being the amount of difference it would have made to the usufructuary if the heir had not neglected the matter; even though the usufruct should have come to an end by the death of the usufructuary.

48 PAULUS (*on Plautius* 9) If, in the absence of the usufructuary, the testator's heir executes repairs, as his voluntary agent, he will have an action against the usufructuary on *negotia gesta,* although in fact the heir had an eye to his own future advantage. But if the usufructuary is prepared to abandon the usufruct, he is not compellable to repair, and he is released from the action on *negotia gesta.* 1. Coppice, even though cut out of season, is quite recognised to be part of the produce, just as olives gathered before they are ripe are part of the produce, or grass cut for hay before the regular time.

49 POMPONIUS (*on Plautius* 7) If a usufruct is bequeathed to you and me at the charge of Sempronius and Mucius, heirs of the testator, then I shall have a quarter of the whole out of the share of Sempronius and another quarter out of the share of Mucius, and you will similarly have two quarters out of their respective shares.

50 PAULUS (*on Vitellius* 3) Titius left the Tusculan estate as a legacy to Mævius, with a *fidei-commissum* that he should convey to Titia the usufruct in half the same estate; Mævius rebuilt a farmhouse which had fallen to pieces from age, but which was required for storing and keeping farm produce: the question was asked whether Titia was bound to undertake part of the expense in proportion to her usufruct. Scævola's answer was that if Mævius was obliged to build before the usufruct was given, he could not be called upon to hand it over except on the terms of[1] the expense being taken into account.

[1] *ut* inserend. before *ejus.*

51 MODESTINUS (*Differences* 9) It is held that the bequest of a usufruct to Titius "when he dies" is inoperative, as it is referred to the very time at which the usufruct ceases to belong to the person named.

52 THE SAME (*Rules* 9) Where a usufruct in a thing is left by testament, then, if taxes are payable for the thing, there is no doubt that the usufructuary is bound to pay them, unless it is shown that the testator directed by way of express *fidei-commissum* that these charges as well as others should be paid by the heir.

53 JAVOLENUS (*Epistles* 2) If the usufruct bequeathed is in a block of chambers, then, as long as any portion of the block remains, the legatee has the usufruct in the whole site.

54 THE SAME (*Epistles* 3) The usufruct of an estate was bequeathed to Titius on a contingency at your charge as heir; you sold and delivered the estate to me, with a reservation of the usufruct: I wish to know, supposing the contingency fails to happen, or it happens and the usufruct has expired, to whom it belongs. Answer: I understand your question to refer to the usufruct which was bequeathed. I should say then that if the contingency on which the legacy depends comes to pass, there is no doubt that the usufruct in question will belong to the legatee, and that, if by any chance it should be lost to him, it is merged in the bare ownership of the estate; but if the contingency does not come to pass, the usufruct will belong to the heir, all rules of law holding good with reference to the heir which regard the loss of usufruct and which are commonly put in force. However, in a sale of this kind, we ought to look at the precise terms of the agreement between the vendor and the purchaser, so that, if it is shown that it was for the sake of the legacy that the usufruct in question was reserved, then, even if the contingency does not come to pass, it ought to be given up by the vendor to the purchaser.

55 POMPONIUS (*on Quintus Mucius* 26) Should there be a bequest of the *usus* in an infant slave and nothing more, then, although for the present the *usus* amounts to nothing, still as soon as the child outgrows the age of infancy, it begins to be in force.

56 GAIUS (*on the provincial Edict* 17) It has been made a question whether an action in respect of a usufruct ought to be allowed to a municipal body; the point being that there seemed to be a danger of the usufruct becoming perpetual, as it would not

be lost by death, and hardly by *capitis diminutio*, and the consequence would be that the ownership would be valueless in consequence of the usufruct being always outstanding. However the law now is that an action must be allowed. This leads to a further doubt, viz. as to how long the municipality is to be protected in the enjoyment of the usufruct; but it is held that it will be protected for a hundred years, because that is the utmost extent of the life of a man, however long he lives.

57 PAPINIANUS (*Responsa* 7) A landowner left by testament to a usufructuary the estate in which the latter had the servitude of usufruct, but this estate the legatee was compelled, after being in possession for a considerable time, to give up to the son of the testator, who had carried through successfully a case of inofficious testament: it was clear from the event that ensued that the right of usufruct remained untouched. 1. The produce of certain portions of land being left by *fidei-commissum* to various freedmen by way of alimentary provision, on the death of any beneficiaries the profits of their respective shares revert from them to the bare owner.

58 SCÆVOLA (*Responsa* 3) A woman who had a usufruct in land died in the month of December, all the produce procurable from the land having been already carried by the tenants in the month of October. Hereupon the question arose whether rent ought to be paid to the heir of the usufructuary, although she herself died before the first of March, which was the day on which rents became due, or it should be apportioned between the heir of the usufructuary and the municipality (*res publica*), to which the ownership was bequeathed. I replied that the municipality had no right of action against the tenant, but that, upon the facts as stated, the heir of the usufructuary would have a right to receive the whole rent on the regular day. 1. "I give and bequeath to Sempronius a sixth part of the produce of the crops of cabbage and leeks which I have in the field of the Farrarii." The question is whether these words can be held to amount to a bequest of the usufruct. My answer was:—"No, not of the usufruct, but of the particular portion of the produce gathered which was mentioned in the bequest." 2. It was further asked, assuming that it was not a case of usufruct, whether the bequest was one of the sixth part of the produce for every successive year. I answered that it must be held to be left for every year, unless the contrary were expressly proved by the heir.

59 PAULUS (*Sentences* 3) Where trees are overturned by the force of a tempest without any negligence on the part of the usufructuary, it is not the law that he must put others in their place. 1. Whatever is produced on the land or is gathered from it goes to the fructuary, and so do the rents of farms already leased, if such rents are expressly included. But, as in the case of a sale, if the rents were not expressly excepted, the usufructuary can eject the lessee. 2. Profit derived from cutting reed or stakes goes to the fructuary, where this has formed part of the usual returns from the land.

60 THE SAME (*Sentences* 5) The usufructuary of any estate may, if warned off or ejected, bring an action to have restored to him everything which was seized on the occasion; moreover, if the usufruct should meanwhile be terminated by some independent event, then too an *utilis actio* is allowed, to recover any produce already got in. 1. Where it is sought to recover a usufruct in land, and the land is in possession of someone who is not owner, an action is allowed. Consequently, if there is a question between two persons as to the ownership in the land, the usufructuary has none the less a right to be in occupation (*in possessione*), but if the usufructuary's own title as such should be disputed, his enjoyment as usufructuary is postponed for the time, but an undertaking has to be given him[1] for making over to him whatever he would receive out of the profits, or, if [such] security is not furnished, he is allowed to take the profits himself, and then security must be given him by the person in possession (*possessor*) that he will not prevent the person to whom the usufruct was left from taking such profits, so long as he is himself endeavouring to establish his legal rights[2].

61 NERATIUS (*Responsa* 2) A usufructuary cannot put a fresh gutter on the walls; [and,] where a building is only begun, the law is that a fructuary is not at liberty to complete it, even if he cannot make any use of that part of the property without doing so; indeed, it is held that there can be no usufruct in such a building itself; unless, in both cases, when the usufruct was created or bequeathed, it was expressly added that the things above mentioned might be done.

[1] After *caveri* read or understand *oportet*.

[2] The above translation is more or less conjectural. Mommsen puts the clause from *satisque ei* (and then security) down to *de jure suo probet* at the end, instead of after *in possessione esse debet* (a right to be in occupation), and I have followed him. The words *ipse frui permittitur* betray the hand of the interpolator.

62 TRYPHONINUS (*Disputations* 7) It is quite correctly said that a usufructuary may hunt in the forests or on the moors on a landed estate ; and if he captures a boar or a stag, he is not taking any property of the bare owner's, but he makes what he takes his own either by the law of usufruct or else by universal law. 1. If wild animals were kept on the estate, confined in preserves when the usufruct began, is the fructuary at liberty to train them, but not to kill them? and if there are any which he confined by his own exertions at the outset, or which afterward were caught in a snare, or slipped into one, are these in law the usufructuary's property? The most convenient rule is, in order to avoid the uncertainty which there would be as to the right enjoyed by the usufructuary in cases of different animals, owing to the difficulty of establishing sound distinctions, that it is enough to assign to the bare proprietor on the expiration of the usufruct the same numbers of the different kinds respectively as he had at the time when the usufruct began.

63 PAULUS (*on exceptional law*) It is possible for people to transfer to others what they have not got themselves ; for instance, when a man has an estate, then, though he has not got a usufruct, nevertheless he can grant a usufruct to someone else.

64 ULPIANUS (*on the Edict* 51) Where a usufructuary is prepared to abandon his usufruct, he cannot be compelled to repair the house, even in those cases in which this duty would fall on the usufructuary. Indeed, after issue has been joined with the fructuary, it must be held that, if he is prepared to abandon the usufruct, the judge ought to dismiss the action.

65 POMPONIUS (*Extracts from Plautius* 5) However, as the fructuary is [absolutely] bound to repair anything which has been damaged by his own act or that of any member of his household, the action ought not [in such a case] to be dismissed, even though he should be prepared to abandon the usufruct; and in fact he is himself bound to do whatever a careful householder would do in his own house. 1. The heir is no more bound to repair anything which was left by the testator in a ruinous condition from age than he would be if the testator had bequeathed the full proprietorship.

66 PAULUS (*on the Edict* 47) There may be a good right of action against a usufructuary not only on the *lex Aquilia*, but also for spoiling a slave (*servi corrupti*) and for *injuria*, in any case where he reduces the value of the slave by torture.

67 JULIANUS (*extracts from Minicius* 1) The legatee of a usufruct can sell it to a stranger, even against the will of the heir.

68 ULPIANUS (*on Sabinus* 17) It was a question in old days whether the child of a female slave belongs to the fructuary; but the opinion of Brutus came to prevail, to the effect that the law[1] of usufruct has no application to the case, as a human being cannot be treated as produce of a human being; and, on this principle, the fructuary will not even have a usufruct in the child. Suppose however the usufruct were left in the expected child itself, would the legatee have this usufruct? As to this, seeing that expected offspring can be bequeathed, so can the usufruct therein. 1. The young of cattle, however, Sabinus and Cassius were both of opinion would belong to the fructuary. 2. No doubt, where there is a bequest of the usufruct in a flock of sheep or a herd of cattle, the usufructuary will be bound to fill up the flock out of the young that are born from time to time, that is to supply the place of dead

69 POMPONIUS (*on Sabinus* 5) or useless animals by means of others which he provides for the purpose, so that, after these are put in the place of the old ones, these latter may become the property of the usufructuary, so as to prevent the bare owner from making a profit by the whole thing. Of course, just as the substituted animals at once become the property of the bare owner, so too the old ones cease to belong to him, in accordance with the legal character of produce; in fact the general rule is that whatever is produced belongs to the fructuary, and, when he puts it in the place of something else, it ceases to be his.

70 ULPIANUS (*on Sabinus* 17) How then, if he does not act in the way described and does not fill up the number? According to Gaius Cassius (*Jus civile* 10) he is liable to be sued by the bare proprietor. 1. In the meantime, however, until they are reared and the number of the animals that are dead is filled up, the question arises to whom these young belong. To this Julianus says (*Dig.* 35), that the ownership in them is in suspense; so that, if they are set apart, they belong to the bare proprietor, if not, to the usufructuary, and this is a sound opinion. 2. According to this, if the young die, the loss will fall on the usufructuary and not

[1] Ins. *jus* after *optinuit.* M.

on the bare proprietor, and he will be obliged to rear other young. Hence Gaius Cassius declares (b. 8) that the flesh of any young that die belongs to the fructuary. 3. With regard however to the rule above given, that the usufructuary is bound to rear animals to set apart, this is only so in cases where the usufruct bequeathed is of a flock or a herd or a stud of horses, in short of some collective unity; if it is of such and such individual animals, there will be no number for him to fill up. 4. Again, suppose that, at the time when the young were born, nothing had occurred to make it necessary for any to be set apart, but something has[1] occurred now, subsequently to their birth; a point to consider is whether he will be bound to take animals to set apart only from among those born later or he must take them from those born already. I should say however that the better opinion is that such as are born at the time when the flock is complete are the property of the fructuary, and the fructuary will suffer only in the case of some subsequent falling off in the flock. 5. Setting apart is matter of fact, and Julianus calls it expressly parting off, separating, making a separation, as the ownership in the creatures set apart is in the bare proprietor.

71 MARCELLUS (*Digest* 17) Where a man builds on a vacant plot in which someone else has a usufruct, then, if the right to the surface is taken away before the expiration of the period required for the usufruct to be lost, according to what the old lawyers laid down, the usufruct is restored.

72 ULPIANUS (*on Sabinus* 17) If the owner of the bare property bequeaths a usufruct, the true view is, as is stated by Mæcianus (Questions on *fidei-commissa* 3), that the bequest is valid, and, if it chance that it [the preceding usufruct] is merged in the bare property in the lifetime of the testator, or before entry is made on the inheritance, then it [the later usufruct] goes as bequeathed. Mæcianus is ready to go further still; in his opinion even where the [preceding] usufruct only falls in after entry is made on the inheritance, it [the later usufruct] is validly vested and goes as bequeathed.

73 POMPONIUS (*on Sabinus* 5) Where there is a bequest to me of the usufruct in a vacant plot, I can build a shed there for the purpose of keeping in it goods of mine which are on the spot.

[1] For *et* read *est*. Cf. M.

74 GAIUS (*on the provincial Edict* 7) If a usufruct is bequeathed to your slave Stichus and my slave Pamphilus, such a bequest is equivalent to one made to you and me; accordingly there is no doubt that the usufruct belongs to us in equal shares.

II.

ON ACCRUAL OF USUFRUCT.

1 ULPIANUS (*on Sabinus* 17) Whenever there is a bequest of usufruct, the right of accrual as between two usufructuaries exists only where the usufruct was left jointly (*conjunctim*); but if a usufruct in a share was left to each separately, there is no doubt that the right of accrual does not exist. 1. Hereupon the question is asked in Julianus's *Digest* (b. 35), supposing a usufruct is left to a slave who is owned by two persons in common, and so a right to it is fully acquired by the two owners, whether, if one of the two declines the usufruct or loses it, the other has the whole; as to which Julianus's opinion is that it belongs to the other; and, even if the usufruct came to the owners of the slave not in equal shares but in shares equal to their respective shares in the slave, nevertheless you look at the person of the slave and not of the owners, so that it goes to one of the owners, and does not become an accession to the bare property [in the thing]. 2. The same writer says, supposing a usufruct is bequeathed to a slave owned by two persons in common and to Titius separately, then, if one of the two co-owners loses the usufruct, it will not belong to Titius, but to the other co-owner alone, as being the only person who was entitled jointly; and this is the proper view, since so long as even one only [of the two joint owners] is using the thing, you may say that the usufruct is still lodged where it was. The rule is the same if the usufruct should be left to two jointly and a third separately. 3. In some cases, however, even if the two legatees did not take jointly, still the usufruct bequeathed may come to one of them by accrual; for example, suppose the usufruct in the whole estate is left to me separately and is left to you in similar terms. For, as Celsus himself says (*Dig.* 18) and Julianus too (b. 35), the fact of concurrence (*concursus*) makes us own shares, and the same would be the case even with the bare property itself, as, if one declined, the other would have the whole estate. But, in the case of usufruct there is this in addition, that[1] even when the usufruct has been

[1] For *quia* read or understand *quod*.

created and afterwards lost, it may none the less be the subject of a right of accrual ; indeed all writers cited by Plautius agree upon this point, and, as Celsus and Julianus cleverly put it, usufruct is created and bequeathed every successive day, and not necessarily, like the bare property, only at the time when [it can be first] sued for. Accordingly, so soon as either legatee finds no one else in concurrence with him, he will enjoy the usufruct to its full extent by himself and it matters not whether the bequest was joint or several. 4. Again, Julianus says (*Dig.* 35) that if a testator appoints two heirs, and bequeaths the bare property with a reservation of usufruct, the heirs have no right of accrual ; the usufruct is held to be created [in shares[1]], it does not become divided by concurrence ;

2 AFRICANUS (*Questions* 5) consequently any share in the usufruct which may have been lost will revert to the legatee, that is the owner of the bare property.

3 ULPIANUS (*on Sabinus* 17) Neratius himself holds that the law of accrual will have no application [in such a case] Responsa 1) ; and with this view agrees the principle laid down by Celsus, where he says that the right of accrual occurs only when, two persons having the usufruct for the whole, it is divided between them by their concurrence. 1. Hence Celsus declares (b. 18) that if two co-owners of an estate both convey the bare property with a reservation of usufruct, then, whichever of the two loses his usufruct, it reverts to the bare property, not, that is, to the whole property, but rather the usufruct of each [conveying party] becomes an accession to the share which he himself conveyed ; in short it must needs merge in the particular share from which it was originally parted. 2. Moreover, the right of accrual exists not only where a usufruct is bequeathed to two persons, but equally where a usufruct is bequeathed to one and the estate to another ; as, if the one to whom the usufruct was bequeathed should lose it, it thereupon belongs to the other rather by right of accrual than in virtue of its merger in the bare property. This was to be expected, seeing that, if a usufruct is bequeathed to two, and, in the hands of one of the two, it comes to be merged in the bare property, this does not put an end to the right of accrual either for the benefit of the one in whose hands the merger takes place or from him [for the other], and in whatever way he might have lost [his usufruct] before the merger, he may lose [it] in the same way now. This is the view of Neratius and Aristo, and Pomponius confirms it.

[1] M.

4 JULIANUS (*Digest* 35) If the bare property in an estate is bequeathed to you, and the usufruct of the same estate to me and Mævius and you, I and Mævius will have third parts respectively of the usufruct, and the remaining third part will be merged in the bare property. But if either Mævius or I should suffer *capitis diminutio*, a third will be divided between you and the other of us two, so that the one of us two who has not suffered *capitis diminutio* will have half the usufruct and you will have a right to the property together with [the other] half of the usufruct;

5 GAIUS (*on the provincial Edict* 7) and, if you convey away the bare property, reserving the usufruct, Julianus is of opinion that it is still a case of accrual, and that you are not held to acquire a fresh usufruct.

6 ULPIANUS (*on Sabinus* 17) The law is the same where the usufruct is merged in the property in the hands of one of three fructuaries. 1. Again, if the property is bequeathed to anyone with a reservation of usufruct, and a share in the usufruct is bequeathed to me, it is worth considering whether the law of accrual applies as between me and the heir; however, the correct view is that, if either of us loses the usufruct, it falls into the bare property. 2. If the usufruct in an estate is left to me absolutely and to you on a condition, it may fairly be said that the usufruct in the whole estate belongs to me in the meantime, and that, if I suffer *capitis diminutio*, I lose the whole; but, if the condition is fulfilled, then, should I have suffered *capitis diminutio*, you have a right to the whole usufruct, but, if I keep my status, the usufruct must be shared between us.

7 PAULUS (*on Sabinus* 3) If a man leaves a usufruct to Attius and his heirs, Attius will have half and his heirs will have half; but if the words are "to Attius and Seius with my heirs," the usufruct will be divided into three parts, so as to give one to the heirs, one to Attius, and one to Seius; it makes no difference whether the bequest is "to *A* and *B* with Mævius" or "to *A* and *B* and Mævius."

8 ULPIANUS (*on Sabinus* 17) If a usufruct is bequeathed to a woman "with her children," then, if she lose her children, she has the usufruct; on the other hand, if the mother herself dies, still her children have the usufruct by the law of accrual. Julianus himself says (*Dig.* 30) that we must adopt the same construction in the case of a testator appointing heirs his children only, even where he does

not name them as legatees, but only desires to make it clear that his wish is that the mother's enjoyment should be one in which she has her children associated with her. Here, however, Pomponius asks the question, "How if the heirs are children and outsiders mixed up?" To this he says the sons (*sic*) must be held to be legatees, and, conversely, if his desire was that the children in question should be associated with their mother in the enjoyment, the proper rule is that the mother must be regarded as a legatee, and thereupon the legal result will be in all respects similar to that in the other case.

9 AFRICANUS (*Questions* 5) If the bare property in an estate is bequeathed to two and the usufruct to one, the three persons do not take third parts respectively in the usufruct, but the two take a half and the usufructuary has the other half; and a corresponding rule holds if there are two fructuaries and one legatee of the estate.

10 ULPIANUS (*on the Edict* 17) In some cases a share of usufruct goes by accrual even to a person who has no share of his own, but has lost it; for example, suppose a usufruct is bequeathed to two persons, and one of these, after joinder of issue [in an action to recover it] loses his right of usufruct, shortly after which his co-legatee, who has not joined issue, loses his right of usufruct too; in this case the one who joined issue in the action against the person who came forward to defend the case will [by such action] get from the person in possession only the half part which he lost; as for the share lost by his co-legatee he gets that by accrual, and it does not go to the bare proprietor: the accrual of usufruct is to the person, though it [his original share] should be lost.

11 PAPINIANUS (*Definitions* 2) Where the usufruct in one and the same thing is bequeathed to different individuals at the charge of different heirs respectively, such usufructuaries are regarded as being just as truly separate as if the usufruct of the same thing had been bequeathed to the two in equal shares; and the consequence is that there is no right of accrual between them;

12 ULPIANUS (*on Sabinus* 17) as one legatee will bring his action for the usufruct against one heir and the other against the other.

III.

WHEN THE BEQUEST OF A USUFRUCT VESTS.

1 ULPIANUS (*on Sabinus* 17) Although usufruct involves the taking of produce, in short, some active behaviour on the part of the person who has the usufruct, still it vests once for all; the case is not like that of a thing being bequeathed a man for every separate month, or day, or year (*in menses* etc. *singulos*); in such cases the legacy vests daily (*per dies singulos*), or monthly, or annually. Hence arises this question:—supposing a usufruct is bequeathed a man from day to day or for every year, does it vest once for all (*semel*)? As to this I should say that it does not vest all at once (*simul*), but at the different times mentioned, so that there are so many different legacies. This view is upheld by Marcellus (*Dig.* 4) in the case of a man to whom a usufruct was bequeathed for every other day (*alternis diebus*). 1. Accordingly, if the bequest is of a usufruct such as cannot be taken advantage of every day, the bequest is not void, but the legacy will apply to those days on which the party can take the produce. 2. However, a usufruct, and, similarly, an *usus*, will not vest before entry is made on the inheritance, as a usufruct is only fully created when a person is able to enjoy it at once. On this principle it is that, according to Julianus, if a usufruct is bequeathed to a slave who is part of an unclaimed inheritance, however much any other kind of legacy would be acquired to the inheritance, in the case of usufruct we wait for the person of an owner who can enjoy the use and produce. 3. Again, if the bequest of usufruct is from and after a given day, the usufruct will not vest until it is immediately claimable (*dies nondum cedet nisi cum dies venit*); it is of course settled law that a usufruct can be bequeathed from and after a given day or until a given day. 4. Not only is it true that the usufruct does not vest before entry on the inheritance, but the right of action for usufruct does not vest sooner, and the same rule holds where the usufruct is bequeathed from and after a given day; Scævola says plainly that a man who sues before the day of the usufruct will get nothing by it, though indeed in any case a man who sues before the day sues to no good purpose.

IV.

THE WAYS IN WHICH USUFRUCT OR *Usus* IS LOST.

1 ULPIANUS (*on Sabinus* 17) It is settled law that by *capitis diminutio* not only is usufruct lost but the right of action for usufruct as well, and it matters little whether the usufruct was created by direct law or by the aid of the prætor; on the same principle, where usufruct is created by delivery, or, contrary to strict law, is in land let on a perpetual lease (*fundus vectigalis*) or in a *superficies*, it is lost by *capitis diminutio*. 1. Usufruct however can be lost by *capitis diminutio* only where it is already created; if a man suffers *capitis diminutio* before entry on the inheritance or before the usufruct has vested, there is no doubt it is not lost. 2. Where an estate in land is bequeathed to you from and after a certain day, and you are requested to hand over the usufruct to me, we may fairly consider whether it is not really the fact that, if I suffer *capitis diminutio* before the day mentioned in the legacy to you, my usufruct is perfectly safe, on the ground that the *capitis diminutio* takes place before the usufruct vests; and upon an indulgent construction this may be held. 3. Indeed, so true is it that *capitis diminutio* only destroys a usufruct which is already created, that if the usufruct is bequeathed for every separate year, month, or day, the only usufruct that is lost is the one which is already running, so that, for example, if it is bequeathed for separate years, the usufruct for the current year alone will be lost, if for separate months, that for the current month, and if for separate days, that for the current day.

2 PAPINIANUS (*Questions* 17) If a usufruct is left to two persons separately for every other year (*alternis annis*), the right of property runs on year after year without the enjoyment, whereas, if, instead of this, we suppose one legatee only, to whom the usufruct is bequeathed for every other year, the heir will have the property with the enjoyment during such time as the legatee is not entitled to have the usufruct. If however [in the case first mentioned] one of the two should die, then the property will be coupled with enjoyment for the odd years (*per vices temporum*); there can be no accrual for the benefit of the survivor, since each party had his own times of undivided usufruct without the other being in concurrence with him. 1. If what occurs is not death, but *capitis diminutio*, then, seeing that it is a case of distinct

bequests, the only usufruct lost will be that of the current year, if, that is, he [the party who suffered *capitis diminutio*] had the right of usufruct [in that year]; indeed, even in the case of a single legatee to whom the usufruct was given for so many separate years respectively, this is the proper rule to maintain, so that the express mention of periods is equivalent to a renewal of the usufruct. 2. Where the usufruct is bequeathed to separate persons for every other year, then, if they agree that they shall both take in the same year, they obstruct one another, as it does not appear to have been intended that they should take in concurrence; and of course it makes a great deal of difference whether a usufruct is given to two persons together for every other year, (in which case the enjoyment cannot continue over the end of the first year, any more than it could if the usufruct had been given in the same terms to one person,) or it is given to separate persons for every other year, in which case, if they choose to have it concurrently, either they will be in one another's way, considering what was the testator's intention, or else, if such intention is really not inconsistent with it, it will come to pass that one year's profits will [every other year] go a-begging.

3 ULPIANUS (*on Sabinus* 17) Just as a usufruct can be bequeathed for each of so many separate years, so too it can be made the subject of a further bequest [to take effect] after loss by *capitis diminutio*, some such words being added as "whenever so and so shall suffer *capitis diminutio* I bequeath to him" etc. or "whenever it shall be lost": and, in such a case, if it should be lost by *capitis diminutio*, it will be held that it is renewed. Hereupon this question has been discussed: a usufruct being bequeathed to a man for as long as he shall live, must it be considered to be renewed [for] every time that it is lost? This view is suggested by Mæcianus, and I should say that it must be held to be so renewed. Hence, where a usufruct is bequeathed for a definite term, say, for example, for ten years, we must lay down the same rule. 1. With regard to the renewal mentioned which takes effect after a usufruct has been lost by *capitis diminutio*, the question has been asked whether it carries with it the undiminished right of accrual: for instance, suppose a usufruct was bequeathed to Titius and Mævius, and the testator, in case Titius should suffer *capitis diminutio*, bequeathed him the usufruct over again; hereupon it is asked, if Titius takes the usufruct by renewal, whether the right of accrual will still be preserved between the two. To this Papinianus says (Questions 17) that it is

preserved, just as it would be if some third person had been put in the place of Titius to receive the usufruct; as the legatees [Titius and Mævius] must be held to be joint by the fact (*re*), though not by the words. 2. Papinianus proceeds to raise a further point. Suppose the testator, after bequeathing the usufruct to Titius and Mævius, should, in a renewed bequest of usufruct, give Titius not the whole, but a part,—would the two legatees be held [after that] to be joint? To this what he says is: should Titius lose his usufruct, his co-legatee will get the whole by accrual, but, if Mævius lost, the whole would not go by accrual, part would go to Titius (*eum*), and part fall into the bare property. This is a reasonable view, as it cannot be maintained that the ground (*momentum*) on which a man loses his usufruct and then takes back usufruct will actually entitle the same man by accrual to any portion of what he lost, as what we hold is that a man who loses a usufruct will get nothing by accrual out of what he loses. 3. That death is one of the ways in which usufruct is lost does not admit of doubt, seeing that the right of enjoyment is put an end to by death, just like any other right which is attached to the person.

4 MARCIANUS (*Institutes* 3) If the legatee of a usufruct is requested [in the testament] to hand it over to someone else, the prætor ought to take care that, if it is lost, it should be rather in the person of the fidei-commissary than in that of the legatee.

5 ULPIANUS (*on Sabinus* 17) A usufruct which is bequeathed can be renewed, however it may be lost, so long as it is not by death, unless, indeed, the testator renew the bequest in that event to the heirs. 1. If a man who has acquired a usufruct through a slave conveys away to another a usufruct in such slave and nothing else, there is no doubt that he retains the usufruct which he acquired through him. 2. Usufruct is held to come to an end by a complete change in the thing which is the subject of it; for instance, say a bequest was made to me of the usufruct in a house, and the house has fallen to pieces or has been burnt down, the usufruct in the house is undoubtedly extinguished. Is that in the site too? [As to this,] it is quite certain that, when the house is burnt down, no usufruct exists in either the site or the materials. Julianus himself has this. 3. If there is a bequest of the usufruct in a site, and [then] a building is erected on the site, it is well settled that the subject-matter is changed and the usufruct is extinguished. No doubt, if it was the bare proprietor who erected the building, he will be liable in an action on the testament or for *dolus*,

6 POMPONIUS (*on Sabinus* 5) (besides which the usufructuary has a right to the Interdict *quod vi aut clam*,)

7 JULIANUS (*Digest* 35) unless such bare proprietor takes the building down and grants me a usufruct in the site; I am assuming that the time has passed lapse of which puts an end to the usufruct.

8 ULPIANUS (*on Sabinus* 17) The usufruct of an estate being bequeathed, if the residence should be destroyed, the usufruct will not be extinguished, as the residence is an accession to the land; this would no more follow than it would if trees were to fall.

9 PAULUS (*on Sabinus* 3) It should be added that I still have a usufruct in the ground on which the residence stood.

10 ULPIANUS (*on Sabinus* 17) Suppose however the estate was an accession to the residence; how then? let us consider whether in that case the usufruct in the estate itself would be extinguished; but, as to this, we must say, as before, that it will not be extinguished. 1. The usufruct is extinguished not only where the house is reduced to the bare site, but also where the testator pulls down the house and puts a new one in its place; no doubt, if he executes partial repairs here and there, we cannot lay down the same rule, even though at last the whole house should be rebuilt. 2. Where there is a bequest of usufruct in a field or a close, then, if it should be flooded, so as to be turned into a pool or a swamp, beyond doubt the usufruct will be extinguished. 3. Again, if the bequest is of the usufruct in a pool and the pool comes to be dried up and so turned into a field, the subject being changed, the usufruct is extinguished. 4. If however what is bequeathed is the usufruct in an arable field and vineyards are made on it or the converse takes place, I do not think the usufruct will be extinguished. It is true that where the usufruct is in a forest, and thereupon the forest is cut down and the ground sown, the usufruct is undoubtedly extinguished. 5. Should the usufruct of a mass of metal be bequeathed and vessels be made out of it or the converse take place, Cassius, as quoted by Urseius, says that the usufruct is gone; and this view I should say is correct. 6. On the same principle where an ornament is destroyed or its form is altered, this puts an end to the usufruct in it. 7. Sabinus too tells us, in connexion with the usufruct of a ship, that if the ship is repaired now in one part and now in another, the usufruct is not destroyed; but if the ship is taken to pieces, then, though

it should be made up again out of the same timbers without a single piece being added, still the usufruct is extinguished; and this, I should say, is the sounder opinion. In fact, even if a house is rebuilt, the usufruct is extinguished. 8. If the usufruct bequeathed is in a team of four horses, and one of the horses dies, the question may be asked whether the usufruct is extinguished. For my own part, I should say it makes a great deal of difference whether the usufruct bequeathed was in the horses or in the team; if it was in the horses, it will continue with reference to the remaining horses, if in the team, it will not continue at all, as there has ceased to be any team;

11 PAULUS (*on Sabinus* 3) unless another horse is put in the place of the dead one before the legacy vests.

12 ULPIANUS (*on Sabinus* 17) Where a usufruct is bequeathed in a bath room, and the testator turns it into a room to live in, or in a shop, and he turns it into a dwelling-place, then, according to the proper rule, the usufruct is extinguished. 1. On the same principle if a man leaves a usufruct in an actor, and then transfers him to some other kind of service, we must hold that the usufruct is extinguished.

13 PAULUS (*on Sabinus* 3) If the usufructuary has reaped the corn and after that dies, according to Labeo, the crop which is lying cut belongs to his heir, and the ears which are unsevered from the ground belong to the owner of the estate; the produce, he says, is gathered when the ears of corn [are severed], or the grass for hay is cut, or the grapes are plucked, or the olives are shaken down, though the corn should not be ground, or the oil made, or the vintage completed. (But true as is Labeo's remark about olives which are shaken down, still, according to Julianus, the rule is different with respect to olives which fall of themselves.) The produce [Labeo proceeds to say,] becomes the property of the usufructuary when he has gathered it, although it goes to a *bona fide* possessor as soon as it is once severed from the soil.

14 POMPONIUS (*on Sabinus* 5) Setting aside *capitis diminutio* and death, all other grounds of extinction of usufruct will admit of the extinction being even partial.

15 ULPIANUS (*on Sabinus* 18) Sometimes the bare proprietor can bestow freedom on a slave held in usufruct; for instance, where the usufruct was bequeathed till such time as the slave should be manumitted; in which case, as soon as the proprietor proceeds to manumit, the usufruct is extinguished.

16 THE SAME (*Disputations* 5) Where a usufruct is bequeathed to me on a condition, and in the meantime the thing is in the hands of the heir, such heir can bequeath the usufruct to a third person; the result being that, if the condition attached to my legacy comes to pass, the usufruct left by the heir terminates. Should I myself however lose the usufruct, it will not revert to the legatee to whom the heir bequeathed it in absolute terms, because the legal position of joint legatees cannot be acquired under two different testaments.

17 JULIANUS (*Digest* 35) The usufruct in an estate is bequeathed to you absolutely, and the bare property to Titius on a condition; pending the condition, you acquire the right of bare property, and after that the condition is fulfilled. In this case Titius will have the estate with all rights, and it makes no difference that the bare property was bequeathed with a reservation of the usufruct, because when you yourself[1] acquired the property you lost all your right to the legacy of usufruct.

18 POMPONIUS (*on Sabinus* 3) If a usufruct was bequeathed to a slave who was part of the assets of a deceased person, such bequest taking place before entry was made on the inheritance, the better opinion is that, when entry is made, the usufruct passes to you (the heir), and is not extinguished on the ground of change of ownership, as it did not so much as vest before you became heir.

19 GAIUS (*on the provincial Edict* 7) Neither a usufruct, nor a foot-way nor a carriage-way is lost by change of ownership.

20 PAULUS (*on Plautius* 15) Where a man has a usufruct, will he retain it if he only exercises *usus*, his reason being that he believes *usus* to be the only right that he has got? My answer is that if he chooses to exercise the use only, knowing that he has a right to the use and produce (*ususfructus*), he must still be held to be enjoying produce too; if he does not know, I should say he loses the right to produce (*fructus*), as his use is founded not on what he has, but on what he thinks he has.

21 MODESTINUS (*Differences* 3) If a usufruct is bequeathed to a city and, after that, the ground of the city is ploughed up, it ceases to be a city, as it happened to Carthage; consequently it ceases to have the usufruct, as it were by death.

[1] Ins. *tu* before *enim*. M.

22 POMPONIUS (*on Quintus Mucius* 6) If the *usus* of a house is bequeathed to a woman, and she goes beyond seas and is absent for the time which suffices by law for the loss of the *usus*, but her husband uses the house, then there is nothing to prevent the *usus* being retained, just as if the woman had left her slaves at the house and herself stayed abroad. Still more strongly will the corresponding rule apply where a husband leaves his wife in the house in a case in which the *usus* of the house was bequeathed to the husband himself.

23 THE SAME (*on Quintus Mucius* 26) If a field in which a man has a usufruct is inundated by a river or the sea, the usufruct is lost, as, in fact, the bare property itself is lost in such a case; indeed the usufructuary cannot maintain his position even by fishing. At the same time, just as the bare property is reestablished, if the water recedes with the same suddenness with which it came, so too, it must be held, will the usufruct be reestablished.

24 JAVOLENUS (*Extracts from Labeo's Posteriores* 3) I had a usufruct in a garden, and, that being the case, a river spread over the garden and afterwards receded again; here Labeo holds that the right of usufruct itself is restored, as the soil of the garden always remained in the same legal position. I should say that this is only true in case the river spread over the field in the way of inundation; if the river shifted its course and came to flow in that quarter, my opinion is that the usufruct is lost, because the ground occupied by the old channel becomes public property, and I hold that it cannot be put back upon its former footing. 1. The same rule of law, according to Labeo, ought to be observed with reference to a foot- or carriage-way; but I hold with respect to these the same opinion that I do with respect to the usufruct. 2. LABEO. Even if the surface soil is taken off my land and other soil put in its place, the ground does not on that account cease to be mine, any more than if the field were manured.

25 POMPONIUS (*Selections from various passages* 11) The law is that usufruct may be lost by non-user, whether it is the usufruct in a share or is undivided.

26 PAULUS (*on Neratius* 1) Should a field be taken into possession or a slave be captured by enemies and afterwards be relinquished, any usufruct is reestablished by the law of *postliminium*.

27 THE SAME (*Manuals* 1) If a slave in whom someone has a usufruct is surrendered for *noxa* by the bare proprietor to the usufructuary, by the acquisition of the proprietorship the servitude of usufruct is merged and is thereby at an end.

28 THE SAME (*on Plautius* 13) If a usufruct is bequeathed for alternate years, it cannot be lost by non-user [by one legatee], as it is a case of more than one legacy.

29 ULPIANUS (*on Sabinus* 17) Pomponius raises this question. The bare proprietor of an estate [in which I have a usufruct] hires the land from me and sells it to Seius without reserving the usufruct; do I retain the usufruct through the action of the purchaser? The opinion he gives is this: though the proprietor should pay me rent, nevertheless the usufruct is lost, as the purchaser enjoys as of his own right and not in my name: of course the proprietor is liable to me in an action on the lease, to the extent of the interest I had in his not doing what he did. It is true that if a man hires the usufruct from me and lets it to someone else, I retain the usufruct, but where the bare proprietor of the land lets the usufruct in his own name, we must hold that I lose it, as the lessee does not enjoy it in my name. 1. As to whether[1] if the bare proprietor bought the usufruct from me, and then sold it, I should lose it, this is a proper question to ask. But I should say that I should lose it, as, again, the purchaser of the estate does not enjoy it as on a purchase from me. 2. Pomponius asks further this question. Suppose a usufruct is bequeathed to me, and I am requested to hand it over to you; am I held to enjoy through you, so that the usufruct will not be lost [by non-user]? As to this, he says himself that he is in doubt; but the better opinion is, as Marcellus remarks in a note, that there is nothing in the case to prejudice the fidei-commissary, as he has an *utilis actio* in his own name.

30 GAIUS (*on the provincial Edict* 7) The flesh and fleece of dead cattle are not part of the produce, because, as soon as the animal is dead, the usufruct is extinguished.

31 POMPONIUS (*on Quintus Mucius* 4) If the usufruct of a flock is bequeathed and the numbers of the flock are so far reduced that it cannot be called a flock at all, the usufruct is at an end.

[1] After *vendidisset* ins. *an*.

V.

ON USUFRUCT IN THINGS WHICH ARE CONSUMED OR WASTED BY THE USING.

1 ULPIANUS (*on Sabinus* 18) The Senate decreed that it should be possible for a usufruct to be bequeathed in every kind of thing that was understood to be in any person's patrimony; the result of which decree clearly is that a bequest can be made of the usufruct of such things as are destroyed or wasted by use.

2 GAIUS (*on the provincial Edict* 7) But, in the case of money, a proper undertaking must be given to those at whose charge a usufruct in such money is bequeathed. 1. This senatorial decree did not operate so as to make it possible that there should be a usufruct in money, strictly speaking; as the authority of the Senate cannot subvert common sense; still, the above relief being given, the consequence was that there came to be something analogous to a usufruct.

3 ULPIANUS (*on Sabinus* 18) After this a valid bequest can be made of the usufruct in anything whatever. Does this include a usufruct in pecuniary demands? Nerva said No; but the better opinion, which is that held by Cassius and Proculus, is that this also can be bequeathed. However, Nerva himself goes so far as to say that the usufruct in a pecuniary demand can be bequeathed to the actual debtor himself, and that, in that case, he must be excused the payment of interest.

4 PAULUS (*on Neratius* 1) Consequently the debtor too can be called upon to give the undertaking.

5 ULPIANUS (*on Sabinus* 18) This senatorial decree does not refer exclusively to the case of a man who bequeaths the usufruct of money or anything else which he has of his own; it applies equally where he deals with what belongs to someone else. 1. If there is a bequest of the usufruct of money, or of anything else which can only be used by consuming it, and no undertaking is given, a point to consider is whether, when the usufruct comes to an end, the money that was handed over, or whatever else it may be the worth of which is bound up in the diminution of it, can be recovered by a *condictio*. However, as long as the usufruct is still going on, if the heir wishes to bring a *condictio* to have the under-

taking given, it may fairly be said that the omitted undertaking can be sued for by a *condictio* for an unliquidated amount (*incerti*); but if he waits till the termination of the usufruct, then, as Sabinus holds, the *condictio* can be brought for the actual sum. This opinion is approved of by Celsus himself (*Dig.* 18), and it seems to me not to be wanting in acuteness. 2. What is said above as to the usufruct in money or in anything else which is used by consuming it applies equally to the *usus*; we are told by both Julianus and Pomponius (Stipulations 8) that the *usus* and the usufruct of money have the same legal implications.

6 JULIANUS (*Digest* 35) If ten thousand (*aurei*) are bequeathed to you and the usufruct of the same ten thousand to me, the whole ten thousand will become your property; still five thousand will have to be paid to me, on the terms of my undertaking that at the time of my death or *capitis diminutio* the money shall be handed over; as in fact if a landed estate were bequeathed to you and a usufruct in the same estate to me, you would have the property of the whole estate, but you would have part of it with the use and produce (*ususfructus*), and part without the use and produce, and I should give an undertaking to the satisfaction of an impartial arbitrator, not to the heir but to you. 1. Where however the usufruct in the same ten thousand is bequeathed to two different persons, they will both get five thousand, giving undertakings to one another mutually and to the heir as well.

7 GAIUS (*on the provincial Edict* 7) Where the usufruct bequeathed is of wine, oil, or corn, the actual property ought to be transferred to the legatee, and he must be required to give an undertaking to the effect that whenever he dies or suffers *capitis diminutio*, goods of like quality shall be handed over; or else the original goods must be valued and an undertaking must be given to pay a fixed sum of money. This last is indeed the more convenient method, and we may assume exactly the same rule in the case of anything else the worth of which is given by the using thereof.

8 PAPINIANUS (*Questions* 17) A testator appointed three heirs and bequeathed to Titius the usufruct in fifteen thousand (*aurei*), ordering at the same time two of the heirs to give security for Titius. It was held that there was a valid legacy of [the benefit of] the undertaking [for security so ordered to be given], and that the decree of the Senate did not militate against this construction

as there was nothing in it to prevent the [statutable ?] undertaking being given. There were, in fact, it was held, two legacies, the one being for an ascertained sum and the other for an unliquidated amount. Accordingly, on the head of usufruct, a portion of the money might be sued for [by the legatee] at the hand of an heir who had had security given him by his co-heir, and the same defendant was subject also to an action for unliquidated damages, if he had himself failed to give security. With regard to an heir who gave security himself, but owing to the default of his co-heir failed to have security given him, he would not in the meantime be liable in pursuance of the legacy of usufruct under the senatorial decree, nor would he be liable to the action for unliquidated damages, seeing that he had already given the required security to his co-heir. We are further of opinion that the legatee can be compelled to promise [to refund]. When however the usufruct comes to an end, if the co-heirs should be sued as sureties, they will not have a right of action on mandate [to recoup themselves], the fact being that they never contracted a mandate, they only obeyed the will of the testator, and, in any case, they are themselves released from their obligation under the legacy of security. One point there is which did not require a long discussion, viz. that the second legacy, that of the security, was not given to the heirs, but to the person to whom was left the usufruct in the money, whom in fact the testator desired to benefit, and in whose interest he thought it was that he should not be looking about for sureties at his own risk.

9 PAULUS (*on Neratius* 1) In a stipulation for restoring the amount in the case of a usufruct in a sum of money, two eventualities only are referred to, viz. those of death and *capitis diminutio*,

10 ULPIANUS (*on the Edict* 79) as the use of the money cannot be lost in any other way than by one of these two. 1. If the *usus* only of the money is bequeathed, then, seeing that in this particular case we must, on the whole, take it that the term *usus* involves *fructus* as well, the same stipulation must be made. Some say that the stipulation is not made till the money is given; I should say however that the stipulation holds, whether it comes after or before the payment over of the money.

11 THE SAME (*on Sabinus* 18) If a usufruct is bequeathed to anyone in wool, or perfumes, or spices, no usufruct in these things

is held to be legally created, but the matter comes under the decree of the Senate, which prescribes the undertaking to be given.

12 MARCIANUS (*Institutes* 7) Money being left to Titius on such terms that after the legatee's death it was to come to Mævius, it was laid down by a rescript of the divine Severus and Antonius that, although it had been added that Titius was to have the *usus* of the money, nevertheless what was bequeathed him was the property in it, and the reason for making mention of *usus* was that the money was to be handed over from Titius to Mævius on the death of the former.

VI.

ON THE CASE OF USUFRUCT BEING SUED FOR OR THE RIGHT OF IT BEING DENIED.

1 ULPIANUS (*on Sabinus* 18) If some [real] servitude is attached to a landed estate in which there is a usufruct existing, Marcellus (b. 8), as cited by Julianus, upholds the opinion of Labeo and Nerva, to the effect that he (the usufructuary) cannot bring a *vindicatio* to recover the servitude, but he can bring one for the usufruct; the consequence being that if the neighbour does not allow him, say, to walk or drive, he, such neighbour, is liable on the ground that he does not let the other enjoy the usufruct. 1. When a usufruct is bequeathed, it requires [those][1] subsidiary rights without which a usufruct cannot be enjoyed; consequently, in the case of such a bequest, there must needs go with the usufruct a right of access, so much so that, where a man bequeaths the usufruct of some spot on the terms that the heir is not to be compelled to allow a road [over adjoining ground], this addition must be held to be inoperative; again, if a usufruct is bequeathed and a right of pathway is withheld, such withholding is inoperative, because a right of access always goes with the usufruct. 2. Again, if a usufruct is bequeathed and there is no right of access to the estate which is the subject thereof over [other] land which forms part of the inheritance, the usufructuary can certainly bring an action on the testament to procure that the usufruct shall be given him accompanied with means of access. 3. Whether, when the usufruct is bequeathed, the usufructuary has a right of access simply, and so a right to a foot-way, or he can claim a road-way too,

[1] M.

Pomponius hesitates to say (b. 5); but he holds, and that rightly, that he ought to have such accommodation as is required to enable him to get the benefit of his usufruct. 4. Will the heir then be bound to furnish him with further conveniences or servitudes too; for example, servitudes of lights and water, or not? As to this, I should say he is only compellable to furnish those conveniences without which the other cannot "use" the premises at all; if the party can use the premises, though not without some inconvenience, he has no claim to the above.

2 POMPONIUS (*on Sabinus* 5) If a usufruct is sued for on a testament, at the hands of an heir who has cut down trees or pulled down the house or in any way lowered the value of the usufruct, either by subjecting the land to servitudes or releasing the adjoining property from servitudes attached to the land, it is a matter for the conscience of the judge to take into consideration what the condition of the estate was before joinder of issue, so that the usufructuary may be protected by him in the enjoyment of the rights so ascertained.

3 (JULIANUS *Digest* 7) Where a man to whom a usufruct had been delivered in pursuance of a *fidei-commissum* has been out of enjoyment of it for the full period the lapse of which would have caused him to lose it, if it had become his legally, he cannot have an action to have it made good; it would be an absurd thing that people who have acquired the possession only of a usufruct and not the property in it should be in a better legal position.

4 THE SAME (*Digest* 35) An estate was bequeathed to Titius with reservation of usufruct, and the usufruct in the same estate was bequeathed to Sempronius on a condition. In this case I expressed the opinion that, during the interval, the usufruct was joined to the property, though the law is, that when an estate is bequeathed with reservation of the usufruct such usufruct goes to the heir. The reason for the above is, that when the owner bequeaths an estate saving the usufruct, and bequeaths the usufruct to another person on a condition, it is not his intention that the usufruct should remain with the heir.

5 ULPIANUS (*on the Edict* 17) The only person who can assert at law the right to use and produce is one who has the usufruct; the bare owner of the estate cannot do it, because one who has the proprietorship has not got a separate right to the use and produce, as in fact he cannot have a servitude over his own estate, and a

man must bring an action on his own right only; he cannot do it on the right of someone else. It is true that the bare owner has a prohibitive right of action (*actio negativa*) against an [alleged] usufructuary, still he may be held to proceed on his own right rather than that of another, so far as he denies that the [alleged] usufructuary has a right to the use against his will, or [asserts] that he himself has a right to stop him. Should it happen that the plaintiff in the action is not the owner, then, although the [alleged] fructuary will not have the right of use, still this latter will gain his case, in virtue of the principle which puts possessors in the better position, though they should have no legal right. 1. Whether the usufructuary has a good right of action *in rem* against the bare proprietor only, or equally so against anyone in possession, is a matter of question. Julianus says (*Dig.* 7) that he has such a right of action against anyone in possession, as, if you take the case of a [real] servitude being attached to the estate which is in usufruct, the usufructuary ought to lay claim, as against the owner of the adjacent land, not to such [real] servitude, but to the usufruct. 2. If a usufruct is created in a portion of an estate, an action *in rem* can be brought in respect of it, whether the party lays claim therein to the usufruct or denies someone else's right to it. 3. In all actions which are brought in respect of usufruct, it is abundantly plain that the question of produce is included. 4. If, after joinder of issue in an action for usufruct, the usufruct should come to an end, will produce cease to be claimable for any further time? I should say that it will so cease; in fact, Pomponius tells us (b. 40) that, in the case of the death of the usufructuary, his heir will be allowed an action for arrears of produce only. 4 *a*. If the usufructuary is successful, he has a right to recover all incidental benefits (*omnis causa*), consequently, if the usufruct bequeathed was in a slave, the possessor will be bound to hand over any acquisition made by the slave founded on the property of the usufructuary or derived from the slave's own services. 5. Add that if it so happen that the usufruct is lost by lapse of time, the fact being that one man was in possession and another came forward to defend the action, it is not enough for the latter to renew the usufruct, but he must give a guaranty against recovery of the same by superior title; suppose, for example, the party who was in possession had pledged the slave —or the land—for a debt, and the plaintiff should be forbidden by the pledgee to exercise his lawful right. Accordingly a guaranty will have to be given him. 6. Just as, where a usufructuary brings a confessorian action[1] *in rem* (asserting his usufruct), he has a right to have the produce given to him, so too has the bare proprietor, if he has recourse to a negatorian action (denying the other's usufruct); but, in any case, this is only where the party who sues is not in possession; (—it may be observed that there are cases where the possessor himself may sue—;) if either party [being plaintiff] is in possession, he will get nothing under the head of produce. On the whole then, does the duty of the judge comprehend more than this: to see that the usufructuary is held free to take the produce without being molested, and the owner of the property is protected against disturbance?

6 PAULUS (*on the Edict* 21) When a man has joined issue as defendant on a question of usufruct, then, if he gives up possession, and that without fraudulent intent, he will be dismissed from the action, but if he volunteered to take up the defence of the case and joined issue in the action as though he were in possession, there will be judgment for the plaintiff.

VII.

ON THE SERVICES OF SLAVES.

1 PAULUS (*on the Edict* 2) A service consists in something that is done, and it is not an overtly existing thing until the day arrives when it has to be rendered; the case is like that of a man making a stipulation for the child that is to be born of Arethusa.

2 ULPIANUS (*on the Edict* 17) When there is a bequest of the services of a slave, the right thereto will not be lost by *capitis diminutio.*

3 GAIUS (*on the provincial Edict* 7) The usufruct of a slave comprises his services and the hire that can be got for such services.

4 THE SAME (*book two of the urban edict on trials of the question of freedom*) The produce of a slave consists[2] of services, or, to invert the phrase, the services of a slave are comprised in his produce. But as in other cases produce is understood to be what remains over after necessary expenses are deducted, so it is also in the case of services of slaves.

[1] For *confessoriam* read *confessoria.* Cf. M.

[2] For *constitit* read *consistit.* Cf. M.

5 Terentius Clemens (*on the lex Julia et Papia* 18) Where the services of a slave are bequeathed, I have myself always been taught and Julianus is of opinion that the *usus* is understood to be given.

6 Ulpianus (*on the Edict* 55) When an action is brought on a claim to the services of a slave who is an artificer, the compensation to be ordered will be according to their value, but, in the case of a common drudge, they will depend on the nature of his work. This is to be found in Mela. 1. If a slave is under five years of age or is physically weak, or is for any other reason one who could perform no service for his owner, no valuation of his services will be made. 2. Moreover the pleasure or the fondness felt by the owner will count for nothing in the valuation; for example, where the owner has a strong regard for a slave or makes a favourite of him. 3. It must be remembered that in estimating the value necessary expenses should always be deducted.

VIII.

On Usus and Habitatio

1 Gaius (*on the provincial Edict* 7) Let us now consider the question of *usus* and *habitatio*. 1. Besides usufruct there may be such a thing created as bare *usus*, that is use without produce (*fructus*); and this is commonly created in just the same ways as usufruct.

2 Ulpianus (*on Sabinus* 17) When the *usus* is left a man he can use, but he cannot take the produce. Let us consider some cases in detail. 1. The *usus* of a house, say, is left to the husband or to the wife. If it is to the husband, he can live in the house, and that not [merely] by himself, but with his slaves too. Whether he can have his freedmen there also was once a matter of question, but Celsus says that he can have his freedmen, and that he may also take in a guest. This is said by Celsus in his *Digest* (b. 18), and the same opinion is supported by Tubero. I remember that in Labeo, in the book called *Posteriores*, the question is discussed whether he can go so far as to take in a lodger, and Labeo says that a man who lives in the house himself can take in a lodger; he also says he can take in guests as well as his freedmen

3 Paulus (*on Vitellius* 3) and clients,

4 ULPIANUS (*on Sabinus* 17) but that even such persons as these must not occupy the house without him. According however to a note by Proculus, dealing with the subject of lodgers, a person cannot be properly called a lodger (*inquilinus*) when he lives with the other. It follows from the above that, even if the usuary receives a rent, still, as long as he is occupying the house himself, this is not to be grudged him: suppose, for instance, that a man of inferior means has had left him the *usus* of such a spacious house that he is content with a small portion of it. We may add that the usuary may have with him such persons as he has to serve him in the place of slaves, though they should be in fact free or the slaves of another man. 1. If the *usus* is left to a woman, then, as Quintus Mucius was the first to allow, she can have her husband living with her, because otherwise, if she chose to make use of the house, she would have to live unmarried. That, to take the converse case, a wife may live with her husband, [if the *usus* is his,] was never a matter of question. Suppose then the *usus* is bequeathed to a widow, would such a woman, if she contracted a second marriage after the *usus* was created, be at liberty to have her husband living with her? The true rule is, as Pomponius (b. 5) and Papinianus (Questions 19) agree, that she can have her husband to live with her, even if she marries after the *usus* is created. Pomponius goes further and says she can have her father-in-law too.

5 PAULUS (*on Sabinus* 3) Indeed the father-in-law can have his daughter-in-law to live with him; at any rate if her husband is there too.

6 ULPIANUS (*on Sabinus* 17) A woman may have living with her not only her husband but her children and freedmen or freedwomen, also her parents: Aristo himself makes a note on Sabinus to this effect. In fact we must go so far as to say that women can admit the same kind of persons as men can;

7 POMPONIUS (*on Sabinus* 5) still a woman is not at liberty to admit an inmate where he is not one who can live with propriety in the same house as the woman herself who has the *usus*.

8 ULPIANUS (*on Sabinus* 17) But those who are entitled to *usus* cannot let the house for exclusive occupation, nor allow persons to live in it without them, nor can they sell the *usus*. 1. Should however the *usus* of a house be bequeathed to a woman on condition that she should be divorced from her husband, she must

be excused the condition, and she can have her husband living with her in the house. This is approved of by Pomponius (b. 5).

9 PAULUS (*on Sabinus* 3) Moreover, where the *usus* of anything at all is bequeathed, the rule is that the wife can have the *usus* of it in common with her husband.

10 ULPIANUS (*on Sabinus* 17) Where what is bequeathed is a *habitatio*, it is asked whether such a bequest is the same thing as that of an *usus*. That the two bequests, of *usus* and *habitatio* respectively, operate to much the same effect Papinianus himself admits (Questions 18). For example, the legatee of a *habitatio* cannot give it away, and he can only take in the same kinds of persons as a usuary can; but the *habitatio* does not pass to the heir, as such, nor is it lost by non-user or *capitis diminutio*. 1. Where what is left is *chresis*, it may be fairly considered whether this is an *usus*; as to which Papinianus says (Responsa 7) that in this case the *usus* is left but not the *fructus* (produce) too. 2. But if it is left in such words as the following: "to such a one the usufruct of the house so that he can live in it," let us consider whether the legatee will have a *habitatio* and no more or will have the usufruct too. As to this, Proculus and Neratius hold that it is a legacy of the mere right of *habitatio*, which is a sound view. No doubt if the testator had said "the *usus* so that he can live there," no one would hesitate to say that it was a good legacy [of *usus*]. 3. It was a question among the old lawyers whether the *habitatio* was a right of dwelling for one year or would last for the party's lifetime; but Rutilius says that the right of *habitatio* is good for a lifetime, which view is confirmed by Celsus (*Dig.* 18). 4. If the *usus* of an estate is left, this, as all agree, is less than the *fructus* (produce), indeed far less. However let us consider what are the rights involved. According to Labeo the legatee is free to live on the estate, and he can forbid the owner to enter; but he cannot forbid a tenant to enter, nor the owner's gang of slaves, that is to say, such as are there to cultivate the land; still, if the owner should send his domestic slaves there, such slaves can be forbidden to enter, on the same principle as that on which the owner himself can be forbidden. Labeo also says that the usuary can make exclusive use of the places that serve for storing wine and oil, but the owner cannot use them without the usuary's consent.

11 GAIUS (*Everyday points or golden things* 2) The usuary has a right to remain on the land for so long only as he causes no

annoyance to the owner and is not in the way of the persons who carry on agricultural operations; moreover he cannot sell or let or give away for nothing to anyone else the right which he possesses.

12 ULPIANUS (*on Sabinus* 17) He has a right to have the full use, if the *usus* of the country-seat and mansion are left him. No doubt we must on the whole say that the proprietor can[1] come and take produce and, during the time required for getting the produce together, it must be allowed that he is at liberty to take up his abode there. 1. In addition to his right of living on the spot (*habitatio*), a legatee of the *usus* will also have the right of walking about, as well as of riding or driving; Sabinus and Cassius add that he may use wood for ordinary daily purposes, also the garden, and take apples, kitchen vegetables and flowers, as well as draw water, not however so as to make a profit, his right is to use only, in short, it does not go so far as using up. Nerva says the same thing, but adds that he can use straw and sticks, though not leaves or oil or corn or agricultural produce. Sabinus, Cassius, Labeo, and Proculus go further, and say that he may in fact take enough to maintain himself and his family out of what is grown on the estate, and that in cases where Nerva says he may not; Juventius goes so far as to let him share the use with guests and friends, and this is, I think, the true view, as a usuary may be treated a little more liberally, in accordance with the consideration due to a person to whom a bequest of *usus* has been made. But the things last mentioned he can, I should say, only use in the country-house; as to apples, kitchen vegetables, flowers and wood, it is worth considering whether he can only use them on the spot or they can be actually brought into the town to him; but we had better take the rule to be that they can be brought into the town, as this amounts to no great burden, if the estate yields a plentiful supply. 2. Where the bequest is of the *usus* of domestic animals, say a flock of sheep, according to Labeo, he can only use them for manuring purposes, he cannot take wool or lambs or milk, as these are rather of the nature of produce. He may, I should say, go further and take under the head of *usus* a small quantity of milk, as the will of deceased persons is not to be construed with such extreme strictness. 3. If what is left is the *usus* of a herd of cattle, the legatee will have a right to every kind of use, whether for ploughing or any other purpose for which cattle are fit.

[1] Insert *posse* before *plane*. Cf. M.

4. Where the *usus* bequeathed is that of a stud of horses, we may consider whether the legatee can break them in and use them in harness for draught. Should the man to whom the *usus* of the horses is left be a charioteer, I should say that he cannot use them for the races in the circus, as this might be held to amount to letting them out; at the same time, if, when the testator left them, he knew that such was the legatee's profession and way of life, he may be supposed to have contemplated the very thing. 5. If the *usus* of an attendant (*ministerium*) is left anyone, he can use the slave to attend upon himself (*ad suum ministerium*) and his children and his wife, and he will not be held to have made his right over to another, if he makes use of the man along with them; although, if the *usus* of a slave is left to a son under *potestas* or to a slave, then, inasmuch as such *usus* will belong to the father or the owner, as the case may be, it imports a right of use on their part only, and not on the part of those subject to their *potestas*. 6. The legatee cannot let out the services of a slave held in *usus* nor make them over to another; this is maintained by Labeo; how, indeed, can a man make over services to another when he has to use them himself? However, Labeo himself holds that, if a man hires a farm, a slave in whom he has an *usus* may work on it; what does it matter, he asks, in what way it is that he makes use of his services? Accordingly, if a usuary should contract to work up wool, he can very well carry out the work by means of slave women in which he has the *usus*, and again, if he contracts to make woven garments or to build a block of chambers, or a ship, he can employ for the purpose the services of a slave in whom he has the *usus*; and this does not clash with the known opinion of Sabinus that, where the *usus* of a female slave is given, she cannot be sent to a wool factory, nor her services be let out for money, but the legatee must, as a matter of law, make the woman work the wool for himself; of course, where the party does not let out the slave's services, but simply executes the work which he undertook to do, he does work it for himself. This view is upheld by Octavenus too.

13 GAIUS (*on the provincial Edict* 7) However Labeo holds that the slave himself or the slave woman can be required to pay money instead of rendering service.

14 ULPIANUS (*on Sabinus* 17) If I make a stipulation or take delivery of something by means of a slave whom I hold in *usus*, the

question arises whether I acquire anything, assuming that what is done is founded on my property or on the slave's services. If it is founded on the slave's service, it will be void, because a usuary cannot let out the slave's services; but, if it is founded on my property, the rule is that a slave whom I hold in *usus* will, by stipulating or taking delivery, acquire for me; in fact, I should in the case supposed be using his services. 1. It makes no difference whether usufruct is bequeathed or *fructus* (produce) only; *fructus* includes *usus*, but *usus* does not include *fructus*, and though there cannot be any *fructus* without *usus*, there may be *usus* without *fructus*. To take a plain case:—if you have a bequest of the *fructus* with reservation of the *usus*, the bequest is void, so Pomponius says (on Sabinus 5); and he also says that in the case where there is a bequest of usufruct, but the *fructus* is revoked, the whole legacy must be held to be revoked, but where there is a bequest of *fructus* without *usus*, the *usus* must be held to be created too, just as it might be expressly created at the outset. If usufruct is bequeathed and then the *usus* is revoked, according to Aristo, this is no revocation at all, and this is the more indulgent view. 2. If the *usus* is first bequeathed and then the *fructus* to the same person, Pomponius says the latter is united to the *usus*. He says also that if the *usus* is bequeathed to you and the *fructus* to me, then we take in common as far as the *usus* is concerned, but I alone am entitled to the *fructus*. 3. It is possible, however, for the *usus* to go to one, *fructus* without *usus* to another, and the bare property to a third; suppose, for example, the owner of the estate bequeaths the *usus* to Titius, and after that his heir bequeaths the *fructus* to you or makes it over to you in some other way.

15 PAULUS (*on Sabinus* 3) When the *usus* of land is bequeathed, the usuary will have a right to take of the edible produce thereof enough for a year, though not more, even if by that means the produce of an estate of average size should be consumed; on the principle on which he might enjoy the *usus* of a house or a slave in such a way as to leave nothing over for anyone else under the head of produce. 1. Just as, where there is a bequest of the *usus* of land, the legatee cannot prevent the proprietor from being frequently on the spot with a view to agricultural operations, by doing which he would in fact be preventing the proprietor from enjoying the produce itself, so too the heir cannot do anything to prevent the legatee of the *usus* from making use of the land in the way in which a prudent householder ought to use it.

16 POMPONIUS (*on Sabinus* 5) If the *usus* of an estate is bequeathed in terms which require it to be properly stocked and equipped, the legatee will have as full a claim to the use of the things constituting the equipment of the estate as if the *usus* of the things themselves had been bequeathed him expressly. 1. The actual proprietor is at liberty to keep guard over the estate or the house by means of a forester or a town-agent, [as the case may be,] even without the leave of the usufructuary or the usuary, as he has an interest in preserving the boundaries of the property. All this applies equally in whatever way the usufruct or the *usus* may be created. 2. When people have the *usus* of a slave and not the *fructus* too, it is admissible that they should make him some present or that he should carry on some business with their money on the terms that whatever the slave acquires thereupon shall be his *peculium* with reference to them (the usuaries).

17 AFRICANUS (*Questions* 5) If the *usus* of a house is bequeathed to a son under *potestas* or to a slave, I should say this is a valid legacy, and the same kind of procedure is available for recovering it as would be if the produce had been bequeathed as well. Consequently the father or the owner, [as the case may be,] may live in the house just as well when the son or the slave is absent as when he is on the spot.

18 PAULUS (*on Plautius* 9) If the *usus* of a dwelling-house is bequeathed without the *fructus*, the obligation to execute repairs so as to keep the property wind and water-tight falls on the heir and the usuary equally. We may consider, however, whether the real rule is not this, that if the heir takes the produce he is[1] himself bound to repair, but if the thing the *usus* of which is bequeathed is of such a kind that the heir cannot take the produce, the legatee is compellable to repair it himself. This is in fact a reasonable distinction.

19 THE SAME (*on Vitellius* 3) There can be no bequest of a share in an *usus*; a man can take produce to the extent of a share, but he cannot make use to the extent of a share.

20 MARCELLUS (*Digest* 13) If I am bequeathed the *usus* of a slave, the slave acquires for me if he acts as my commercial agent (*institor*) and I make use of his services in a shop; in short, he acquires for me in buying and selling wares; and so he does by taking delivery of anything by my order.

[1] Read *sit* for *est*. Cf. M.

21 MODESTINUS (*Rules* 2) The *usus* of a water is a personal right, consequently it cannot be transmitted to the heir of the usuary.

22 POMPONIUS (*on Q. Mucius* 5) The Divine Hadrian, in a case where the *usus* of a forest was bequeathed to certain legatees, laid down that the produce too must be held to be bequeathed to the same persons; because, unless the legatees were at liberty to cut and sell the timber in the way that usufructuaries are, they would take nothing by their legacy. 1. Although a legatee to whom the *usus* of a house is bequeathed should keep up such a small establishment that he cannot avail himself of the *usus* of the whole house, nevertheless the unoccupied part cannot be used by the proprietor, because the usuary will have a right to use the whole from time to time as occasion may arise, the fact being that not uncommonly the very proprietor of a house uses some parts and leaves other parts unused, according to the requirements of the particular occasion. 2. When an *usus* is bequeathed, if the legatee makes ampler use of the thing than he has a right to make, what does the duty of the judge prescribe who determines the question how far the right of use extends? It comes to this, he must see that the legatee do not use otherwise than as the law allows.

23 PAULUS (*on Neratius* 1) NERATIUS. The person who has the bare property cannot in any way change the specific character of the thing held in *usus*. PAULUS. The fact is that he is not at liberty to alter the position of the usuary for the worse; but he may alter it for the worse even where he changes the condition of the subject-matter[1] for the better.

IX.

WHAT KIND OF UNDERTAKING IS GIVEN BY THE USUFRUCTUARY.

1 ULPIANUS (*on the Edict* 79) Where there is a usufruct bequeathed in anything, the prætor thought it most in accordance with justice that the legatee should give two undertakings; one to the effect that he would use the thing in such a way as would satisfy an impartial arbitrator, and the other that when the usufruct should cease to belong to him he would restore what was left of it.

[1] Insert *re* before *etiam*. Cf. M.

1. This stipulation is required to be made, whether the property is moveable or consists of land; 2. and it must be added that the undertaking ought to be used for *fideicommissa* too. Again, there is no doubt that, if a usufruct is created by a donation *mortis causa*, the undertaking ought to be given, as in the case of legacies; and if the usufruct is created in any other way the rule is the same. 3. The party must promise that the usufruct shall be enjoyed in such wise as to satisfy a reasonable arbitrator, that is to say, that he will not bring down the prospective value of the usufruct, and that he will act in all respects as he would if the thing were his own property. 4. However the heir and the legatee will do well, if as soon as the legatee begins to take the produce, they have an attestation made as to the present state of the property, so that it may be made clear thereby whether the legatee has diminished its value, and, if so, how far. 5. It was thought best that an undertaking should be given to the effect above mentioned by means of a stipulation, in order that, if the party should not use the thing in question agreeably to the judgment that would be given by a reasonable arbitrator, it might be possible to sue on the stipulation at once; and thus people do not have to wait till the usufruct expires. 6. The stipulation refers to two occasions in which it may come into operation; there is first the case of the party using in some way which would not be approved of by a reasonable arbitrator, secondly the case in which the usufruct is to be surrendered; the former clause will take effect as soon as ever the usuary commits an irregularity in respect of the use such as is described, and it may take effect again and again; the second takes effect on the termination of the usufruct. 7. With regard to the above statement that what there shall be left of the thing will have to be surrendered, the proprietor is not therein stipulating for the actual thing, as he would not be held to be capable of making any valid stipulation for his own property, he only stipulates that what there shall be left of it shall be surrendered. Still the engagement may comprise the putting a valuation on the property, for instance, [in view of a case] where a usufructuary who has it in his power to interrupt the acquisition of the property by use omits to do so; as he undertakes thorough care of the thing;

2 PAULUS (*on the Edict* 75) in fact, the usufructuary is bound to answer for the custody.

3 ULPIANUS (*on the Edict* 79) This stipulation embraces every kind of contingency in which the usufruct would be lost. 1. We must regard the usufruct as ceasing to belong to the party even where it has never yet begun to belong to him at all, although it was given him as a legacy, and the stipulation can none the less be sued on, it being assumed that a thing ceases to belong to a man to whom it never did belong. 2. Where the usufruct is renewed by the legacy [for] every time it is lost, the stipulation can be sued on, unless the undertaking is worded so as to meet the case, but an *exceptio* will have to be raised. 3. Again, where the testator leaves you a usufruct, and, subject to the condition of your having children, the full proprietorship, then, if the usufruct should be lost, the above stipulation will be enforceable, but it will be a case for an *exceptio.* 4. If the heir disposes of the bare property, and after that the usufruct is lost, let us consider whether he can sue on the stipulation. Strictly speaking it may be held that in actual law the stipulation is not enforceable, because the thing cannot be handed over to the heir or his successors, and the person to whom it can be handed over, that is, the person who has become owner, was not privy to the stipulation; however this last-mentioned person must look out for himself by making a separate stipulation at the time when his ownership is acquired; indeed, even if he has not done so, he can still have recourse to an action *in rem.*

4 VENULEIUS (*Stipulations* 12) If the [usu]fructuary acquires the property, then, as the usufruct is merged, it ceases to belong to him; but if an action is brought against him on the stipulation, the proper rule is that either the action fails, even in direct law, if we go so far as to apply to this case the principles which guide a reasonable arbitrator, or else the defendant must raise a special *exceptio.*

5 ULPIANUS (*on the Edict* 79) The stipulation contains an assurance that no malicious fraud has been committed or will be committed, and, the reference to such fraud being drawn *in rem*, it is held to include fraud on the part of anyone, whether a successor or an adoptive father. 1. If the bequest is of *usus* without *fructus*, the prætor orders security to be given without the article of produce being referred to; and quite rightly, the object being that the undertaking should relate to use only, not produce as well. 2. Consequently it is equally true that if what is acquired

is the right to *fructus* without *usus*, the stipulation is in place. 3. And where a right of *habitatio* is left or the service of a man or of any animal at all, the stipulation is required, although these rights are not modelled on usufruct altogether.

6 PAULUS (*on the Edict* 75) The same rule applies to returns from an estate, for example when there is a bequest of vintage or harvest; as if the things which on the death of the legatee revert to the heir were taken in pursuance of the bequest of a usufruct[1].

7 ULPIANUS (*on the Edict* 79) Where something was delivered in pursuance of a usufruct, but security was not given, then, according to Proculus, the heir can sue to recover the thing, and if he is met with an *exceptio* to the effect that the thing was delivered in pursuance of a usufruct, he has a good replication. This view is sound in principle; but a personal action can still be brought to compel the giving of the actual undertaking. 1. Where there is a bequest of the usufruct of a sum of money, the stipulation ought to make express mention of the two cases referred to in the words "shall be given when you die or suffer *capitis diminutio*." The reason why these two cases alone are to be mentioned is that it is in such cases only that the use of a sum of money can be lost.

8 PAULUS (*on the Edict* 75) If the usufruct is bequeathed to you and the bare property to me, the undertaking must be given to me; but if the bare property is bequeathed to me on a condition, some authorities, including Marcianus, hold that the undertaking should be given both to the heir and to me; and this is a sound view. Again, if the property is bequeathed to me, and, when it should cease to belong to me, to another, then again the undertaking should be given to both, as was held in the case mentioned above. If the usufruct is bequeathed to two jointly, they will be bound to give undertakings to one another and also to the heir, such undertakings containing a reference to the contingency expressed in the following form of words; "to give up the usufruct to the heir, if the right to the same does not pertain to the other co-legatee."

9 ULPIANUS (*on the Edict* 51) If a usufruct is bequeathed to me, and I am requested to hand it over to Titius, it is worth considering who is bound to give the undertaking; is it Titius or I, the

[1] Read *quasi* for *quamvis* and transpose *quæ* and *legato*. So M. suggests, rather than despair of the passage.

legatee? or shall we say that the heir can sue me and that I must sue the beneficiary? The simplest rule is the following:—if I have any contingent interest in the usufruct left in my hands, so that it may possibly revert to me, in other words to the legatee, when you lose it, the matter can be disposed of by you, [Titius,] giving the undertaking to me and my doing the same to the bare proprietor. But if the usufruct was left me for the sake of the beneficiary, and there is no chance of its reverting to me, then the beneficiary ought to give the undertaking to the bare proprietor directly. 1. One thing is certain, that whether a man has a usufruct by direct law or even by the help of the prætor, in any case the usufructuary is compellable to give the undertaking or defend any actions brought. 2. It is true that if the bare property is bequeathed to anyone from and after a given day, but the bequest of usufruct is immediate, then the rule is, according to Pomponius, that the usufructuary should be excused the undertaking, because it is certain that the property will come to him or his heir. 3. If what is bequeathed is a usufruct in dress, then, according to Pomponius, though the heir should stipulate that the dress should be given up on the termination of the usufruct, still the promisor does not incur any liability if he gives it up in a worn condition without deliberate ill intention. 4. Where several persons are bare proprietors, each will stipulate with reference to his own share.

10 PAULUS (*on the Edict* 40) If you and I have a slave in common, and I bequeath the usufruct in him to you, the undertaking will be required for the benefit of my heir; it is true that he can take proceedings with regard to the actual property by an action *communi dividundo,* but the matter of a usufruct to which you have an undivided title does not come within the scope of the judge's duty who hears the action in question.

11 PAPINIANUS (*Responsa* 7) Where the *usus* of a house is left, an undertaking ought still to be given to use in such manner as to satisfy a reasonable arbitrator; and it would not alter the case if the father desired that his sons, being heirs, should occupy the house along with his widow, who is legatee.

12 ULPIANUS (*on Sabinus* 18) If what is left is the usufruct of actual vases the undertaking mentioned in the senatorial decree will not be required, but only the one which says that the party will use and take profit so as to satisfy a reasonable arbitrator. If then the

vases were delivered in order that the deliveree may get the profit of them, no one hesitates to say that the property in them does not pass to the person who received them; as in fact it was not intended in the delivery of them that the person who delivered should part with the property, but that the legatee should use and take the profit. Accordingly, the vases not becoming the property of the fructuary, they can be recovered by the owner by means of a *vindicatio*, though no undertaking was given. It is of course established that no one can recover his own property by a personal action except from a thief.

EIGHTH BOOK.

I.

On Servitudes.

1 Marcianus (*Rules* 3) Servitudes are either attached to persons, as in the case of *usus* and usufruct, or to things, as in the case of rustic and urban estates.

2 Ulpianus (*on the Edict* 17) Where a house is owned in common, one of the owners cannot by himself subject it to a servitude.

3 Paulus (*on the Edict* 21) Of servitudes attached to estates some regard the soil and some the surface.

4 Papinianus (*Questions* 7) Servitudes cannot in direct law be created from and after a given day, or to last until a given day, or so as to depend on a condition, or to last until a given conditional event, for example, as long as I choose, still, if any such qualification is made, a person who sues to recover the servitude against the terms agreed upon can be met by an *exceptio* of *pactum*[1] or of *dolus*; this Cassius tells us is to be found in an opinion of Sabinus, and is his own view. 1. It is settled that servitudes can be qualified by expressing certain limitations, as by saying what kind of transport may be used or may not be used, for instance, that it must always be by horse, or that no more than a given weight shall be conveyed, or that such and such a flock shall be driven, or that charcoal shall be carried. 2. Where intervals of so many days or hours are specified, this does not deal with the question when the servitude shall exist, but only with the mode of enjoyment of a servitude legally created.

[1] Ins. *per* before *pacti*. Cf. M.

5 GAIUS (*on the provincial Edict* 7) *Via* (roadway), *iter* (pathway), *actus* (driftway), and *ductus aquæ* (water-course), are created in much the same ways as those in which we have already said that a usufruct is created. 1. The enjoyment of a servitude may be given with particular limitation as to the time for it, for instance, it may be understood that the party is to enjoy the servitude from the third hour until the tenth hour, or that he shall have it every other day.

6 PAULUS (*on the Edict* 21) A servitude can be either released or created as to a certain portion of the land exclusive of the rest.

7 ULPIANUS (*on the lex Julia et Papia* 13) The right to conduct a drain is a servitude.

8 PAULUS (*on Plautius* 15) A servitude cannot be created to the effect that a man shall be at liberty to pluck apples, or to walk about, or to dine on another man's ground. 1. If your land serves me, then if I come to be owner of a share in your land or you of a share in mine, the servitude is in both cases retained as to a part [*per partes*], though it could not have been originally acquired as to a part.

9 CELSUS (*Digest* 5) If a *via* over anyone's land is conveyed or bequeathed to a man without more[1], he will be at liberty to walk or drive without restriction, that is to say over any part of the land that he likes; only, however, in a reasonable way, as the language which people use is always subject to some tacit reservation. The party cannot be allowed to walk or drive through the house itself, or straight across the vineyards, when he might have gone some other way with equal convenience and with less damage to the servient land. It is in fact an established rule that, wherever it was that he directed his course at the outset, he is bound to walk or drive that way only, and he has no power after that to change his direction. This was the opinion of Sabinus himself; that writer argued from the case of a water-course, which, he said, the party could at first carry in any direction he pleased, but, when it had been once made in any particular direction, he was not at liberty to carry it somewhere else; and it is perfectly true that this rule ought to be observed with a *via* as well.

[1] Read *simpliciter* for *simplicius*. Cf. M.

10 THE SAME (*Digest* 18) Where a right of *iter* is bequeathed which cannot be enjoyed without special works being executed, then, according to Proculus, the legatee has a right to make a pathway by means of levelling or substructure.

11 MODESTINUS (*Differences* 6) It is commonly received that a servitude cannot be acquired in respect of a share of ownership; consequently, if a man who has an estate stipulates for a *via* and afterwards disposes of a share in his estate, he vitiates the stipulation by putting matters into a position in which such stipulation could not at the outset have been validly made. Again, a *via* cannot be either bequeathed or revoked in respect of a share, and if either is done [in words], the bequest or revocation is void.

12 JAVOLENUS (*Epistles* 4) I have no doubt that a servitude can be lawfully acquired through a slave, so as to be attached to land belonging to a municipality.

13 POMPONIUS (*on Quintus Mucius* 14) If there is a gift of a *via*, but the space pointed out for it is so narrow that neither a carriage nor a horse can be got into it, it will be held that what is acquired is an *iter*, rather than a *via* or an *actus*: if however a horse could be taken along it, but not a vehicle too, it will be held that what is acquired is an *actus*.

14 PAULUS (*on Sabinus* 15) Servitudes of rustic estates, although attached to corporeal things, are nevertheless incorporeal, and for that reason they are never acquired by use; or the reason may be that they are servitudes of such a character that they are not subjects of determinate and continuous possession; as no one can use a path so constantly and continuously that his possession of it cannot be held to be intermitted for any moment. The same rule is applied to servitudes of urban estates too. 1. The servitude of an *iter* giving access to a burial-place will remain a matter of private property, and consequently it can be released to the owner of the servient estate; moreover it can be acquired even where the religious character of the burial-place is already established. 2. Where a piece of public ground or a public road lies between [two estates], a servitude of drawing water can still be created, though a water-course cannot; however, the practice is to petition the Emperor that the party may be at liberty to make a water-course across a public road in such a manner as not to incommode the public. If what lies in the way is a spot which is consecrated or religious, this prevents even the servitude of an *iter*; as no one can have any servitude over such land.

15 POMPONIUS (*on Sabinus* 33) Wherever a [supposed] servitude cannot belong to any person or attach to any estate, then, inasmuch as no neighbour has any interest therein, it has no valid existence; take, for example, a servitude to the effect that you shall not walk over your own estate or be upon it. Hence, if you grant me a servitude to the effect that you shall have no right to the use and produce of your own estate, this is inoperative; it would be a different thing if it were to the effect that you should have no right to take water on your own estate in order to diminish my supply. 1. It is not of the nature of servitudes that a man should [have to] do anything; for instance, remove shrubs so as[1] to afford a more pleasing view, or, with the same object, paint something on his own ground; but only that he should submit to something being done or abstain from doing something.

16 JULIANUS (*Digest* 49) When a man has taken an estate by way of security for debt, it is not unjust that he should have allowed him an *utilis actio* to enforce a servitude attached to it, just as he will be allowed an *utilis actio* to recover the estate itself. It is quite understood that the same rule is observed as to a man who is a tenant of vectigalian land (a perpetual lease).

17 POMPONIUS (*Rules*) It is impossible for a share in a *via*, *iter*, *actus*, or water-course to be made the subject of an obligation [to grant it], as the use of such rights is undivided; consequently where a man who has stipulated for any such servitude dies leaving several heirs, any one heir can sue for the whole *via*, and, if the promisor dies leaving several heirs, there is a right of action for the whole against any one of them separately.

18 PAULUS (*Questions by Papinianus* 31, *note*) In all cases where servitudes are extinguished by merger on entry by the heir, it has been laid down that a legatee [of the servient estate] will be barred by an *exceptio*, if he decline to let the servitude be created again.

19 LABEO (*Posteriores epitomized by Julianus* 4) I am of opinion that where a man sells an estate, it can be subjected to a servitude [in his favour], even if such servitude should be of no use to him; suppose, for instance, some vendor should have no object in[2] having a water-course, still that servitude might be created [in his favour]; there are some things which people are able to[3] possess even where they are of no use to them.

[1] Read *ut* for *aut*. Cf. M. et Bas.

[2] del. *debere*. M. [3] del. *debere*. M.

20 JAVOLENUS (*Extracts from Labeo's Posteriores* 5) Whenever a roadway or any other right to be attached to an estate is being purchased, Labeo holds that an undertaking should be given to the effect that nothing will be done by you [the vendor] which will prevent the purchaser being able to use the right in question, as there is no such thing as clear delivery of a right of that kind. I should say myself that the exercise of the right must be treated as equivalent to delivery of possession, and for this reason interdicts have been established answering to possessory ones.

II.

ON SERVITUDES OF URBAN ESTATES.

1 PAULUS (*on the Edict* 21) If public ground or a public road comes in the way, this does not hinder the servitude of a *via* or an *actus* or a right to raise the height of a building, but it hinders a right to insert a beam, or to have an overhanging roof or other projecting[1] structure, also one to the discharge of a flow or drip of rain-water, because the sky over the ground referred to ought to be unobscured. 1. If you have the usufruct and I have the bare property in a house which is subject to the servitude of support to the neighbour's building, I am liable to be sued in respect of the whole, and you are not liable at all.

2 GAIUS (*on the provincial Edict* 7) Rights attached to urban estates are such as follows :—that of raising a building higher and stopping the neighbour's lights, that of preventing such raising, also that of discharging eavesdrip on to the roof or the vacant ground belonging to a neighbour, or the servitude of not being free to discharge it ; also the right of letting beams into the neighbour's wall, lastly that of having a projecting house or other structure and other similar rights.

3 ULPIANUS (*on Sabinus* 29) There is also such a servitude as that of a right to enjoy an unobstructed prospect.

4 PAULUS (*Institutes* 2) Where[2] servitudes of lights are created, what people are held to acquire is a right to the effect that some neighbour of theirs shall have to submit to their lights (*lumina nostra excipiat*) ; but, if the servitude imposed is that lights shall not be blocked, what they are on the whole held to acquire is this,

[1] For *prohibendi* read *projiciendi*. Cf. M. [2] del. *in*. M.

that the neighbour shall have no right to raise his own building against their will so as to diminish the flow of light to their building.

5 ULPIANUS (*on the Edict* 17) When we speak of a thing being against a man's will in the matter of a servitude, we must understand this to imply not that he expressly objects, but that he does not consent. Accordingly Pomponius holds (b. 40) that a thing may properly be said to be against the will of an infant or lunatic ; the expression does not refer to the act which is done, but to the existence of a right to do it of the nature of a servitude.

6 GAIUS (*on the provincial Edict* 7) These servitudes, exactly like those of rustic estates, are lost by non-user after lapse of a specific period ; subject however to this distinction, that they are not lost by non-user as a matter of course, but only where the [servient] neighbour acquires freedom by the user of the same. Suppose, for instance, your house serves my house in this way, that your house must not be raised higher, lest it obstruct my lights, and, that being the case, I keep my windows blocked up or built up for the period prescribed ; I still lose my right only in case you have had your house raised and standing higher throughout the same period ; but, if you made no alteration, I retain the servitude. Again, if your house is subject to a servitude of having a beam let into it, and I take the beam out, I do not lose any right, unless you fill up the cavity out of which the beam was taken, and keep things in that condition for the required time ; but, if you make no alteration, the[1] servitude remains unaffected.

7 POMPONIUS (*on Quintus Mucius* 26) With regard to the statement that I may succeed in acquiring freedom for my building by user of the same, it is said by Mucius that I could not have acquired it as well by having a tree planted on the same spot ; and this is perfectly sound, because a tree would not remain in the same precise posture and condition as a wall would, owing to the natural movement of the tree.

8 GAIUS (*on the provincial Edict* 7) Where a wall is on natural principles common [to two houses], it is not lawful for one of the two neighbours to pull it down or repair it, as he is not sole owner.

9 ULPIANUS (*on the Edict* 43) Where a man, by raising the height of his own house, cuts off the flow of light to that of his

[1] del. *suum*. Cf. M.

neighbour, but is not subject to a servitude in respect of the latter, there is no right of action against him.

10 MARCELLUS (*Digest* 4) Gaurus to Marcellus:—I own two houses, and one of them I bequeath to you; [after my death] my heir raises the height of the other, and obstructs your light: can you take any[1] proceedings against him? and do you think that it makes any difference whether the house which he raises was his own or is one which he has as heir? I desire your opinion on another point too; namely, whether the heir is bound to allow access to the property bequeathed through a house which belongs to a different owner [from the legatee][2], a question often asked where there is a bequest of the usufruct in a piece of ground to which there is no access to be had, except through the land of some other person [than the usufructuary]. Marcellus replied as follows:—Where a man who had two houses has bequeathed one of them, there is no doubt that his heir has a right to stop the access of light to the one bequeathed by raising the height of the other; and the same must be said where a man bequeaths a house to one person and the usufruct of another house to another. But we cannot always apply a similar rule to the case of a right of way; because a legacy of usufruct is worth nothing without a right of access, whereas a man can live in a house even where it is darkened. In fact, where there is a legacy of the usufruct of some spot, access ought to be given as well, since if what was left were a right to draw water, a right of way for the purpose of drawing water would be given too. It should be observed that the heir is allowed to build out the light and darken the house bequeathed only to an extent which does not cause the light to be shut out entirely, but leaves remaining so much as the inmates require for reasonable daily use and enjoyment.

11 ULPIANUS (*on the Office of Consul* 1) Where a man wishes to block out his neighbours' lights or to construct anything at all which interferes with their convenience, he must bear in mind that he is bound to observe the form and position of the original buildings. 1. If you have got no agreement with your neighbour as to how high a building which you have taken in hand to construct may be raised, you can have an *arbiter* appointed.

12 JAVOLENUS (*Extracts from Cassius* 10) Where buildings are subject to a servitude to the effect that no part of them is to

[1] Read *numquid* for *quid*. Cf. M.

[2] Probably to the heir himself.

be raised in height, they may very well have shrubs placed upon them in excess of that height, but if the servitude is one of prospect, and the shrubs would be in the way, they cannot be so placed.

13 PROCULUS (*Epistles* 2) A man named Hiberus, who has a block of chambers at the back of my warehouses, built some bathrooms against our party-wall; at the same time a man has no right to have tubes brought up against a party-wall; just as, in fact, he has no right even to build another wall of his own[1] over it. The rule applies the more strongly in the case of the tubes for the fact that they cause the wall to be scorched by the fire: so I wish you would speak to Hiberus about the matter, and prevent him from doing what a man has no right to do. Proculus replied:—"I do not suppose Hiberus has any doubt in this case that he is doing an illegal act in setting up tubes against a party-wall." 1. According to the opinion of Capito, it is lawful to put facing on a party-wall, just as I am at liberty to have on such a wall paintings of very great value; at the same time, if the neighbour pulls the wall down and proceedings are taken for *damnum infectum*, by way of action on [the regular] stipulation, such paintings cannot be valued at a higher rate than ordinary stucco; and the same rule must be observed with the facing.

14 PAPIRIUS JUSTUS (*on Imperial enactments* 1) The Emperors Antoninus Augustus and Severus Augustus declared by rescript, with reference to vacant ground over which no one has a servitude, that the owner, or anyone else with his consent, is free to build on it, if he leaves clear the statutable space between the spot and the neighbouring block.

15 ULPIANUS (*on Sabinus* 29) Various differences are maintained in practice between the servitude of not blocking out lights (*ne luminibus officiatur*) and that of not interfering with the prospect (*ne prospectui offendatur*); as, in the case of the prospect, the dominant owner has this particular advantage, that nothing may be constructed so as to prevent his having a pleasing and unimpeded view, but, in the case of the lights, the right enjoyed is that the servient owner shall erect nothing by which the other's lights would be obscured. Accordingly, whatever he does which tends to impede the light can be put a stop to, if there is a servitude existing, and there can be a "notification of novel

[1] For *suum per* read *super*. Cf. M.

structure" served on him, supposing, that is, that his operations are such as to interfere with the light.

16 PAULUS (*Epitomes of Alfenus's Digest* 2) Light means a view of the sky, and there is a difference between light and prospect; a prospect may exist in respect of places on a lower level, but there can be no light enjoyed from a place on a lower level.

17 ULPIANUS (*on Sabinus* 29) If a man plants a tree so as to shut out [a dominant owner's] light, it may perfectly well be said that he acts in violation of the servitude created; even a tree causes a smaller extent of sky to be seen. But if what is placed on the spot in no respect impedes the light, but only keeps off the sunshine, then, if it is done in a place where it was more agreeable to be without sunshine, it may be said that thè party does not do anything in violation of the servitude; but if he does it over against a room meant to be exposed to the sun (*heliocaminus*), or a sundial, then it must be said that, by causing shade in a place where sunshine was indispensable, he is acting in violation of the servitude created. 1. If a man, on the other hand, should remove a building or, say, branches of trees, with the result that a spot which up to that time was in the shade comes to be fully exposed to the sunshine, he does not violate the servitude; the servitude to which he was subject was to the effect that he should not obscure the light, but, in the case in question, he does not obscure the light, he lets light in to an excessive extent. 2. However, there are cases in which it may be said that even a man who removes or lowers a building does obscure the light, where, for example, light found its way into the house by reflexion or some sort of repercussion. 3. The following clause in an agreement for delivery of a house,—"eavesdrip to be such as it is now,"—imports that neighbours are under the necessity of admitting eavesdrip, it does not go so far as this, that the purchaser himself is to submit to eavesdrip from the adjoining buildings; so that what the vendor engages is that he enjoys a servitude in respect of eavesdrip but that he is subject to none in favour of anyone else. 4. What is here said as to eavesdrip must be understood to be true of all other cases of servitudes too, where no express agreement is made to a different effect.

18 POMPONIUS (*on Sabinus* 10) If pipes through which you conduct water are laid against my house and do me an injury,

I have a good right of action *in factum*, but I can also call upon you to give an undertaking by way of stipulation against *damnum infectum*.

19 PAULUS (*on Sabinus* 6) According to Proculus, a pipe attached to a party-wall and supplied with water from a cistern or from rainfall is a thing which cannot legally be had; at the same time an adjoining proprietor cannot be prevented from having a bath against such a wall, though the wall should contract moisture thereby, any more than he could be prevented from spilling water in his own dining-room or his bedchamber. However Neratius says that if a warm bathroom is used in such a way as to keep up constant moisture, and this is a nuisance to the adjoining owner, it can be put a stop to. 1. A chamber made of earthenware constructed against a party-wall is a thing which may legally be had, if it is so supported as to remain standing even when the wall is taken down, always provided it does not interfere with the repair of the party-wall. 2. Sabinus says very reasonably that I have a right to place a set of steps against a party-wall, because this is a thing which can be taken down again.

20 THE SAME (*on Sabinus* 15) Servitudes which affect only the surface of the soil are kept alive by possession; suppose, for instance, I have a beam reaching from my house and let into yours[1], then, by means of the beam, I possess the easement of having it so let in[2]. A similar result will follow if I have a balcony resting on something on your ground, or I discharge eavesdrip on to your ground, as, in that case, I make use of something which is within your precincts, and so[2] have possession [of an easement] by what may be called an act of mine. 1. If your courtyard is on a higher level than my house, and you have granted me a right of way on foot or by carriage to my house across your courtyard, but there is no level approach across such courtyard, I have a right to construct steps or a sloping approach by my door, so long as I do not, with a view to maintaining the way, break the place up more than is necessary. 2. If a building from which eavesdrip is discharged is taken down with a view to its being replaced by another of the like form and character, it is requisite in the general interest that the latter should be regarded as the same building; whereas,

[1] del. *habendi consuetudinem*. Cf. M.: even so the passage must be corrupt; sense, on the whole, clear.

[2] For *si* read *sic*. Cf. M.

no doubt, if you take a strict view of the matter, what is erected in the second instance is a different building, and, consequently, by the removal of the old building, any usufruct in the same is lost, true as it may be that the site of a building is a part of it. 3. If a servitude of eavesdrip is created, it is not lawful for the owner of the servient ground to build on the spot to which the eavesdrip has reached. 4. If the eavesdrip was originally discharged from the tiles, it cannot afterwards be legally discharged from a floor made of beams or other material. 5. In whatever way a right to discharge eavesdrip is acquired, the discharge may be made from a higher level, as the servitude thereby becomes less burdensome, because water that falls from a height falls with a less forcible impact, and sometimes is carried away and does not reach the place on which the servitude attaches; but the discharge cannot lawfully be carried lower down, because that would make the servitude more burdensome, that is to say, instead of a drip it would be a stream. For a similar reason, the discharge of eavesdrip may be carried back, because then the fall will begin more on the property of the dominant owner, but it cannot be carried forward, because then it would fall on a different spot from that to which the servitude applies; the dominant owner is at liberty to make the discharge more tolerable, but not more burdensome; in short, it ought to be understood that the position of a servient neighbour may legally be altered for the better, but not for the worse, unless some express [provision for an] alteration was made at[1] the creation of the servitude. 6. A man who builds on vacant ground which is subject to a servitude of eavesdrip is at liberty to bring up his building to the place from which the fall comes; indeed, if the fall takes place on to the building itself, he is allowed to carry the building higher, provided always the drip is duly submitted to.

21 POMPONIUS (*on Sabinus* 33) If your house is subject to two distinct servitudes in favour of my buildings, viz. first that it is not to be raised higher, and secondly that it must receive rain-water from off my buildings, and I thereupon grant you the right to raise your house without my consent, the rule which will have to be laid down, as far as my eavesdrip is concerned, is as follows: if, on your house being raised higher, it would become impossible for my rain-water to be discharged on to it, you will for that reason not be at liberty to raise it; but if the discharge would not be interfered with, you are at liberty to raise it.

[1] Ins. *in* after *nominatim*. M.

22 JULIANUS (*Extracts from Minicius* 2) The owner of a building can subject his neighbour to a servitude of such a kind that he gives an undertaking with reference not only to lights actually existing, but to any that may afterwards be created.

23 POMPONIUS (*on Sabinus* 33) If a servitude is created with these words:—"lights now existing to remain as they are," this is not held to involve any provision as to future lights; but if the words of the undertaking are "lights not to be built out," this expression leaves it doubtful whether it is only meant that lights now existing are not to be built out, or subsequent lights are included too. The more indulgent construction is that the expression, being general, refers to all lights, whether they exist at the moment or come to exist after the date of the agreement. 1. Even a building which is yet to be made, but does not at present exist, may be subjected to a servitude or have one attached to it.

24 PAULUS (*on Sabinus* 15) Whoever has a building which is, with good right, superposed on another may lawfully build on the top of his own structure as high as he pleases, so long as this does not [tend to] impose on the buildings underneath a more burdensome servitude than they ought to have to bear.

25 POMPONIUS (*on Sabinus* 33) The above rule applies to cases in which something is inserted from one building into another; this being the only way in which a man can have an upper building superposed on another which is not his. 1. There are three houses standing on an incline, of which the house in the middle serves the uppermost house, but the lowest is subject to no servitude, and a party-wall which divides the middle house from the lowest is raised in height by the owner of the lowest house. In this case, according to Sabinus, the owner last mentioned can legally keep the wall so raised.

26 PAULUS (*on Sabinus* 15) In a case of common property it is not open to either owner, in virtue of a servitude, to construct anything without the consent of the other or to prevent the other from constructing anything; as no one can have a servitude over his own property. Accordingly, seeing the endless contests that might arise, it generally comes to a partition. However, by means of the action *communi dividundo*, one part-owner can prevent works being executed by the other or procure that the other shall remove any work that he has executed already, provided such removal is advisable in the joint interest of both.

27 POMPONIUS (*on Sabinus* 33) But if you and I own the Titian house in common, and something is unlawfully inserted from that house into another belonging to me in severalty, I have a right to bring an action for damages against you on account of it or to have a partition[1] of the property. The same is the case where, in a similar way, some part of your house has been made to reach over a house belonging to you and me in common, as I have an action in my own person against you. 1. If you are going to build upon ground common to you and another, your fellow-owner has a right to stop you, even though you should have a right to build given you by the adjacent owner, as you have no right to build on common property[2] without the consent of the other part-owner.

28 PAULUS (*on Sabinus* 15) An opening made at the bottom of the wall of a [neighbour's] apartment or dining hall and intended [by him] to be used for the purpose of washing the floor is not held to imply the servitude of discharging a stream nor to be a thing a right to which can be acquired by lapse of time. This is true on the assumption that no water comes to the spot in question in the form of rain, as what is effected by human hands has no perpetual cause; but water that falls from the heavens, although it does not keep on without interruption, still has a natural cause, and therefore is regarded as being produced perpetually, and all real servitudes are required to depend on causes that are perpetual, for which reason it is impossible to grant a right to a water-course which is supplied by a reservoir or a standing pool. The servitude of a right to discharge eavesdrip is also required to depend on a natural and perpetual cause.

29 POMPONIUS (*on Quintus Mucius* 32) Accordingly if the adjacent proprietor suffers any damage owing to an opening such as above mentioned, in respect of which there is no servitude, we must say that it is a case for a stipulation against *damnum infectum*.

30 PAULUS (*on Sabinus* 15) If a man purchases and takes delivery of a house which serves his own house, the servitude is merged and taken away, and, should he wish to sell the house again, the servitude must be expressly renewed; otherwise the house will be sold free. 1. If I acquire a share in an estate over which I have a servitude, or in respect of which I am subject to a servitude,

[1] Read *partiri* for *perdere*. Cf. M.: otherwise the translation must be "or to lose my property."

[2] Read *in re* for *in jure*. Cf. M.

it is held that the servitude is not merged, as it still exists in respect of a share. Hence, if my estate serves your estate, and thereupon you[1] deliver to me a share in your estate and I deliver to you a share in mine, the servitude remains. Again, the acquisition of a usufruct in either of the two estates will not interrupt the servitude.

31 THE SAME (*on the Edict* 48) If the heir, being ordered by testament not to obscure the lights of an adjacent owner, but to allow him a servitude, pulls down the [servient] building, the legatee [adjacent owner] must have an *utilis actio* allowed him by which the heir can be stopped, if he afterwards attempts raising the building above the old limit.

32 JULIANUS (*Digest* 7) My house serves the house of Lucius Titius and that of Publius Mævius, [the servitude in both cases being] to the effect that I may not raise the height of my house, whereupon I ask Titius's leave to raise it, and I keep it so raised for the legal period; in this case I acquire by user freedom from the servitude as against Publius Mævius, as Titius and Mævius did not have one servitude between them, but two respectively. This view derives support from the consideration that, if either of the two were to release me from the servitude, I should thereby be free so far only as that one was concerned, but I should be under a servitude in favour of the other just as much as before. 1. Freedom from a servitude is acquired by user where the house is kept in possession [and not otherwise]; accordingly, if a man who has raised the height of a house [in violation of a servitude] goes out of possession of the house before the expiration of the legal period, such acquisition is interrupted; and then anyone else who comes into possession of the same house will acquire freedom by user by lapse of the entire legal period. The fact is that the nature of servitudes is such that they cannot be possessed, but the person who possesses the [dominant] tenement is regarded as possessing the servitude.

33 PAULUS (*Epitomes of Alfenus's Digest* 5) The person who is bound to replace a column which afforded support to an adjacent house in virtue of a servitude is the owner of the servient house, not the party who desires to enjoy the support; as, where part of the written terms of a contract for sale of a house was as follows:— "the wall is to continue to give the same support that is given now,"

[1] Ins. *tu* before *tuorum*. Cf. M.

this very plainly implies that a wall was required to exist in perpetuity; no doubt it is not declared by these words that the same wall is to be there for ever, which in fact would be impossible, but that there should for ever be a wall of the same kind to support the burden; just as, where a man has given an undertaking that[1] he will afford anyone support for his building (*onus*), it follows that supposing the thing which is the subject-matter of the servitude and bears the burden imposed by the other should be destroyed, another thing of the same kind would have to be supplied to take its place.

34 JULIANUS (*Extracts from Minicius* 2) Where a man has two vacant plots, he can convey the one so as to make it serve the other.

35 MARCIANUS (*Rules* 3) Where a man owns two houses, and, in selling one, he declares that it is to be subject to a servitude [attaching to the other], but, when he makes delivery, he says nothing about the servitude, he can either sue on the contract of sale or bring a *condictio* for an unliquidated amount in order to have the servitude created.

36 PAPINIANUS (*Questions* 7) A man had two houses covered by a single timber roof, and bequeathed them to two legatees respectively. What I said was that, inasmuch as it is the better opinion that the timbers of a building may be shared between two persons on the principle of each owning a specific portion of the whole connected structure, therefore the materials in question here will belong to the two owners over their respective houses, and they will not have mutual rights of action the one against the other so as to contest their respective claims to insert beams from one house into the other; moreover it makes no difference, I said, whether the houses are bequeathed to the two men in absolute terms or to one of them subject to a condition;

37 JULIANUS (*Digest* 7) and the same holds where he [the owner first mentioned] conveys the houses to two persons.

38 PAULUS (*Questions* 2) If my house is so distant from yours that they are out of sight of one another, or there is a mountain

[1] Instead of reading "si quis *alicui* cavisset ut *servitutem præberet* qui" M. would like to omit the words in italics and read *cui* for *qui*, and I have followed him above; we at least get the sense.

between them which shuts out the view, there can be no servitude created between them.

39 THE SAME (*Handbooks* 1) In fact no one can subject his own buildings to a servitude, unless both the grantor and grantee have the respective buildings within the field of view, so that the one building could stand in the way of the other.

40 THE SAME (*Responsa* 3) I gave it as my opinion that persons who did not enjoy the servitude of making a window (*luminis immittendi*) had acted illegally in making an aperture in a wall owned in common with the neighbour and making windows in it.

41 SCÆVOLA (*Responsa* 1) A testator bequeathed to Olympicus for his life the right of habitation in a particular house and [the use of] a warehouse which there was in the house; and adjoining the same house there was a garden, and also an upper room which was not bequeathed to Olympicus, but there had always been access to the garden and the room through the house in which the right of habitation was left. The question was asked whether Olympicus was bound to allow such access. My answer was that it was not a case of a servitude, but still that the heir was at liberty to pass through the house to the parts mentioned, provided he did not incommode the legatee. 1. Lucius Titius made an aperture in a wall in his house and opened a doorway leading to public ground, so as not to exceed the limits pointed out by vertical eavesdrip and a projecting[1] eave; I wish to know, seeing that he did not interfere with the access of light enjoyed by Publius Mævius, his neighbour, or with his means of approach, nor do anything to prevent the discharge of rain-water from his house, whether Publius Mævius, the said neighbour, has any right of action to interfere with him. My answer was that on the facts stated he had none whatever.

III.

ON SERVITUDES OF RUSTIC ESTATES.

1 ULPIANUS (*Institutes* 2) The following are servitudes of rustic estates, *iter, actus, via, aquæ ductus* (footpath, drift-way, roadway, water-course). *Iter* is the right of passing or walking for a man, but not of driving a beast of draught as well;

[1] For *protectus* read *projectus*. Cf. M.

actus is the right of driving a beast of draught or a vehicle; so that one who has [only] an *iter* has no *actus*, and one who has an *actus* has an *iter* too, even without a beast of draught. *Via* is the right of passing or driving or walking; *via* in fact includes both *iter* and *actus*. *Aquæ ductus* is the right to convey water over another person's ground. 1. Among rustic servitudes must be reckoned the right to draw water, the right to take cattle to water, the right to pasture, the right to burn lime or to dig for sand. 2. There is no doubt that the delivery of servitudes and acquiescence in them will constitute sufficient ground for the aid of the prætor.

2 NERATIUS (*Rules* 4) Among servitudes of rustic estates are the right to raise the height of a building and thereby to obscure the neighbour's residence, or to maintain a drain under the house or residence of a neighbour, or to maintain projecting eaves. 1. The right to have a water-course or to draw water to be conveyed by a water-course across the same place can perfectly well be granted to a number of persons; again, the grant may be that the water-course should be used on different days or at different hours; and, if the water-course or the means of drawing water should give a large enough supply, the right may even be granted to a number of persons to take the water across the same place, and that on the same days or at the same hours.

3 ULPIANUS (*on the Edict* 17) Again, a servitude may be granted to the effect that[1] oxen used for ploughing the farm may be pastured on neighbouring land; Neratius tells us (Membranes b. 2) that this kind of servitude can be created. 1. The same writer says that there can be a servitude created to the effect that agricultural produce may be collected in a neighbour's country-house and there kept, or that props for vines may be taken from a neighbour's estate. 2. In the same book he says that where a neighbour has stone quarries adjoining your land, you can grant him the right to cast soil or rubbish or bits of rock on to your land and to leave them as they lie, or to let stones roll on to your land and be left as they are, and then afterwards to carry them away. 3. When a man has a right to draw water, he is held to have an *iter* as well, to enable him to draw it, and, according to Neratius, (Membranes 3), if the right to draw and the right of access for the purpose are both given him, he will have them both, and if the

[1] del. *et*. M.

only right granted is that of drawing, this includes that of access too, or if it is only that of access to the spring, this includes that of drawing. This applies to the case of water being drawn from a private spring. In the case of a public river, Neratius says further in the same book, that a right of *iter* up to it ought to be conveyed, though a right to draw need not, and if a man only grants a right to draw, it is inoperative.

4 PAPINIANUS (*Responsa* 2) A servitude of pasturing[1] cattle or of taking them to water, where the main produce of the estate is derived from cattle, is held to be attached to the estate rather than to the person; but if a testator pointed out some particular person to whom he wished the servitude to be given, the same servitude will not be vouchsafed to a purchaser of the land from such person or to the person's heir.

5 ULPIANUS (*on the Edict* 17) Consequently, in his opinion, such a servitude can be recovered by a *vindicatio*. 1. Neratius says in his books on passages from Plautius that there can be no such thing as a right to draw water, or take cattle to water, or to win chalk or burn lime on another man's ground, except where the party has an adjoining estate, and this he says was the doctrine of Proculus and Atilicinus. At the same time he adds that, however true it may be that there can be a servitude created of burning lime and winning chalk, still it cannot be given for a greater quantity than is required for the purposes of the dominant estate;

6 PAULUS (*on Plautius* 15) it might exist, for instance, where a man had a pottery at which earthenware vessels were made which served for carrying off the produce of the same land (just as on some estates it is the practice for wine to be despatched in jars, or for vats to be made), or one at which bricks were manufactured for building a country-house[2]. If however the pottery were worked to produce vessels for sale, this would amount to a usufruct. 1. Again, a right to burn lime or to take stones or dig for sand for the sake of building something which is [to be] on the estate falls a long way short of a usufruct, and so does a right to take coppice in order that there shall be no want of props for vines. How then if the rights described improve the prospective value of an estate? 2. There can be no doubt that they may be the subject of a servitude; Mæcianus himself is so much in favour of this

[1] Read *servitus* for *servitutes*. Cf. M.

[2] del. *vel* after *tegulæ*. Cf. M.

view that he holds that a servitude can be established to the effect that I shall have a legal right to set up a hut on your land, that is to say, assuming that I already have a servitude of pasture there or of watering cattle, so as to enable me to have a place of shelter if a storm comes on.

7 THE SAME (*on the Edict* 21) When a man is carried on a chair or a litter, he is said to have an *iter*, not an *actus*, but a man cannot take a beast of draught where he has only an *iter*. If he has an *actus*, he can take a waggon or drive beasts of draught. But in neither case has he a right to drag stones or timber; and some say that he cannot carry a spear in an upright position, as this he would not do by way of walking or driving, moreover fruit might be damaged by it. A man who has a *via* has an *iter* and an *actus*, and most authorities hold that he has a right to drag things, and also to carry a spear upright, provided he does not damage the fruit. 1. In rustic estates, however, a servitude is barred by a third estate lying between the two concerned which is subject to no servitude.

8 GAIUS (*on the provincial Edict* 7) The breadth of a *via* is by the Twelve Tables eight feet where the road is straight, but in an "anfractus," that is, where the road winds, sixteen.

9 PAULUS (*Sentences* 1) No servitude can be created for conveying or drawing water from any other place than the source or spring; however, at the present day, the practice is to create it so as to start anywhere.

10 THE SAME (*on the Edict* 49) According to Labeo, there can be a servitude created to the effect that a man shall be at liberty to search for water and convey it in a channel when found; in fact, if it is lawful to create a servitude with reference to a building which is not yet constructed, why should it not be equally lawful to create a similar servitude where the water has not yet been found? Again, if we can grant a man a servitude which authorizes him to search for water, it is possible to grant one which authorizes the conveying of the water when it is found.

11 CELSUS (*Digest* 27) The easement of passing or driving across land which belongs to a number of different persons in common can be conveyed to me by the respective owners separately. It follows that, upon strict principles, I shall not get the easement unless all grant, and then, when the last grant is made, and not before, all the

preceding ones will come into force; however the more indulgent construction is that, even before the last man grants, those who have already granted cannot stop me from using the easement granted.

12 MODESTINUS (*Differences* 9) There is some difference between an *actus* and an *iter*; where a man can travel either on foot or on horseback [as he pleases], it is an *iter*, but where he can drive a herd of cattle or take a vehicle, it is an *actus*.

13 JAVOLENUS (*Extracts from Cassius* 10) A servitude may be acquired, to attach to landed estates of some specified kind, for example, vineyards, because in that case it would be a servitude which concerned the soil rather than the surface. Accordingly, if the vineyards are done away with, the servitude will remain; still if, when the servitude was created, a different intention was entertained, there will have to be an *exceptio* of *dolus malus*. 1. If a whole field is subject to a servitude of *iter* or *actus*, the owner is not at liberty to do anything in the field to interfere with the exercise of the servitude, the right being so general that every sod is subject to it; again, if an *iter* or an *actus* is bequeathed, without any special limits to it being given, such limits must be assigned straightway, and where they are first assigned, there will the servitude be[1], and all other parts of the field will be free from it; accordingly, an *arbiter* must be appointed whose duty it will be in both cases to settle the course of the right of way. 2. In the case of an *actus* or an *iter* the breadth will be whatever was pointed out, and if nothing was said on the matter, it must be settled by the *arbiter*. In the case of a *via*, the rule is different; if the breadth was not pointed out, the statutable breadth can be claimed. 3. If the part of the estate is pointed out without the breadth of the way being given, the party may go over such part wherever he likes, but, if the part is left undetermined, and, as before, no breadth is specified, some one roadway may be selected over any part of the estate, but of no greater breadth than is laid down in the statute; and to settle the course itself, if there is a doubt, recourse must be had to the office of an *arbiter*.

14 POMPONIUS (*on Quintus Mucius* 32) If I grant a roadway to one man on certain lines, I cannot then grant another man a watercourse on the same lines; and again, if I grant one man a watercourse, I cannot sell or grant in any way a footpath on the same lines to another.

[1] For *constitit* read *consistit*. Cf. M.

15 THE SAME (*on Quintus Mucius* 31) Quintus Mucius tells us that where a man has a watercourse, yielding a supply either for every day or for the summer, or one serviceable at longer intervals, over another man's estate, he has a right to lay down a conduit of his own of earthenware or of any other material, in the channel, so as to spread the flow of water, and he has a right to make any construction he likes in the channel, so long as he does not make the watercourse less serviceable for the servient owner.

16 CALLISTRATUS (*on Cognitiones* 3) The Divine Pius issued the following rescript to fowlers:—"It is not reasonable that you should snare birds on other people's land without the landowners' consent."

17 PAPIRIUS JUSTUS (*on Imperial enactments* 1) The Emperors Antoninus Augustus and Verus Augustus laid down by rescript that the water taken from a public river ought to be divided for purposes of irrigation in proportion to the dimensions of the respective [riparian] properties, except where anyone could show that he had a special right in virtue of which he was allowed a larger supply. They further laid down that a man was at liberty to convey water only where this would not involve any wrong being done to another.

18 ULPIANUS (*on Sabinus* 14) Where a *via* is created over several servient estates, it is still a single roadway, as it is a single servitude. Hereupon this question is asked:—If I pass over one estate and forbear to pass over another for such length of time as is required for extinguishing a servitude, do I still keep the servitude? As to this, the better opinion is that either the whole servitude is lost or else the whole is retained; consequently, if I did not make use of either estate, the whole servitude is lost; if I made use even of one only, the whole is retained.

19 PAULUS (*on Sabinus* 6) If one of several co-owners stipulates for an *iter* to the common estate, the stipulation is inoperative, as the right itself could not be granted him, but, if they all stipulate, or a slave stipulates whom they hold in common, each of the co-owners can bring an action in which he prays that the right of way should be given him, as a grant can be made to them all in this way: otherwise it would follow that, if the stipulator of the right of way died leaving several heirs, the stipulation would become inoperative.

20 POMPONIUS (*on Sabinus* 33) If you agree with me at one and the same time that I shall have a right to an *iter* and an *actus* over your land and also that I shall have a right of usufruct in the same, and then I agree with you that I abandon the usufruct, you will not be able to have the use and produce yourself, except on the terms of my having a full right to the *iter* and *actus*. Again, where I have a good right to convey water across your estate, and you have no right to build upon it without my leave, if I agree that you shall have the right to build, nevertheless you will be bound to give me a servitude to this effect, that you shall build only in such a way as will allow of my watercourse being kept up; and the whole state of things will have to be such as it would have been if at the outset only one grant had been made. 1. A servitude may [lawfully] injure the servient estate through something that happens in the natural course of things, though not through anything caused artificially; as, for example, where the water in a channel is increased by a shower of rain, or water flows into it from neighbouring fields, or a spring is subsequently discovered by the side of the channel or within it. 2. If there is a spring close to the boundary of the Seian estate and I enjoyed a right to a watercourse from the spring across that estate, then, should the Seian estate become mine, the servitude will remain. 3. A right to draw water is not attached to a person but to an estate.

21 PAULUS (*on Sabinus* 15) If you grant me a watercourse (*iter aquæ*) across your estate, without assigning the particular quarter in which I am to conduct it, your whole estate will be subject to the servitude.

22 POMPONIUS (*on Sabinus* 33) At the same time, the only parts of the estate which will accordingly be affected by the servitude are such as were not occupied by buildings trees or vines at the time when the grant was made.

23 PAULUS (*on Sabinus* 15) A *via* may be created more than eight feet in breadth or less, provided always it is broad enough for a vehicle to pass along it; otherwise it will be an *iter*, not a *via*. 1. If there is a permanent lake on your land, there may be created over it a servitude of boating, so as to afford access to a neighbouring estate. 2. If a servient estate, or the estate to which the servitude is attached, should become State property, in either case the servitude remains unaffected; land which comes to the hands of the State does so without its condition being changed.

3. Wherever there is a servitude attached to an estate, it is attached to all parts of it alike; consequently, even if the dominant estate is sold piecemeal, the servitude goes with every part, with the result that the different owners have a right to bring actions respectively in which they claim [for example] to have a right of way. But where land to which a servitude is attached has been divided into portions marked out by metes and bounds among a number of owners in severalty, then, although the servitude attaches to all parts alike, still it is requisite that those owners whose portions do not adjoin the servient estate should have a legal right of passage across the other portions of the divided land or should be able to pass, with the leave of the respective adjoining owners.

24 POMPONIUS (*on Sabinus* 33) We read in Labeo that if I have a watercourse, I can lend the use of it to any neighbour I please; Proculus, on the other hand, says that I[1] cannot even use it myself for a different part[2] of my estate from that for which the servitude was acquired. The opinion of Proculus is the sounder of the two.

25 THE SAME (*on Sabinus* 34) If I sell you a particular part of my estate, the right to a watercourse will come to you with it as well, even though the watercourse should be chiefly used for the sake of some other portion; and no account need be taken, in respect of that portion, either of the goodness of the soil or of the use which is made of so much of the water, so as to make out that the right to convey the water goes with that part of the estate only which is the most valuable or is the most in need of the use of the water: the rule is that the water must be divided in proportion to the amounts of land retained and conveyed away respectively.

26 PAULUS (*on the Edict* 47) Where a *via*, an *iter*, an *actus*, or a watercourse across an estate is bequeathed without more, the heir has a right to create the servitude in any part of the estate that he likes, provided it puts the legatee to no unfair disadvantage in respect of the servitude.

27 JULIANUS (*Digest* 7) If the Sempronian estate serves an estate which you and I own in common, and we thereupon purchase it to hold in common, the servitude is extinguished, because both

[1] Read *possim* for *possit*.

[2] Read *partem mei* for *meam partem*. Cf. M.

owners have come to have the same rights over the two respective estates. But if the land which is purchased was serving my several estate and also your several estate, then the servitude will remain; as an estate which a man owns in severalty can have attached to it a servitude over one which he shares with another person.

28 THE SAME (*Digest* 34) Where an *iter* is bequeathed leading to an estate which is common to two persons, then, unless they both agree as to the course which the path is to take, the servitude is neither acquired nor lost.

29 PAULUS (*Epitomes of Alfenus's Digest* 2). A man had two estates abutting on one another, and sold the upper one. One term of the agreement for sale was that the purchaser should be at full liberty to discharge water through an open trench on to the lower estate. Hereupon this question was asked:—If the purchaser receives water from a third estate and wishes to discharge it on to the lower estate, can he do so in pursuance of the right acquired as above, or not? My answer was that the lower neighbour was not bound to admit more water than the purchaser discharged for the purpose of draining his own estate.

30 THE SAME (*Epitomes of Alfenus's Digest* 4) A man who had two properties in selling one of them reserved [the use of] water the source of which was on the land sold, and round the same a breadth of ten feet. The question was asked whether he had thereby the ownership in the space in question, or only the right of access over it. The answer given was: if the reservation was expressed to be of "ten feet round such water," it must be held that the vendor had only a right of way.

31 JULIANUS (*Extracts from Minicius* 2) Three properties lying side by side belonged to three owners respectively[1], and the owner of the lowest of the three had acquired for such lowest estate as against the highest estate a servitude of watercourse, which watercourse he conducted into his own land across the intervening estate with the consent of the owner thereof. After this he bought the uppermost estate, and then he sold the lowest estate on to which he had conducted the water. The question was asked whether the lowest estate had lost the right of watercourse in question, on the ground that, the two estates having come into the hands of the same owner, there could be no servitude between

[1] del. *adjecta*. M.

such two estates themselves. The answer of our authority was that the lowest estate had not lost the servitude, because the [intervening] property, across which the water was conducted, belonged to another person, and just as there was no way in which the uppermost estate could be subjected to a servitude to the effect that water should come to the lowest estate, except by the water being conducted across the intervening estate as well, so too this servitude, when once existing in favour of the same [*i.e.* the lowest] estate, could not be lost without the watercourse at the same time ceasing to be conducted across the middle estate itself, or all three properties coming to be in the hands of one owner.

32 AFRICANUS (*Questions* 6) You and I have an estate in common; you convey to me your share and also a roadway to the estate across neighbouring land which belongs to you in severalty. Our authority declares that by this means a servitude is properly created, and that in such a case the common rule that servitudes can neither be acquired nor imposed for a share (*per partes*) has no application; as here the servitude is not acquired for a share, being acquired with reference to a time at which I shall be sole owner of the estate.

33 THE SAME (*Questions* 9) You and I having two estates in common, the Titian and the Seian, and having agreed, on making a partition, that the Titian estate should go to me and the Seian to you, we made mutual deliveries of our respective shares in the estates, and it was specified, when we did so, that each party was to have a right to a watercourse across the estate of the other: the servitude, he says, was well created, especially if the informal agreement was followed by a stipulation. 1. You conduct water across the lands of a number of different owners in virtue of a servitude created some way or other; in this case, you cannot convey to any one of such owners or to any other neighbouring owner the right to draw water from the channel, unless some pact or stipulation was added to that express effect; in fact such a right is not uncommonly given by some pact or stipulation being interposed, though of course no estate can serve itself, and there cannot be such a thing created as the usufruct of a servitude.

34 PAPINIANUS (*Questions* 7) If one co-owner of an estate held in common allows anyone to have an *iter* or an *actus*, this is inoperative; consequently, if two estates which serve one another become the common property of the two owners, then, seeing that

the law is that servitudes can be retained in respect of a share (*pro parte*), the servitude cannot be released by one party to the other; for, although each co-owner having a right to a servitude has it to himself in severalty, still, as the subject burdened with the servitude was not the person but the estate, it is impossible for exemption from the servitude to be acquired, or for the servitude to be released, for a share (*per partem*). 1. If a spring dries up from which I have a watercourse, but the same spring begins to flow again after the expiration of the legal period, the question arises whether the watercourse is lost:

35 PAULUS (*on Plautius* 15) as to which Atilicinus says that the Emperor issued a rescript to Statilius Taurus in these words:—"The persons who were in the habit of getting water from the Sutrine estate came before me and stated that they had been unable to convey from the spring which is to be found on the Sutrine estate the water which they had used for a number of years, because the spring had dried up; but that afterwards water began to flow again from the same spring; and their petition was that, whereas they had lost their right through no default or negligence of their own, but because they could not possibly get any water, it might be restored to them. This request seemed to me not to be unjust, and accordingly I held that relief ought to be given them. I therefore decide that the legal position which they had on the day when it was first impossible for them to get a supply of water be restored to them."

36 THE SAME (*Responsa* 2) When one of two estates is retained by a vendor [of the other], and is subjected by him to a servitude of watercourse [in favour of the other], the servitude thus acquired for the estate which is purchased will follow that estate on a subsequent sale; and it is immaterial that the stipulation by which the parties agreed that a penal sum should be promised referred to the purchaser personally and provided for the case of his not being allowed to use the servitude.

37 THE SAME (*Responsa* 3) "Lucius Titius sends best wishes to his brother Gaius Seius. Of the water which flows into the reservoir constructed on the isthmus by my father I give and present to you one inch in depth [to be conducted] into your house on the isthmus or wherever else you like." My question is whether on these words the use of the water passes to the heirs of Gaius Seius as well. Paulus answered that the use of the water being personal would

not pass to the heirs of Seius, the latter being in the position of a usuary.

38 THE SAME (*Handbooks* 1) A *via* can be created though there is a river in the way, provided the river can be crossed by a ford or there is a bridge over it; but it is different where the only passage is by a ferry (*pontonibus*). This is so on the assumption that the river passes through the lands of one person; but, if we suppose the following case,—your land adjoins mine, after your land comes the river, then lands belonging to Titius, and then a high-road to which I wish to acquire a right of way,—let us consider whether there is anything to prevent your giving me a *via* up to the river, and Titius one from it up to the high-road. It is a fair question however whether the legal position is [not] the same, even where you are owner of the lands beyond the river on this side of the high-road; the fact is that a complete *via* generally reaches as far as some town, or up to a high-road, or to a river which is crossed by a ferry, or to some other land under the same ownership [with the dominant estate]; and, this being the case, it cannot be held that the servitude is barred even by a public river flowing between two estates which belong to the same person.

IV.

RULES COMMON TO URBAN AND RUSTIC ESTATES.

1 ULPIANUS (*Institutes* 2) Buildings are called urban *prædia*, and it may be observed that, even where buildings are part of a country-house, it is still possible to create servitudes of urban *prædia*. 1. The reason why these servitudes are said to be of *prædia* (estates, tenements), is that they cannot be created without *prædia*, as no one can acquire a servitude over urban or rustic *prædia*, unless he has got a *prædium* himself.

2 THE SAME (*on the Edict* 17) With regard to the taking or drawing of water from a river with a wheel, or the case of a man creating a servitude over a cistern, some have been in doubt whether these were servitudes at all; but, in a rescript of the Emperor Antoninus to Tullianus, there is an observation to the effect that, although there were no valid servitude in law, still, if the party obtained such a right under an agreement to the effect in question, or acquired it by any other lawful means, a man who

has been in possession of such an easement must receive protection.

3 GAIUS (*on the provincial Edict* 7) If a man who owns two pieces of land conveys one of them to you with an agreement that the land so transferred shall serve the property which he retains, or the converse, a servitude is held to be legally created.

4 JAVOLENUS (*Extracts from Cassius* 10) No valid assurance can be given that a [sepulchral] monument shall not be built so as to exceed a given height, because that which is no longer under human law cannot be subjected to a servitude, just as no such servitude can exist as one to the effect that only some specified number of bodies shall be buried on one spot.

5 THE SAME (*Epistles* 2) I am selling land which belongs to me: can I lay a servitude on such land in terms expressing that I myself and my neighbour shall have the benefit of it? Again, if I am selling land which I own in common with someone else, can I procure that it shall be subject to a servitude in favour of me and my fellow-owner? My answer was:—No one can reserve a servitude in favour of any other person than himself; consequently the mention of the neighbour must be treated as void, so that the whole servitude will belong to the person who reserved it. Moreover, on the sale of land owned in common, I cannot put it under a servitude in favour of me and my fellow-owner, as, where land is owned in common, no servitude can be procured in favour of it by the act of one co-owner.

6 ULPIANUS (*on Sabinus* 28) If a man has two houses and conveys away one of them, he can express in the terms of his conveyance either that the house which he does not convey is to serve the one which he conveys, or, conversely, that the one conveyed is to serve the one which is retained; and it matters little whether the two houses adjoin or do not. The rule is the same with rustic *prædia*; if a man has two estates, he can, by the terms of his conveyance (*tradendo*) put one under a servitude to the other. But if he conveys two houses at the same time, he cannot put one under a servitude to the other, as he cannot acquire a servitude for another man's house nor can he subject such a house to a servitude. 1. If a man conveys away a share in a house or a share in an estate, he cannot subject it to a servitude, as servitudes cannot be imposed nor yet acquired in respect of shares (*per*

partes). No doubt, if he has divided an estate into two parts by metes and bounds, and then conveys away a divisional part, he can impose a servitude on either of the two ; in fact, such a part is not a portion of an estate, it is an estate. The same thing may be said in the case of a house, supposing the owner of a single homestead builds a wall across the middle of it, and so divides it into two, as is often done ; here, too, the house must be treated as two houses. 2. Again, suppose we are two persons who own two houses in common, we can, by joining in a conveyance, bring about the same effect as I could by myself, if I had two houses of my own. But even if we make separate conveyances, the result will be the same, it being always held that the later conveyance gives effect to the one first made. 3. If, on the other hand, one of the houses belongs to one of two persons, and the other is common to both, then, according to Pomponius (extracts from Sabinus *b.* 8), I cannot create a servitude in favour of either or over either. 3*a*. If a man makes it a term in a contract of sale that the house which he sells shall be subject to a servitude, he is not obliged to convey the house free from all servitudes ; accordingly he can either impose a servitude in favour of his own house or give a servitude to a neighbouring proprietor, so long, that is, as no delivery has taken place. No doubt, if he expressly said that there was to be a servitude in favour of Titius, and he grants a servitude to Titius, there is an end of the matter, but if he gives it to anyone else, he will be liable on the contract of sale. This is not inconsistent with what is said by Marcellus (*Dig.* 6) ; [that writer asks this question :—] supposing a man, on delivery of land, declares that it is subject to a servitude in favour of Titius, whereas this is not the case, but the vendor is under an obligation to Titius to confer it on him,—can the vendor sue the purchaser on his contract of sale, to call upon him to allow the servitude to be imposed on the land which he bargained for?—and his opinion is, on the whole, that he must be allowed to bring the action. The same author also says that, even if the vendor should be able to sell the servitude to Titius, he must none the less be allowed to bring the action. The above is on the assumption that the declaration was made in the conveyance with a view to reserving the servitude ; but if, as Marcellus proceeds to say, the vendor only had a misgiving that Titius might have a good claim to the servitude, and made the above provision on that account, he will not have a right to sue on the contract of sale, if he had really made no promise to Titius about it.

7 PAULINUS (*on Sabinus* 5) Whenever one house is conveyed by a man who owns two, the precise servitude [which he wishes to create] ought to be expressed, or else, if it is simply said in general terms that the house is to serve, either the words will produce no effect, because it does not appear what kind of servitude is reserved, or there is no kind of servitude which it may not be obligatory to create. 1. Even where a house which belongs to a third person is between the two in question, [a servitude] can be imposed, as, for example, one to the effect that the height of either house may be raised or may not be raised, or even, in the case of a right of way, [with a clause providing] that it shall only come into force if, at any time thereafter, a servitude should be imposed on the intervening house; as, in fact, a servitude [of this kind] can be created over the lands of several owners, and that even at different times. Still it may fairly be said that if I have three estates forming one continuous piece of ground and I convey the estate at one end to you, a servitude may be acquired for either your estate or my [remaining two] estates; but if it is acquired for the estate which is furthest from yours, which I retain, the servitude will hold good, seeing that the middle estate too belongs to me; whereas, if I afterwards dispose of either the estate in favour of which the servitude was acquired or the one in the middle, the right will be interrupted until a servitude is imposed on the middle estate itself.

8 POMPONIUS (*on Sabinus* 8) If I have two blocks of chambers and I convey them to two purchasers respectively at the same moment, it may fairly be considered whether any servitude imposed on either of the two is valid, seeing that no one can impose a servitude on, or acquire one for, another man's house. However, so long as the conveyance is not completed, the party conveying acquires the servitude for, or imposes it on, his own house rather than another's, so that it will be valid.

9 THE SAME (*on Sabinus* 10) If I have become heir to a man over whose land I had a servitude, and I have thereupon sold you the inheritance, the servitude must be established again, such as it was before, as the understanding is that you yourself, as it were, are to be deemed heir to the deceased.

10 ULPIANUS (*on Sabinus* 10) Whatever a vendor wishes to reserve to himself by way of servitude ought to be reserved expressly; a general reservation in such words as these: "whatever

persons have any servitudes, they are still to have them"—only refers to strangers, it makes no provision for the vendor himself in the way of preserving his rights, as, in fact, he had no rights, seeing that no one is subject to a servitude to himself; moreover, even if there was once a servitude existing in my favour, and then the ownership of the servient land came to me, the necessary construction is that the servitude is extinguished.

11 POMPONIUS (*on Sabinus* 33) Persons who have a right of servitude are allowed freedom of access, for the sake of executing repairs, to parts which are not affected by the servitude, but access to which is a necessity for them; assuming that no express provision was made, when the servitude was created, defining the quarter in which access should be allowed. Accordingly the owner of the [servient] land is not at liberty to make the ground "religious" either close to a watercourse or above one,—supposing, for example, the water should be conducted in an underground channel,—lest the result should be that the easement is lost. This is a correct statement of the law. In fact, if you have a legal right to carry a stream of water through a particular channel, you may either lower or raise such channel, except where provision has been made that you should not do so. 1. If I have a right to conduct water in a channel close to your land, this gives me by tacit implication the following rights as well:—I can repair the channel; I and my workmen may, for the purpose of such repair, get as near to the spot as we can; moreover, I may claim that the landowner shall leave me sufficient free space to admit of my approaching the channel on both the right and left banks and throwing down soil, mud, stones, sand or chalk.

12 PAULUS (*on Sabinus* 15) Where one plot (*fundus*) serves another, if either plot is sold, the servitudes pass too; and, where buildings serve plots or plots serve buildings, the rule is the same.

13 ULPIANUS (*Opinions* 6) The vendor of the Geronian estate made it a term of the sale in favour of the Botrian estate, which he kept in his hands, that no tunny-fishery should be carried on off the latter. It is true that no servitude can be imposed on the sea by private agreement, seeing that it is by nature free to every one, still, as the good faith of the contract requires that the terms of agreement of sale should be carried out, [it follows that] the individuals who are in possession at the time or who succeed to their legal position are bound by the terms of the stipulation or the sale

[contracted by the parties]. 1. If it is understood that there are stone quarries on your land, no one can hew stone there, either as a private person or in the Government service, without your consent, where he has no easement (*jus*) allowing him to do so; unless indeed there is a custom existing in those quarries to the effect that, should anyone desire to hew any such stone, he is to be at liberty to do it, if[1] he first gives the owner of the land the customary payment in consideration thereof. Even then he must first give security to the owner that the latter's use of such stone as he requires shall not be barred by the other's exercise of his right, nor his enjoyment of his property spoilt.

14 JULIANUS (*Digest* 41) There is nothing to be said against a right of way being created in such terms as to allow of its being used by day only; indeed such a restriction is almost necessary in the case of urban property.

15 PAULUS (*Epitomes of Alfenus's Digest* 1) Where a man has granted anyone an *iter* or *actus* across a particular close, there is no doubt that he can grant either of such easements across the same close to a number of persons; just as, where a man has laid a servitude on his house for the benefit of his neighbour, he is none the less able to lay a similar servitude on the same house for the benefit of as many other persons as he likes.

16 GAIUS (*Everyday matters or golden things* 2) A man may in his testament order his heir not to raise the height of his house, lest he obscure the lights of the neighbouring house, or [order him] to suffer the neighbour to let a beam into the wall, or discharge eavesdrip on to the land, or to allow the neighbour to walk or drive over his land or conduct water from it.

17 PAPINIANUS (*Questions* 7) If a neighbour carries a wall across your land by leave asked of you, no proceedings can be taken against him by way of interdict "*quod precario habet*" (whereas the defendant has by leave asked), nor, when the wall is built, can it be held that there is a completed gift of a servitude, nor can there be a valid claim made at law on the neighbour's part to the effect that he has a right to maintain the structure without your consent, seeing that the building takes the legal position of the land and so makes the claim void. But if a man who was under a servitude existing in your favour carries a wall across his

[1] In the text—"he is not to be at liberty etc. unless."

own property on leave asked from you, he will not acquire by user freedom [from the servitude] and proceedings can be effectively taken against him on the interdict "*quod precario habet.*" Should you however allow him to build by way of gratuitous bounty, then you cannot sue for the interdict, moreover the act of bounty puts an end to the servitude.

18 PAULUS (*Manuals* 1) It is established law that different co-owners, even without joining in the grant of a servitude, may still impose one on their estate, or may acquire one, the construction being that, when the last grant is made, the previous grants come into force along with it, and the result is the same as though all the co-owners had granted at the same moment. It follows that if the man who first granted should die or[1] should dispose of his share in some other form or manner, and then, after that, his fellow proprietor should grant, the whole will be inoperative. The reason of this is that, when the last man grants, it is not held that the servitude was acquired by relation back, but the construction is that things are on the same footing as though, at the moment when the last grant was made, all had granted; accordingly this last grant itself will still be in suspense until the new co-owner grants. A similar rule applies where a grant is made to one of the co-owners and then some event such as above mentioned comes to pass in respect of another person among the number. On the same principle, on the other hand, if anything such as mentioned happens to a co-owner who has not made a grant, they will all have to grant afresh, as they are excused for so long a time from executing whatever[2] gift or act it is in their power to execute as[3] to be still able to execute it, even though at different times, and accordingly the grant cannot be made to one person nor by one person. A similar rule holds where one man grants a servitude and another leaves it by testament, as, if every co-owner leaves a servitude by testament, and all their respective inheritances are entered upon at the same moment, it may be said that the servitude is duly bequeathed, but if the entries are at different times, the legacy vests to no purpose; the acts of living persons may have their operation suspended, not so those of persons deceased.

[1] Or perhaps "or *succession to his estate should take place* in some other form or he should dispose of his share in some other manner." This is preferred by M. who would insert after *genere* the words *in bona ejus successum sit.*

[2] For *quo* read *quod.* Cf. M.

[3] Ins. *ut* before *vel.* M. would read *ut* for *vel.*

V.

WHERE AN ACTION IS BROUGHT TO RECOVER A SERVITUDE OR TO CONTEST ANOTHER'S RIGHT TO ONE.

1 ULPIANUS (*on the Edict* 14) Rights of action in respect of servitudes, whether rustic or urban, belong to the persons who have the property in the land; but a place of sepulture is not a subject of private property at all: it is true that a man can lay claim to a right of way up to a sepulchre.

2 THE SAME (*on the Edict* 17) People may have an action *in rem* for a servitude framed on the same lines as one relating to a usufruct, whether such action be confessory or negatory, the former being used by one who maintains that he has a right of servitude, and the latter by an owner who denies [that some other person has such a right]. 1. The confessory action *in rem* can belong to no one else than an owner of land; nobody is at liberty to sue to recover a servitude except a man who is owner of adjoining land and who claims that the servitude is attached to it. 2. Neratius tells us quite correctly, that if there is a bequest of the usufruct in ground surrounded [by other land of the testator], a right of way must needs go with it, I mean, that is, across those parts of the surrounding land across which a man who granted [the usufruct] would establish it,—so far as right of way is necessary for enjoyment of the usufruct; it should always be remembered that a right of transit which is allowed to a usufructuary to enable him to enjoy his usufruct is not a servitude, indeed no [real] servitude can belong to one who has a usufruct in the land; though, if there is one attached to the land, then the usufructuary can make use of it. 3. Pomponius says that a usufructuary can sue for the Interdict *de itinere* (for a right of way), if he has used the way within the year, as there are two kinds of inquiry, one into a matter of law, as in a confessory action, and another into a matter of fact, as in the case of the Interdict referred to; the same thing is said by Julianus (*Dig.* 48). The opinion of Julianus is confirmed by a passage of Labeo, who says that even where the testator who bequeathed the usufruct was himself the person who made use of the way, an Interdict founded on equitable principles should be allowed the usufructuary, just as these Interdicts are available to an heir or a purchaser.

3 THE SAME (*on the Edict* 70) We may add that the rule applies equally where what is purchased is part of an estate.

4 THE SAME (*on the Edict* 17) The actual material place does not fall within the proprietorial right of the person who has a servitude; what belongs to him is a right of way. 1. A man who has *iter* without *actus* or *actus* without *iter* can bring an action for a servitude. 2. In a confessory action which is brought for a servitude profits can be included in the order. Let us consider, however, what profits there can be of a servitude; and, as to this, the better opinion is that the only thing that can be reckoned as coming under the head of profits is such interest, if any, as the plaintiff has in not being prevented from using the servitude. Even in a negatory action, so Labeo says, profits are included, namely, the interest the plaintiff has in the opposite party not using a way over his ground; and this opinion is approved by Pomponius himself. 3. If the land to which a right of way is attached belongs to several co-owners, each of them has a good right of action for the whole, as indeed Pomponius himself says (b. 41), but, in assessing damages, interest will be taken into account, the interest, that is, of the person who takes proceedings. Accordingly, as to the bare right to the easement, any owner can proceed separately, and, if he succeeds, the others will get the benefit of it, but the assessment will be confined to the question of his interest; though, of course, the servitude cannot be acquired through one person. 4. Similarly, if there are two owners of the servient land, the action in question can be brought against either of them, and, as Pomponius has it in the same book, whichever defends the action must make good the whole, as this is a thing which does not admit of division. 5. Where my case is, not that a man raises any dispute as to my right to some *iter* or *actus* or *via*, but that he will not suffer me to make repairs or lay down gravel, then, according to Pomponius in the same book, I must bring a confessory action; indeed, even where a neighbour has a tree which reaches over so as to make the *via* or the *iter* impassable or unusable, then, according to Marcellus in a note on Julianus, there may be an action for the *iter* or an action to recover the *via*. With regard to the repair of the *via*, recourse may also be had to an Interdict, namely, the one given for the repair of an *iter* or *actus*; which, however, is not available where the applicant wishes to lay down flints, except where such right was expressly agreed for. 6. Add to this that a right to draw water too, being a servitude, is a thing for which people may have an action *in rem*. 7. On the other hand, the owner of a building may bring an action in respect of a servitude, in which he denies that he is subject to any servitude for the

benefit of his neighbour, where his house is not free altogether, but is subject to no servitude for the benefit of the defendant. For instance, suppose I have a house, adjoining which there are the Seian house and the Sempronian house; I am under a servitude appertaining to the Sempronian house, but I wish to take proceedings against the owner of the Seian, because he hinders me from raising the height of my house. My course will be to bring an action *in rem*; it is true my house is under a servitude, but it is not under a servitude in favour of the defendant, accordingly my contention is that I have a right to raise the height without the consent of the defendant, since, as far as he is concerned, my house is free. 8. Where a man is not at liberty to raise the height of his house at all, an action may very well be brought against him in which it is contended that he has no right to raise it. This kind of servitude may exist even for the benefit of a man whose house is not the adjoining one;

5 PAULUS (*on the Edict* 21) and, consequently, if your house comes between my house and Titius's, I can put Titius's house under a servitude to the effect that he shall not be at liberty to raise the height of it, though your house should be put under no such servitude; as, so long as you forbear to raise the height of your house, I derive benefit from the servitude.

6 ULPIANUS (*on the Edict* 17) And if it happen that the intervening owner, seeing that he is under no servitude, raises the height of his buildings, the result being that I cannot now be held to obstruct your light if I build myself, it is in vain for you to contend that I have no right to keep up such building without your consent; at the same time, if within the prescribed period, the neighbour takes his building down again, your right of action (*vindicatio*) will be resuscitated. 1. It should be understood that in these servitudes the person who is in possession of the easement may still be plaintiff.[1] Now, if it so happen that I have not raised the height of any building on my land, then the other party is in possession of the easement, as, no innovation being yet made, he has got possession, and, if I proceed to build, he can resist me by a civil action or by an interdict *quod vi et clam*, or he can stop me equally well by the throw of a pebble. But if I build without any interference on his part, then I myself will become the possessor. 2. Furthermore, a right of action exists in respect of a servitude

[1] del. *eum*. Cf. M.

which was imposed with a view to support (*oneris ferendi causa*), the object being to make the servient owner keep up the support and also keep his building in repair in such manner and form as was defined at the time when the servitude was created. Gallus, no doubt, is of opinion that no servitude can be created to the effect that a man shall be compelled to do anything, but only that he shall not prevent me from doing something; in fact, in every servitude, the execution of repairs is the business of the person who claims the servitude, not of the person whose property is subject thereto. However, the view of Servius has prevailed, to the effect that he has a right to compel the other party to repair his wall so as to support his burden: though what Labeo says is that this servitude binds not the person, but the property, and he makes it come to this that the owner is free to abandon the property. 3. And in fact the action is *in rem* and not *in personam*, and is open only to the owner of the [dominant] house and against only the [other] owner, agreeably to the statement of claim in servitudes in general. 4. If a [dominant] house belongs to several co-owners,—such is the question discussed by Papinianus (Questions 3),—can proceedings be taken in respect of the servitude in its entirety? To this his answer is that the co-owners can proceed each separately in respect of the whole, as in the case of other servitudes, setting aside usufruct. But this, he says, is not the right answer to give where the house which has to support a burden which a neighbour lays upon it belongs to several co-owners. 5. The kind of repair that can be sued for in this action depends on the question what kind of repair was mentioned when the servitude was created: the arrangement may have been that the party should repair with rectangular blocks or with built up stones, or any kind of work that was mentioned in the terms of creation. 6. Profits are taken into account in the action, in short the advantage which the plaintiff would have gained if the neighbour [*i.e.* the defendant] had furnished support to the weight imposed by the plaintiff's house. 7. The servient owner is at liberty to make the wall better than was required by the terms in which the servitude was created; but, if he proceeds to make it worse, he can be stopped, either by means of this action or by "notification of novel structure."

7 PAULUS (*on the Edict* 21) The outcome of these actions is that the successful plaintiff, by motion to the judge (*officio judicis*), gets either specific relief or else an undertaking. The specific relief is this,—the judge orders the defendant to amend the defective

condition of the wall and to put it into a serviceable state. As for the undertaking, the judge orders him to engage that the wall shall be repaired and that neither he nor any of his successors will prevent the plaintiff from building on it and keeping up the building so made; and, on giving this undertaking, the defendant is discharged. But if he will give neither specific satisfaction nor the undertaking, the judge must order him to pay damages on a scale determined by the plaintiff's oath as sworn for the purposes of the trial.

8 ULPIANUS (*on the Edict* 17) The repair of the wall being thus incumbent on the neighbour, it is equally true that the business of propping up the building of the owner who has a right to the servitude, during the execution of the repairs, need not be undertaken by the owner of the lower building; if the superior [*i.e.* dominant] owner does not care to prop his buildings up himself, he can take them down and rebuild them when the wall is restored to its previous condition. In this case too, just as in that of servitudes in general, the converse action will be allowed, that is to say, an action in which it is asserted that you [the dominant owner] have no right to compel me [to prop up your building]. 1. I have a good right of action against anyone who grants me a servitude to the following effect:—that I shall be at liberty to insert beams into his wall, and upon such beams to construct, say, a gallery to walk up and down in, with built up columns placed on the top of the wall to support the roof of such gallery. 2. The actions above mentioned differ from one another in this respect;—the first action (*oneris ferendi*) may be used even for the purpose of compelling the adjoining owner to repair my wall, but the other can be brought only to make him admit my beams; and this is not inconsistent with the rules governing servitudes. 3. Should the question be asked which party is in the position of possessor and which in that of demandant, the answer is that, if the beams are already inserted, the character of possessor is borne by the party who claims to have a right to the servitude, but, if they are not inserted, by the party who denies the right. 4. If, in such a case, the party who claims the right to the servitude gains his case, no servitude will have to be granted to him; for the reason, if the judgment is sound in law, that he has got it already, and, if it is unsound, because the proper object of the decree is not to create a servitude, but to declare one already existing. No doubt, if, after joinder of issue, the plaintiff lost the

servitude by non-user, owing to the malicious contrivance of the owner of the house, it ought to be restored to him, just as a similar rule is held in the case of the owner of a house. 5. Aristo says, in an opinion given to Cerellius Vitalis, that he does not think that smoke can lawfully be discharged from a cheese factory on to buildings which are overhead, unless the buildings are subject to a servitude of that particular kind[1], and such a servitude he recognised. The same author declares that it is not lawful to discharge water or anything else from the building above to the building below, as a man is at liberty to carry on operations within his own premises in such a manner only as not to discharge anything on those of anyone else; and it is, he adds, just as possible to discharge smoke as to discharge water; accordingly, he says, the upper owner can bring an action against the lower owner in which he asserts that the latter has no right to act in the way described. Lastly, he says that we are told by Alfenus that an action may be brought in which what is asserted is that such a one has no right to hew stone on his own ground so as to let broken bits fall on the plaintiff's property. Aristo therefore maintains that the person who hired a cheese factory from the town authorities of Minturnæ could be prevented by the upper owner from discharging smoke, but the town authorities are liable to the lessee on the contract of hiring; he says further that the declaration he can make in his action against the person who discharges the smoke is that he has no right to discharge smoke. Conversely, therefore, there may be an action in which the declaration is that the plaintiff has the right to discharge smoke, and this too Aristo clearly approves. Besides this, the Interdict '*uti possidetis*' may be employed, if a man is prevented from using his own property in the way that he likes. 6. We find in Pomponius (*Lectiones* 41) a doubt expressed whether a man can make such a claim in an action as this:—that he has a right, or that another has no right, to cause smoke to a moderate extent on his own ground, say, for instance, smoke from a hearth. On the whole, he says, no such action can be brought, just as no action can be brought to maintain that a man has a right to light a fire, or to sit down, or to wash on his own ground. 7. The same writer approves of a decision to a dissimilar effect; as he says that, in a case of vapour from a bath, where one Quintilla had made an underground passage which penetrated to the premises of Ursus Julius, it was held that such a servitude could be created.

[1] After *rei* ins. *serviunt, nam.* M.

9 PAULUS (*on the Edict* 21) If you build on a spot over which I have a right to an *iter*, I can bring an action in which I claim that I have a right to walk and drive there; and if I establish this, I can stop your operations. Julianus says further,—If an adjoining owner to me, by building on his ground, contrives to avoid admitting the eavesdrip which I have a right to discharge, I can bring an action to maintain my right, that is, the right to discharge such eavesdrip on his ground: the case is like that of the *via* above mentioned. But, if the party has not yet built, the other, whether he has a usufruct or a *via*, can claim by action that he has a right to walk and drive or a right of usufruct [as the case may be], whereas, if the owner in question has built already, then one who has an *iter* or an *actus* can still claim by action that he has such a right, but a usufructuary cannot make a claim [as such], because he has lost the usufruct; consequently in this case, according to Julianus, an action *de dolo* must be allowed. If, on the other hand, you build across the course of an *iter* in respect of which my estate is subject to a servitude in your favour, I have a good right of action in which I can declare that you have no right to build or to keep up a building, just as I could if you built on a vacant space belonging to me. 1. Where a man has been using a broader or a narrower *via* [than he had a right to use], he will have kept the [actual] servitude on foot, just as a man who has a right to take water and uses it mixed with other water at the same time keeps up his right.

10 ULPIANUS (*on the Edict* 53) Where a man has acquired a right of watercourse by lasting user and, so to speak, long possession, he is not required to bring evidence to show the legal title on which his right to the water was founded, such, for example, as a legacy or any other ground of title; he has a good right of action if he can show that he had the use of the watercourse, say for such and such a number of years, and that not by force or by stealth or by leave and license. 1. Proceedings can be taken in this action not only against the person who owns the land where the spring is, or over whose land the water is conveyed, but equally well against anyone whomsoever who seeks to prevent the party[1] from conducting the water, just as in the case of servitudes generally. The rule in short is that whoever it is that tries to prevent me from conducting the water, I can take proceedings against him by this action.

[1] Read *nos* for *non*. Cf. M.

11 MARCELLUS (*Digest* 6). The following questions have arisen. Can one of several co-owners lawfully build on the common ground without the consent of the others? that is to say, if his fellow-owners try to stop him, can he take proceedings against them, and therein contend that he has a right to build? or, on the other hand, can his fellow-owners bring an action against him in which their contention is that they have a right to stop him or that he has no right to build? Furthermore, if the building is raised already, can they[1] take proceedings in which they say: "You have no right to have such a building there"? To this the best answer may be said to be that a co-owner has a right to prevent construction rather than a right to construct; as, on the whole, a man who is attempting to construct in the way described, if he aims at making use of the common property[2] at his own pleasure, as if he were sole owner, is more or less snatching for himself a right which belongs to others as well.

12 JAVOLENUS (*Epistles* 2) I brought an action in which I contended that the defendant had no right to have his beams let into my wall: will he have to undertake in addition that he will not let any into it in future? My answer is:—I hold it to belong to the judge's office to see that an undertaking is given with reference to future operations as well.

13 PROCULUS (*Epistles* 5). I have got pipes by which I conduct water laid on a public road; these pipes have burst and your wall is in consequence drenched with water; I should say you have a good right of action against me in which your claim will be that I have no right to have a discharge of water from my ground flowing on to your wall.

14 POMPONIUS (*on Sabinus* 33) If I am the owner of a wall and I suffer you to let into the wall the same beams that you have had so let into it for some time past, and, this being the case, you wish to let in fresh beams, I have a right to stop you; not only so, but I have a right of action to compel you to remove any fresh beams that you have let in. 1. If a wall which you and I own in common should, in consequence of some operations of yours, lean over towards my house, I have a right of action against you in which my claim will be that you have no right to have the wall in that position.

[1] For *non possit* read *num possint*. Cf. M.

[2] For *jure* read *re*. Cf. M.

15 ULPIANUS (*Opinions* 6) A man raised his house in such a way as to make it obstruct the lights of a person under twenty-five, or under the age of puberty, to whom he was himself curator or guardian: in this case, it is no doubt true that the man in question and his heirs will be liable to an action, because he had no right to commit in his own person the very act which in consequence of his position he was compellable to stop anyone else from committing; at the same time the boy or the minor ought to be allowed an action against anyone who should be in possession of the house in question, to make him remove a structure which was wrongfully put up.

16 JULIANUS (*Digest* 7) If I purchase from you the liberty of discharging eavesdrip from my house on to yours, and, after that, I discharge it with your knowledge in pursuance of such purchase, I wish to know whether I can, on the strength of these facts, protect myself by an action or an *exceptio*? The answer was that I can have recourse to either defence.

17 ALFENUS (*Digest* 2) Should there in any case be, between two houses, a wall which so protruded as to lean over half a foot or more towards the adjoining house, the proper action would be one in which it is claimed that the defendant has no right to have the wall encroaching in the way described over the plaintiff's precincts without his consent. 1. A portion of the house of Gaius Seius being under a servitude in favour of the house of Annius to the effect that Seius was not to have a right to have anything placed on that portion, Seius planted trees there, and underneath the same had basins, vessels[1], and kettles. Hereupon Annius was advised by all those learned in the law to bring an action against Seius and claim therein that the defendant had no right to have the above objects placed on the spot without his leave. 2. A dunghill had been put against someone's wall by an adjoining owner from which moisture came through the wall; whereupon the aggrieved party asked for a legal opinion as to how he could compel the other to remove the dunghill. My answer was that, if the other had set up the nuisance in a public place, he would be compelled to remove it by an Interdict, but if it was in a private place, the proper course was to bring an action raising the question of servitude; again, that if the applicant had stipulated in respect of *damnum infectum*, he would, if he had suffered any damage

[1] For *et tenes* read *lenes et*. Cf. M.

from the cause mentioned, protect himself by means of the stipulation.

18 JULIANUS (*Extracts from Minicius* 6) A man whose slaves prevented an adjoining owner from using a watercourse kept out of the way in order to avoid being sued: the plaintiff seeks to know what is his proper course. My answer was that the prætor ought, after hearing the application, to order that the other party's property should be taken into possession and not be given up until he had created in favour of the applicant a servitude of watercourse; and, if such applicant, in consequence of being prevented from conveying water, had suffered any harm through drought,—for instance, his meadows or his trees were dried up [,—had made it good][1].

19 MARCIANUS (*Rules* 5) Where a man brings an action about a servitude which he has in common with others and therein frames his claim to the same in due form, but he in some way or other loses the case by his own negligence, it is not fair that this should cause any loss to his fellow-owners; but, if he colludes with the opposite party and abandons the suit, then, according to Celsus, the others must be allowed to bring an action *de dolo*, and this, he says, was the opinion of Sabinus.

20 SCÆVOLA (*Digest* 4) A testatrix who bequeathed a certain estate had some houses close to such estate: the question was asked whether, assuming that the houses did not go with the estate, and the legatee sued to recover it[2], the estate would be subject to any servitude in favour of the houses; or, supposing the legatee claimed to have the estate conveyed to him in pursuance of a *fideicommissum* the heirs ought to reserve a servitude in favour of the houses. The answer was—Yes (*sic*). 1. Several members of a municipal body who respectively possessed estates purchased a piece of forest land to hold as co-owners, in order to have common rights of pasture, and the same position of things was kept up by their successors; but after this some of those who were in enjoyment of the right of pasture sold the estates above mentioned which they respectively owned. I wish to know whether after the sale the right referred to still follows the respective estates, seeing that the intention of the vendors was to convey this right too? The answer was that the understanding which there was

[1] For *exaruisset* read *exaruissent, restituisset.* Cf. M.

[2] For *cum* read *eum.*

between the contracting parties must be adhered to; but if their intention was not clear, the right in question would go to the purchasers with the rest [of what was sold]. I also wish to know, supposing a part of any one of the above-mentioned estates held in severalty should pass to a legatee, whether it would carry with it any portion of the common right of pasturage. The answer was that, inasmuch as the right in question was one which must be held to be attached to the estate bequeathed, such right would equally go to the legatee.

21 LABEO (*Pithana epitomised by Paulus* 1) Where no water so far appears, no way thereto nor conduit thereof can be established. *Paulus*: on the contrary, this, I should say, is not the fact, for the reason that it is quite possible for a grant to be made to the effect that you [the grantee] shall be at liberty to search for water, and, if you find any, to convey it by a watercourse.

VI.

HOW SERVITUDES ARE LOST.

1 GAIUS (*on the provincial Edict* 7) Prædial servitudes are lost by merger, if the same person comes to be owner of both estates.

2 PAULUS (*on the Edict* 21) When a man has an *iter* and an *actus*, if he should for the period required by law use the *iter* only, then, according to Sabinus, Cassius, and Octavenus, the right of *actus* is not extinguished, but holds good; a man who has a right of *actus* is at liberty to use that of *iter* as a matter of course.

3 GAIUS (*on the provincial Edict* 7) It is generally received that easements attached to estates are not lost by death or *capitis diminutio*.

4 PAULUS (*on the Edict* 27) An *iter* existing at law by way of access to a burial-place is never lost by non-user.

5 THE SAME (*on the Edict* 66) A man can keep up a servitude through a fellow-owner or a usufructuary or a *bona fide* possessor;

6 CELSUS (*Digest* 5) it is enough that an *iter* has been used as attached to the land. 1. If you and I have a *via* across the land of

an adjoining owner, and I make use of it, but you, for the regular period, forbear to use it, will you have lost your right? Conversely, if an adjoining owner who has a *via* across our land should walk and drive over my portion, but should not enter your portion, will this exempt your portion from the servitude? Celsus's answer was this:—if the estate is divided between the co-owners in distinct portions, then, with regard to the servitude which was attached to the land, the legal position is the same as if it had been attached originally to two separate estates; accordingly, each of the two owners can keep up his own servitude, and each may lose his servitude by non-user, and the legal implications affecting the respective estates are no further mixed up in the matter; moreover this construction does no wrong to the man whose estate serves, indeed, if anything, he is the better off, because user by one of the two owners benefits that owner only and does not benefit the whole united estate. 1 *a*. If, on the other hand, it is the servient estate which is divided in the way mentioned, the matter then involves a little more uncertainty. If the right of way has a distinct and specific course, then, if the whole land is divided in the line of the way, the same consequence in all respects must follow as if there had equally been two distinct estates in the case when the servitude was originally created; but if the land is divided by a line which crosses the way,—and it makes very little difference whether it is divided into equal or unequal parts,—then the same right of servitude remains as was existing before the division was made, moreover what is retained by user or lost by non-user will be nothing short of the whole right of way; and if it should happen that the dominant owner used so much only of the way as lay across one of the two estates, it will not follow that the other estate becomes free, as the right of way is one single right and so indivisible. 1 *b*. At the same time the parties can exempt either of the estates, provided they expressly agree to do so; at any rate, if the person who has a right to the servitude should purchase one of the two estates which resulted from the division, can it be said that the servitude to which the other is subject will be any the less still on foot? I do not see how any absurd consequence will follow from this view, so long as one of the estates remains subject to the servitude, assuming that from the first a more restricted right of way could have been created than was defined in the agreement, and that, in the estate as to which the servitude was not released, there is space enough left to allow the right of *via* to be exercised; but if there is not space enough left for such exercise of the right, then both estates will be exempt, one because it was purchased [by the dominant owner], and the other because the space left is such that no right of way could be established over it. 1 *c*. If however, lastly, the nature of the *via* constituted was such that the party entitled could walk or drive over any part of the estate at his pleasure, and there was nothing to prevent his changing his course from time to time, and, after that, the land was divided, if [as I say] he is free to walk or drive through all parts equally, in that case we shall have to treat the matter in the same way as if at the outset there had been two servitudes imposed on the two estates respectively, so that the one could be kept up and the other could be lost by non-user. 1 *d*. I am quite aware that upon this view of the matter one man's right would be impaired by another man's act, because, before the division, it was enough[1] that the party entitled walked or drove over one part of the land for him to retain the same right over the other part, but we must remember that the party who was entitled to the *via* has gained this advantage that he is able to walk or drive along two roadways equally, and enjoys twice over a road which is eight feet wide where it extends in a straight course and sixteen where it bends.

7 PAULUS (*on Plautius* 13) If the right to a watercourse is given under circumstances such that it can only be enjoyed in the summer or only in one month, the question arises how it can be lost by non-user, as there is no continuous period to be shown during which the party was[2] able to use it but did not do so. Accordingly, if a man enjoys a watercourse only every other year, or every other month, the right is lost by lapse of twice the regular period; and the same rule is followed as to a right of way. But if he has a right which he can exercise every other day, or only[3] by day, or only by night, this will be lost by lapse of the time laid down by the statute, because it is all one servitude; and if he has a servitude which he can use every other hour, or for one hour every day, then, according to Servius, he will lose the servitude by non-user [for the regular period], because what he has is available every day.

8 THE SAME (*on Plautius* 15) If I have the right to discharge rain-water on to a vacant place belonging to you, and I allow you the right of building on the space in question, I lose the right to

[1] For *satius* read *satis*. Cf. M.
[2] del. *non*.
[3] For *toto* read *tantum*. Cf. M.

discharge rain-water. Similarly, if I have a right of *via* over your land, and I allow you to do anything on a spot across which the roadway runs, I lose the right. 1. A man who passes along a portion of an *iter* to which he has a right is held to keep up the user of the whole right of way.

9 JAVOLENUS (*Extracts from Plautius* 3) If water flows into a portion of a channel for conveying water, though it does not go as far as the extreme end of it, still the user is maintained as to every part.

10 PAULUS (*on Plautius* 15) If I and my ward have land in common [to which a right of way is attached], then, though we should not both use it, [but only the ward,] still, in the interest of the ward, I retain the right of way myself. 1. If a person who has a right to draw water by night draws it by day only, for the period laid down for loss by non-user, he loses the right to draw it by night, because he failed to use it. A similar rule applies to a man who, having a right to the use of a watercourse for certain specified hours of the day, uses it at other hours and not for any portion of the hours specified.

11 MARCELLUS (*Digest* 4) A man who had a right to a *via* or an *actus*, provided he used vehicles of a particular kind, used a vehicle of some other kind ; in this case we may fairly consider whether he has not lost his servitude, and whether it is not a different case where a man has been conveying a greater load than he had a right to convey ; the position of this latter being that he may be held to have used the roadway to excess rather than used it in the wrong way, just as if[1] he had used a greater breadth of road than he ought, or driven too many horses, or added water from some other source [than that to which he had a right]. Accordingly, in all the cases mentioned, the servitude is not lost ; but the party is not to have by way of servitude a more extensive right than is embraced by the terms of the agreement. 1. Land being given by way of legacy, on a condition, the heir subjected it to certain servitudes ; if the condition is fulfilled, the servitudes will be extinguished. We may consider whether, supposing the servitudes had been created in favour of the land bequeathed, the legatee would not get the benefit of them ; and the better rule is that he would.

[1] Ins. *si* after *sicuti*.

12 CELSUS (*Digest* 23) A *bona fide* purchaser of land which did not belong to the vendor made use of a right of way attached to the land; here the right of way will be maintained; and that even if he should be in possession on *precarium*, or after forcibly ejecting the owner; as the fact is that when an estate which has acquired a particular bent and character (*qualiter se habens*) is in that character taken into possession, such a right is not lost, and it is immaterial whether one who possesses it, such as it is, possesses lawfully or not. For this reason, still more is it true that, if there has been a natural flow of water through some channel, the right of watercourse is kept up. This is held by Sabinus very reasonably, and it is to be found in Neratius (*Membranes* 4).

13 MARCELLUS (*Digest* 17) If a man who has an estate to which there is attached a right of way over adjoining land should sell a part thereof abutting on the servient estate, without imposing the servitude, but he should, before the expiration of the statutable time by lapse of which servitudes are lost, acquire once more the part which he sold, he will enjoy the servitude to which the adjoining owner was subject.

14 JAVOLENUS (*Extracts from Cassius* 10) Where a space of ground over which there exists a *via* or an *iter* or an *actus* is submerged by the influx of a river, but, before the expiration of the period which suffices for the extinction of servitudes, the spot of ground is recovered by soil being deposited by the stream, the servitude is restored too, such as it was before; but if so much time passes that the servitude is lost, the owner of the ground can be compelled to renew it. 1. Where a public road is effaced by the flow of water from a river or by the fall of a building, the nearest landowner is bound to afford a passage.

15 THE SAME (*Epistles* 2) If I have a right of servitude over several estates, and, that being the case, I acquire one of such estates which lies between two others, I should say that the servitude is not lost, as a servitude can be lost only when the person to whom it belongs is unable to use it; but, if that person has acquired an estate between the two, it may very well be the case that he has a right of way over the estates that come first and last.

16 PROCULUS (*Epistles* 1) A number of persons were in the habit of conducting along one and the same channel, in virtue of

a right so to do, water which came to the surface on the land of an adjoining owner ; the arrangement being that each one on his own particular day conducted the water from its source first of all along one channel which was used by all in common and then along a special channel of his own, the parties coming one after the other in the order of distance. One of the number took no water for the whole of the regular period by lapse of which servitudes are lost. My opinion is that he lost the right to take water, and that his right was not made the subject of user on the part of those who took water, as such right belonged to each one as his own separate property and could not be exercised by user on the part of another. But if a watercourse had been attached to an estate belonging to several persons, it would have been exercised by user on the part of one for the benefit of all the persons who shared in the ownership of the estate. It may be added that if [in the case first mentioned] one of the persons who were entitled to a servitude for conducting water and who conducted water along the same channel should lose the right to conduct it by failing to exercise it, no portion of right would accrue on that ground to the others who used the channel, and the benefit would go to the landowner across whose estate the watercourse lay[1] which, as to the share of one person, was lost by non-user ; the landowner enjoying liberty in respect of so much of the servitude.

17 POMPONIUS (*Extracts from various readings* 11) Labeo says that if a man who has a right to draw water should for the period required for the loss of a servitude by lapse of time go to the spring but draw no water, he loses the right of way too.

18 PAULUS (*on Sabinus* 15) Where a man uses some other water than the one intended when the servitude was created, the servitude is lost. 1. Any period of time during which the last owner of land to which a servitude is attached failed to use it is reckoned against the person who succeeds to his place. 2. Where you have a right to insert a beam, but the adjoining owner has allowed the regular period to pass without any building of his being there, and you in consequence are not able to insert anything, you will not thereby any the more lose your servitude, because the adjoining owner cannot be held to have acquired by *usus* exemption from the servitude affecting his house, as he never interrupted your exercise of the right.

[1] Insert *est* after *aquæ*. M.

19 POMPONIUS (*on Sabinus* 32) If I sell part of my land and provide in the agreement that I shall have a right to conduct water over that part to the rest of my estate, and the regular time passes by without my making a channel, I do not lose any right, as there is[1] no watercourse, and my right to a servitude remains unimpaired; but if I had made a channel and not used it, I should lose it. 1. If I bequeath to you a *via* over my land, and, after the time when my inheritance is entered upon, you should, for the whole of the period which is required for loss of a servitude, be unaware that the bequest was made, you will lose the *via* by non-user. But if, before the expiration of the period, you should sell your land, without having yet become aware that the servitude was bequeathed you, the purchaser will have a good title to the right of way, if he should use it for the rest of the time, because, in short, it had already begun to belong to you; one result being that you could never become entitled even to repudiate the legacy, as the land [to which the servitude would be attached] would not belong to you.

20 SCÆVOLA (*Rules* 1) A servitude is kept up by user when it is enjoyed by the actual person who has a right to it or who is in possession of it, or his hired servant, or his guest, or his doctor, or someone who comes to visit him, or a tenant of his, or a usufructuary;

21 PAULUS (*Sentences* 5) even though, in the case of the usufructuary, he should be in occupation in his own name;

22 SCÆVOLA (*Rules* 1) in short, whoever it is that uses the roadway as if he had a right to it,

23 PAULUS (*Sentences* 5) whether he uses it for the sake of access to another man's estate or of exit from it,

24 SCÆVOLA (*Rules* 1) and that even as a *mala fide* possessor,—it will keep the servitude alive.

25 PAULUS (*Sentences* 5) A man is not regarded as using a servitude except where he thinks he is using a right of his own; consequently where a man uses it by way of using a public road or of using a servitude belonging to someone else, there is no available interdict or action open to him.

[1] The text has *fuerit*. I think the sense must be as above, though that seems more to agree with *fuit*, which some would read.

NINTH BOOK.

I.

On alleged Commission of *Pauperies* by a Four-footed Animal.

1 Ulpianus (*on the Edict* 18) Where a four-footed animal is alleged to have done *pauperies* (damage), there is a right of action which has come down from the Twelve Tables: that Statute lays down that either the offending subject, that is, the animal which committed the *noxia* (harm), should be handed over or pecuniary damages should be given equivalent to the amount of harm done. 1. The word *noxia* signifies the actual delict. 2. The action is given in the case of every kind of four-footed animal. 3. The prætor's words are "have done *pauperies*." *Pauperies* means damage done without legal wrong on the part of the doer, and of course an animal cannot do any legal wrong, as it is devoid of reason. 4. Accordingly, as Servius says, this action lies where an animal does harm because its savage nature is excited; suppose, for instance, a horse given to kicking actually kicks, or an ox butts with its horns which is in the habit of butting, or mules [do some mischief] owing to exceptional vice; but if an animal should upset a load on some passer by, owing to the roughness of the ground or the negligence of the driver, or because it was too heavily laden, this action will not be allowed, but the proceedings will be for wrongful damage. 5. Again, suppose a dog that someone is leading should out of a vicious disposition break loose and injure anyone, in such a case, if it could have been better held by another person, or it ought not to have been taken along that particular way, this action will not lie, and the person who was holding the dog will be liable. 6. Furthermore, the action will not lie if the creature does damage through someone setting it on. 7. To give a general rule, this action lies whenever a creature does

pauperies under some excitement which is contrary to the nature of such animals; consequently, if a horse kicks out because it is excited by pain, then the action will not lie, but the person who struck or wounded the horse is liable, the action against him being *in factum* rather than on the *lex Aquilia,* were it only for this reason, that the person did not do the damage with his own body. But if a horse kicks a man when he stroked or patted it, there is ground for the action. 8. If one animal provokes another so that it does damage, the action must be brought in respect of the one which provokes. 9. This action will lie whether the animal did *pauperies* with its own body or through some external object with which it was in contact; say, for example, that an ox crushes someone by upsetting a waggon or anything else. 10. The action will not apply in the case of wild beasts, because they are savage by nature; consequently, if a bear has got loose and so done harm, there can be no action against the late owner, because, now that the wild beast has got away, he ceases to be owner; accordingly, if I kill the bear, the carcase will be mine. 11. Where two rams or two bulls fight and one kills the other, Quintus Mucius draws a distinction; if, he says, the animal killed is the one who first attacked, there will be no action, but if it is the one who gave no challenge, there is a good right of action, and consequently the party [who owns the other] must either make amends for the mischief or surrender the animal for *noxa.* 12. We may add that as the rule is that *noxa* follows the offending subject, even in the case of four-footed animals, this action will be allowed not against the party to whom the animal belonged when it did the damage, but against the one to whom it belongs at the moment, 13. and, no doubt, if the creature dies before joinder of issue, there is an end of the right of action. 14. Surrender for *noxa* means handing over the live animal. If it belongs to several persons in common, the rule is that there is a right to a noxal action against each co-owner for the whole amount, just as in the case of a slave. 15. In some cases however the action against the owner will not be brought to make him surrender for *noxa,* but will be for the whole amount; for example, where, on being asked before the magistrate whether the animal is his, he replies that it is not; as, after that, if it should be shown that it is his, he will be ordered to pay the whole amount [without the alternative]. 16. If some third person should kill the animal after joinder of issue, then, seeing that the owner has the right of action on the *lex Aquilia,* account will be taken of the *lex Aquilia* [by the judge] in the action [against the owner], because the owner has lost the power of surrendering for *noxa*; consequently in the action which we are discussing he will have to tender the damages assessed, unless he is prepared to assign his right of action against the man who killed the animal. 17. This action, as no one will hesitate to say, is allowed to the heir and to every kind of successor; moreover it is available against the heir and other successors, not, that is, by right of succession, but on the ground of their position as owners.

2 PAULUS (*on the Edict* 22) This action is open not only to the owner of the property injured, but equally to anyone who has the requisite interest, for example, to a person to whom the property was lent, also to a fuller, as these persons clearly suffer damage owing to their own liability. 1. If a man should be trying to get away from somebody, say from a magistrate, and should betake himself to the nearest shop, and there be injured by a savage dog, then, according to the opinion of some, the action cannot be brought in respect of the dog; though it could, if the dog were at large.

3 GAIUS (*on the provincial Edict* 7) There is no doubt that an action can be brought on this statute by or on behalf of free persons, supposing, for example, an animal wounds a *paterfamilias* or a son under *potestas*; not, that is to say, that disfigurement can be taken into account, as no valuation can be made in respect of a free individual, but there may be account taken of expenses incurred for medical treatment and the loss of employment which the party has had to give up or has lost an opportunity of taking in consequence of being disabled.

4 PAULUS (*on the Edict* 22) This action is open as an *utilis actio*, where it is not a four-footed animal that did the *pauperies*, but one of some other kind.

5 ALFENUS (*Digest* 2) A groom was leading a horse into an innyard, when the horse snuffed at a mule; whereupon the mule kicked out and broke the groom's leg; an opinion was desired as to whether there could be an action brought against the owner of the mule, because the mule did *pauperies*. My answer was Yes.

II.

ON THE LEX AQUILIA.

1 ULPIANUS (*on the Edict* 18) The *lex Aquilia* was a partial repeal of all the statutes which before it dealt with illegal damage, whether it were the Twelve Tables or any other enactment; which statutes need not now be rehearsed. 1. The *lex Aquilia* is a plebiscite; Aquilius, a tribune of the plebs, having moved it before the plebs.

2 GAIUS (*on the provincial Edict* 7) It is provided by the *lex Aquilia* in Chap. I as follows:—"If anyone slays unlawfully a slave of either sex belonging to another person, or a four-footed animal of the class of '*pecudes*,' then, whatever was the greatest value of the same in the year then last past, let the party be ordered to pay brass to that amount to the owner;" 1. and then, further on, it is provided that, against one who denies the fact, the action shall be for double the amount. 2. It appears therefore that the statute puts a man's four-footed animals on a level with his slaves, such animals being of the class of *pecudes* and kept in herds, as, for instance, sheep, goats, kine, horses, mules, and asses. Whether swine are included under the term *pecudes* is a question sometimes asked, and Labeo holds very properly that they are. But the term does not comprise dogs: much less are wild beasts members of this class, such as bears, lions, and panthers. Elephants and camels are, so to speak, half and half, as they do the work of beasts of draught and, at the same time, their nature is wild, consequently they must be held to be included in the first chapter.

3 ULPIANUS (*on the Edict* 18) If a slave of either sex should be killed unlawfully, the *lex Aquilia* applies. It is very properly added that the killing must be unlawful, as it is not enough that the slave should be killed, but the act must be done unlawfully.

4 GAIUS (*on the provincial Edict* 7) Accordingly, if a slave of yours is a robber and lies in wait for me, and I kill him, I need be under no apprehension;—common sense allows a man to defend himself from danger. 1. The statute of the Twelve Tables allows anyone to kill a thief who is caught at night [in the act of thieving], provided always the party gives notice of his intention with a shout; if the thief is caught by day, the statute only allows him to be

killed where he defends himself with a weapon, provided, again, the party gives notice with a shout.

5 ULPIANUS (*on the Edict* 18) However, when a man kills anyone who seeks to attack him with a weapon, he will not be held to kill him unlawfully, and if a man should kill a thief to save his own life, no one will hesitate to say that he is not liable on the *lex Aquilia*. Still, if, where he had it in his power to apprehend the thief, he chose to kill him, he must, on the whole, be held to have done it unlawfully; consequently he will be liable on the *lex Cornelia* too. 1. By *injuria* we must not here understand some kind of insult, as we do in connexion with an action for *injuriæ*, but something which is done not according to law, in short, against the law, that is to say a case in which a man kills by negligence (*culpa*); consequently sometimes the two actions, the one on the *lex Aquilia* and the one for *injuriæ*, are both admissible, but there will be two assessments of damages, one for damage and the other for insult. Accordingly we must here understand *injuria* to mean damage done by negligence, even by a person who had no desire to do harm. 2. Hence arises the question whether there is an action on the *lex Aquilia* where damage is done by a lunatic. Pegasus said there was none: what negligence, he asked, can there be in such a person, seeing that he is not in his right mind? This is perfectly sound. Accordingly there will be no action on the *lex Aquilia*; just as there is none where an animal does the damage, or where a tile falls. Again, if a child (*infans*) does the damage, the same rule applies. If a boy under age (*impubes*) does it, then, according to Labeo, seeing that he would be liable for theft, he is liable under the *lex Aquilia* too, and this I should say is true, if he has reached sufficient intelligence to commit a legal offence. 3. If an instructor wounds or kills a slave in the course of teaching him, will he be liable under the *lex Aquilia*, on the ground that he did unlawful damage? Julianus tells us that a man was held liable under the *lex Aquilia* who, in the course of giving instruction, blinded his pupil of an eye; much more, therefore, must the same be held if he kills him. We find the following case given by him. A shoemaker, he says, when a boy whom he was instructing, a freeborn *filius familias*, executed rather badly what he gave him to do, hit him on the neck with a last, with the result that his eye was destroyed. Here Julianus says that there is no right of action for *injuriæ*, because the man did not strike the blow with the intention of committing any *injuria*, but in order to correct

and instruct; but he hesitates to say there is no action on the contract, because a person who gives instruction is only allowed to chastise his pupil to a moderate extent; however I have no doubt that an action can be brought on the *lex Aquilia*,

6 PAULUS (*on the Edict* 22) as excessive brutality on the part of a teacher is counted for negligence.

7 ULPIANUS (*on the Edict* 18) In this action, according to Julianus, the father will get an amount equivalent to the falling off in the gains he makes from his son's services occasioned by the destruction of his eye, besides the cost the father incurs for medical attendance. 1. The word "slay" must be taken to apply whether the party took a sword or, it may be, a stick or some other weapon or used his hands; as, for instance, where he strangled the man or killed him by a kick or by butting at him with his head or in any way whatever. 2. If a man who is carrying a burden which is too heavy for him throws it down and kills a slave, the *lex Aquilia* applies, as it was open to him to avoid taking so great a load: we may observe that it is said by Pegasus that, if a man falls and crushes someone else's slave with a load which he is bearing, he is not liable under the *lex Aquilia*, unless he either loaded himself more heavily than he ought to have done or walked in a slippery place without taking proper care. 3. Similarly where a man does damage in consequence of someone else pushing him, Proculus tells us that neither the man who pushed is liable, because he did not kill, nor the man who was pushed, because he did not do wrongful damage; from which it follows that an action *in factum* must be allowed against the man who pushed. 4. If one man kills another in a wrestling match or in the *pancratium* or in a trial of strength between two boxers, if the man is killed, the *lex Aquilia* does not apply, because the damage must be held to be done for the sake of distinction and prowess, and not with any wrongful intent. But this rule has no application in the case of a slave, as the practice is that only freeborn persons contend; it does apply where a *filius familias* is wounded. Of course, where a man injures someone who is trying to get out of the way, the *lex Aquilia* applies, or where he kills a slave without there being any contest, unless it takes place in a case where the owner set the slave on; there the *lex* would not apply. 5. If a person gives a slight blow to a sick slave, and the man dies, then, as Labeo truly says, he is liable under the *lex Aquilia*, as a blow that will kill one man very often will not kill another. 6. Celsus says that it makes a great

deal of difference whether the party kills or furnishes the cause of death, one who furnishes the cause of death not being liable under the *lex Aquilia* but to an action *in factum*; and, in this connexion he mentions the case of a man who gave poison by way of a medical drug, who, he says, furnished the cause of death, just like one who puts a sword in the hand of a lunatic; this latter, he says, like the first, not being liable under the *lex Aquilia*, but *in factum*. 7. But when a man throws someone off a bridge, whether the latter is killed by the shock itself, or is at once drowned or is overpowered by the force of the current and dies from exhaustion, the offender, according to Celsus, is liable under the *lex Aquilia*, just as he would be if he had dashed a boy against a rock. 8. Proculus says that if a surgeon operates on a slave unskilfully, there is a good right of action, either on the contract or under the *lex Aquilia*.

8 GAIUS (*on the provincial Edict* 7) The same rule applies where a doctor makes a wrong use of a drug; but, in fact, where a man operates properly, but omits further treatment, he will not get off free, but is held guilty of negligence. Again, where a mule-driver, through want of experience, is unable to hold in his mules as they rush off, if they run over someone else's slave, the driver is commonly said to be liable on the ground of negligence. The law is the same where he is unable to hold the mules in because he is not strong enough; and it cannot be held unjust that want of strength should bear out a charge of negligence, because no one ought to undertake a task in which he knows or is bound to know that his want of strength will be a source of peril to others. The same law holds in the case of a man who from want of experience or from want of strength cannot keep in a horse on which he is riding.

9 ULPIANUS (*on the Edict* 18) Again, where a midwife gives a drug to a woman who dies in consequence, Labeo makes this distinction: if she administered the drug with her own hands, she must be held to have killed the woman; but if she gave it to the woman for her to take it herself, there must be an action allowed *in factum*; and this is a sound opinion, as in this case the midwife furnished the cause of death rather than killed. 1. Where a man, either by force or suasion, administers a drug to any person, either as a draught or by injection, or rubs him with some poisonous preparation, he is liable under the *lex Aquilia*, just as the midwife is who gets a woman to swallow a drug. 2. Where a man starves

a slave to death, according to Neratius, he is liable to an action *in factum.* 3. If my slave is riding on horseback, and you frighten the horse, and so cause the man to be thrown into the river, and he is drowned, then, as we read in *Ofilius,* it is a case for an action *in factum* ; just as it would be if my slave were inveigled into an ambush by one man and killed by another. 4. ***[1] But if persons are hurling spears by way of sport and a slave is killed, the *lex Aquilia* applies ; (though if, when a number of persons were hurling spears on the exercise ground, the slave passed that way, the statute does not apply, because the slave had no business making his way at an improper time across the ground used for hurling spears ; at the same time [even then] anyone who should deliberately aim at the slave would certainly be liable under the statute ;)

10 PAULUS (*on the Edict* 22) because the practice of a mischievous sport is a piece of negligence.

11 ULPIANUS (*on the Edict* 18) Again, Mela says this :—If several persons are playing at ball, one of whom gives the ball rather a hard stroke and so drives it against the hand of a barber, and thereby a slave whom the barber has in his hands has his throat cut, in consequence of the razor being knocked against it, whichever party was guilty of negligence is liable on the *lex Aquilia.* Proculus says the negligence is the barber's ; and certainly, if he was carrying on his trade on a spot where the sport above mentioned was usually practised, or where people were constantly passing, he is to some extent accountable, though, on the other hand, there is some sense in the remark that where a man puts himself in the hands of a barber who has set up his stool in a dangerous place, he has himself to blame. 1. If one man held a slave and another killed him, the one who held him you may say furnished the cause of death and consequently he is liable to an action *in factum.* 2. But if a number of persons struck him, it is a point to consider whether all are not liable, as having all killed him. As to this, if it is known who struck the fatal blow, that one is liable, as having killed him ; but, if it is not known, then, according to Julianus, all are liable, as having slain, and if an action is brought against one, this does not release the others, because, under the *lex Aquilia,* payment by one man is no

[1] Probably words referring to an accident occurring in the course of regular drill are omitted by an oversight. Cf. J. 4. 3. 4 : *v.* M.

discharge to another, as it is a case of penal damages. 3. Celsus tells us that if one man gives [a slave] a mortal wound, and, after that, another kills him outright, the former is not liable for slaying but for wounding, because the slave died from a different wound; but the latter is liable for slaying. Marcellus takes the same view, and it is the more reasonable opinion. 4. If a number of persons let fall a piece of timber and crush a slave, the old lawyers hold that they are all equally liable under the *lex Aquilia.* 5. Again, Proculus gave the opinion that there was an action on the statute against a man who set his dog at someone and made it bite him, though he was not holding the dog; but Julianus says that a man would be liable under the statute only where he held the dog and so caused it to bite someone; whereas, if he did not hold it, the action must be *in factum.* 6. The right of action under the *lex Aquilia* belongs to the "*erus,*" that is the owner. 7. If wrongful damage is done in the case of a slave whom I was going to restore to you by way of "redhibition," then, according to Julianus, I have a good right of action under the *lex Aquilia,* and, when I proceed to make the redhibition, I must assign it over to you. 8. Suppose, however, the slave is held to service in good faith by someone [who is not his owner], will the latter have the right of action? Here, on the whole, the action to be allowed is *in factum.* 9. Where clothes have been lent to a person, according to Julianus, if they should be torn, the borrower cannot bring an action on the *lex Aquilia*; the right of action is with the owner. 10. Julianus discusses the question whether a usufructuary or a usuary has an action on the *lex Aquilia*; my own opinion is that in such a case what will have to be allowed is an *utilis actio.*

12 PAULUS (*on Sabinus* 10) We may add that if the bare proprietor wounds or kills a slave in whom I have the usufruct, I have a right to have an action allowed me against him on the analogy of the *lex Aquilia,* the damages to be in proportion to the value of my usufruct, and, in assessing such damages, that part of the year is to be included in the account which was anterior to my usufruct.

13 ULPIANUS (*on the Edict* 18) A free man has an *utilis actio* on the *lex Aquilia*; he has not the direct action, as no one can be called owner of his own limbs. The owner can sue on account of a runaway slave. 1. Julianus says that if a free man acts as a *bonâ fide* slave to me, he is liable towards me in his own person under the *lex Aquilia.* 2. Where a slave is killed who is part of

the assets of a deceased person, the question may be asked who can bring the action, as there is no owner of such a slave? Celsus says that the statute requires that damage should always be made good to the owner; so here the inheritance will be deemed the owner; consequently, when the heir enters on the inheritance, he can take the requisite proceedings. 3. Where a slave who was left as a legacy is killed after entry on the inheritance, the right of action on the *lex Aquilia* is in the legatee, unless[1] it was only after the death of the slave that he accepted the legacy; if he declined it, then, according to Julianus, it follows that we must say that the right of action goes to the heir.

14 PAULUS (*on the Edict* 22) But if the heir kills the slave himself, the view has been maintained that the legatee must be allowed an action against him.

15 ULPIANUS (*on the Edict* 18) It would follow from the passage [in Julianus] that the rule is that if the slave bequeathed is killed before entry is made on the inheritance, the right of action on the *lex Aquilia* remains with the heir, having come to him through the inheritance: but if the slave was wounded before the entry, then the right of action remained part of the inheritance, but the heir is bound to assign it to the legatee. 1. Where a slave receives a mortal wound and then is killed by the fall of a house or by shipwreck or by a blow of any kind sooner than he would have died of the wound, there can be no action for killing him [against the man who first wounded him], but only one for wounding him; but if he was manumitted or disposed of to someone else and after that died of the wound, in that case, according to Julianus, an action can be brought as for killing him. The reason of the above discrimination is that it is a fact that he was killed by you at the moment when you wounded him, though it was made manifest only when he died, but, in the first mentioned case, the fall of the house made it impossible to ascertain whether he was killed or not. Where your slave is mortally wounded, and you [in your testament] make him free and appoint him your heir, and after that he dies, your heir cannot sue on the *lex Aquilia*,

16 MARCIANUS (*Rules* 4) because the matter is brought into a position in which the right could not have arisen.

17 ULPIANUS (*on the Edict* 18) If an owner kills his own slave,

[1] For *non* M. is inclined to read *vel*; which gives "even if" instead of "unless."

he will be liable to an action *in factum* at the hands of a *bonâ fide* possessor or one who held the slave as pledgee.

18 PAULUS (*on Sabinus* 10) We may add that if the pledgee kills or wounds the slave, he can be sued under the *lex Aquilia* and by the action on the pledge, but the plaintiff is bound to be content with one or other of the two actions.

19 ULPIANUS (*on the Edict* 18) But if a man kills a slave whom he owns in common with someone else, according to Celsus he is liable on the *lex Aquilia*; and the rule is the same if he wounds him:

20 THE SAME (*on Sabinus* 42) he is liable, that is, in respect of such share in the slave as belongs to the plaintiff.

21 THE SAME (*on the Edict* 18) The words of the statute are:—"whatever was the greatest value of the slave in that year." This clause prescribes a valuation of the amount of damage done. 1. The year is to be reckoned back from the day when the slave was killed; but if he was only mortally wounded and died after a long interval of time, then, according to Julianus, we must reckon the year from the time when he was wounded, though Celsus gives a different rule. 2. Do we however merely estimate the intrinsic value borne by the slave himself when he was killed, or do we not rather consider the interest his owner had in his not being killed? According to the present practice what is estimated is the interest mentioned.

22 PAULUS (*on the Edict* 22) Accordingly, if you have killed a slave whom I had engaged to deliver to someone else under a penalty, the difference it makes to me is a relevant consideration in the case. 1. Indirect elements of value (*causæ*) attached to the particular individual must be brought into the account too; for instance, where a man kills one slave out of a troop of players or singers, or one of twins, or one horse out of a team, or one animal, male or female, of a pair of mules; as in such cases a value must not be set only on the individual killed, but account must be further taken of the extent to which the others are depreciated.

23 ULPIANUS (*on the Edict* 18) On this principle Neratius tells us that if a slave is killed who is appointed heir [by a stranger], the value of the inheritance itself will be considered in assessing damages. 1. Julianus says that if a slave is killed who had been manumitted by testament and appointed heir [by his owner],

neither the substituted heir nor the statutable heir can by means of an action on the *lex Aquilia* recover the amount of a value set on the inheritance, such inheritance not having been open to the slave; and this opinion is sound. Accordingly, he says, the only thing to be estimated is the market value of the slave, as that is all in which the substitute can be held to have any interest: but my own opinion is that even the market value will not be considered, because, if the slave had been heir, he would have been free too. 2. Julianus says further that if I am appointed heir on condition that I manumit Stichus, and then Stichus is killed after the testator's death, the assessed amount that I shall get will include the value of the inheritance, because the act of killing prevented the fulfilment of the condition; but if the slave is killed in the testator's lifetime, the value of the inheritance will not be taken into account, because the question is put retrospectively what was the greatest value the slave bore. 3. Again Julianus says that the valuation of the slave is made with reference to the time at which he was worth most in that year; it follows that, if there is some valuable painter whose thumb is cut off, and within a year's time after this injury he is killed, his owner can sue on the *lex Aquilia*, and the painter must be valued at such a sum as he was worth before he lost his thumb and with it his power of painting. 4. Again, if a slave of mine should be killed who had been guilty of extensive falsification in my accounts, and accordingly it was my intention to examine him by torture, in order to extract from him the names of his accomplices, Labeo says very properly that the value which ought to be put on the slave is one representing the interest I had in the frauds[1] committed through him being detected, not the amount of direct loss occasioned by the man himself. 5. If a well-conducted slave should change his character and then be killed within the year, the value to be taken in assessing the damages will be what he was worth before such change. 6. In short, the rule is that any advantages which enhanced the value of the slave at any time within the year ending at the moment when he was killed form an element in the valuation to be put on him. 7. If an infant is killed which is not a year old, the better opinion is that this action will meet the case, the valuation being referred to the portion of the year during which the infant existed. 8. It is settled that the action is allowed to the heir and to all other successors; but it will not be allowed against the heir or other successors [of the wrongdoer], as

[1] del. *servi*. M.

it is a penal action, unless such heir chance to have become the richer by the damage done. 9. Where a slave is killed with malice, it is settled that the owner can proceed on the *lex Cornelia* too; and if he brings an action on the *lex Aquilia*, this ought not to bar the action under the *Cornelia*. 10. The right of action is for simple damages, where the defendant admits his guilt, and for twofold where he denies it. 11. If a person confesses falsely that he killed a slave who is really living, and afterwards he is prepared to show that the man is alive, then, as we learn from Julianus, no action lies under the *lex Aquilia*, though the party has confessed that he killed; because, where the action is founded on a confession, all that the plaintiff is excused thereupon is the necessity of proving that the person who killed the man is the defendant, but it is still necessary that the man should have been killed by someone or other.

24 PAULUS (*on the Edict* 22) This comes out more clearly where a slave is [alleged to be] wounded; if the defendant confesses that he wounded him, but the man was not wounded, what wound is to afford the basis of the valuation, or what day are we to go back to?

25 ULPIANUS (*on the Edict* 18) Accordingly, if the slave was not killed, but still is dead, the better opinion is that the party is not liable in respect of the slave so dead, in spite of his confession. 1. If an agent or a guardian or a curator or anyone else confesses that the absent principal [or the ward or the minor] wounded a slave, an *utilis actio* founded on confession must be allowed against the party so confessing. 2. It should be observed that in the action which is allowed against a party who confesses, the judge is appointed not for the purpose of deciding the question but of assessing the damages, there is nothing to be done in the way of deciding the question against those who confess.

26 PAULUS (*on the Edict* 22) Suppose, for instance, that the party who is sued should confess that he killed the slave and should be prepared to pay the sum assessed, but the plaintiff puts the matter in question at a very high figure.

27 ULPIANUS (*on the Edict* 18) If a slave should carry off another slave belonging to a different owner and kill him, then, according to both Julianus and Celsus, there is a right of action for theft and one for wrongful damage too. 1. If a slave who is owned in common, say by you and me, should kill another slave belonging

to me, the *lex Aquilia* will apply against you, if the man acted with your consent; and this, so we learn from Urseius, was the opinion of Proculus. If, he added, the slave did it without your consent, there is no noxal action, lest it should be in the power of the slave to make himself the property of one of us only[1]; and this, I should say, is sound. 2. Again, if a slave owned in common by you and me should be killed by a slave belonging to Titius, Celsus says that if one of us two sues, either he will get a part of the damages assessed corresponding to his share in the slave, or else there will be an order that the slave be surrendered to him for *noxa* absolutely, as such delivery does not admit of division. 3. The person bound in respect of the slave who killed is the owner; a person whom he is serving as slave in good faith is not bound. Whether a man whose slave has run away is bound in respect of him, if he is sued on the *lex Aquilia*, is a question asked; Julianus says that he is bound, and this is perfectly sound, as Marcellus too is of the same opinion. 4. The second chapter of the statute has gone out of use. 5. In the third chapter the *lex Aquilia* continues thus:—"In respect of all other things besides slaves or cattle killed, where anyone does damage to another by wrongful burning, breaking or breaking up, whatever was the worth of the property[2] in the last thirty days, the offender must be ordered to give that sum of money to the owner." 6. If therefore a man should, in the case of a slave or an animal, not kill, but burn, break, or break up, there is no doubt that the action must be brought under the above words. Accordingly, if you throw a torch at my slave and scorch him, you will be liable to an action at my hands. 7. Again, if you set fire to my plantation or my country-house, I shall have an action under the statute. 8. If a man's object is to burn down my[3] block of chambers, but the fire spreads to the neighbour's block too, he will be liable to an action under the *lex Aquilia* at the hands of the neighbour as well, and he will still be answerable to the tenants too for the burning of their moveable goods. 9. Where a tenant has a slave whose duty it is to look after a furnace, but the man goes to sleep at the fireside and the house is burnt down, Neratius tells us that, if an action is brought against the tenant on

[1] Meaning apparently "my property." The text says "*your* property," *tibi*: but this is probably a bad case of shifting the pronoun. M. however proposes *utri* instead of *ut tibi*.

[2] *quanti ea res erit*: perhaps "whatever is the estimate of the damage, if assumed to have been done on the day when it would have been greatest."

[3] Perhaps del. *meam*, and read here "his" for "my." Cf. *Collatio*.

his lease, he is bound to make it good, if he was negligent in the selection of men to do the work ; if, however, one man lit the fire in the furnace, and another was negligent in attending to it, will the man who lit the fire be liable? The fact is that the one who had to attend to the fire did nothing at all, and the one who lit the fire in the proper way did nothing wrong. What is the upshot? I should say that there is an *utilis actio* both against the man who went to sleep beside the furnace and the man who was negligent in looking after the fire; and no one ought to say, in the case of the man going to sleep, that he was overtaken by a natural human weakness, as his duty was either to put the fire out or else to guard it in some way that would prevent it from spreading. 10. If you have an oven against a wall belonging to you and your neighbour, will you be liable for wrongful damage? Proculus says no such action can be brought, because none can be brought even against a man who has an [ordinary] hearth; accordingly, it would, I think, be fairest that an action should be allowed *in factum*, supposing, that is, that the wall is burnt, but if you have so far done me no damage, but you have simply got your fire in such a position that I apprehend that you will do damage, then I think that the case would be met by the undertaking against *damnum infectum*. 11. According to Proculus, where the slaves of a tenant have burnt down the residence, the tenant is liable, either on the contract of lease or else under the *lex Aquilia*, it being open to the tenant to surrender the slaves for *noxa*, and if the case has been decided in one of the two actions, no further proceedings can be taken in the other. This is always provided there was no negligence in the tenant; but if he had slaves given to such offences, he is liable to an action for wrongful damage for having such slaves. A similar rule, he says, must be observed as to persons who are lodgers in a building, and there is much to be said for this view. 12. If my bees fly off to join your bees, and you fire them, according to Celsus I have a good right of action on the *lex Aquilia*. 13. The statute says *ruperit* (breaks up). This word is understood by nearly all the old lawyers to be equivalent to *corruperit* (destroys). 14. Accordingly Celsus gives this [answer to a] question [on the subject];—If you sow tares or wild oats in the middle of your neighbour's corn so as to spoil his crop, then not only can the landowner, or, if the land is let, the tenant, take proceedings by way of Interdict *quod vi aut clam*, but there is an action *in factum* too, and, if the tenant brings it, he is bound to give an undertaking that no further action shall be brought, the object being that the owner shall give no further trouble; as it is one kind of damage to destroy or spoil something in itself, and so give ground for an action on the *lex Aquilia*, but quite another case where, without affecting the thing in itself, you mix something else with it which it would cost trouble to get rid of. 15. Where a man contaminates wine, or spills it, or makes it turn sour, or spoils it in any other way, according to Celsus, an action can be brought on the *lex Aquilia*, as the term "*corrumpere*" (destroy) extends to spilling wine or making it turn sour. 16. The same writer agrees that breaking and burning are included in the term destroying, but there is nothing new, he says, in a statute enumerating certain things specifically and then adding some general term which comprises the specific things; and this is a sound remark. 17. We must certainly hold that the word "*rumpere*" applies where a man wounds a slave or strikes him with a rod or a thong, or his fist, or a weapon, or anything whatever, so as to draw blood or cause a bruise; but only so far as it is a case of wrongful damage to property; where the party does not lower the value of the slave to any extent or make him less serviceable, the *lex Aquilia* does not apply, and there will only be an action for *injuriæ* (insult etc.), as the statute deals with those cases of "breaking up" which occasion loss. Hence, even if the slave is none the worse as a matter of market value, but expense has been incurred to have him cured and made sound, it must be held that I (the owner) am so far damnified, and consequently that proceedings can be taken under the *lex Aquilia*. 18. Where a man tears or befouls someone's clothes, he is liable as though he had "broken up." 19. Again, if a man throws my millet or corn into a river, an action on the *lex Aquilia* will meet the case. 20. Also where a man mixes sand or anything else with my corn, so that it is difficult to get rid of it, an action can be brought as it were for spoiling. 21. If anyone knocks coins out of my hand, there is, as Sabinus holds, an action for wrongful damage, supposing the coins are lost in such wise that they do not come into anybody's hands; for instance, by falling into a river, or the sea, or a drain; but, where they come into someone's hands, the action must be for theft aided and encouraged; this was held by the old lawyers themselves. 22. If you hit a female slave with your fist or strike a mare and the result is a premature birth, you are liable, according to Brutus, under the *lex Aquilia*, as it were for "breaking." 23. He adds that if a man overloads a mule and ruptures any part of its body, the statute will apply. 24. Where a man scuttles a merchant ship carrying a cargo, Vivianus tells us there is a right of action under the *lex Aquilia*, as it were for breaking. 25. If a man picks unripe olives, or cuts an unripe crop of corn, or gathers grapes before the proper time, he will be liable under the *lex Aquilia*; if the fruit is ripe, the statute does not apply, as there is no wrong done; in fact the man makes you a present of the cost which would have to be incurred for the purpose of gathering the particular kind of crop; but, if he abstracts the crop which has been so gathered, he is liable for theft. Octavenus adds, as to the case of the grapes, the words—"unless the party throws the grapes on the ground so that they are scattered about." 26. The same writer (Vivianus) says with respect to the taking of coppice, that, if the twigs are not mature, the party is liable under the *lex Aquilia*, but, if he takes them when they are mature, he is liable for theft and also for trees cut by stealth. 27. If you [cut and] carry away a fully grown willow plantation, but do not injure the stocks, the *lex Aquilia* does not apply. 28. If a man castrates a slave boy and so raises his value, according to Vivianus, the *lex Aquilia* does not apply, but the action must be for *injuriæ* (insult—to the owner), either on the Edict of the Ediles or for fourfold. 29. If you send anyone a cup to be pierced with holes, then, if he breaks it through want of skill, he will be liable for wrongful damage; but if he breaks it through no want of skill, but the fact is that it had cracks which spoilt it for the above treatment, he may well get off. In consequence of this, it is a practice of workmen, when articles of this kind are put in their hands, to make an agreement that they shall not do the work at their own risk, and this bars any right of action either on the contract or under the *lex Aquilia*. 30. A husband gives his wife a number of unstrung pearls to use; should the wife thereupon, without the husband's consent or without his knowledge, perforate the pearls in order to wear them, when so bored, on a thread, she is liable under the statute, whether she is divorced or is still the man's wife. 31. If a man breaks down or breaks open the doors of a building belonging to me, or demolishes the building itself, he is liable under the *lex Aquilia*. 32. If a man demolishes a watercourse belonging to me, then, although the materials which are thrown down are my property, still, as the ground across which I conduct the water is not mine, the best conclusion to come to is that an *utilis actio* must be allowed. 33. If a stone falls off a waggon and breaks to pieces or fractures anything, it is held that the waggoner is liable on the statute, if the reason the stones gave way was that he packed them badly. 34. A man hires a slave to lead a mule and puts the animal under his charge; the slave thereupon ties the line by which he is holding the mule to his thumb, and the mule breaks away, tears the slave's thumb off, and then throws itself over a height: here Mela holds that if an unskilled slave was let out on the understanding that he was a skilled one, an action on the contract can be brought against the owner of the slave on account of the mule being destroyed or disabled, but if the mule was excited by being struck or frightened, then the owner, I mean the owner of the mule, and the owner of the slave will have a right of action under the *lex Aquilia* against the man who excited the mule. My own opinion is that, even in the case in which there is a right of action on the contract, there is a good right of action on the *lex Aquilia* too. 35. Again, if you put a vat full of wine in the hands of a plasterer, under an agreement that he shall do what is wanting with it, and he knocks a hole in it, so that the wine runs out, Labeo says that the proper action is *in factum*.

28 PAULUS (*on Sabinus* 10) Where persons make pits in order to catch bears or deer, if they make them on a place where people commonly pass and something falls in and is injured, such persons incur liability under the *lex Aquilia*; but, if they dug in some other place where pits are usually made, no liability is incurred. 1. However, the action is allowed only on special grounds, that is to say, only where no warning was given and the owner had no knowledge and was not able to take precautions. There are in fact a great many cases of this kind to be met with, in which an applicant is refused relief if it was in his power to avoid the danger.

29 ULPIANUS (*on the Edict* 18) The rule is like that applied in a case in which you put snares on some spot where you had no right to put them, and a neighbour's cattle have been caught in the snares. 1. If you break down a projecting roof of mine which I allowed to extend above your house without any right to do so, then, as we learn from Proculus, I can bring an action against you for wrongful damage; as your proper course was to bring an action against me averring that I had no right to have a projecting roof; and it is not fair, Proculus proceeds to say, that I should have to suffer damage by your breaking down my materials. There is a rescript of the Emperor Severus which varies the rule: the Emperor, where a watercourse was carried through a man's house without any right of servitude, told him by rescript that he was at liberty to break it up without asking leave; and this is quite sound,—the point

of difference is that in the former case the party built the projecting roof on his own property, but, in the latter, a man made a construction on somebody else's ground. 2. If your vessel comes into collision with my boat, the question is asked what kind of action I have. According to Proculus, if it was in the power of the persons navigating the vessel to prevent the collision and it took place by their negligence, there ought to be an action brought against them under the *lex Aquilia*, as it makes but little difference whether you do the damage by steering straight at the boat, or drawing the steering-oar towards the ship, or do it with your own hands directly, as in all these cases alike I suffer damage by your act; but if the ship drifted against the boat because there was a rope broken or there was no one at the helm, no action can be brought against the owner. 3. Again, Labeo says that where a ship is driven by the force of the wind against cables which hold the anchors of another ship, and the sailors [on board the former] cut the cables, then, if there was no other way in which the first ship could get loose except by cutting the cables, no action will be allowed. Labeo and Proculus held the same opinion with reference to fishermen's nets in which a fishing-boat belonging to others was entangled; of course, if this happened through the negligence of those navigating the fishing-boat, there would be an action on the *lex Aquilia*. Where, however, an action is brought for wrongful damage to nets, no account is taken of the fish which the owner of the nets fails to catch in consequence, as it is a matter of uncertainty whether any would have been caught or not, and a similar rule is maintained in the case of hunters and fowlers. 4. If one ship collides with and disables another which is coming in the opposite direction, according to Alfenus, there is a good right of action against either the pilot or the skipper (*ducator*); but if the vessel was impelled with too strong an impetus to be restrained, no action can be allowed against the owner (*sic*); though, if the mischief took place through the negligence of the sailors, I should say the action under the statute will meet the case. 5. Where a man cuts a rope by which a vessel is made fast, and the vessel is lost, there can be an action *in factum*. 6. Under this section of the statute the action can be brought for injury done to any animals that are not "*pecudes*" (gregarious), for instance, to a dog; and the same may be said of boars and lions, and of wild beasts and birds generally. 7. Municipal magistrates, it is held, can be held liable under the *lex Aquilia*, if they do wrongful damage: there is no doubt that, even if such a magistrate were to take your cattle in execution, and then, by not letting you give them food, cause them to die of starvation, an action would have to be allowed (*in factum*). Again, where such an officer thinks that he is levying an execution in accordance with the statute, but he does not really do it in accordance with the statute, and he allows the things taken to be worn and spoilt, it is said that the *lex Aquilia* applies; indeed the same thing may be said even where the execution was in accordance with the statute. But if a magistrate uses some violence against a man who resists, he will not be liable under the statute; as, even in a case where a magistrate took a slave in execution and the slave hanged himself, no action was allowed. 8. The words "whatever was the value in the last thirty days" do not say expressly the greatest value; however, it is settled that they must be taken as if they did.

30 PAULUS (*on the Edict* 22) A man who kills someone else's slave whom he detects in the act of adultery [with his wife] will not be liable under this statute. 1. If a slave is killed who was pledged for debt, the debtor has a good right of action. Whether the creditor himself has a right to an *utilis actio*, because he may have an interest [in the slave's life], on the ground that the debtor is insolvent, or that he himself has lost his right of action by lapse of time, is a question sometimes asked. However, it is not fair that the offender should be liable to be sued both by the owner and by the creditor: unless indeed anyone choose to say that the debtor would not in that case suffer any wrong, as [whatever the creditor receives] the debtor is credited with to the extent of his debt, and anything paid in excess he can recover from the creditor, or, at the outset, the debtor will be allowed an action for so much of the damages as is in excess of the debt. Accordingly, in those cases in which the creditor is allowed an action [against the offender] because the debtor cannot pay, or because he has lost his right of action [against the debtor], the creditor will have an action under the *lex Aquilia* [against the offender] to the extent of the debt, the debtor being credited with the amount recovered, and the debtor himself has a good right of action on the *lex Aquilia*, for the amount to which the statutable damages exceed the debt. 2. If a man should consume wine or corn belonging to someone else, he cannot be held to do wrongful damage; consequently an *utilis actio* must be allowed. 3. In the action arising on this section, as in the other, it is malice and negligence that are penalized; consequently, if a man should set fire to his stubble or his thorns, in order to burn them up, and the

flames increase and spread so as to injure the corn or vines of some one else, we have to ask whether it took place through his negligence or his want of skill. If he did it on a windy day, he is guilty of negligence, as a man who gives an opening for damage to occur is held to commit it, and he exposes himself to the same charge if he did not take means to prevent the fire from spreading. But if he took all proper precautions, or a sudden gust of wind caused the spread of the fire, he is not guilty of negligence. 4. If a slave is wounded, but not mortally, and he dies from neglect, an action can be brought for wounding him, not for killing.

31 THE SAME (*on Sabinus* 10) If a pruner who throws down a branch from a tree or a man on a scaffolding kills a passer-by, he is liable only where the object thrown falls on a spot open to the public, and he did not call out so that the person might be able to get out of the way. Mucius, however, says that an action could be brought on the ground of negligence, even if the same thing should have happened on private property,—in fact, he said, it is a case of negligence where a man fails to foresee what a diligent person could have foreseen,—or notice should only have been given when it was too late to avoid the danger. On this principle it makes no great difference whether the party was going across public or private ground, as it very often happens that numbers make their way across private ground. If people do not pass there, a man is answerable for malice only, being bound not to let anything fall on one whom he sees going across; he cannot be called to account for negligence, as he cannot possibly guess whether anyone is going to pass that way.

32 GAIUS (*on the provincial Edict* 7) The following question has been asked:—Is it necessary that the same rule should be observed in an action for wrongful damage as is observed by the proconsul in a case of theft committed by a gang of slaves, viz., the rule that a demand for the whole damages is not to be allowed in respect of every separate slave, but it will be enough for so much to be paid as would have to be paid if the theft had been committed by a single freeman? The view on the whole held is that the same rule must be observed, and this is very reasonable; for the principle being in the case of an action for theft that an owner ought not to be deprived of his whole household of slaves in consequence of one delict, and that principle applying equally to an action for wrongful damage, it follows that the same kind of assessment should be made, especially considering that not infrequently the case of a delict

such as we are discussing is less grave; for example, where the damage is done by negligence and not maliciously. 1. If the same man first wounds a slave and afterwards proceeds to kill him, he will be held liable both for wounding and for killing, as there are two offences committed. The case differs from that of a man killing a slave by inflicting a number of wounds in the course of the same attack, as there will then be one action only, viz. for killing.

33 PAULUS (*on Plautius* 2) If you kill my slave, I should say that my personal feelings cannot be taken into account; suppose, for example, a man should kill a natural son of yours whom you would be glad to buy at a high price [if he were another man's slave]; the question is what he would be worth to people in general? Sextus Pedius agrees that the prices of things are not determined by personal feelings or convenience, but by average circumstances; so that a man who has his own natural son in his possession as a slave is none the richer for the fact that, if someone else had him, he would himself be ready to buy him for a very large sum; and a man who is in possession of someone else's son has not got an amount of wealth equivalent to what he could sell such son for to his father. The fact is that under the *lex Aquilia* people recover the amount to which they have suffered damage; and they will be held to have lost either gain that they were prevented from making or expense that they were compelled to incur. 1. In respect of damage which is not comprised in the *lex Aquilia* the action allowed is *in factum*.

34 MARCELLUS (*Digest* 21) A testator bequeathed Stichus to Titius and Seius; while Seius was making up his mind, but after Titius had brought a *vindicatio* for the legacy, Stichus was killed, after which Seius declined the legacy. In this case Titius is in the same position for suing the wrongdoer as if he had been sole legatee,

35 ULPIANUS (*on the Edict* 18) as he is held to have been full owner by accrual by relation back;

36 MARCELLUS (*Digest* 21) and just as, where a legatee declines the legacy, the right of action is in the heir as if the slave had never been bequeathed, so here the right of action is in Titius, as if he had been sole legatee. 1. If the owner of the slave to whom Titius gave a mortal wound orders in his will that he shall be free and his heir, and, after that, Mævius becomes heir to him (the slave), Mævius will not have a right of action under the *lex Aquilia*

against Titius; not, that is, in the opinion of Sabinus; the point he took being that no right of action would be transmitted to the heir which could not have been possessed by the deceased; and it certainly would be an absurdity that an heir should get damages representing the value of the person whose heir he was, on the ground that that person was killed. If, however, the testator gave the slave a share in the inheritance and gave him his liberty too, then on the death of the manumitted man, his coheir can sue on the *lex Aquilia*.

37 JAVOLENUS (*Extracts from Cassius* 14) If a free man has committed wrong with his own hand by the order of another, an action under the *lex Aquilia* can be brought against the person who gave the order, provided he had had a lawful right of command; if he had not, the action must be brought against the man who did the act. 1. Where a right of action exists against a man in respect of some fourfooted animal owned by him which has done "pauperies" (damage), and the animal is killed by a third person who is thereupon sued on the *lex Aquilia*, the damages must be assessed, not by reference to the intrinsic value of the animal, but to the legal implications which attach to it (*causa ejus*), which include the liability under an action for "pauperies"; and in the action on the *lex Aquilia* the person who killed will be ordered to pay a sum representing the extent to which it would have been in the interest of the plaintiff to dispose of the case against him by surrendering the animal for "*noxa*" rather than paying the damages assessed.

38 THE SAME (*Epistles* 9) If, at a time when a slave belonging to me of whom you are *bonâ fide* purchaser is acting in your service, he is wounded by a slave of yours, it has been decided that I have in any case a full right to proceed against you under the *lex Aquilia*.

39 POMPONIUS (*on Quintus Mucius* 17) Quintus Mucius has the following. A mare was turned out to graze on land that did not belong to her owner, and, as the landowner was driving her off, she slipped her foal; the question was asked whether the owner of the mare could bring an action on the *lex Aquilia* against the man who drove her off, for injuring her when he struck her[1]? It was held that, if the party struck her or deliberately drove her too violently, the owner could bring an action. 1. POMPONIUS. Even where a man finds another's cattle on his own land, he is bound to drive

[1] *in iciendo:* M suggests *in ejiciendo*, "through the above mishap."

them away in the same way as he would if the cattle he found were his own, because, if he has suffered any damage by their being there, he has the appropriate right of action. Consequently, where a man finds someone else's cattle on his own land, he has no right to impound them, and he is not allowed to drive them in any other way than, as above mentioned, as if they were his own; he must either drive them away without causing any loss to the owner or call upon the owner to fetch his cattle off.

40 PAULUS (*on the Edict* 3) Under the *lex Aquilia*, if I aver that there has been an obliteration of a chirograph (note of hand) of mine importing that a sum of money was owed me on a condition, and I am able at the time to prove this by the testimony of witnesses as well, who may, however, be unable to bear witness at the time when the condition comes to pass, whereupon I make a short statement of the facts to the judge, and convince him of the truth of my story,—I ought to win my case; still the money to be paid me by the terms of the order made in my favour can be demanded only when the condition on which the original debt was owing comes to pass; and, if it fails altogether, the order will fall to the ground.

41 ULPIANUS (*on Sabinus* 41) Where a man obliterates a testament, let us consider whether there is not an action for wrongful damage. As to this, Marcellus says (*Dig.* 5), on consideration, that there is no such right of action; in fact, he says, what can you go upon to assess the damages? I made a note myself to Marcellus's work to the effect that this is quite true as far as the testator is concerned, as no valuation can be made of his interest; but with reference to an heir or to legatees the case is different, as for them a testament is almost equivalent to a note of hand; [and] Marcellus himself tells us in the same passage that, if a note of hand is obliterated, there is a good right of action under the *lex Aquilia*. We may add that if a man should obliterate a testament left in his charge, or should read it out before a number of persons, the best plan is for an action to be brought *in factum* and also for *injuriæ*, assuming that the party published the secret dispositions of a man's will with intent to commit a legal wrong (*injuria*). 1. Pomponius makes the discriminating remark that it sometimes happens that a man who obliterates a written document does not thereby become liable for theft, but only for wrongful damage, for example, where he did not obliterate with the intention of committing theft, but only of doing damage; in

such a case, he says, he will not be liable for theft, as theft requires not only the act of thieving but the intention thereof.

42 JULIANUS (*Digest* 48) Where a man so obliterates a written testament left in his charge or any written document of title that it is impossible to read it, he is liable to an action on *depositum* and also to one *ad exhibendum* (for production), on the ground that he returned or produced the thing entrusted to him in a spoilt condition. There is also in the same case a good right of action on the *lex Aquilia*; even where a man falsifies a document he is very properly said to have spoilt it.

43 POMPONIUS (*on Sabinus* 19) Where damage was done to property left by a deceased person before you entered on the inheritance as heir, you have a right of action on the *lex Aquilia*, although[1] the mischief was done after the death of the person whose heir you are; as the *lex Aquilia* by the term owner does not mean simply the person who was owner when the damage was done; indeed, if it did, it would follow that, even where a man succeeds someone as heir, the right of action in question could not pass to him from the deceased; and, similarly, that if you had been in the hands of the enemy and came back by *postliminium*, you would not be able to sue in respect of a wrong which was done during your absence; and no other rule than the above can be laid down save at the cost of great injustice to posthumous children who eventually become heirs to their fathers. A similar observation applies equally to the case of trees being cut by stealth during the same period; and I should say that the rule will also apply to the Interdict[2] *quod vi aut clam*, assuming that either the party committed the trespass after being warned not to do so, or it is shown that he was bound to know that he would have been warned by the persons who had a right to the inheritance, if they had been aware of his intention.

44 ULPIANUS (*on Sabinus* 42) Under the *lex Aquilia* the smallest negligence counts. 1. Whenever a slave wounds or kills with the knowledge of his owner, there is no doubt that the owner is liable under the statute.

45 PAULUS (*on Sabinus* 10) Knowledge [on the part of the owner] is understood to mean sufferance, so that, where the owner

[1] For *quod* read *quamvis*. Cf. M.

[2] For *hac actione* read or understand *Interdicto*. Cf. M.

is able to prevent the offence, he is liable if he does not do so. 1. An action can be brought on the *lex Aquilia* even though the slave wounded should be cured. 2. If you kill my slave believing him to be a free man, you will be liable under the *lex Aquilia*. 3. Two slaves try to leap over a heap of burning straw, they come into collision, both fall and one of the two is burnt to death ; here no action can be brought for what happens as long as it is not ascertained which of the two was upset by the other. 4. Where persons cause a certain amount[1] of damage because they have no other means of protecting themselves, they are free from guilt; all statutes and all rules of law allow people to repel force by force. But if, in throwing a stone at my adversary by way of defending myself, I miss him, but hit a passer-by, I shall be liable under the *lex Aquilia*, as you are only allowed to strike the party who commits the assault, and even him only when you do it in self-defence, not where your object is revenge. 5. A man who removes a serviceable wall is liable to the owner thereof for wrongful damage.

46 ULPIANUS (*on Sabinus* 50) If an action has been brought under the *lex Aquilia* where a slave is wounded, and after that the slave dies of the wound, there is nothing to prevent an action under the statute [for the death].

47 JULIANUS (*Digest* 86) Still, if a valuation was made in the first action, and subsequently to that, the slave being dead, the owner takes proceedings for the killing, then, if the defendant raises the *exceptio* of *dolus malus*, care will be taken that the plaintiff shall not get more damages by the two actions than he would have had a right to get if his action had been at the first for the slave being killed.

48 PAULUS (*on the Edict* 39) If, before entry made on some inheritance, a slave does damage to property forming part of the inheritance, and, having been set free, he does further damage to the same property, he will be liable to both the consequent actions, as the two matters depend on two distinct acts respectively.

49 ULPIANUS (*Disputations* 9) Where a man by raising smoke drives away or say even kills someone else's bees, he must be held to have not so much killed as furnished the cause of death; consequently he will be liable to an action *in factum*. 1. With regard to the saying, that the Aquilian action deals with damage wrongfully

[1] For *culpam* read *quiddam*. Cf. M.

done, we must hold in applying these words that damage is done wrongfully when it inflicts wrong in addition to the damage; [which can hardly fail to be the case[1],] unless the act was done under the stress of urgent physical danger, as in the case we read in Celsus of a man who broke to pieces an adjoining house in order to keep off a fire; there, Celsus says, there would be no action under the *lex Aquilia*, because the party broke down the adjoining house under the influence of reasonable alarm lest the fire should extend to where he was himself; and he holds that whether the fire reached him or was extinguished before it got so far, the action on the *lex Aquilia* will not lie.

50 ULPIANUS (*Opinions* 6) Where a man demolishes another man's house without the leave of the owner and erects baths on the spot, then, to say nothing of the rule of natural law to the effect that the surface belongs to the owner of the soil, the offender is exposed to an action on the mere ground of damage done.

51 JULIANUS (*Digest* 86) A slave was so badly wounded that he was sure to die of the injury inflicted; but in the interval of time before his death he was appointed heir, and afterwards died of a wound inflicted by another assailant; I wish to know whether an action for slaying can be brought under the *lex Aquilia* against both offenders? The answer was:—A man is commonly held to slay where he furnishes the cause of death in any way whatever; but, under the *lex Aquilia*, the only person who is held to be liable is the one who furnished the cause by direct violence, and, so to speak, with his own hands, the interpretation of the word "*occidere*" (slay) being got at by taking the meaning of the words *cædere* and *cædes*. On the other hand, the persons who are held to be liable under the *lex Aquilia* are not only those who may have wounded a slave so severely as at once to deprive him of life, but those are included who inflict such a wound as to make it certain that the man will die. Consequently where one man inflicts a mortal wound on a slave, and then after a while another man gives the same slave a stroke which puts an end to him sooner than he would have died from the first wound, the rule to lay down is that both assailants are liable under the *lex Aquilia*. 1. This is in keeping with the view handed down from the old lawyers, who, where the same slave was wounded by several persons under such circumstances that it did not appear by whose hand it was that he died, came to the con-

[1] Cf. M.

clusion that they were all liable under the *lex Aquilia*. 2. The damages assessed for killing the man will not be the same for both assailants in the above case; as the one who first wounded him will have to pay a sum representing the best value the man bore in the year then last past, and this is found by counting back three hundred and sixty-five days from the day of the wound; the later assailant will be liable for a sum amounting to the utmost that the man would have fetched in the year immediately preceding the day when his life ended, and this will take in the value of the inheritance. Accordingly one man will pay a larger sum and another a smaller by way of damages for killing the same slave; but there is nothing strange in this, seeing that the two offenders are understood to have killed the man in different ways and at different times. If anyone should think this an absurd decision for us to come to, let him reflect that it would be a much more absurd decision still if we held that neither of them was liable under the *lex Aquilia* or that one was more liable than the other, seeing that, on the one hand, misdeeds ought not to go unpunished, and, on the other hand, it is not at all easy to decide which of the two is more plainly hit by the statute. The fact is that it can be shown by innumerable instances that a great many rules have been adopted in the civil law in the general interest which are contrary to strict logic; I shall content myself at present with mentioning one of them. Where several persons carry off a piece of timber belonging to someone else with intent to steal it, but no individual of them all could have carried it by himself, every one is held to be liable to an action for theft, although it may be said, upon a nice view of the matter, that not one of them is liable, as it certainly is the fact that not one carried the timber off.

52 ALFENUS (*Digest* 2) Where a slave dies from blows inflicted on him [by a stranger], and this result is not attributable to the medical attendant's want of skill or to neglect on the part of the owner, an action may properly be brought for his death as for a case of unlawful killing. 1. A shopman had set down his lantern at night on a stone by the wayside, some one who was passing by took it away, the shopman went after him and asked him to give the lantern up, and, as the man tried to run off, held him back. Thereupon the man took a whip which he had in his hand, a lash with which would inflict severe pain, and began belabouring the shopman to make him let go. This gave rise to a serious scuffle, in the course of which the shopman knocked out the eye of the man who had taken his lantern; and upon these facts he asked for an opinion as to whether he could not be held to have done no unlawful damage, seeing that he had been first struck with the whip. My answer was that, unless he knocked the man's eye out of set purpose, he could not be held to have done unlawful damage, because the fault remained with the party who first struck him with the whip; but that if he, the shopman, had not been first beaten, but had fought with the other in trying to get the lantern out of his hands, the act in question must be held to be his own fault. 2. Two loaded waggons were being dragged by mules up the Capitoline steep, and, the foremost being tilted over, the drivers were pushing it behind so as to make it easier for the mules to drag it; at the same time[1] the upper waggon began to go back, and the drivers, who were between the two waggons, having thereupon come out from that position, the hindmost waggon was struck by the one in front, and so was driven back, thereby crushing a slave-boy, the property of someone or other. The owner of the boy consulted me on the question whom he should bring an action against. My answer was that the law depended on the circumstances of the case: if, I said, the drivers who were supporting the front waggon got out of the way without necessity, and it was in consequence of this that the mules could not hold up the waggon and so were dragged back by the mere weight of the load, then no action could be brought against the owner of the mules, but there was a good right of action under the *lex Aquilia* against the men who had been supporting the waggon when it came to be tilted over; because, I said, if a man deliberately let go something which he was supporting and thereupon it struck someone, in that case the damage done was none the less his own act; in the same way as if anyone were to be driving an ass and did not hold it in, he would be just as much doing unlawful damage as if he were to discharge a weapon or anything else out of his hand. But if, I said, the mules [backed[2]] because they were frightened at something, and thereupon the drivers left the waggon in desperate fear lest they should be crushed, then there could be no action brought against the men, but there could be one against the owner of the mules. If, lastly, neither the mules nor the men were the cause of the mishap, but the mules could not sustain the weight, or, in the course of struggling to do so they slipped and fell, and so the

[1] M. would omit *inter*: we may perhaps read *interea.*
[2] Cf. M.

waggon had gone back, and the men had been unable to support the weight as the waggon was tilted over, then no action could be brought against either the owner of the mules or the men. One thing, I said, I could affirm, viz. that however the matter were, there could be no action against the owner of the mules that drew the hindmost waggon, since they did not go back of their own motion, but because they were struck. 3. A man sold some oxen, it being a term in the agreement that he should let the purchaser have them on trial; accordingly he handed them over to be tried; and a slave of the purchaser in the course of the trial was gored by one of the oxen: the question was asked whether the vendor was bound to make good the damage to the purchaser. My answer was, that if the purchaser had got the oxen in pursuance of the terms of the purchase, the vendor was not bound to make good the damage; but, if he had not got them on that footing, then, if it was through the man's own negligence that he was gored by the ox, the damage would not have to be made good, but if it was through the vice of the ox, it must. 4. A number of persons were playing at ball, and as a small boy, a slave, was attempting to pick up the ball, one of the players pushed him, whereupon the slave fell and broke his leg. The question was asked whether the owner of the boy could bring an action under the *lex Aquilia* against the man who pushed him and so made him fall? My answer was No, as the thing appeared to have happened by accident rather than negligence.

53 NERATIUS (*Membranes* 1) You drove another man's oxen into a confined spot, and the result was that they fell over a precipice: an action *in factum* will be allowed against you modelled on that under the *lex Aquilia*.

54 PAPINIANUS (*Questions* 37) A debtor [who is bound as such to deliver an animal] has a good right of action under the *lex Aquilia* where the party who has stipulated for the delivery wounds the animal promised before the debtor is in fault; and the case is the same if he kills it. But if the party who stipulated kills the animal after the promisor's default, the debtor, no doubt, is discharged; but in this case he will not have a right to take proceedings under the *lex Aquilia*, as the creditor must be held to have done the wrong to himself rather than to anyone else.

55 PAULUS (*Questions* 22) I promised Titius to give him either Stichus or Pamphilus, Stichus being worth ten thousand and

Pamphilus twenty [thousand]; the promisee killed Stichus before there was any default on my part: an opinion was asked as to the action on the *lex Aquilia*. I answered:—"It being a fact in the case that Titius killed the less valuable slave of the two, the creditor [*i.e.* Titius] for the purpose of this inquiry is in exactly the same position as any third person." Then what is to be the measure of damages? is it ten thousand, the value of the slave killed, or is it the amount which the slave is worth whom I must needs hand over, in other words, the amount representing the difference which the act makes to me? Again, what are we to say if Pamphilus himself should die without there being any default on my part? will the sum to be paid for Stichus be thereupon the less on the ground that the promisor is discharged? As to this, it will be enough to say that Stichus was worth the higher value when he was killed, or had been worth it within the year; and, on this principle, Stichus must be held to have been of the higher value even if he was killed after the death of Pamphilus, but within the year.

56 THE SAME (*Sentences* 2) If a wife does damage to her husband's property, she can be sued in accordance with the terms of the *lex Aquilia*.

57 JAVOLENUS (*Extracts from Labeo's Posteriores* 6) I lent you a horse; as you were riding it, and several other persons were riding in your company, one of these rode against the horse you were on and threw you off, the result of the incident being that the horse's legs were broken. Labeo says that there is no right of action against you; but if the thing happened through the negligence of the horseman, there is one against him; it is certain, he adds, that there can be none against the owner [as such] of the horse which he rode. With this I agree.

III.

ON THE CASE OF PERSONS POURING OUT OR THROWING OUT.

1 ULPIANUS (*on the Edict* 23) The Praetor lays down the following as to persons who throw out or pour out anything:—"If anything should be thrown out or poured out from any place on a spot where people commonly pass or where they stand, I will allow an action for twofold the damage caused or done thereby to be

brought against the person who lives in that place. If it is averred that a free man was killed when struck by anything so falling, I will allow an action for fifty *aurei.* If he [the person struck] is living, and it is averred that he is injured, I will allow an action for whatever sum it shall seem fair to the judge that the party against whom proceedings are taken should be ordered to pay. If it is averred that a slave did the act in question without his owner's knowledge, I will add to the terms of the prayer the words 'or surrender the slave for *noxa*[1].'" 1. No one will deny that the above Edict of the Prætor is highly beneficial, as it is in the public interest that people should move about where they lawfully may without fear or danger. 2. It must be treated as a matter of small account whether the spot [where mischief is done] is public ground or private, so long as people commonly pass there, as the object of the Edict is to protect persons who are pursuing their way, and there was no thought of maintaining public roads; and any places over which people commonly pass ought to be at all times equally safe. If, however, in the case of such a road, there was once a time during which people in general did not pass that way, and then something was thrown down or poured out, while the spot was still closed, but, after that, it began to be used as a place of passage, there will be no liability incurred under this Edict. 3. Where a thing falls down while it is being hung up, it is on the whole regarded as thrown down, but, even where a thing falls down after it has been hung up, the better opinion is that it is to be regarded as thrown down. Similarly, if something is poured out of a suspended vessel, though the pouring of it out is not the act of anyone, we must still hold that the Edict applies. 4. The above action *in factum* is allowed to be brought against whoever occupies the house when the matter is thrown down or poured out, and not against the owner of the house; because the negligence is on the part of the former. The Edict does not go on to mention negligence or the case of the defendant denying the fact, so as to give a right of action for double damages, though, in the action for *damnum injuria* (unlawful damage), both these things are declared to be grounds of charge. 5. Where a free man is killed, there is no assessment of damages for the mischief at double the amount, because, in the case of a free man, no valuation of his person can be made at all; but the order will be for payment of fifty *aurei.* 6. The words "if he is living and it is averred that he is injured"

[1] For *noxam* read *noxæ.* Cf. M.

do not refer to any damage done in respect of the property of a free man, for example, where his clothes or anything else belonging to him should be torn or spoilt, but only to the infliction of bodily hurt. 7. If a *filius familias* has a hired upper room and something is thrown down or poured out therefrom, there is no action *de peculio* allowed against his father, because there is no claim made on the ground of contract, accordingly the right of action is against the son himself. 8. If the person who occupies the house is a slave, will a noxal action be the one to be allowed, seeing that there is none on *negotia gesta*? Or will there be an action *de peculio*, as no claim is made on the ground of the slave's delict? Of course we cannot properly speak of *noxa* (damage) on the part of the slave, where the slave himself did no harm. However, for my own part, I think that the slave ought not to be unpunished, but he should be corrected on motion (*officio judicis*) under the extraordinary power of the Court. 9. A man may be said to occupy a house whether it is his own or is let to him or he is there by favour. A guest will certainly not be liable, because he does not occupy, but is only entertained; the party liable is the one who gives the entertainment; there is as much difference between an occupier and a guest as between a person who is at home on the spot and one who comes from a distance. 10. If a number of persons occupy the same lodging (*cenaculum*), and something is thrown down from it, the action is admissible against any one of them,

2 GAIUS (*on the provincial Edict* 6) as it is quite impossible to know which person threw out or poured out anything;

3 ULPIANUS (*on the Edict* 23) and the action will be for the whole penal sum, but, where it has been brought against one person, the rest will be discharged;

4 PAULUS (*on the Edict* 19) that is, when the money is received [by the plaintiff], not merely on joinder of issue; the others being compellable by an *actio societatis* to contribute their share in [what is due for] the damage to the one who paid.

5 ULPIANUS (*on the Edict* 23) But if a number of persons occupy separate divisions of a lodging, the action is allowed only against the person who occupied the particular part from which the pouring out took place. 1. If a person gives free occupation to his own or his wife's freedmen and clients, then, according to Trebatius, he is liable on their account, and this is true. The law

is the same where a man accommodates a number of friends with quarters to lodge in on a small scale, as where one who carries on the business of letting out lodgings occupies the greater part of the lodging himself, he will be the only person liable, but if[1] he reserves only very limited quarters for his own use and lets out the rest to a number of different persons, they will all be liable, on the ground that they occupy the lodging from which the matter was thrown down or poured out. 2. In some cases, however, so long as it involves no injustice to the plaintiff, the Prætor ought, on principles of fair dealing, rather to allow the action against the person from whose sleeping-place or recess the matter was thrown down, even though there should be a number of persons living in the same lodging, but if something should be thrown from the middle of the apartment, the sounder view is that all are bound. 3. If the person by whom something is thrown is a warehouseman or a man who has hired a store-room or has hired a place for the sole purpose of carrying on some work or for seeing pupils, there will be ground for an action *in factum*, [and the rule is the same] even though it should be one of the workmen or one of the pupils who threw down or poured out. 4. When, however, a man has suffered adverse judgment in an action under the *lex Aquilia* (*sic*) on the ground that his guest or anyone else threw something from his lodging, it is a reasonable thing, in the opinion of Labeo, that[2] he should have an [action] *in factum* allowed him against the party who threw it, and this is perfectly true. No doubt, if he had let the room to the person who threw the matter down, he has a right of action on his contract too. 5. The action which the law allows for things poured out and thrown down cannot be barred by lapse of time, and it is open to the heir [of the party injured], but it is not allowed against the heir [of the wrongdoer]; but the one which can be brought on the ground that a free man, as it is alleged, has been killed is available for a year only, and it is not allowed against the heir nor on the part of heirs and successors generally, as it is a penal action and one which anyone may bring (*popularis*); it being always borne in mind that where a number of persons all wish to bring the action, it ought to be allowed by preference to one who has an interest in the matter, or who was connected with the deceased by marriage or blood. If, lastly, [the action is founded on the fact

[1] Omit *quis cenaculariam exercens* where it occurs the second time. M.

[2] Omit *qui ob hoc* and transpose *merito ei* and *quod hospes...dejecit.*

that] a free man was injured, he has a right of action himself which is not liable to be barred, but if any other person chooses to bring the action, the right to bring it will expire in a year; it is not open to the heirs of the party wronged as a matter of hereditary right, the rule being that where any injury is done to the body of a free person, no claim passes by hereditary right to his successors, as it is not a case of pecuniary loss, but the action is founded on principles of justice and fairness. 6. The Prætor says, "No one is to keep anything placed on an eave or a projecting roof over a spot where people commonly pass or collect which would injure anyone if it fell. Whoever transgresses this regulation, I shall allow an action *in factum* against him for ten *solida*. If it is alleged that a slave did it without the knowledge of his owner, I will order that [either the above sum be paid[1]] or else the slave be surrendered for *noxa*." 7. This pronouncement is a portion of the Edict already mentioned; it was in keeping with what preceded that the Prætor should provide for this case too, so that, if anything should be in a dangerous position in any part of the house named, it might do no harm. 8. The Prætor's words are:—"No one etc. on an eave or a projecting roof." The words "no one" apply to persons of every kind, whether they live in the house or not, so long as they have something placed in the position described. 9. "Anything placed over a spot where people commonly pass or collect." We must take the word "placed" to apply whether [the roof is[2]] of a private room or lodging or, say, a warehouse or any other building. 10. A man may be said to keep a thing placed even if he did not place it himself, but suffers it to remain where somebody else placed it; accordingly, if a slave places it, and the owner allows it to remain as placed, he, the owner, will be held responsible, not by liability to a noxal action, but directly. 11. The words are further "which might injure anybody if it fell." It is clear from these words that the Prætor takes measures to prevent harm being done, not by everything which is placed [in the position described], but everything which is so placed [there] that there is a possibility of its doing harm; moreover the law does not wait till the harm is done, the Edict applies at once if the harm is possible; and the party who kept the thing placed is punished, whether the thing so placed has actually done harm or not. 12. If the thing that was placed falls down and does harm, the action is admissible against the person who *placed* and not against

[1] Ins. after *fecisse dicetur* the words *aut idem dari*. M.

[2] Ins. after *edificii* the word *protecto*. M.

the one who *occupies the house*, on the ground that this action is not enough, as the person who placed the object cannot as a matter of course be said to have kept it placed, unless he was either owner or occupier of the house[1]. Thus, where a painter had a shield or a picture exhibited in a booth, which fell and did some[2] hurt to a passer-by, Servius laid down that an action ought to be allowed framed on the analogy of the present one; the present one itself, he said, clearly was not available, as the picture had not been placed on an eave or a projecting roof. The same rule he declared should be observed where a jar which was suspended in a net had fallen and done harm; as there was no statutable or prætorian action. 13. The action under discussion can be brought by anyone and is open to the heir of the party and successors generally, but it is not open against the heir of the party liable, because it is penal.

6 PAULUS (*on the Edict* 19) This Edict does not refer only to cities and villages, but applies equally to any roads where people commonly pass. 1. Labeo says that it applies only where something is thrown down in the daytime, not by night; however there are places where people pass even by night. 2. The occupier is bound to make good his own negligence and that of his family. If the matter is thrown out of a ship, there will be an *utilis actio* allowed against the person in charge of the ship.

7 GAIUS (*on the provincial Edict* 6) Where bodily hurt is inflicted on a free man by something which is thrown down or poured out, the judge takes into account the cost of medical attendance as well as any other expense incurred for his cure, and he reckons in besides these the value of any employment which he has lost or will have to lose in consequence of being disabled; but no estimate is made of scars or disfigurement, as the body of a free man cannot be made the subject of any valuation.

[1] The above follows the text. Cujas would transpose *posuerit* and *habitaverit*, —that is "placed" and "occupies the house." M. is inclined to follow him, and also to add some such words as "accordingly an *utilis actio* must be allowed against the one who placed"; inferring this, no doubt, from what follows.

[2] Ins. *quid* after *damni*. M.

IV.

On Noxal Actions.

1 Gaius (*on the provincial Edict* 2) Actions are called noxal which are put in force against people not in connexion with any contract, but in consequence of some "*noxa*" (*damage*) or misfeasance committed by a slave; and the force and effect of such actions is that, if judgment is given against the defendant, it is open to him to avoid having to pay the damages assessed by surrender of the individual who committed the wrong.

2 Ulpianus (*on the Edict* 18) If a slave has killed with the knowledge of his owner, this makes the owner liable for full damages, as the owner himself must be held to have killed; but if it was done without the owner's knowledge, the action is noxal, as it was not right that the owner should incur liability from the misfeasance of his slave, except so far as this, that he should have to surrender him for *noxa*. 1. If an owner did nothing to prevent the act, then, whether he remains owner or ceases to be owner, he is liable to this action; it is enough that he was owner at the time when he declined preventing the act, so much so that Celsus holds that, if the slave should come to be disposed of, in whole or in part, or should be manumitted, the *noxa* does not follow the individual, as in fact the slave committed no wrong, having obeyed his owner's order. This may, no doubt, be said, if the owner did so order; but if he simply failed to prevent, how can we say that there is no guilt in the slave? Celsus, however, makes a distinction between the *lex Aquilia* and the statute of the Twelve Tables; under the old statute, he says, where a slave has committed a theft or been guilty of any other *noxa* with the knowledge of his owner, there is a noxal action on the slave's account, and the owner is not liable on his own account; but under the *lex Aquilia* the owner is liable on his own account, and not on account of the slave. He proceeds to give the principle of each of the two statutes; that of the Twelve Tables being, he says, that the law desired that, where such a case arose, slaves should refuse to obey their owners, whereas that of the *lex Aquilia* was that the statute excused a slave who obeyed his owner, as he would have lost his life if he did not do as he was ordered. But if we must take for law what Julianus says (*b.* 86), that the words "if a slave commits theft or

is guilty of mischief" etc. are to be applied in connexion with subsequent statutes too, the inference will be that [besides the direct action] there can be noxal proceedings taken against an owner on his slave's account; so that the fact that an Aquilian action is allowed against the owner does not exonerate the slave, it simply is a burden on the owner. For my own part I have come to a conclusion agreeing with that of Julianus; his view is in accordance with principle, and is upheld by Marcellus, as Julianus himself informs us.

3 THE SAME (*on the Edict* 3) In all noxal actions, where knowledge on the part of the owner is required, the word "knowledge" must be taken to imply that the owner was able to prevent [the wrong being done] and failed to do so; there is, of course, a difference between instigating a slave to the commission of a delict and simply suffering him to commit one.

4 PAULUS (*on the Edict* 3) In the case of the delicts of slaves, what are we to understand by the expression "the owner's knowledge"? does it imply guilty intention? does it apply if the owner simply sees the deed done, although he is unable to prevent it? Suppose, for example, a slave who is taking proceedings to assert his freedom at law commits an offence with his owner's knowledge, or take the case of his disregarding his owner; again, suppose the slave is at the further side of a river, and commits some injurious act under his owner's eyes, but against his will. On the whole it is better to say that we must take knowledge to mean that of a person who is able to prevent the act; and this must be understood throughout the whole Edict, wherever the word "knowledge" occurs. 1. Where the slave of a stranger commits an offence with my knowledge, and I purchase him, a noxal action will be allowed against me; the man cannot be held [as against me] to have acted with the knowledge of his owner, since at the time of the offence I was not his owner. 2. Where the owner is held liable in virtue of his knowledge, it may be fairly asked whether an action will not be allowed in respect of the slave himself as well; unless indeed the Prætor intended that the owner should be called upon to pay one penalty only. Then is the slave's malicious behaviour to go altogether unpunished? That would be unjust: the rule rather is that the owner is to be held liable in both ways, but still, when one penalty is paid, namely, whichever the plaintiff chooses, the other is not demandable. 3. If nothing is said as to surrender for *noxa*, and the action is brought against the owner as

being privy to the offence, but in fact the owner was not really privy to it, then, if the case is dismissed and the trial ended, the plaintiff will be barred by an *exceptio* of *res judicata* (plea of "judgment given"), if, after that, he attempts further proceedings in which he gives the defendant the option of surrender for *noxa*; because the matter was brought to an issue in the previous trial and has been disposed of. But so long as the first trial is going on, it is open to the plaintiff, if he would rather give up the attempt to prove knowledge on the part of the owner, to alter his procedure and make it a noxal action. Conversely too, if he has carried through an action against an owner who really had knowledge and given him therein the option of surrender, he will not then be allowed to take further proceedings against such owner in which he omits the alternative of surrender for *noxa*; but if, in the course of the trial, he chooses to go on to establish the owner's knowledge, he must be allowed to do so.

5 ULPIANUS (*on the Edict* 3) If a slave belonging to several persons in common commits a delict of which all the co-owners are ignorant, a noxal action will be allowed against any one of them; but, if they all knew, then any one of them may be held liable without the alternative being given of surrender for *noxa*, just as if they had all committed the offence; and proceedings against one [of two such co-owners] will not release the other. If however one knew and the other did not know, the one who knew will be sued without the alternative of surrender, and the one who did not know with that alternative. 1. What distinguishes these two cases from one another is not merely the fact that the owner who knows is liable for the absolute amount, it has to be added that, in the case of the one who knows, if he should dispose of the slave, or should manumit him or the slave should die, the owner in question remains liable; though, if such owner himself dies, his heir is not liable.

6 THE SAME (*on the Edict* 18) However, the slave himself, if manumitted, will be liable too;

7 THE SAME (*on the Edict* 3) but a noxal action is not allowed [as against me], unless the slave is in my hands, and, if he is in my hands, though he was not so at the time when he committed the delict, I am liable, and my heir will be liable [after my death], if the guilty slave is living. 1. Pomponius says that, if a purchaser of the slave is sued in a noxal action, the vendor who had

knowledge of the act when it was done is no longer liable to be sued.

8 THE SAME (*on the Edict* 37) If a slave who belongs to several co-owners commits a theft, any one of the co-owners is liable to a noxal action for the whole amount, and this is the present practice. But the one who is sued cannot avoid paying the damages assessed except by surrendering for *noxa* the whole undivided property in the slave, and, if he is ready to surrender a share only, he is not to be indulged. It is true that, if, in consequence of the fact that the other co-owners are not prepared to surrender the slave, he should be ordered to pay the whole damages, he can proceed against them by an action *communi dividundo* or *familiæ erciscundæ*. No doubt, before issue is joined in the noxal action, he can procure immunity by assigning [to the injured person] his share in the slave, so as not to be under the necessity of sustaining the action; although it might be maintained that, when a share is once assigned[1] to the person in question, he loses his right of action, as when he has become owner of a share he cannot proceed by way of noxal action against a fellow-owner. Perhaps indeed he could not even bring an action *communi dividundo* against a fellow-owner on the ground of an offence which was committed before the co-ownership began. If he really cannot, he will suffer a plain legal wrong; but the better rule is that he has a right to an action *communi dividundo*.

9 PAULUS (*on the Edict* 39) Where a gang of slaves or a single slave, belonging in either case to co-owners, commits a theft with the knowledge of one of them, the party who knows will be liable in the name of both[2], and, if he is sued, it is a discharge to the other, and he will have no right to any contribution from his fellow-owner, as he incurred the penalty on account of his own act. But if the one who had no knowledge pays double damages, he will get simple damages from his fellow-owner.

10 THE SAME (*on the Edict* 22) We may add that a man can bring an action against his fellow-owner on the ground that he brought down the value of a slave owned in common, just as he might against anyone else who brought down the value of a piece of common property. However, if, after the slave has been

[1] For *eive data* read *ei cedatur*. Cf. M.

[2] *omnium*: but the text, by an apparent slip, confuses the cases of two and several.

surrendered for *noxa*, there is nothing else remaining which he owns in common, there can be an action *pro socio* (partnership action), or, if the parties were not partners, an action *in factum*.

11 ULPIANUS (*on the Edict* 7) The *bona fide* possessor of a slave will be liable for theft on the slave's account, and the owner is not liable. It is, of course, true that he cannot, by surrender for *noxa*, pass the property in the slave to the plaintiff; still, if the owner brings a *vindicatio* to recover the slave, he will be barred by an *exceptio* of *dolus*, or [the defendant] can procure that he shall be saved harmless by motion to the judge.

12 PAULUS (*on the Edict* 6) If a *bona fide* possessor gets rid of the slave so possessed, in order to avoid the possibility of an action against him on noxal grounds, he is liable to the action which is allowed against all such as have a slave in their power or have taken fraudulent means to avoid having him, the rule being that, in this last case, they are deemed to be still in possession.

13 GAIUS (*on the provincial Edict* 13) Noxal actions are allowed, not only against *bona fide* possessors, but also against those who possess *mala fide*; in fact it is deemed an absurdity that persons who are in possession in good faith should have to stand an action and mere plunderers be safe.

14 ULPIANUS (*on the Edict* 18) If a man should be sued by a number of persons owing to the offence of one slave, or by one person only on the ground of several distinct offences, then the fact that he cannot surrender the slave to all the plaintiffs does not put him under the necessity of offering the amount of damages assessed to those to whom he cannot make surrender. Then how does the matter stand, where he is sued by several persons? If one of them has got before the others, will that one be in a better position, and the surrender thereupon be made to him alone, or is the answer this, that either the slave must be surrendered to them all or else the defendant must give an undertaking that the one to whom he is surrendered shall be defended against the other plaintiffs? To this the truer answer is that the one who comes first is in the better position. The slave will therefore be surrendered, not to the plaintiff who first sued, but to the one who first got judgment in his favour; and accordingly the rule is that action on the judgment is refused to anyone who wins his suit later on. 1. We may add that if the slave is a *statuliber*, and, before the surrender, the condition is fulfilled [on which he is to become free], *or, again,*

before surrender, liberty is given in pursuance of a trust, or a condition is fulfilled subject to which the man was left as a legacy, and thereupon the property in him is transferred to the legatee, the defendant must by the judge's order be dismissed from the action; besides which it will be a thing for the judge to order on motion that he should guarantee the surrenderee against the man being recovered by superior title owing to any act of the defendant[1].

15 GAIUS (*on the provincial Edict* 6) The Prætor ought to order that the proceedings against the [late] owner should be transferred so as to be carried on against the [late] *statuliber*; but if, at the time when the case comes on, the slave's liberation is still in expectancy, then, in the opinion of Sabinus and Cassius, the heir is discharged from liability by delivering the slave, as, by so doing, he would assign all his own rights; and this is a sound view.

16 JULIANUS (*Dig.* 22) Should the heir contrive maliciously to avoid having the *statuliber* in his power, and the result be that he joins issue in an action which does not give the option of surrender for *noxa*, judgment ought to be given against him, even if the condition on which the man was to become free should have come to pass, just as it would be if the slave were to die.

17 PAULUS (*on the Edict* 22) Where a slave who belongs to two persons commits an offence with the knowledge of one of his owners, but without the knowledge of the other, whereupon an action is brought against the one who was ignorant and he surrenders the slave for *noxa*, it is not right that the other co-owner should be discharged by the surrender of some utterly worthless slave; accordingly proceedings will be taken against such other as well; and, if the action to make good the damage brings in anything over and above, the plaintiff will get the balance after giving credit for the value of the slave surrendered for *noxa*. But the co-owners themselves should compound their mutual claims on an action *communi dividundo* as follows:—If the one who was privy to the act of the slave pays the damages, he will not be credited with a proportion of the whole payment so made, but with his proportion of the amount which the slave is worth; and, if the other [who was ignorant] pays anything, he will be credited with a share on the same principle [viz. everything except his own proportion of the value of the

[1] Section 15, in the opinion of M., was meant to carry on the sense from the point where the above words in italics begin.

slave]. What would be quite unjust is that the one who ordered the slave to commit the offence should get anything from his fellow-owner, seeing that the loss which he suffers is owing to his own misfeasance. 1. If a number of different persons wish to bring a noxal action against me in respect of the same slave, or one person sues in a number of different actions in respect of the same slave, the slave being one in whom you have the usufruct and I have the bare property, it will fall within the duty of the judge, when I surrender the slave for *noxa*, to see that I give the plaintiff the usufruct as well; at the same time, I, the bare proprietor, can, by application to the Prætor, procure that the Prætor himself shall compel you either to contribute towards the whole assessed value an amount proportional to the value set on the usufruct, or else to assign the usufruct, if this is more convenient. On the other hand, if I, the bare proprietor, do not choose to defend the action brought in respect of the slave, you must yourself be allowed to defend it, and if you should hand over the slave in pursuance of the order of the Court, you will have nothing to fear from me.

18 POMPONIUS (*on Sabinus* 18) A person who has the usufruct in a slave has a right of action for theft against the bare proprietor, just as much as if he were any third person;—though there can be no action against him [for a theft committed by the slave], although the man is in his service;—accordingly, if judgment is given against the bare proprietor, he can get off by surrender for *noxa* to the usufructuary.

19 PAULUS (*on the Edict* 22) If a slave belonging to Titius does damage to property which you and I have in common, then, if we both wish to sue Titius, there is ground for a noxal action on the *lex Aquilia*, but not with the result that, if we get judgment against him, he can be compelled to surrender the slave in undivided ownership to each of us separately. It may however be said, on the analogy of the case in which the damage is suffered by one only and one claim for redress is acquired, that either the money should be offered to both jointly, or else, on motion made to that effect (*ex officio judicis*), the slave should be surrendered to both of us at once; still, even if the slave is surrendered for *noxa* to either of us in undivided ownership, and thereby the owner is quit as regards both of us, it is maintained quite correctly that the one to whom the surrender was made can be sued by the other in an action *communi dividundo*, to compel him to give up a share in the slave surrendered, as this is a case in which something has

come to the hands of a co-owner through the property owned in common. 1. Where the bare proprietor of a slave in whom someone else has a usufruct hires the services of the slave, the very terms [of the Edict?] import that judgment given against him will be with the option of surrender for *noxa*. 2. If your slave is *exercitor* of a ship, and his underslave, being a sailor belonging to the ship, does damage on board, an action must be allowed against you, just as if the *exercitor* were free and the underslave were his slave, so that you will be ordered to surrender the underslave for *noxa* out of the *peculium* of your slave; though, at the same time, if the underslave did the damage by the order of your slave or with his knowledge and sufferance, there ought to be a noxal action against you in respect of your slave. The same will also be the case if your slave orders any sailor to do the damage.

20 GAIUS (*on the provincial Edict* 7) If a man brings actions at different times on the ground of several distinct offences [committed by the same slave], then, if he acquires ownership in the slave in consequence of some one offence, he will have no further right of action against the previous owner, because a noxal action follows the delinquent subject; still, if the owner at the time of the offence preferred paying the damages assessed when sued in the first action, there is nothing to prevent him from being liable at the suit of the same plaintiff or of anyone else, if he brings an action on some other offence.

21 ULPIANUS (*on the Edict* 23) Whenever an owner is sued on noxal grounds, if he does not choose to defend the action, the position is such that he is bound to surrender for *noxa* the slave in respect of whom he declines to defend the action; and, if he will not surrender him, he is absolutely bound to defend the action; at the same time, judgment will be given against him only in case he has the slave in his power, or has contrived fraudulently not to have him. 1. When proceedings are taken by way of noxal action in respect of any slaves, it is received law that their case can be defended even without their being present; but this is only where they are the defendant's own property; should they belong to anyone else, they must be present, and the same is the case if there is any doubt whether they belong to the defendant or to another. We must, I think, take this rule subject to the proviso that even if it is ascertained that they are serving the defendant only as *bona fide* slaves, their case can still be defended without their presence. 2. The Prætor's words are:—"If the party in

whose power the slave is said to be denies that he has him in his power, I shall either order him to swear that the man is not in his power and that he did not contrive fraudulently that he should not be, or else I will grant an action without the alternative of surrender for *noxa*: whichever of these two things the plaintiff prefers." 3. By the words "in his power" we must understand to be meant the case of the defendant having the means and power of producing the slave; of course, if the slave should be on his flight or abroad, he cannot be held to be in the defendant's power. 4. If the defendant refuses to swear, he is in the same position as one who will neither defend the case of an absent slave nor yet produce him; and such persons suffer adverse judgment as contumacious. 5. If there is a guardian or *curator*, he is bound to swear that the slave is not in the power of his owner; in the case of [the defendant being] a *procurator*, the owner himself must swear. 6. If the plaintiff has required the defendant to swear and the latter has sworn, and after that the plaintiff chooses to proceed by a noxal action, we may consider whether there ought not to be an *exceptio* of "oath sworn" allowed in bar of the action. Sabinus holds that no such *exceptio* will be allowed, on the ground that the oath was on a different question, in other words, the defendant swore that the slave was not in his power at that time; now however, the slave being discovered to be in his power, an action can be brought for what he did. Neratius himself laid down that, after the oath has been required, the plaintiff can sue without giving the option of surrender for *noxa*, provided, that is, his contention is that it was only after taking the oath that the defendant came to have the slave in his power.

22 PAULUS (*on the Edict* 18) If the slave is in someone's hands on the footing of deposit or loan, a noxal action can be brought against the owner, as the slave is regarded as being in his service, and, as far as this Edict is concerned, he is in his power, especially if the owner can easily get him back. 1. A person who has taken a slave in pledge or who has leave to hold him at the will of the owner (*precario*) is not liable on a noxal action; persons in either situation, however true it may be that they are in lawful possession, still are not in possession in the belief that they are owners; accordingly, even then the slaves are regarded as in the power of their owners, if the owners have the means of recovering them. 2. What is meant by having the means of recovering them? It means that they have the amount of ready money required to enable them

to extricate themselves from their position; of course the owner cannot be compelled to sell his effects so as to pay the money and ask for the return of the slave. 3. An owner who confesses that he has a slave in his power is bound either to produce him or to defend the case in respect of him, though the slave is absent; and, if he will not do either, he is punished in the same way as if the slave were present, but he declined to surrender him. 4. If the owner declares that the slave is not in his power, the Prætor allows the plaintiff to choose whether he would prefer to settle the matter by tendering an oath or to proceed by action without offering the alternative of surrender for *noxa,* and, if he does the latter, he will win his case, if he proves that the slave is in the defendant's power, or that the defendant has fraudulently contrived that he should not be; but a plaintiff who cannot prove that the slave is in his opponent's power loses his case;

23 GAIUS (*on the provincial Edict* 6) at the same time, if his opponent should come to acquire possession of the slave at some subsequent time, he is liable on the ground of fresh possession and the *exceptio* is refused him.

24 PAULUS (*on the Edict* 18) A point to be considered is whether the action[1] is admissible only against one who fraudulently contrives not to have the slave in his power,—supposing that it happens through his fraud that a noxal action cannot be brought, for example, where he orders the slave to take to flight,—or whether proceedings can still be taken against some other party just as well, as in fact they might be if the slave were manumitted or disposed of. This latter is the sounder view; and, that being the case, the plaintiff has the choice which party he will sue. Julianus, we know, says that if the manumitted man is prepared to defend his own case, the party who manumitted ought to be allowed an *exceptio*; and Labeo says the same thing.

25 GAIUS (*on the provincial Edict* 6) The same rule holds if the new owner of the slave is made defendant in the action.

26 PAULUS (*on the Edict* 18) The election of one as defendant is a release to the other; as the Prætor introduced the right of election in order to prevent the plaintiff being baulked, but not in order to enable him to make a positive profit; consequently, if he

[1] The text has *actio noxalis*: I have followed Cujas in omitting this last word. Cf. M.

brings the other action, he will be barred. 1. It is a further application of the same principle that if a number of persons fraudulently contrive to avoid having the slave in their power, the plaintiff is bound to choose which of them he prefers to sue. 2. Moreover, if, among several co-owners, some fraudulently contrive to cease to be in possession of their respective shares, the plaintiff will have a right to elect whether he will bring a direct action against the party who is in possession or a prætorian action against the one who has ceased to be in possession. 3. If a man confesses before the Prætor (*in jure*) that some slave is his who in fact belongs to another, then, if either of the two pays, the other is discharged. 4. If a slave whom you have put out of your possession with a fraudulent intent should die before you are sued in this action[1], you will be thereupon discharged, because this action takes the place of the direct action; the rule would be different if it were through your default that issue was not joined sooner. 5. No action will be allowed *to an heir*[2], *nor* against an heir, on the ground that the deceased said what was not true, nor yet against the person originally liable himself, simply at any distance of time; as it ought to be open to a party who takes up the defence of an absent slave to avoid the penalty imposed by this Edict, that is to say, the liability to be sued without the alternative of surrender for *noxa*. Accordingly, if you should declare that the slave is not in your power, you may afterwards declare that he is, unless the case against you has already got so far as joinder of issue; after that your confession will not be heard, so Labeo says; Octavenus, however, holds that you will get relief even after issue has been joined, on cause shown, at any rate if your years are such that you have a claim to indulgence. 6. If the slave is carried off in the absence of his owner, or even in his presence, and the circumstances of his case are not changed, so that a *restitutio in integrum* is admissible, leave is given to defend the case in respect of the slave so taken; as, if an application is made for his production for the purposes of the defence, the Prætor ought to accede to it. The same relief ought to be given to a usufructuary or to one to whom the slave was pledged for debt, in cases where the owner is present and declines to take up the defence, so as to avoid one man's malice or indifference injuring another. The same must be allowed in the case of a slave belonging to two co-owners, if one of them is present and declines to defend. It should be added that

[1] Meaning apparently before joinder of issue.

[2] The words *neque heredi* can hardly be Paulus's. M.

relief ought in these cases to be given to the plaintiff too, because the law is that the acquisition of ownership in the slave puts an end to the right of action, the fact being that when he is once taken off by the order of the Prætor, the property in him passes to the party who took him.

27 GAIUS (*on the provincial Edict* 6) If proceedings are taken by way of noxal action in respect of a slave who is held by someone as security for debt or of a slave in whom some other person has a usufruct, it must be borne in mind that if the creditor or the usufructuary is present and declines to undertake the defence, the proconsul will intervene, and will refuse to allow proceedings to be taken to realise the security or an action on the usufruct to be brought. In which case it may be said that the security is at once released (in fact a security on which no proceedings can be taken is no security at all), but a usufruct continues as a matter of course (*ipso jure*), even if proceedings are not allowed to be taken in pursuance of it, until the regular period has elapsed and it is lost by non-user. 1. From what has just been said as to a slave whom someone holds as a security, or a *statuliber*, or a slave in whom someone has a usufruct, it is clear that when a defendant declares before the Prætor that a slave is his who really belongs to someone else, then, although he is[1] liable to a noxal action, still he cannot as a matter of course be discharged of liability by surrender for *noxa*, because, not being owner himself, he cannot transfer any ownership to the plaintiff. It is true, however, that, when a slave has been handed over under these circumstances, if the owner afterwards brings an action to recover him, but does not offer the damages assessed in the action, he can be met by an *exceptio* of *dolus malus*.

28 AFRICANUS (*Questions* 6) And, to give a general rule, if I sue you in a noxal action, in respect of a slave who belongs to a third person, but is serving you as a *bonâ fide* slave (*justam servitutem*), and you surrender him to me for *noxa*, then, if I am in possession and the true owner brings an action to recover him from me, I can bar him by an *exceptio* of *dolus malus* unless he offers the damages assessed; but should the owner be in possession himself, I am allowed the Publician action, and if the defendant raises the *exceptio* expressed in the words "unless the defendant is owner," there will be a good *replicatio* of *dolus malus* in my favour. From this it follows that I can acquire the ownership by

[1] The text has *they are*, etc.

usus, although I am in possession of another man's property with knowledge of the fact; indeed, if the law were laid down otherwise, the result would be that a *bonâ fide* possessor would suffer extreme injustice, because, whereas in plain law the only right of action against him was noxal, he nevertheless would be put under the necessity of submitting to payment of the value assessed. The rule is the same where the same person (*i.e.* the owner) declines to defend the case in respect of the slave and I carry him off in pursuance of the Prætor's order, as, in that case too, I have a lawful ground of possession.

29 GAIUS (*on the provincial Edict* 6) Not only is a person free to decline the noxal action when he has not got the man in his power, but, even where he has him in his power, it is open to him to avoid the action, if he chooses to leave the case of that particular person undefended; but in that case he is bound to transfer his own rights to the plaintiff, just as if the case had been decided against him.

30 THE SAME (*on the Edict of the Prætor, tit. de damno infecto*) In the case of noxal actions the rights of persons who are absent *bonâ fide* are not interfered with, as when they return they are allowed full liberty of defending the case on principles of justice and fairness, whether they are owners or persons who have some partial rights over the property in question, such as creditors and usufructuaries.

31 PAULUS (*on Plautius* 7) With reference to the pronouncement of the Prætor, to the effect that, when a gang of slaves commits a theft, he will allow an action of such scope only that the plaintiff will get the same relief as he would have got if the offence had been committed by a free man, the question has been asked whether this refers to the payment of pecuniary damages or includes surrender for *noxa*; so that, for example, if double damages are made up out of the sum of the values of the slaves who are surrendered, no further action is allowed. Sabinus and Cassius hold that the defendant ought to be credited with the values of the slaves surrendered for *noxa* as well [as with money paid], which is approved of by Pomponius, and this is in fact true; indeed, even where a slave is taken off [by the plaintiff] because he is undefended, the owner must be credited with the value. No doubt Julianus holds that we must take into account not only the double damages but the value recoverable on a *condictio*. *With*

regard to the case in which a gang of slaves commits theft, we must, *he holds*[1], look at the time when the theft was committed in order to answer the question whether they were of the same gang, as the Edict does not apply in a case where slaves who belong to different owners come afterwards to be the property of one only.

32 CALLISTRATUS (*Monitorian Edict* 2) If a slave who is in the power of someone who is not his owner is alleged to have committed an offence, then, if he is undefended, he is taken off, and, if the owner is present, he ought to deliver him over and give an undertaking against *dolus malus.*

33 POMPONIUS (*on Sabinus* 14) Nobody can be compelled against his will to defend anyone else in a noxal action; a man must, however, go without anyone whom he declines to defend, if such person is his slave; but if the person subject to *potestas* is a free man, he ought to be allowed to make his own defence without further question;

34 JULIANUS (*on Urseius Ferox* 4) as wherever no one is found to take up the defence of a *filius familias* in the matter of a delict, an action is allowed against the *filius familias* himself,

35 ULPIANUS (*on Sabinus* 41) and, if judgment is given against him, the *filius familias* ought to obey the order, as he is bound by the decision. Moreover this must be remembered, that the father himself can be sued in an action *de peculio,* but only after judgment has been given against the son.

36 THE SAME (*on the Edict* 37) Where a slave is pledged for debt and then stolen by the debtor and someone purchases him from the debtor, the purchaser will be liable in respect of the theft after he has acquired the property in the slave, and this in spite of the fact that the slave can be recovered from him by the Servian action. The rule is similar in the case of such as purchase from one who is under twenty-five years of age, or in fraud of the vendor's creditors; as, although such persons may be deprived of the property in what they have purchased, nevertheless in the meantime, they can legally be sued [for damages].

37 TRYPHONINUS (*Disputations* 15) If a slave belonging to another steals my goods and afterwards I acquire the property in him, the right of action for theft which was open to me is at an

[1] Words equivalent to those in italics seem to have been omitted by a slip. Cf. M.

end, if it has not yet been brought to an issue; and if, after that, I should dispose of the slave, having bought him before joinder of issue, the action for theft will not be set up again; but if I only bought the slave after joinder of issue, the vendor is liable to be ordered to pay,

38 ULPIAN (*on the Edict* 37) just as he would be if he had sold him to someone else; in fact, it makes very little difference who it is to whom he sells him, whether it is to the plaintiff in the suit or to some other person, and it will be his own fault that he has to submit to pay the damages assessed, as, by selling him, he put it out of his own power to surrender him for *noxa*. 1. Julianus, however, says (*Dig.* 22) that, if I abandon a slave who stole your goods, I am discharged from responsibility, on the ground that the slave at once ceased to belong to me, so that, were it not for this rule, there would be an action for theft in respect of a slave whom nobody owned. 2. If my slave steals your goods and sells them, and you forcibly take from him money which he has in his hands which was part of the price, there will be ground for an action of theft on both sides; as you can bring a noxal action against me in respect of the slave, and I can bring an action against you in respect of the money. 3. Again, if I pay money to a slave of my creditor, for him to give it to his owner, there will equally be ground for an action of theft if the slave embezzles the money he received.

39 JULIANUS (*Digest* 9) If a slave belonging to several co-owners commits a theft, and all the co-owners contrive fraudulently to avoid having him in their power, the Prætor ought to follow the model of the action which is open in the civil law and allow the honorary action which he offers in such circumstances against whichever owner the plaintiff selects, as he ought not to give the plaintiff any further advantage than this, that he should be able to bring an action, without giving the defendant the option of surrender for *noxa*, against whomsoever he would have been able to sue in a noxal action, if the slave had been produced. 1. Where a man confesses that a slave is his own who in fact belongs to someone else, then, although he is liable to a noxal action, nevertheless, on due cause shown, he is compellable to give security, but a man who is sued on account of a slave of his own ought not to be burdened with security, as he is not offering himself as defendant on behalf of another man's slave. 2. If anyone should allege that the owner of a slave has fraudulently

contrived to avoid having him in his possession [and should sue such owner accordingly], but the owner should contend that the action ought to be defended by someone else, who would give security, this is a case for an *exceptio* of *dolus malus*. 3. Even if issue is joined with the owner and, after that, the slave comes forward, and, not being defended, he is carried off, the owner will be discharged if he raises an *exceptio* of *dolus malus*. 4. We may add that if the slave dies before joinder of issue, the owner will escape all liability on this action.

40 THE SAME (*Digest* 22) If a slave who is left by way of legacy should, before the inheritance is entered upon, steal the goods of the future heir, the latter can bring an action for theft against the legatee, if he accepts the legacy; but, if the same slave misappropriated something which is part of the inheritance, there will be no action for theft, because there can be no theft committed of such things; but there is a good right of action to have the thing produced.

41 THE SAME (*on Urseius Ferox* 2) If a slave who belongs to two co-owners does unlawful damage to one of them, there is no right of action under the *lex Aquilia*; for the reason that, if he had done the damage to a stranger, proceedings could have been taken under the statute for the whole amount claimed against the other co-owner; just as, when a slave owned in common commits theft [against one owner], there cannot be an action for theft brought against the other owner, but there can be an action *communi dividundo*.

42 ULPIANUS (*on the Edict* 37) If a man in respect of whom issue has been joined in a noxal action claims his liberty, the action ought to be stayed until judgment is given on the question of status; accordingly, if he is pronounced a slave, the noxal action will proceed, but if he is pronounced free, it will clearly be to no purpose. 1. If one undertakes to defend a noxal action in respect of a slave who is dead, where he is unaware of the fact, the case ought to be dismissed, as it has ceased to be true that it is his duty to hand over anything on account of the slave. 2. These rights of action are not subject to lapse, and there is good ground for bringing them so long as it is in the power of a proposed defendant to surrender the slave; moreover they are available not only for the party injured, but for his successors too, and also against the

successors of the party originally liable, not however as succeeding to his obligation, but because they are owners. On the same principle, if it is a fact in the case that a slave has come to the hands of someone else, the new owner, as being owner, can be sued in a noxal action.

43 POMPONIUS (*Epistles* 8) Slaves in whose case the *noxa* follows the delinquent subject must be defended in the place in which it is averred that they committed the delict, accordingly the owner is bound to produce such slaves in the same place as that in which they are alleged to have done the act of violence, and he may have to lose his property in all of them, if he declines to defend them.

TENTH BOOK.

I.

1 Paulus (*on the Edict* 23) The action for settling boundaries (*finium regundorum*) is *in personam*, although it is an action for recovering a thing as owner (*pro vindicatione rei*).

2 Ulpianus (*on the Edict* 19) This action deals with "rustic estates" though there should be buildings between them ; in fact, it makes very little difference whether a man plants trees on the boundary or places buildings there. 1. The judge in a case of determining boundaries is at liberty, if he cannot settle[1] the boundary, to settle[1] the dispute by a vesting order, and, if the judge chooses, by way of getting rid of a doubt of long standing, to draw the line of demarcation in a fresh direction, he can do so by means of a vesting order and an order [on the party acquiring thereby] to pay money.

3 Gaius (*on the provincial Edict* 7) In any case in which it is requisite that an order should be made assigning a portion of the land of one party to the other party, the[2] one in whose favour such order is made must be directed to pay a sum of money in consideration of the land assigned to him.

4 Paulus (*on the Edict* 23) We may add that, where the dispute is as to a single plot of ground, the property can still be divided up into distinct portions by vesting orders, corresponding to the proprietorial rights which the judge finds that the respective parties have. 1. In a suit for settling boundaries, the court takes into account any incidental advantage enjoyed (*id quod interest*).

[1] *dirimere—dirimat.* [2] del. *quo nomine.* M.

Suppose, for instance, one of the parties was deriving some benefit from a piece of ground which turns out to belong to another; there would be no injustice in an order for payment which took such benefit into account. Again, suppose a surveyor had been engaged by one of the parties to measure the land, an order for payment of part of the remuneration for the service rendered ought to be made on the party who did not join in the engagement. 2. After joinder of issue, profits will be taken into account in a case of this kind; in fact, from that moment, malice and negligence can be charged; but profits realized before joinder will not as a matter of course be included; either the party took them in good faith, and then he ought to be allowed, if he has consumed them, to make a clear gain by them, or else he took them in bad faith, and then they must be recovered by a *condictio* (express personal action). 3. Moreover where a party refuses to obey the order of the court as to cutting down a tree or pulling down a building which is placed on the boundary or some portion of it, he can be ordered to pay money. 4. Where boundary marks are averred to be removed by throwing anything down or digging it up, the judge who hears the charge can entertain an application for settling the boundary as well. 5. If one estate belongs to two persons and the other to three, the judge can assign by order the particular plot about which the question arises to one of the two sides, though such side comprises several owners, as, in fact, an order settling boundaries is regarded as made in favour of an estate rather than a person; in such a case, however, though the order is in favour of several persons, each person will take the same fractional share which he has in the original estate; (6) and as for the persons who have such undivided shares in the common estate, no order will be made on any one of them in favour of another, as among these persons themselves no judicial contention was raised. 7. If you and I are part-owners in common of an estate, and I am sole owner of an adjoining estate, can there be judicial proceedings between us for settling boundaries? Pomponius says that there cannot; my co-owner and I cannot be opposite parties in such an action, but are counted as one person. Pomponius also says that even an *utilis actio* cannot be allowed, as it is open to the one who has property in severalty to dispose either of his share or of the part which he holds in severalty and then take proceedings. 8. There can be an action brought for settling boundaries not merely between two estates, but even among three or more; suppose, for instance, cases in which one estate abuts on several estates, say on three or four. 9. A right of action for settling boundaries may be good even in respect of lands let on perpetual lease (*agri vectigales*), or between parties who have usufructs in the respective lands, or between a usufructuary and a bare proprietor of adjacent land, or between parties who are in possession in virtue of a pledge made as a security for money. 10. This kind of action is applicable where the boundary runs between "rustic estates," it has not been held admissible between "urban estates"; in the case of the latter the parties are not said to be owners with a common boundary (*confines*), but neighbours (*vicini*), and their properties are, for the most part, separated from one another by common walls. Accordingly, where buildings are contiguous, even in the country, there is no room for this action; and, conversely, in a town there may be an extent of garden ground, so that parties can, in fact, have recourse to an action for settling boundaries. 11. Where a river or a high-road comes in there can be no such thing as a common boundary; consequently no action can be brought to settle boundaries,

5 THE SAME (*on Sabinus* 15) as what adjoins my land is rather the high-road or the river than the land of my neighbour;

6 THE SAME (*on the Edict* 23) but, if it is a private stream that makes the division, there can be an action for settling boundaries.

7 MODESTINUS (*Pandects* 11) Arbiters are appointed to ascertain the dimensions of the land, and whoever is declared to have the larger plot in the whole space is compelled to assign a distinct portion to the others who have smaller plots; there is a rescript to this effect.

8 ULPIANUS (*Opinions* 6) Where a river overflows, and so a flood effaces the boundaries of a field, so as to afford certain persons an opportunity of encroaching on land over which they have no legal right, the governor of the province will order that they should leave other people's property alone, and that the true owner should get back what belongs to him, and the boundary marks should be made clear by the surveyor. 1. It is part of the duty of the judge in a case of boundaries to send surveyors, and through them to settle the actual question of the boundary line in the way required by justice, and with the place before his eyes, if the occasion requires it.

9 JULIANUS (*Digest* 8) The case for settling boundaries can still be tried, though the part-owners should have brought an action for partition, or should have disposed of the land.

10 THE SAME (*Digest* 51) The action for partition among co-owners, or division among heirs, or settlement of boundaries is such that in it each party stands in the twofold legal position of plaintiff and defendant to the action.

11 PAPINIANUS (*Responsa* 2) In inquiries into boundaries, in default of[1] old memorials, the parties must be guided by the authority of the census last made before the proceedings were begun, provided that there is nothing to show that since that time, owing to frequent changes of ownership on death and the deliberate acts of persons in possession, portions of land have been added or taken away and the boundaries have consequently been disturbed.

12 PAULUS (*Responsa* 3) In connexion with an inquiry into ownership, those boundary lines ought to be maintained which were pointed out by someone who owned both estates on the occasion of his selling one of the two; as it is not required that those boundaries should be observed which used to divide the different plots, but the indications given as to who are adjoining owners must be held to lay down a fresh boundary between the estates.

13 GAIUS (*Law of the Twelve Tables* 4) We must bear in mind that in the action for settling boundaries we ought to follow the rule which was set down, so to speak, after the model of that law which Solon is said to have passed at Athens. The words of it are as follows:—If a man makes[2] a rough wall[3] close to another person's land, he must not go beyond the boundary; if it is a mortared wall[4], he must leave a foot clear; and if it is a house, two feet. If he digs a grave or a trench, he must leave a clear space as broad as the depth; if it is a well, space to the extent of a fathom. Olives and fig-trees he must plant nine feet from the adjoining property, all other trees five feet.

[1] After *monumenta* read *ubi deficiunt, proximi*. M.

[2] Gr. ὀρύγῃ. [3] αἱμασία. Cf. Roby, *R.P.L.* I. 451. [4] Cf. Roby.

II.

On Dividing an Inheritance (*familiæ erciscundæ*).

1 Gaius (*on the provincial Edict* 7) This action is derived from the Law of the Twelve Tables, the fact being that it was deemed necessary that, where co-heirs were desirous of giving up ownership in common, some form of action should be provided by means of which the assets might be divided among them. 1. At the same time the action is open, in direct law, even to a man who is not in possession of his share; but if the heir who is in possession avers that the plaintiff is not a co-heir with him, he can bar the action by an *exceptio* worded thus:—"provided that the question of heirship is not prejudged in connexion with the matter which the action is about." If the applicant is in possession of his share, then, even though it should be averred that he is not a co-heir, the above *exceptio* will be no bar; the consequence of which is that, in that case, the judge himself who tries the action entertains the question whether the applicant is a co-heir or not; in fact, if he is not a co-heir, no vesting order will be made in his favour, nor will his opponent be ordered to pay him anything.

2 Ulpianus (*on the Edict* 19) By the action *familiæ erciscundæ* an inheritance can be divided, whether it is testamentary or on intestacy, and whether it is given by the Twelve Tables, or by some other[1] statute, or by a decree of the Senate, or even by an Imperial enactment; and, as a rule, the only persons whose inheritance can be divided are those on whose decease there can be a *petitio hereditatis* (action to recover the inheritance). 1. If there is a quarter share coming by law to someone who was arrogated in pursuance of the enactment of the Divine Pius, then, as such a person does not become either heir or *bonorum possessor*, an *utilis actio familiæ erciscundæ* will be required. 2. Again, if the estate is the [*castrense*] *peculium* of a son under *potestas* who was a soldier, there is good ground for maintaining that there is an inheritance created by Imperial enactments, consequently this[2] action will be applicable. 3. In an action *familiæ erciscundæ*, each of the heirs acts the part of both defendant and plaintiff. 4. It is also beyond question that the action is admissible even where the parties are a few heirs out of a larger number. 5. True

[1] For *aliqua* read *alia*. Cf. M. [2] Read *huic* for *hoc*. Cf. M.

as it is that claims against debtors are not taken into account in this action, still, if stipulations have been made as to the division of any such, it being understood that such division is to be adhered to and each party has to assign rights of action to the other and make him procurator on his own behalf, the parties must abide by the division.

3 GAIUS (*on the provincial Edict* 7) No doubt it is often a matter within the competence of the judge to assign different debts and demands in their entirety to different heirs respectively, as it often happens that the business both of discharging and getting in shares is attended with no small inconvenience. But it must always be understood that the result of an assignment of this kind is not that any single heir owes the whole debt or has a right to realize the whole demand, but only this, that, if an action is to be brought, the heir brings it partly in his own name and partly as *procurator* [for his co-heirs]; and, again, if an action has to be defended, he is sued partly in his own name and partly as *procurator*. The creditors, no doubt, are still fully entitled[1] to take proceedings against any heir separately; at the same time the heirs themselves are equally empowered to put in their own places those persons to whom the brunt of the action has been assigned by the judge's discretion.

4 ULPIANUS (*on the Edict* 19) Accordingly, everything, setting aside pecuniary demands, is taken into account in this action. But if a pecuniary demand is bequeathed to some one of the heirs in particular, such heir will get it by the action *familiæ erciscundæ*. 1. Noxious drugs and poisons are included in the action; but the judge ought not to offer to have anything to do with things of that kind, as his duty is to discharge the office of a good and inoffensive person. He ought to act in the same way in respect of books which it is objectionable to read, for example, such as deal with magic arts or any similar books; everything of that kind ought to be at once destroyed. 2. Again, where anything turns out to have been acquired by embezzling public money (*peculatus*) or sacrilege, or violence or robbery or acts of brigandage, it will not be divided. 3. It may be added that the judge ought to order that the testament itself either should be left in the hands of whoever is heir for the largest share or should be deposited in a temple. Labeo himself says that on a sale of the inheritance a copy of the

[1] del. *esse* after *potestas*. M.

testament ought to be deposited; the heir, he says, ought to hand over a copy, but the original testament he should keep in his own custody, or else deposit in a temple.

5 GAIUS (*on the provincial Edict* 5) If there are among the assets any heritable bonds (*cautiones hereditariæ*), the judge should take means to make sure that they shall remain in the hands of the person who is heir for the largest share,—*the others are to have a copy made and verified*[1],—an undertaking being given by such heir that, when the occasion arises, the originals will be produced. If all the heirs take equal shares, and they do not come to any agreement on the question with whom the documents are to be left, they ought to draw lots, or some friend must be chosen by agreement or vote with whom they can be placed, or else they should be deposited in a consecrated temple;

6 ULPIANUS (*on the Edict* 19) the plan of settling the question by competitive offers, so that the highest bidder shall have the custody of the heritable papers, does not commend itself either to me or to Pomponius.

7 VENULEIUS (*Stipulations* 7) If one particular heir, in a case where another heir either was added on some condition, or is in the hands of the enemy, should declare that he is himself the heir and should succeed in proceedings taken thereupon, and, after that, the conditional event should take place on which the other becomes entitled, or the other should return by *postliminium*, will the former be bound to let the latter share the fruits of his successful application? There is, of course, no doubt at all that he has an undivided right to an action on the judgment. Here the co-heir [who was added] ought to be allowed to elect, that is to say, either he must have a share given him in the inheritance or he must be enabled to take proceedings, the fact being that he is a man who became heir himself—or returned to the city—subsequently to the judgment given in favour of his present co-heir. The same rule will hold where a posthumous child is born after the death of the testator. That these persons failed to apply before is no ground of objection, considering that they only acquired the inheritance after the other heir had been successful.

8 ULPIANUS (*on the Edict* 19) Pomponius tells us that, if the account books are bequeathed (*prælegatæ*) to some one of the heirs in particular, they ought not to be handed over to him until his

[1] Text in bad Latin, probably interpolated.

co-heirs have copied them. Suppose, he says, the bequest is of some slave who was a bailiff, the man need not be handed over until he has brought in his accounts. It may fairly be asked whether there ought not in fact to be an undertaking given that whenever the accounts, or the bailiff bequeathed as above, should be required, they should respectively be forthcoming; as very often it is necessary to have the original accounts—or the actual bailiff[1]—before you, in order to elucidate points which subsequently crop up and which bear on the question of the man's knowledge; and it is in fact necessary that the co-heirs should have an undertaking given them on the subject by the heir first mentioned. 1. Pomponius says further that pigeons which are habitually allowed to leave the pigeon-house come within the scope of the action *familiæ erciscundæ*, because they belong to their original owner so long as they keep up the habit of returning to his premises; accordingly, if anyone should take them, the owner has an action for theft. The same rule applies to bees, as they are reckoned a subject of property. 2. Again, if one out of a man's cattle should be carried off by a wild beast, the same writer holds that if it escapes from the beast it is included in the action *familiæ erciscundæ*; the better opinion, he says, is that a creature which is carried off by a wolf or some other wild animal does not cease to be a piece of property so long as it is not devoured.

9 PAULUS (*on the Edict* 23) The action includes things which the heirs have acquired by user, in cases where they were delivered to the deceased, also things which were delivered to the heirs, but which had been purchased by the deceased,

10 ULPIANUS (*on the Edict* 19) also lands which are held in ownership and, besides these, land let on perpetual lease, and rights to surfaces (*prædia vectigalia* and *superficiaria*); the rule applies equally to things of which the deceased had possession in good faith, though they were the property of another.

11 PAULUS (*on the Edict* 23) The child of a female slave, if born after entry on the inheritance,

12 ULPIANUS (*on the Edict* 19) or even after joinder of issue, can, so Sabinus tells us, be reached by the action *familiæ erciscundæ* and be assigned by the order. 1. The same is the case as to anything given by a stranger to slaves which are part of the estate.

[1] For *actori* read *actorve*. Cf. M.

2. Anything bequeathed subject to a condition is the property of the heirs in the meantime, consequently it is included in the action, and it can be assigned by the order, subject, that is, to the liabilities attaching to it (*cum sua causa*), so that, if the condition comes to pass, it will be taken away from the heir to whom it was assigned, and, if the condition fails, it will revert to the heirs at whose charge it was left. The same principle applies in the case of a *statuliber*; he is for the time the property of the heirs, but, if the condition comes to pass, he acquires his liberty:

13 PAPINIANUS (*Questions* 7) as the transfers of property which are forbidden to be made after issue is joined are only such as are voluntary, and not those which were required in virtue of some antecedent ground and have a legal origin which acts with compulsory force.

14 ULPIANUS (*on the Edict* 19) But if, on the other hand, the period for acquiring a thing by user should have begun to run before joinder of issue in favour of someone who was not heir, and should be completed afterwards, this takes the thing out of the scope of the action. 1. It has been a matter of question whether a usufruct comes within the scope of the action; suppose, for instance, land was bequeathed away from the heirs, the usufruct being reserved:

15 PAULUS (*on the Edict* 23) or a usufruct was bequeathed to a slave who is part of the assets: it should be remembered that a usufruct cannot shift from the holder without terminating altogether.

16 ULPIANUS (*on the Edict* 19) My own view is that it is part of the duty of the judge that, if the heirs wish to break up their part-ownership of the usufruct, he should comply with their wish, making them give mutual undertakings. 1. Julianus says that, if the judge vests the land in one heir and the usufruct therein in another, this does not make the usufruct common property. 2. A usufruct can be assigned by the order from and after a given time, or until a given time, or for alternate years. 3. Land which a river adds to some estate by alluvion after joinder of issue is fully included in the action. 4. If, moreover, anything should be done by one of the heirs by malice or negligence so as to impair the [value of the] usufruct, this too Pomponius says is included in the action; as, in fact, anything whatever that the heir does to the injury of the inheritance by malice or negligence

will be taken into account in the action *familiæ erciscundæ*, provided always that he does it as heir. Accordingly, if one of the heirs took away money in the lifetime of the testator, this money does not come within the scope of the action, because at that time the party was not yet heir; but where he did it as heir (*quasi heres*) then, although the party complaining should have some other right of action as well, still, as Julianus tells us, he is liable to the action *familiæ erciscundæ*. 5. Lastly, he says that if one of the heirs should obliterate or falsify the amounts of the testator's estate, he is liable under the *lex Aquilia* on the ground of destruction; but nevertheless he is liable to the action *familiæ erciscundæ* too. 6. Again, if a slave who is part of the estate steals something belonging to one of the heirs, Ofilius says that there are the actions *familiæ erciscundæ* and *communi dividundo*, and there is no action for theft; and, accordingly, if the heir brings the *familiæ erciscundæ*, he will either get an order vesting the slave in him or else one to the effect that the damages assessed in the case shall be given him, that is, simple damages.

17 GAIUS (*on the provincial Edict* 7) Where damage is committed by a single heir, the rule which meets the case is that the simple amount should be taken into account in the action *familiæ erciscundæ*.

18 ULPIANUS (*on the Edict* 19) In keeping with this is what is said by Julianus:—If there are several heirs, and a legacy is made to one of them simply of a slave, in general terms, with liberty of option, whereupon the [other] heirs declare that Stichus has falsified the testament or badly damaged it, their object in giving this information being to prevent that slave being chosen, but, after that, he is chosen, and then an action is brought to recover him, they can, if they are defendants in the action, have recourse to an *exceptio* of *dolus malus* and examine the slave by torture. 1. The question has been asked whether in an action[1] *familiæ erciscundæ* the heirs have a right to examine by torture with reference to the death of the testator or his wife or his children; as to which Pomponius says very properly that these matters have nothing to do with the division of the testator's assets. 2. The same writer holds[2] that where a person directs by testament that a slave shall be sold in order that he may be taken away, it is within the duty of the judge to see that the will of the deceased shall

[1] For *judicium* read *judicio*. Cf. M.

[2] In the text, "asks."

not fall through. Again, in a case where the testator directs that a monument should be set up, there can be an action *familiæ erciscundæ* to have it done. He suggests, however, besides this, that, inasmuch as the heirs have an interest in the matter, seeing that they acquire a right over the monument, any one of them can have an action in special terms (*præscriptis verbis*) to have the monument erected. 3. Where one of the heirs goes to expense in good faith, he can get interest from a co-heir from the date of default [on the part of the latter], according to a rescript of the Emperors Severus and Antoninus. 4. Celsus goes so far as to add the following discriminating remark, viz. that a co-heir, even where he does not pay a debt himself, still has a right to an action *familiæ erciscundæ* to compel his co-heir to pay, on the ground that the creditor will not relinquish some piece of property until he is paid in full. 5. Where a *filius familias* was heir to his father to the extent of a share and is sued by creditors who have a claim on his *peculium*, he being ready to pay the whole debt, he can, by means of an *exceptio doli,* make the creditors assign to him their rights of action; but, besides this, he has a good action *familiæ erciscundæ* against his co-heirs. 6. Where one of the heirs has paid a legacy to a legatee who had got an order putting him in possession in order to preserve legacies, Papinianus holds, and so the law is, that he has a good action *familiæ erciscundæ* against his co-heirs, because the legatee would never relinquish possession which he had once taken as being equivalent to security for his debt, until the whole of his legacy was paid him. 7. Again, if an heir should pay Titius a debt to prevent a pledge being sold, Neratius says that he can proceed by an action *familiæ erciscundæ.*

19 (GAIUS *on the provincial Edict* 7) Conversely also, the judge ought to take care in the same way that where one of the heirs has made some gain out of part of the assets or acquired a claim by stipulation at the expense of the estate, this shall not be for his exclusive benefit. The judge will secure these objects by either taking debtor and creditor accounts among the different heirs, or compelling them to give undertakings to one another by means of which both profits and liabilities may be shared equally among them.

20 ULPIANUS (*on the Edict* 19) Where a married daughter [being one of the heirs of her father,] was bound to bring her *dos*

into hotchpot (*dotem conferre*), and, through a mistake on the part of her co-heirs, she gave an undertaking to the effect that she would pay them in proportion to their respective shares in the inheritance whatever she recovered from her husband, Papinianus has it that, in spite of this, the *arbiter* in the action *familiæ erciscundæ* must rule that, even if the wife herself should depart this life without the married state having ended, the *dos* must still be brought in; no inadvertency, he says, on the part of the co-heirs can make any difference as to the course which the legal proceedings will have to take. 1. If a son under *potestas* has incurred an obligation at his father's request, he must retain the amount out of the assets; indeed, if he spent money in his father's interest, the same rule applies; and, if [the right of action was[1]] *de peculio*, the son will retain his *peculium* [to the extent of the amount of the debt[2]]. All this was laid down by rescript by the present Emperor. 2. Besides this, where a son under *potestas* is appointed heir, he can retain his wife's *dos*; and this is reasonable, as it is he who has to bear the expense entailed by the married state. Accordingly, he can retain the whole *dos*, and he must give an undertaking to his co-heirs, who are liable to an action on stipulation, that the action shall be defended on their behalf. A similar rule holds where a stranger gave the *dos* and made a stipulation. [The rule applies to] not only the *dos* of the son's own wife, but to that of his son's wife, on the ground that this too is an expense entailed by the married state which falls on him, as he is obliged to answer for the expense which will be incurred by his son and his daughter-in-law. According to Marcellus, the son will retain the *dos* not only where it was given to his father, but where it was given to himself, such son; so far, that is, where it was given to himself, as his *peculium* covers it, or as it was spent in his father's interest. 3. Where a father divides his property among his sons without any writing and apportions the burden of his debts among them according to what they respectively get, this, Papinianus says, is not to be treated as a mere gift, but rather as a distribution in virtue of a man's last will. Of course, he says, if the creditors bring actions against them for amounts corresponding to their respective shares in the inheritance, and one of them declines to be bound by the terms of the arrangement, an action can be brought against him *præscriptis verbis*, on the ground that they made an exchange

[1] After *peculio* ins. *sit actio*. M.
[2] Before *peculium* ins. *eatenus*. M.

on definite terms, provided, that is, all the property was included in the division. 4. The action *familiæ erciscundæ* cannot be brought more than once, save on special cause shown; and, if there are some things left undistributed, in respect of these there can be an action *communi dividundo.* 5. Papinianus says that if the duty of paying a debt is laid on one of the heirs without its being done by way of a legacy [to the creditor], then, in virtue of the office of the judge who hears the case on *familiæ erciscundæ*, the heir is compelled to undertake the payment—though not to the extent of more than three-quarters of his share, in order that he may have one clear quarter; accordingly, he will have to undertake to save his co-heirs harmless. 6. The same writer says further that where a son is liable on a balance of accounts in respect of public offices which his father consented to his exercising, and is then appointed heir to the extent of a share, he will have a right to retain the amount of his liability, because this was one of the debts owed by his father; but, as for any offices which he undertook after his father's death, the father's heirs are not liable in respect of them. 7. There is, however, an opinion given by Neratius to this effect. A man, he says, who had several sons offered that one of them should undertake an *agonothesia* (superintendence of public games), and, before the son had discharged the office, the father died, having appointed heirs all his sons; whereupon the question was asked whether the son first mentioned could, by an action *familiæ erciscundæ*, recover the amount he had expended in the matter; to which, he said, his reply was that there was no action by which he[1] could recover it. This is, very properly, not admitted; so that the expense in question must be held to be within the scope of the action *familiæ erciscundæ.* 8. Again, Papinianus says that, if a husband directs one of his two heirs to bear the burden of paying the *dos*, where the same is due in pursuance of a stipulation, but the widow brings her action for *dos* against both, the heir who was directed to undertake the burden must defend his co-heir in an action so brought. But, if legacies are left at the charge of both heirs to take the place of the *dos* and, in consequence of the widow electing to be paid the *dos* as such, they are retained by the heirs, such retention ought not to profit the co-heir who is relieved of the payment of the debt; [that is, the *dos*;] the intention being that the co-heir who undertook the burden of the debt, should, by the exercise of the judge's office,

[1] For *idem* read *id eum.* Cuj.

get the legacy [charged on the other]. All this is perfectly correct, unless the testator directed otherwise. 9. The same writer says that where a *statuliber* pays money to one of several co-heirs out of his *peculium*, by way of fulfilling the condition on which he is to become free, the money is not included in this action, and it need not be shared.

21 PAULUS (*on the Edict* 23) The same rule holds in the action *communi dividundo*.

22 ULPIANUS (*on the Edict* 19) Again, Labeo tells us that, if one of the heirs digs up a concealed hoard which the testator left as it was, he is liable in an action *familiæ erciscundæ*, even though he should have divided the hoard with a stranger who was aware of the facts. 1. The judge in the action *familiæ erciscundæ* can assign property in the same thing to several persons in those cases only in which either the right of retainer was left [by the deceased] to several persons in respect of the same thing—where, indeed, as Pomponius says, the necessity of the case requires that the assignment should be to a number of persons—or else he [the judge] apportions definite shares in the thing to the different respective co-heirs. He can however, if he chooses, let the thing be bid for and vest it by an order in one single heir; 2. again, it will not be disputed that he can divide the land into so many distinct portions and assign these by order to the various persons respectively according to the division so made. 3. Moreover, when he makes such assignments he can impose a servitude, so as to make one plot among those which he assigns serve another plot; still, if he once gives a plot to any heir in absolute terms, he cannot, after that, in giving another, proceed to make the former subject to a servitude attaching to the latter. 4. Proceedings in the action *familiæ erciscundæ* deal with two kinds of subject-matter, questions of property and questions of transfer, the latter being matters *in personam*[1]. 5. Papinianus finds fault with Marcellus with reference to property in the hands of an enemy, in regard that the latter does not hold that[2] transfers of such property as is in the hands of an enemy are embraced by the action *familiæ erciscundæ*. How, indeed, can there be any objection to the action embracing acts which may be required with reference to any kind of property where it embraces that very property itself,

[1] del. *actiones*. M. [2] del. *in*. M.

23 PAULUS (*on the Edict* 19) in virtue of the possibility of *postliminium*? Of course an undertaking would have to be given, as it is possible that the party should not return; unless, indeed, there was simply a valuation put on the chance itself as an expectancy.

24 ULPIANUS (*on the Edict* 19) Indeed, even where a thing has ceased to exist at all, the question of transfer may still come within the scope of the action; I agree with Papinianus as to this. 1. The action *familiæ erciscundæ* applies among *bonorum possessores,* also as between a person to whom the inheritance was handed over in pursuance of the Trebellian decree of the Senate, and all other Prætorian successors.

25 PAULUS (*on the Edict* 23) The heirs of one who died in the enemy's hands can proceed by way of this action. 1. If a soldier makes one person heir to his castrensian property and another to everything else, there is no occasion herein for an action *familiæ erciscundæ,* because, in such a case, the property is divided between the two successors in virtue of imperial enactments; just as the action is not available where there is no corporeal property at all, but the inheritance consists entirely of debts owing to the estate. 2. In connexion with the question whether a man is qualified to undertake to defend the action *familiæ erciscundæ,* it makes no difference whether he is in possession of his inheritance or not. 3. Where a number of different inheritances are held by several persons in common by different titles, they can have one action *familiæ erciscundæ* in respect of them all. 4. If you and I have Titius's inheritance in common and you and I and Titius (*sic*) have that of Seius, Pomponius tells us that a single action may be had to which three persons are parties [embracing both cases]. 5. Again, if several inheritances belong to you and me in common, we can take proceedings by way of an action *familiæ erciscundæ* as to one of them by itself. 6. If a testator had property in common with a stranger, or bequeathed to anyone a share in property of his own, or his heir, before meeting an action *familiæ erciscundæ,* disposed of his own share, it falls within the duty of the judge to order that the share which was the property of the testator should be made over to some one person. 7. Where a co-heir is in possession of anything as purchaser or, say, as donee, according to Pomponius, it is not embraced by the action *familiæ erciscundæ.* 8. The same writer has the following:—You and I having become heirs to Titius, if you sue Sempronius to recover

part of an estate the whole of which you declare is included in the inheritance, and you are defeated, and I thereupon purchase the part in question from Sempronius and take delivery of it, then, if you bring the action *familiæ erciscundæ*, this will not only fail to embrace what I possess as heir, but will not reach even what I have as purchaser[1]; in fact, as it was made clear by the previous judgment that the whole estate lay outside the inheritance, how can it come within the scope of the action *familiæ erciscundæ*? 9. It is a matter of doubt whether the action will include a stipulation such as gives each separate heir a right of action for the whole; for example, where a man dies after stipulating for a roadway, pathway or drive[2], the fact being that such a stipulation is by the Twelve Tables not allowed to be divided, as indeed it cannot be. However, the better opinion is that the action does not embrace this stipulation, but every heir has a right of action for the whole, and if the roadway is not furnished, the order made on the defendant should be for damages proportional to the plaintiff's share in the inheritance. 10. Conversely, where the man who promised a roadway dies, having appointed several heirs, the obligation is not divided, and there is no doubt that it continues to hold good, seeing that a roadway can be promised even by a man who has no land. Since therefore each separate heir is liable for the whole, undertakings should be called for, in exercise of the judge's office, in order that if any one of the heirs should be sued and should thereupon pay the damages assessed, he may recover part of the amount from the others. 11. The rule is the same where the testator bequeaths a roadway. 12. In the case of another stipulation also, viz. where the testator's promise was that nothing should be done by him or by his heir to prevent the promisee from being able to walk or drive—seeing that, if a single co-heir impedes access, the stipulation can be sued upon for the whole sum—provision has to be made on behalf of the co-heirs, to prevent the act of one of them being injurious to the others. 13. A similar rule holds in the case of a sum of money promised by the testator, if it was promised under a penalty; it is true that, in that case, the obligation is divided by the Statute of the Twelve Tables, still, inasmuch as the fact of one co-heir paying his share will be of no avail to prevent the penalty being incurred, [it follows that,] if, on the one hand, the debt has not yet been paid nor become demandable, the case must be met by an undertaking [to which all

[1] The Basilica transpose "purchaser" and "heir."

[2] Read *actum* for *actus*.

are parties[1]], so that [either] the one by whose fault it eventually happens that the money is not all paid engages to keep the rest harmless, or else [each[2]] engages that he will make good a portion to whoever pays the whole; while, if, on the other hand, the whole sum which was promised by the testator has been paid by one of the co-heirs, in order to prevent the penalty being demandable, he will be able to recover from his co-heirs their respective shares by the action *familiæ erciscundæ*. 14. A similar rule is observed with reference to the redemption of pledges; unless there is a tender of the whole sum due, the pledgee can lawfully sell the thing pledged. 15. If one of several co-heirs defends a noxal action in respect of a slave who is part of the estate and tenders the damages assessed, where that is the best course to take, he can by means of this action recover a portion of the money. The rule is the same where one co-heir gives an undertaking in respect of legacies to prevent the legatees getting an order to be put in possession. And, to give a general rule, wherever a matter cannot be disposed of by partial performance, if one party should, under pressure of necessity, discharge the whole, there is room for an action *familiæ erciscundæ*. 16. A co-heir is bound to answer not only for malice but for negligence too in respect of property which is part of the estate, *seeing that a person has not contracted with a co-heir but has simply chanced upon him; but the co-heir is not bound to answer for as much diligence as is a diligent paterfamilias, since, in this case, the co-heir had good reason for acting in the matter on account of his own share, and he consequently has no right of action on* negotia gesta (voluntary agency); accordingly he is bound to use the same amount of diligence that he does in his own affairs[3]. The same may be said where a thing is bequeathed to two legatees; in their case too, what brought them into co-ownership

[1] Cf. Bas. "the co-heirs must give an undertaking to one another." This appears to me to make better sense. (See Bas. 42. 3. 25. 9. 7. τὸ πλάτος.)

[2] I put "each" in place of "he" to avoid a contradiction, again following the Basilica. See Bas. 42. 3. 25. 9 (*sic*, not 13).

[3] The above follows the text, but the text cannot be what Ulpian wrote, as the conclusion from the fact mentioned would be to the opposite effect. M. proposes a version in which a number of words are transposed and which may be Englished as follows:—"but, seeing that a person does not contract with a co-heir but chances upon him, he is not bound to answer for as much diligence as a diligent *paterfamilias*; for since, in this case, the co-heir had good reason for acting in the matter, on account of his own share, he consequently has no right of action on *negotia gesta*" etc. This is founded on the Basilica, but, in M.'s opinion, it implies a deliberate emendation on the part of the Greek writer.

was not their own agreement but the circumstances of the case. 17. Where there is a bequest of a slave who is not expressly specified, and afterwards, the legatee dying, one of his heirs, by refusing to concur [in the choice of a slave], obstructs the discharge of the legacy, the party so obstructing can, by means of this action, be ordered to pay the others the amounts of their respective interests. A similar rule holds where, to take the converse case, one of several heirs at whose charge a bequest has been made in general terms of such slave as they shall themselves choose, refuses to agree to the particular slave being handed over whom it would be advantageous to all of them to have transferred, and thereupon the heirs are sued at law by the legatee and ordered to pay something over and above. 18. Again, a man is liable on the ground of negligence who, having entered on an inheritance before others [entitled along with him], has allowed servitudes which attached to land included in the estate to be lost by non-user. 19. Where a son who defends an action on behalf of his father suffers adverse judgment and thereupon pays, either in his father's lifetime or after his death, the fairest rule to give is that he has a right to sue to recover [part] from his co-heir in an action *familiæ erciscundæ*. 20. The judge in the action *familiæ erciscundæ* ought not to leave anything undivided. 21. He ought also to see that an undertaking is given to the persons in whom he vests the property to secure them against its being recovered by superior title. 22. If money which was not left in the house is bequeathed [to one of the heirs] *per præceptionem* (to be taken by retainer), it is a matter of question whether the co-heirs ought to pay the whole amount or only pay in proportion to their shares in the inheritance, just as if the money had been left so as to be found among the other assets; but on the whole the proper view is that the amount which must be paid is what would be paid if the money had been found.

26 GAIUS (*on the provincial Edict* 7) But it is within the competence of the judge to order that something or several things included in the estate should be sold, and that the money arising from the sale should be paid to any legatee to whom such money was bequeathed.

27 PAULUS (*on the Edict* 23) In this action an order must be made or the application dismissed with reference to every party; consequently, if the order is omitted in the case of any party, there will be no validity in anything done by the judge with reference to the remaining parties, as it is impossible for a decision

pronounced in some one case to be in force with reference to part of the matter in question and not with reference to another part.

28 GAIUS (*on the provincial Edict* 7) If a testator should bequeath *per præceptionem* something which he has pledged for debt, it is open to the judge to order that the pledge should be redeemed out of the common funds and that the party to whom the thing was bequeathed as above should have it.

29 PAULUS (*on the Edict* 23) If a thing was given to the deceased by way of pledge, we must hold that it will be included in the action *familiæ erciscundæ*; but the person to whom it is assigned by the judge in this action must be ordered to pay his co-heir for it in proportion to the latter's share in the inheritance; moreover he (the latter[1]) need not give his co-heir any undertaking that he shall be kept harmless in the case of an action [to redeem] on the part of the pledgor, as things will be in the same kind of position as if a hypothecarian or Servian action had been brought and the assessed amount at stake had been tendered [by a stranger], where the person [so] offering the money would thereupon have a right to be protected by an *exceptio* against the owner [pledgor], if the latter brought an action to recover the property. We may add, on the other hand, that if the heir to whom the thing pledged has been assigned wishes to restore the whole, he will get a hearing, even if the pledgor should object. Where the creditor (*i.e.* one heir) buys the thing pledged [from his co-heir], the rule is not the same, because assignment by the Court takes effect compulsorily, but purchase is a matter of choice; unless indeed, [in the case of the assignment,] the creditor should be charged with bidding for the possession of the thing greedily. The reason why the above is taken into consideration is that what the creditor did is to be treated as if the debtor had done it through an agent, and any expense that such creditor was obliged to incur he can recover by an original action.

30 MODESTINUS (*Responsa* 6) I have a piece of land in common with a girl *sui juris* who is under age and co-heir with me; in the same land human remains are buried to which veneration is due on the part of both[2], in fact, the girl's own parents are buried there. Her guardians, however, wish to sell the land, to which I do not

[1] This is assumed without comment, and must be correct. See Bas. and Pothier; but we miss the word *ille*.

[2] Read *partibus* for *patribus*. Glück.

consent, preferring, as I do, to keep in my hands my own portion, as I cannot afford to buy the whole piece of land, and I should like to discharge the duty which we owe to the dead (*jus religionis*) at my own pleasure. I wish to know whether my proper course is to ask for an *arbiter* by an action *communi dividundo* to partition the piece of land in question, or the same *arbiter* as is appointed for the purposes of the action *familiæ erciscundæ* can discharge the office as well, and so divide this property too between us in accordance with our respective rights apart from the rest of the assets. Herennius Modestinus replied that there was nothing in the facts stated to prevent the person who was appointed *arbiter* in the action *familiæ erciscundæ* from extending the exercise of his function to the business of dividing the piece of land in question; at the same time "religious" spots could not be brought within the scope of the action, and rights over them appertained to each separate heir in respect of the whole.

31 PAPINIANUS (*Questions* 7) If a slave who is pledged for debt is redeemed by one of the heirs, then, even though after that the slave should die, still the *arbiter's* official position in respect of him will continue; there is sufficient ground for this furnished by the fact of common ownership which was previously existing and would be continuing at this day if the property had not perished.

32 THE SAME (*Responsa* 2) Such things as a father has not divided among his children, after[1] giving them rights of action by way of making a division, belong to the children in proportion to their respective shares in the inheritance; provided always he did not bestow them under one general description on a single child, and they are not accessory to the things given.

33 THE SAME (*Responsa* 7) Where a father, in bequeathing different parcels of land to his respective heirs, desired to execute a partition as if he were an *arbiter*, one co-heir will not be compelled to hand over his share save on the terms of getting in return a share which is free from the burden of a pledge.

34 THE SAME (*Responsa* 8) Where slaves were valued as between co-heirs at the time of partition, it is held that prices are put upon them not with a view to purchase but to division; consequently, if any die while a condition is still pending [on

[1] M. would insert after *datas* the words *res et collatas*; making the whole equivalent to "after making over property and giving rights," etc. He refers to 20. 3 above.

which they were to go to someone in pursuance of a testamentary trust], the loss is held to fall on both the heir and the fidei-commissary.

35 THE SAME (*Responsa* 12) Pomponius Philadelphus delivered certain plots of ground by way of *dos* to a daughter whom he had under his *potestas*, and requested that the rents and profits of the same should be handed over to his son-in-law [her husband]; the question was asked whether the daughter could retain the land for herself on the father appointing all his children (*filios*) heirs. My answer was that the daughter had good ground to retain the possession; as the father desired the lands in question to go for *dos*, and the married state had continued even after the father's death; the fact being, I said, that the case being defended was that of a daughter who remained in *de facto* possession, as though in virtue of a *dos* which she was capable of taking.

36 PAULUS (*Questions* 2) Being of opinion that you were my co-heir, whereas the fact was not so, I brought an action *familiæ erciscundæ* against you, and vesting orders and orders to pay were made by the judge on both of us: I wish to know whether, on the real facts being discovered, there are mutual rights of action for reconveyance or actions on claims of ownership; also whether one rule applies in the case of the party who is heir and another in the case of the party who is not heir? My answer was as follows:—If a man is sole heir, and, under the idea that Titius is co-heir along with him, he joins issue in proceedings *familiæ erciscundæ* between them, and, on orders for payment being made, pays accordingly, then, seeing that he paid in pursuance of a judgment of the Court, he cannot sue to have the money back. But your point seems to be that no action *familiæ erciscundæ* can be entertained save between co-heirs; still, even if the proceeding is no [legal] action, nevertheless it is a sufficient obstacle to the action to recover what was handed over that the party believed himself to be [legally] ordered to pay it. If, on the other hand, neither party was heir, but they join issue in the action *familiæ erciscundæ* as if they were heirs, the rule as to recovering the property just laid down in respect of one party will apply to both. No doubt, if they divided the property without applying to a judge, then it may be said that there is a good right even to bring a personal action for redelivery of those things which went to the party whom the actual heir took to be his co-heir; it cannot be held, where the

heir [only] thought that the other was his co-heir, that the matter was compounded between them.

37 SCÆVOLA (*Questions* 12) A man who takes proceedings by way of action *familiæ erciscundæ* admits[1] that the other party is his co-heir.

38 PAULUS (*Responsa* 3) Lucius and Titia, brother and sister, being emancipated by their father, had, when adult, curators appointed them, and these supplied both of them separately with money which was their common property, being derived from rents and profits. They afterwards divided the whole property between them, and, this being done, Titia, the sister, began proceedings against her brother Lucius on the alleged ground that he had received more than she had. Now as Lucius the brother did not get more than his proper portion, indeed got less than half the whole estate, I wish to ask whether Titia has a good right of action against her brother. Paulus replied:—"Upon the facts stated, if Lucius did not receive from the rents and profits of the lands owned in common more than what he had a right to in virtue of his share in the inheritance, I should say that his sister has no right of action against him." He gave a similar answer in a case where it was maintained that an alimentary provision having been ordered by the Prætor, a brother had received more than his sister, but not more than half the whole.

39 SCÆVOLA (*Responsa* 1) A man who was appointed heir in respect of a share defended an action relative to the whole estate, the action being against all the heirs and founded on the alleged fact of their not having avenged [the testator's[2]] death,—and he got judgment; hereupon a co-heir brought an action to recover his share from the heir above mentioned, but declined to pay his portion of the expense incurred in defending the [previous] action. The question was asked whether the co-heir's action would be barred by an *exceptio* of *dolus*. My answer was that if additional expense had been incurred [by the present defendant] in consequence of a defence which he had made in the interest of [the present plaintiff] himself [as well as his own], such expense ought to be taken into account; and even if the present defendant did not raise the *exceptio* of *dolus*, he could bring an action to be

[1] Omit *non*, M.: who follows the Basilica, and relies on the logical bearing of the affirmative on s. 36.

[2] M.

reimbursed a portion of the expenditure incurred. 1. A man who died intestate made codicils in which he divided all his landed estates and other property between his [two] children in such a way as to leave a great deal more to his son than to his daughter; the question was asked whether the sister was bound to bring her *dos* into hotchpot for the benefit of her brother. My answer was that, upon the facts as stated, if the deceased left no property undivided, the more correct view was that the right to ask to have the *dos* brought into hotchpot was taken away by the deceased's own wish. 2. A testator gave a slave of the age of fifteen years his freedom when he should reach the age of thirty, and also signified his wish that there should be given him from the day of his own death for the rest of the slave's life ten *denarii* [a month[1]?] for his food and twenty-five *denarii* [a year[1]?] for his clothing. Stichus [the slave in question] having died before the day when he was to be free, the question was asked whether the legacy providing food and clothing was valid, and also whether, in case it were not valid, the heir who had paid it could recover it from his co-heir in whose house the slave had been living. My answer was that the money had not been due and payable, but still, if what was given had been spent on aliment, that it could not be recovered. 3. A man cannot charge his brother in proportion to the share of the latter in the inheritance of their father with debts owing to the municipality which he himself contracted after the father's death, unless the two brothers were partners in respect of their whole property; even though they possessed their father's estate in common and the father before his death had discharged a magistracy in his municipality on behalf of his other son. 4. A man named his two sons heirs, and bequeathed to each of them by way of *prælegatum* certain specified slaves, including, in the case of one of the sons, a slave named Stephanus, with his *peculium*. This slave was manumitted and died in the lifetime of the testator, then the father died; and the question was asked whether what Stephanus had in his *peculium* before he was manumitted belonged to both sons, or only to the one to whom Stephanus was bequeathed by way of *prælegatum* with his *peculium*. My answer was that, on the facts as stated, it belonged to both. 5. A father divided his property amongst his sons, and confirmed the division by testament, providing further that whatever debt any one of his sons had incurred or should incur he should remain liable for the whole of it; after this, on one of the sons borrowing money, the

[1] Cf. M. and D. 34. I. 18. pr.

father came forward, and, with his consent, the land which he had assigned to the son was pledged [as a security for the money]. After the death of the father, the same son was in possession of the land and paid interest on the debt; I wish to know, supposing the creditor sells the land given in pledge, whether anything will have to be paid to this son by a co-heir which could be realised by an action *familiæ erciscundæ*. My answer was that, taking the facts as stated, nothing need be paid.

40 GAIUS (*Fideicommissa* 2) If a person who is appointed sole heir is requested to hand over a particular portion to me, for example, half, an *utilis actio familiæ erciscundæ* can properly be brought between us.

41 PAULUS (*Decrees* 1) A woman appealed from the decision of a judge on the ground, as she alleged, that, in an action *familiæ erciscundæ* between her and a co-heir, he had divided not only the property but the freedmen too, and also the [liability to pay an] alimentary provision which the testator had ordered to be given to particular freedmen; this, she said, he had no right to do. It was replied on the other hand that both parties had agreed to the division and had paid the alimentary provision for a great number of years in accordance with the terms agreed upon. The decision was that they must abide by the alimentary provision; but the judge added that the division of freedmen was of no force.

42 POMPONIUS (*on Sabinus* 6) If a legacy is made to one of the heirs as follows:—"let him retain out of his share what he owes me," it comes within the duty of the judge of the action *familiæ erciscundæ* to forbid the co-heirs from demanding from the heir in question payment of the debt; as, even where one heir is told to retain what is owed by another, rights of action ought, in pursuance of the duty of the judge, to be assigned to him in proportion to the share of a co-heir.

43 ULPIANUS (*on Sabinus* 30) An *arbiter* may be asked for in the action *familiæ erciscundæ* even by one party only, as it is well known that an appeal to the judge may be made even by a single heir; consequently a single heir can ask for an *arbiter*, even though the others are present and refuse their consent to the application.

44 PAULUS (*on Sabinus* 6) Among co-heirs there may be proceedings taken *communi dividundo* in such wise that the only

things embraced by the action are such things as belong to the parties in common, and questions which can be raised in respect of these things, the right of action *familiæ erciscundæ* being left untouched with reference to everything else. 1. If an action *familiæ erciscundæ* or *communi dividundo* has been carried through, the Prætor allows exceptions or actions so as to maintain any assignments made by the Court. 2. If co-heirs have sold property in the absence of one of their number, and have therein fraudulently contrived that they should get more than their share, they can be called upon to make good the loss to the one who was absent by means of either an action *familiæ erciscundæ* or a *petitio hereditatis*. 3. Any produce which an heir takes before entry on the inheritance from land included in the deceased's estate he does not, according to Julianus, have to give up pursuant to an action *familiæ erciscundæ*, save where he took it with knowledge of the fact that the land was part of the deceased's estate. 4. Persons who bring the actions *familiæ erciscundæ*, or *communi dividundo*, or *finium regundorum* are both plaintiffs and defendants; consequently they are bound to swear that they do not take contentious proceedings vexatiously nor deny their liability vexatiously. 5. Wherever a single co-heir, in pursuance of a promise on stipulation binding the heirs, makes a payment incurred through his own act, he cannot recover it from his co-heir; for example, where the deceased promised that no malicious act (*dolus malus*) should be committed by himself or his heir or that nothing should be done by himself or his heir which should prevent some specified person from using a footpath or a drive. Indeed, even where the other heirs incur liability through the act of one, on the ground that the condition mentioned in a stipulation binding the heirs has come to pass, they will have a good right of action *familiæ erciscundæ* against the one through whom it happened that an action could be brought on the stipulation. 6. Where a man stipulates that Titius and his heir shall ratify some act of his, and Titius dies leaving several heirs, [it is held] that the heir who failed to ratify is alone liable; and [similarly, in case the promisee dies[1],] that, of the promisee's heirs, the one against whom proceedings have been taken can alone enforce the liability. 7. Where a man bequeaths a usufruct to his widow till such time as her *dos* shall be duly made over to her, then, according to Cassius, by order of the *arbiter* in the action *familiæ erciscundæ*, anything that may have

[1] M. suggests *uterque* instead of Titius, where the name occurs the second time: *i.e.* "both die" instead of "T. dies."

been given by way of *dos* on behalf of a co-heir can be recovered[1] [from him] and, on the other hand, a co-heir can be made to pay [his proportion of] the *dos*; which is quite correct. 8. If two co-heirs are ordered by testament to erect a statue, whereupon one does nothing and the other sets up the statue, Julianus says that there is no injustice in an action *familiæ erciscundæ* being allowed, so that a portion of the expense may be paid to be determined by the judgment of a reasonable arbitrator.

45 POMPONIUS (*on Sabinus* 13) If you maintain that some part of the inheritance of a deceased person is common to you and me which I, on some other ground, declare to be my own in severalty, the question does not come within the scope of the action *familiæ erciscundæ.* 1. Ill practice on the part of a slave of an heir is not embraced by the action *familiæ erciscundæ,* unless there was so far negligence in the owner of the slave that he employed an untrustworthy slave about the common property.

46 PAULUS (*on Sabinus* 7) If the husband is appointed heir by his father subject to a condition, [the rule is] that in the meantime the wife's right of action for *dos* is suspended. No doubt, if a divorce takes place after her father-in-law's death, though at a time when the condition on which her husband was to be heir is still pending, the rule is that he has a right of retainer as to the *dos,* because, on the death of the father, some things go with his sons even before they become his heirs, such as [duties connected with the expense entailed by] marriage or [with] children or guardianship. Accordingly, a son who, after the death of his father, bore the expense entailed by marriage has a right to retain the *dos*; and this was the opinion of our friend Scævola himself.

47 POMPONIUS (*on Sabinus* 21) In the action *familiæ erciscundæ* or *communi dividundo,* if, while the matter is before the *arbiter,* there is a dispute as to a servitude, the rule is that all those amongst whom the *arbiter* has been appointed can bring actions or make a "notification of novel structure" according to their respective shares in the property; and, when vesting orders are made by the *arbiter,* then, if the whole estate should be assigned to one heir, undertakings ought to be given that anything that might be won by means of the actions [brought in connexion with the dispute] should be made over [to him], and any cost incurred in them should be made good [by him]; and, in case no action was brought with reference to the land while the case was before the

[1] Read *reciperari* for *reciperare potest.*

arbiter (*in judicio*), the original right of action should go with the person to whom the whole piece of land is assigned by order of the *arbiter*, or the right of action connected with whatever share it is in respect of which the assignment is made. 1. Again, as to things which are movable and which can be made the subject of the actions in question, should any such things come to be stolen while the case is proceeding, actions for theft can be brought by those persons at whose risk the things were.

48 PAULUS (*on Sabinus* 12) If proceedings are taken, either *familiæ erciscundæ*, or *communi dividundo*, or *finium regundorum*, and one of the parties dies leaving several heirs, the case cannot be split up into parts, but either all the heirs must accept the matter as it stands or they must appoint some one person as procurator against whom the case may proceed, as representing them all.

49 ULPIANUS (*Disputations* 2) A person was appointed heir for a particular share, and was ordered by the Prætor to bury the testator. Accordingly he sold a slave who had been given his liberty by the testament, and gave the purchaser the promise of twice the value [in case of recovery by superior title], after which, being sued in pursuance of his engagement, he paid the money. The question is asked whether he can get back by an action *familiæ erciscundæ* the amount which he is out of pocket through his promise of twice the value. As to this, let us first consider whether he was bound to undertake to pay the double value. For my own part I should say that he was not bound; the only persons who are bound to promise the double value are those who sell of their own accord; but if the party selling[1] is discharging a duty, he ought not to be constrained to make the promise, any more than a person who sells where the Prætor appointed him to carry out a judgment; even there the party is not in such a position that he is compellable to do everything which is required of those who sell at their own pleasure; persons who undertake a duty and persons who sell voluntarily[2] are in very different positions. Consequently at the outset the party was not bound to make the promise for the double value, but it is for the Prætor to rule that the purchaser has a good right of action as such against the person who becomes heir, if the thing sold should be recovered by a third person. If however the heir has made the mistake and given the

[1] For *distrahentis* read *distrahens*. Cf. M.

[2] Read *suscipientes et voluntate distrahentes* for *suscipientis et voluntatem distrahentis*. Cf. M.

undertaking, and, after that, the slave acquires his liberty, an action may be brought on the stipulation, and, should it be brought, it is only fair that the heir who sold should have an *utilis actio* allowed him against his co-heir,—the direct action *familiæ erciscundæ* being inapplicable,—so as to prevent the heir from having to abide by the loss. The fact is that, for a man to be in a position to bring the action *familiæ erciscundæ*, it is required not merely that he should be heir, but that he should be a party, either as plaintiff or defendant, in consequence of some matter constituting an act or default on his part subsequent to his becoming heir: otherwise the action *familiæ erciscundæ* is not applicable. The consequence is that if a man should do any act in connexion with an inheritance before he knew that he was heir, there is no room for an action *familiæ erciscundæ*, because he clearly did not do it with intent to act as heir; so that a man who has done anything before entry on the inheritance, for example, buried the testator, has no action *familiæ erciscundæ*; but if he did it after entry, it follows that we must hold that he can by means of an action *familiæ erciscundæ* get back the expenditure which he made on the funeral.

50 THE SAME (*Opinions* 6) Where a father has furnished assistance to an emancipated son who is spending his time abroad with a view to study, if it should be shown that the father forwarded the supplies in question not by way of a loan, but moved thereto by natural feeling, justice will not allow them to be reckoned as included in the portion of the goods of the deceased [father] which come to the same son.

51 JULIANUS (*Digest* 8) Land having been delivered to the father-in-law [of a bride] by way of *dos*, if such father-in-law should appoint his son [the husband] heir with respect to any share in his inheritance, the land ought to be taken in advance (*præcipi*) in pursuance of an order of the *arbiter* in an action *familiæ erciscundæ*, so as to make the legal position of the son the same as[1] it would have been, if the *dos* had been bequeathed to be taken in advance. Consequently produce realized after joinder of issue must go to him, allowance being made for outlay; but that which is realized before joinder will belong to all the heirs equally.

[1] I venture to read *quæ* for *in qua*. M. suggests *qua futurus* instead of *in qua futura*: the resulting English would, I suppose, be this:—"so that it (*i.e.* the land) will belong to the son subject to the same implications as those to which it would have been subject," etc. On the whole the sense is the same.

Outlay again must be allowed for, as no case can occur which would stand in the way of an abatement on that score. 1. Should I desire to bring a *petitio hereditatis* against you, and you to sue me in an action *familiæ erciscundæ*, we ought both to be gratified, on sufficient cause shown ; as, when I am in possession of the whole inheritance and admit that you are heir to the extent of half, but I wish to give up the common ownership, I ought to have an action *familiæ erciscundæ* allowed me, because there is no other way in which the inheritance can be divided between us. Again, if you have a sufficient reason for desiring to settle the matter by a *petitio hereditatis*, rather than an action *familiæ erciscundæ*, then you must yourself be allowed to bring a *petitio hereditatis*, as some things are embraced in that form of procedure which have no place in the other; suppose, for example, I am a debtor to the estate, you will not recover by an action *familiæ erciscundæ* my debt to the deceased, but, by a *petitio hereditatis*, you will.

52 THE SAME (*on Urseius Ferox* 2) Mævius, who appointed us heirs by his testament, had some property in co-ownership with Attius ; supposing after that we bring an action *communi dividundo* against Attius, and the above property is vested in us by order of the judge, then, according to Proculus, it will be embraced in an action *familiæ erciscundæ* [between us]. 1. A slave as to whom it is provided [by his owner's testament] that he shall be free and heir is compellable by an action *familiæ erciscundæ* to make good to his co-heirs any balance which he retains in his hands from accounts which he kept for the deceased owner. 2. An *arbiter* whom you and I took to be judge between us in an action *familiæ erciscundæ* wished to assign some things to me and others to you, and considered that with reference to these things each party ought to be ordered to make a payment to the other ; but it was asked whether it was not open to him to set off one amount against the other and to make one order, confined to the party who owed the larger sum, simply to pay the amount of the excess. It was thereupon held that it was open to the *arbiter* to take this course. 3. In proceedings *familiæ erciscundæ* or *communi dividundo* the valuation to be made is that of the whole of the assets, not of the different shares in the specific things.

53 ULPIANUS (*Responsa* 2) A sum of money which was lent by an emancipated son, on the understanding that it should be repaid to his father, will, it was held, be reckoned part of the father's

inheritance only where the father had a good right of action against the son in respect of the same sum.

54 NERATIUS (*Membrana* 3) You and I being heirs in common to Lucius Titius, I disposed of my share in a piece of land forming part of the assets, and, after that, an action *familiæ erciscundæ* was taken between us. Hereupon no account will be taken in the trial of the share which once was mine, seeing that, when it was disposed of, it ceased to be part of the inheritance, nor will any be taken of your share, because, however true it is that it is still held by its old title and is part of the inheritance, still, by the disposition made of my part, it is taken out of the common ownership. Whether one heir only forbears to dispose of his portion or more than one do the same is a matter of no importance, so long as there is some portion or other which is disposed of by one of the heirs, and consequently has ceased to be part of the inheritance.

55 ULPIANUS (*on the Edict* 2) If an action *familiæ erciscundæ* or *communi dividundo* is brought and the business of division is so difficult as apparently to be almost impossible, it is open to the judge to make the whole decree in favour of one person and to vest [in him] the whole of the assets.

56 PAULUS (*on the Edict* 23) Not merely in an action *finium regundorum*, but in one *familiæ erciscundæ* too, arrears of produce will be included along with present produce.

57 PAPINIANUS (*Responsa* 2) Even after an *arbiter* has been accepted, brothers who divide by agreement a common inheritance are discharging a duty enjoined by family affection, and the division[1] ought not to be given up, even if, when the hearing is ended, the *arbiter* should deliver no judgment; provided there is no case for giving relief on the ground of immature age.

[1] Ins. *divisionem* after *quam*. M.

III.

PARTITION OF COMMON PROPERTY.

1 PAULUS (*on the Edict* 23) The action *communi dividundo* (for partition of common property) is one that was required for the reason that the action *pro socio* rather deals with personal renders and transfers on both sides than with the division of common property. Of course the action for partition cannot be brought where there is no property held in common.

2 GAIUS (*on the provincial Edict* 7) But it makes no difference whether it is with partnership or without partnership that property is held among sundry persons in common, as the action *communi dividundo* is applicable in both cases. Common property occurs with partnership where, for example, the parties are persons who have jointly purchased the same thing; it occurs without partnership where, say, they are persons to whom the same thing was bequeathed by testament. 1. In respect of the three double actions, viz. *familiæ erciscundæ, communi dividundo* and *finium regundorum,* the question has been raised which party is to be regarded as plaintiff, as all parties seem to be in the same position; however the view on the whole adopted is that the person that must be held to be the plaintiff is the one who challenged the others to legal proceedings.

3 ULPIANUS (*on Sabinus* 30) In an action *communi dividundo* nothing is admitted save the question of the division of the actual things which are owned in common and that of any damage caused or done to any of these things or of any loss or expenditure being incurred by one of the co-owners or of anything coming to his hands out of the common property. 1. If the parties themselves have made any mutual agreement in good faith, the judge in the action *familiæ erciscundæ* or *communi dividundo* is bound to maintain it in the first place.

4 THE SAME (*on the Edict* 19) By means of this action a division is made of corporeal things, these being such as persons are owners of; it does not go on to give any partition of an inheritance. 1. The question has been raised whether there can be an action *communi dividundo* brought with reference to a well; to which Mela says that it can only be where the soil in which the

well is sunk is owned in common. 2. The action is *bona fide*; consequently, if some one thing should be left undivided, both the partition of all the rest will be perfectly valid and further proceedings *communi dividundo* can be taken in respect of the thing which remained undivided. 3. As the partition of an actual thing may be made the subject of an action *communi dividundo*, so also may renders and payments; accordingly, where a co-owner has laid out money, he can recover [a portion of] it; moreover, even if his action is not against an actual fellow-owner, but against the heir of a fellow-owner, Labeo holds very properly that both expense [incurred] and produce realized by the deceased are brought into account. No doubt produce realized before the property was owned in common and outlay made before the same date are not embraced by the action *communi dividundo*. 4. Accordingly Julianus tells us that, if you and I get an order putting us into interim possession for *damnum infectum*, and, before the final order to take possession, I shore up the building, I cannot recover the cost of doing so by an action *communi dividundo*.

5 JULIANUS (*on Urseius Ferox* 2) But if no defence was made and accordingly we have got a final order from the Prætor for possession of the house and in pursuance of it we have become owners, it is laid down by Proculus that by means of an action *communi dividundo* I can recover a part of the expense which I incurred.

6 ULPIANUS (*on the Edict* 19) If a man believes that he owns a piece of land in common with Titius, whereas he really owns it in common with someone else, and thereupon he takes produce from it or makes an outlay on it, proceedings can be taken by way of an *utilis actio communi dividundo*[1]. 1. Consequently, even if he[2] should dispose of [his share in] the land, then, although thereupon an action *communi dividundo* would be inadmissible, because the ownership in common is broken up, still it is held that it is a case for an *utilis actio*, such an action being allowed in respect of [previous] payments, where [the property] has ceased to be owned in common. 2. But where a co-owner makes any profit out of the land owned in common, either by letting it or by cultivating it, he can be sued in an action *communi dividundo*, and, if he was acting on behalf of the co-owners in general, he ought not to make [the whole] gain or bear [the whole] loss, but, if he did not act on behalf

[1] See note at the end of this title.

[2] The text has Titius, but M. following Cujas, would omit this name, and so attribute the disposition to the other party. This seems necessary.

of the co-owners, but with a view to his own exclusive gain, it is, on the whole, right that loss should fall on him. The reason why he has to account for his gains in an action *communi dividundo* is that it is recognized that he could not have found it an easy matter to let his own share. However an action *communi dividundo*, as Papinianus himself tells us, will be in place only where he did no more than what was indispensable for properly managing his own share; if he did more than that, he can bring an action for *negotia gesta* and he is liable to a similar action himself. 3. If any outlay should be made after joinder of issue in an action *communi dividundo*, Nerva is very properly of opinion that this will be included as well. 4. We may add that Sabinus and Atilicinus lay it down that children of a female slave are included in like manner. 5. Moreover, the same authors held that the scope of this action lends itself to accessions or reductions. 6. If a man buries a body in common ground, a question to consider is whether he makes the ground "religious." As to this, there is no doubt that each co-owner has the full right of burying in a place of sepulture, but one of the two by himself cannot make ordinary ground religious. But Trebatius and Labeo, though they hold that the place is not made religious, are still of opinion that there is a right of action *in factum*. 7. If you give an undertaking in respect of a house against *damnum infectum* for the full amount, Labeo says that you have no right of action *communi dividundo*, because you were not obliged to give the undertaking for the full amount, but it was enough[1] to give it for an amount proportional to your share; and this view is correct. 8. If you and I have a piece of land in common, but it [*i.e.* my share] is pledged by me for debt, it will be embraced by the action *communi dividundo*, but the creditor's right as pledgee will remain unaffected, even though the land should have been assigned by the Court, as, in fact, the security would be unaffected even if one co-owner had delivered his share to the other. But the *arbiter* in the action *communi dividundo* is bound, according to Julianus, to value the share at so much the less in consideration of the fact that the creditor is able to sell that particular subject-matter in pursuance of the agreement to that effect. 9. Julianus also tells us that if a man with whom I had a slave in common pledges his share to me and thereupon proceeds to bring an action *communi dividundo*, he could be barred by an *exceptio* of pledge; should I however not raise this *exceptio*, it will then be the duty of the judge,

[1] Read *sufficeret* for *sufficere*. Cf. M.

after assigning the undivided slave to the debtor, to order him to pay me the estimated value of my share, as my right as pledgee remains unaffected; but if the judge assigns the slave to me, then he can only order me to pay a sum equal to the excess of the value of the property pledged over the money that I lent, and he must order that the debtor be discharged of his debt to me. 10. It is within the attributions of the judge that the order made should be one which vests the land in one party and a usufruct therein in the other. 11. The remaining points are the same as we have dealt with in connexion with the action *familiæ erciscundæ*. 12. According to Urseius, where a neighbour has given the "notification against executing any works" in respect of a building which two persons own in common, then, if an order is made on one of the co-owners in pursuance thereof, he can recover the damages paid from his fellow-owner to the extent of the share [of the latter]; but Julianus observes quite correctly that this is true only where it was beneficial to the house that the thing should be done.

7 THE SAME (*on the Edict* 20) An action *communi dividundo* will lie even in respect of land let on perpetual lease (*ager vectigalis*). Whether such land can be divided into distinct plots is a question to consider; but, on the whole, the judge ought to avoid making a division of that kind, otherwise the perpetual rent will get into confusion. 1. Neratius tells us that where the *arbiter*, after dividing an estate not leased in perpetuity into [two] distinct plots, assigns them to two persons respectively, he can impose servitudes, just as if there were two separate estates. 2. Persons who are in a position to bring the Publician action *in rem* can equally take proceedings *communi dividundo*. 3. There are some cases in which, though[1] there may be no right of action to recover property as owner, still, if there is good ground for holding possession, an *utilis actio communi dividundo*[2] is open; for example, suppose a case where property is in someone's possession in pursuance of a payment made where none was due[3]. 4. The action is not available among mere plunderers, nor will it lie where persons are in possession on

[1] Ins. *ubi* before *vindicatio*. M.

[2] See note at the end of this title.

[3] This translates the text, but M., following Keller, would read *debiti* for *indebiti*. This would make it "in pursuance of payment off of the money owed"; the case supposed is that of a mortgagor who pays the mortgage debt without taking a reconveyance and remains in possession, the mortgage being of the old-fashioned kind by *fiducia*. Cf. Gaius, 2. 60.

precarium (on request, at will) or by stealth; in the case first mentioned the possession is simply wrongful, in the case of *precarium* it is legal, no doubt, but it is not substantial enough to give ground for an action. 5. Julianus tells us that if one possessor challenges a division, but the other alleges that the applicant is in possession by force, this action ought not to be allowed, in fact, not even after the lapse of a year, because the law is that even after the year an interdict will be granted against a person who turned another out by force. Even, he adds, where the allegation is that the party applying is in possession on *precarium*, this action is still out of place, because an interdict is equally allowed in a case of *precarium*. Again, if the applicant is alleged to be in possession by stealth, the proper rule, he says, is that the action cannot be brought, since the interdict, as he informs us, is obtainable where the possession is by stealth. 6. If there are two persons who have taken property in pledge as a security for a debt, it is, he holds, perfectly fair that they should be allowed an *utilis actio communi dividundo*[1]. 7. Similarly, if there is a dispute between two persons with reference to a usufruct, the same action ought to be allowed. 8. Again, where two persons are put in possession by order of the Prætor to preserve legacies, the rule is the same; there is a good ground of possession in regard of the custody to be exercised. Consequently, where there are two unborn children, the rule still holds, and this is reasonable. 9. No doubt, where a man who is put in possession on the ground of apprehended damage has already got a final order to possess, there will be no room for the *utilis actio*[1] on his behalf, as he is in a position to bring a *vindicatio* (action to recover *as owner*). 10. Where an action *communi dividundo* is brought in respect of a usufruct, the office of the judge may be exercised in any one of the following ways:—he may allow the parties to exercise usufructs in distinct portions respectively, or he can let the usufruct [in the whole] to one of them, or he can let it to some third person, so as to enable the parties to draw the rents and have no further dispute, or, if the property is movable, he can do this,—he can make the parties come to an agreement and give mutual undertakings that they will enjoy the use and produce for limited periods, that is to say, that the usufruct is to go to the two alternately, each taking it for a specified time. 11. The action is not available for agricultural tenants nor for persons who have taken property on deposit, though in both cases the parties have natural possession. 12. Where persons have taken

[1] See note at the end of this title.

something in common as a pledge for debt, the division which ought to be made among them is one in which a share is not estimated at its real value, but only in respect of the amount of debt secured on that particular share, and the property pledged is assigned to one of the creditors, but the debtor is left at full liberty to tender the amount of his debt and so to redeem his pledge. The same principle is applied where the debtor brings an *actio pigneratitia*[1] (action to redeem) *in rem*, and the person who is in possession of the property offers to pay him the amount assessed. 13. If a debtor has pledged his share in a plot of ground which he has in common with another, and his creditor, being called upon [to make a partition] either by the owner of the other share or by another creditor, viz. one of another debtor, outbids his rival [in an auction for the property pledged and so takes an assignment of the whole plot], after which the debtor of the man to whom the plot has been [so] assigned[, *i.e.* the debtor first mentioned,] desires to get back his share of the plot on payment of his own debt, it is held, in accordance with strict principle, that he will not get a hearing unless he is prepared to take in addition the share which his creditor bought under the assignment. In fact, even if you sell a share in something, and, before you have delivered it to the purchaser, you are sued in an action *communi dividundo*, and an order is made vesting in you the other share [too], there is a corresponding rule, to the effect that there can be no action brought in pursuance of the purchase, unless the plaintiff is prepared to take the whole property, because the additional share came to the vendor through the first share; and not only so, but the purchaser can be himself sued in pursuance of the sale to make him take the whole; the only point to make sure of is whether there is any fraud in the case on the part of the vendor. On the other hand, if, after selling your share, you should yourself be outbidden, and [have to] resign [to your fellow-owner the share which you sold], you will be liable on a similar principle to an action by the purchaser to make you refund the purchase-money. The same rule applies to the case of *mandatum* and other actions arising under circumstances of this kind.

8 PAULUS (*on the Edict* 23) And if it is not the whole number of co-owners but only some of them in particular who wish to have a partition, this action may be had amongst them. 1. Should it be uncertain whether the *lex Falcidia* applies as between a legatee

[1] Read *pigneratitia* for *pigneratitiam*. Cf. M.

and the heir, there can be an action *communi dividundo,* or a *vindicatio* is allowed for an unascertained share. The like is the case where there is a legacy of a *peculium,* because it is uncertain how far a debt to the owner reduces the contents of the *peculium.* 2. The action *communi dividundo* includes the case of a co-owner spoiling a piece of common property, as, for example, by wounding a slave or corrupting his character, or by cutting down trees on the land. 3. If a man pays on behalf of a slave owned in common a larger sum by way of damages for the slave's misfeasance [than he need have paid], a value will be set on the slave and he will get part of it [from his fellow-owner]. 4. Again, if one co-owner is sued *de peculio* for the whole of a debt and judgment is given against him, he has an action *communi dividundo* against his fellow-owner by which he can recover part of the *peculium.*

9 AFRICANUS (*Questions* 7) But where one co-owner has been ordered, in pursuance of an action *de peculio* brought in respect of a slave owned in common, to pay the whole debt, then, if things which are contained in the *peculium* are lost in [such] co-owner's hands, there will still be an *utilis actio communi dividundo*[1] to recover part of the money paid; because it would be an injustice if the whole matter operated to the loss of the man who sustained the action, considering that the risk, as to things contained in the *peculium,* ought to fall on both the owners. It will be remembered that where a man takes up the defence of a slave at his owner's request, he will be indemnified as to all outlay he makes in good faith, although the *peculium* should afterwards be lost. This is on the assumption that no negligence occurs in the case on the side of either party; as our authority held that, if the owner who is sued in the action *de peculio* is prepared to cede the contents of the *peculium* to the plaintiff, his application will be entertained on sufficient cause shown, provided, that is, he would cede without any fraudulent or vexatious intention.

10 PAULUS (*on the Edict* 23) Moreover, although the action on the *lex Aquilia* is not available against the heir, nevertheless in the action under consideration the heir of a fellow-owner must make good any damage done by the deceased to the common property for which there is a good right of action created under the *lex Aquilia.* 1. Where a man has only an *usus,* a thing which

[1] See note at the end of this title.

cannot be either sold or let, let us consider how a partition can be made in an action *communi dividundo*. However, as to this, the Prætor interposes and brings the matter into shape, the understanding being that if the judge vests the actual *usus* in one, it will not be held that the other, who accepts a value, is not exercising *usus*, on the alleged ground that the one who is seen to be in actual enjoyment goes further than the other; the fact being that that state of things is a necessity of the case. 2. In an action *communi dividundo* the judge is bound to value the property at its true worth, and security will have to be given against recovery in virtue of superior title.

11 GAIUS (*on the provincial Edict* 7) We must remember generally that if, after the destruction of the common property, a party who has a right to receive something on the ground of common ownership wishes to bring an action in pursuance thereof, he is allowed an *utilis actio communi dividundo*[1]. Suppose, for example, the plaintiff went to some expense on the common property, or his fellow-owner got the whole benefit of something derived from the property, such as the services of a slave or money paid for his hire, there is an account taken in this action of every such case.

12 ULPIANUS (*on the Edict* 71) If there is a house owned in common or a common wall and it is necessary to repair the wall or to pull it down or to let something into it, the proper course will be to bring an action *communi dividundo*, or proceedings can be taken by way of an interdict *uti possidetis*.

13 THE SAME (*on the Edict* 75) An action *communi dividundo* includes everything, save where anything is expressly excepted by common agreement in order to prevent it from being included.

14 PAULUS (*on Plautius* 3) This action includes whatever has been done on the common behalf or ought to have been done by a man who knew that he had a fellow-owner. 1. With regard however to any outlay which I made under the impression that the land was all my own, and the amount of which, in short, in case a *vindicatio* were brought to recover a share in the land, I should be in a position to retain by raising an *exceptio* of *dolus*, it is a matter for consideration whether, if I am sued in an action *communi dividundo*, I cannot still retain it in virtue of the equitable character of the action itself. On

[1] See note at the end of this title.

the whole, I should say that I can, because the action *communi dividundo* is a *bona fide* action; but this is only so where it is against me that proceedings are taken. Should I, on the other hand, dispose of my share, there will be nothing out of which I can retain the amount. Let us see however whether the purchaser from me has not the right to retain it; there is no doubt that, if a *vindicatio* were brought to recover a share from him, he would be in a position to exercise a right of retention on the ground of the outlay made by me, just as I should myself, and the better opinion is that in this case too the outlay can be retained; and, this being so, it is very properly held further that *I ought to be allowed an* utilis actio *against my fellow-owner on the ground of outlay, even if the common ownership still continues*[1]. It is a different thing where I spend money on property, treating it as my own, when it is really another's, or is common to me and another; in such a case as that, where I spend money on a thing as if it were my own, I have only a right of retention, because it was not my desire to impose an obligation upon anyone. But where I believe a thing to belong to Titius which really belongs to Mævius, or to be owned by me in common with someone who is not my real fellow-owner, my object is to put another person under an obligation towards me, and, just as an action on *negotia gesta* is allowed me against a party on whose behalf I acted as a voluntary agent under the impression that I was acting on behalf of someone else, so too is it in the case which we are considering. Consequently, even if I convey away the plot of land to another, still, as the state of things was such that I could claim to have an action allowed me, I ought, as Julianus himself says, to be allowed one on *negotia gesta*. 2. Should the parties agree that no partition at all shall be made, it is perfectly clear that such an agreement has no force, but should it be that none shall be made within a specified time, and this tends to improve the character of the property itself, it is a valid agreement. 3. If it should be agreed by co-owners that

[1] The clause in italics has given some trouble. Mommsen in a note offers a version which, as it appears to be meant for an emendation, I proceed to give in English. "It is very properly held further that *in that case*" (that is, as M. adds, where the party knows that he has a fellow-owner, but does not know who he is, as in 14. pr.) "I ought to be allowed an *utilis actio* against my fellow-owner on the ground of outlay, even if the common ownership should *not* continue." The English words in italics represent M.'s insertions, but, in reading "not," he follows Cujas.

the co-ownership should not be broken up within a specified time, there is no doubt that one who is bound by such an agreement is free to sell; accordingly even a purchaser from him who should bring an action *communi dividundo* will be barred by the same *exceptio* by which his vendor would have been barred. 4. If a co-owner agrees not to sue for his share, this practically puts an end to the co-ownership.

15 THE SAME (*on Plautius* 5) If a co-owner is sued in respect of a slave who is owned in common, and judgment is given against him, he will have a good right of action *communi dividundo* even before he complies with the judgment, as, if proceedings are taken against one co-owner by way of noxal action, he can at once sue his fellow-owner to have the [defendant's] share delivered to him, giving an undertaking at the same time that, if he does not hand over the slave, he will give the share back.

16 THE SAME (*on Plautius* 6) Where co-owners break up (*dividunt*) the co-ownership, the practice is to give undertakings with regard to any debt which should be owing on a condition.

17 MODESTINUS (*Rules* 9) Where a man is one of several co-heirs, if he purchases from a creditor of his testator a plot of land which the testator had given such creditor by way of pledge, he is not liable to be sued in an action *communi dividundo* by his co-heirs.

18 JAVOLENUS (*Epistles* 2) The *arbiter* cannot order that land which is part of the estate of a deceased person should be subject to a servitude attached to land which is not part of the estate; as the powers of the judge cannot extend beyond the matter which is the subject of the trial.

19 PAULUS (*on Sabinus* 6) A tree which grows on a boundary and similarly a stone which lies over two plots, as long as they adhere to the land, belong to the respective owners so far as they are vertically over their territories, and they are not included in the action *communi dividundo*; but as soon as the stone is taken up or the tree is rooted up or cut down, it becomes common property in undivided shares, and it will be included in the action *communi dividundo*; in short, what was a thing of distinct portions now becomes indiscriminate.

On the same principle, where two masses of stuff, belonging to two respective owners, are fused together, the whole mass is common property, even though some portion of the stuff, as it was originally, should remain unmixed with the rest; and so too, when a tree or a stone is detached from the soil, the proprietary rights over it are no longer distinct. 1. An *arbiter* for the purpose of partition ought not to be appointed in the case of a common entrance court (*vestibulum*) to two houses against the will of either owner, because, where a man is compelled to bid for such a court, he may sometimes have to offer a price for the whole house, if he has no other means of approach. 2. If two persons have a right of way over the same spot, and one has made an outlay on the road, it is rather a hard saying of Pomponius that there can be an action *communi dividundo* or *pro socio*; how is it, in fact, possible to recognize such a thing as co-ownership in an easement which each uses separately[1]? The proper action is rather that on *negotia gesta*. 3. The judge in the action *communi dividundo*, as also *familiæ erciscundæ*, in the case of a slave who has taken to flight, ought to call upon the persons who are parties in the case before him to bid, and then he should make an order vesting the slave in the person[2] who made the last offer; and there will be no danger lest the penalty laid down by the *lex Fabia* should be incurred in pursuance of the decree of the Senate. 4. A watercourse, according to Labeo, is not included in the action *communi dividundo*: either it is attached to the plot of land itself, and consequently does not come in question in the action, or else it is separated from the plot, but is divided in respect of amount or times of user. However, servitudes may sometimes be separated from the plot and yet not divided in respect of amount or times, for example where the person to whom they belonged left several heirs; and, when this occurs, it is consistent therewith that they too should be taken account of in an action *familiæ erciscundæ*; to which Pomponius adds that he does not see why they should not be as much included in a case of *communi dividundo* as in one of *familiæ erciscundæ*. Accordingly, in cases of this kind, it comes to pass, even in an action *communi dividundo*, that the servitudes are divided in respect of amount or times of user.

[1] *communio juris separatim.* I read *separati*: cf. M.

[2] Insert *ei* after *eum*. M.

20 POMPONIUS (*on Sabinus* 13) If a man with whom you have a plot of land in common fails to answer to a charge of tort[1], and thereupon, by the action of the judge, the house is demolished or the plantations cut down, the damage can be made good to you by an action *communi dividundo*, as that action embraces every loss incurred by the fault of a co-owner.

21 ULPIANUS (*on Sabinus* 30) It is a good principle that the judge in a question of dividing plots of land should be guided by consideration of what is most beneficial to all who are concerned or what the parties prefer.

22 POMPONIUS (*on Sabinus* 33) If I build a wall on behalf of my neighbour and myself, either on the understanding that I can recover the expense from him in proportion to his share, or by way of making him a present, the wall will be common property.

23 ULPIANUS (*on the Edict* 32) If you and your fellow-owner agree that you may take the produce in alternate years, and your fellow-owner refuses to allow you to take that which appertains to your year, it is worth considering whether your proper action is *ex conducto* (on a contract of hiring) or *communi dividundo*. This question arises equally where a co-owner who agreed that he should enjoy the produce of every second year turns in his cattle and so causes the crop for the next year to be spoilt which his fellow-owner ought to get. I should say on the whole myself that the action *communi dividundo* applies rather than the action *ex conducto*,—how can there, in fact, be a contract of letting if there is no rent in the case?—or, at any rate, that there ought to be a civil action allowed for unliquidated damages.

24 JULIANUS (*Digest* 8) If a slave owned by two persons makes any acquisition through the property of one of the co-owners, what is acquired will still be owned in common; but the one on whose property the acquisition is founded can get the amount by means of an action *communi dividundo*, because it is in keeping with the principles of good faith that every one should have a claim in advance to any acquisition which a slave makes through his property. 1. I am on the point of bringing an action *communi dividundo*, when you dispose of your share to Titius, in order to change the conditions of the trial; upon this you

[1] Some would read *delectum*, call to military service: contra Florentine MS and Basilica, in which the word is taken to be *delictum*.

are liable to a Prætorian action at my hands, on the ground that you took measures to prevent an action *communi dividundo* being brought against you.

25 THE SAME (*Digest* 12) Stichus, a slave owned by you and me in common, has an underslave Pamphilus who is worth ten *aurei*, and an action *de peculio* is brought against me in which I suffer judgment and pay ten; in this case, though Pamphilus should afterwards die, still, if I sue you in an action *communi dividundo* or *pro socio*, you will have to pay me[1] five, because I have freed you from that amount of debt. Much more should I recover this sum, if Stichus, after the death of Pamphilus, had got another underslave.

26 ALFENUS VARUS (*Digest* 2) A slave owned in common, being in the hands of one of the co-owners, broke his leg in the course of some work he was doing; the question was asked what sort of action the other owner had against the person in whose employment the slave had been. My answer was:—if the common property was in any respect injured by the negligence of the owner last mentioned rather than by chance, damages can be recovered through the *arbiter* by an action *communi dividundo*

27 PAULUS (*Epitomes of Alfenus's Digest* 3) A single co-owner is not at liberty in law to examine by torture a slave owned in common, except in reference to some matter in which all the co-owners are concerned.

28 PAPINIANUS (*Questions* 7) Sabinus declares that no co-owner can legally make any structure on common property against the will of the other. It is plain from this that the other has a right to stop him; where parties are on the same footing, the position of the one who objects is unquestionably superior. Still, although where the property is common, one co-owner may be prevented by another from constructing anything, he cannot be compelled to take down anything which he has once set up, supposing the other omitted to stop him when he was able to do so; consequently the mischief can be made good [only] by an action *communi dividundo*. If however the party [who could have objected] consented to the other man's act, he cannot bring an action, even for positive damage. On the other hand, if the man erected something to the injury of his co-owner while the latter was absent, he can even be compelled to take down what he set up.

[1] For *milia* read *mihi*. Bas.: cf. M.

29 PAULUS (*Questions* 2) If a man who is co-owner of a plot of ground in common with Titius lays out money upon it under the impression that he is co-owner with Mævius, it is said, very correctly, that the simple action *communi dividundo* is all that he requires ;—this in fact holds where I know that the land is owned in common, but do not know in common with whom ;—as the fact is that I am not volunteering to act on behalf of a fellow-owner but am looking after my own property, and the action depends rather on the subject-matter on which the money is laid out than on the person of the co-owner. It may be added here that this is the action to which, in our opinion, a ward will be liable, if the object is to get him to make good some outlay, by application in that behalf to the judge. A man is in a different position where he thinks he is spending money on his own property, when the property is really owned in common ; in that case he has no right to the action *communi dividundo,* nor will an *utilis actio* be allowed him either ; of course a man who knows property to be owned in common or to belong to another[1] acts with the intention of subjecting someone else to an obligation, and is mistaken about the person. 1. Pomponius tells us that any one of the co-owners can call for a judge ; but that, even where one of the co-owners takes no step, an action *communi dividundo* may very properly be brought against him.

30 SCÆVOLA (*Responsa* 1) An action *communi dividundo* can be properly brought both where neither of the parties is in possession of the estate and where one party is out of possession.

31 PAULUS (*Responsa* 15) Where two slaves had by order of the Prætor been reserved out of an inheritance to wait upon each of so many wards, children of the deceased, it was held that no division of property was made, but the slaves remained common to all[2].

[1] For *aliena* read *alienam.* M.

[2] *Note.* I have written *utilis actio* where the original is *utile judicium* ; the word *judicium* is in fact always used of the proceeding under discussion in this title. Both expressions are untranslatable, but I have treated the word *actio,* in an English sentence, as bearing a somewhat more general rather than an opposed sense.

IV.

ACTION FOR PRODUCTION.

1 ULPIANUS (*on the Edict* 24) This is an absolutely necessary action and recourse is had to its agency every day; it was introduced chiefly with a view to aid proceedings for recovery of property (*vindicationes*).

2 PAULUS (*on the Edict* 21) To produce (*exhibere*) is to put a thing[1] at a person's command in a public place, so as to enable him to have ample facility for bringing a matter to a trial.

3 ULPIANUS (*on the Edict* 24) In this action the plaintiff is bound to know and to mention all the evidence identifying the thing which is the subject of the application. 1. A man who brings an action for production does not, as a matter of course, allege that he is owner, and need not prove ownership, as there are many different grounds on which the action may be brought. 2. A further observation to be made as to the action is that, with a contumacious defendant, an order may be made upon him founded on the plaintiff's oath as to the matter in issue, the amount being determined by the judge. 3. This action is personal, and the right to bring it is given to anyone who intends to bring an action *in rem*, no matter what the nature of that action may be, *e.g.* the Servian action on a pledge, or the hypothecarian action, these being open to creditors. 4. According to Pomponius, where a man intends to sue for a usufruct he has a good right of action *ad exhibendum*. 5. We may add that, if he asks to have a thing produced with a view to moving for an interdict, his application will be entertained. 6. Again, if I wish to choose a slave or any other piece of property out of a number in pursuance of a bequest giving me the option, there is no doubt that I can have an action *ad exhibendum*, so that, when the things are produced, I can bring a *vindicatio*. 7. If a man wishes to take proceedings by way of noxal action, he requires an action *ad exhibendum*; indeed, what is to be said, if the owner of the slave wishes to defend the action, but the plaintiff cannot fix on the man unless they are all there, either because he does not recollect the particular slave, or he has not got his name? Is it not the fairest plan that the whole number should be produced

[1] After *facere* ins. *rei*. M.

before him, so that he may recognize the guilty individual? Accordingly, this must be ordered, on due cause shown, so that the particular man in respect of whom the noxal action is being brought may be pointed out, a view of the slaves being had for the purpose. 8. If anyone other than the heir desires that the actual testament, or the codicils, or anything else connected with a testament should be produced, the rule to lay down is that proceedings ought not to be taken by way of the action under consideration, as the party needs no more than the interdicts which are available for the above purpose; this we find in Pomponius. 9. It must be understood however that the action *ad exhibendum* is open not only to the persons above mentioned, but equally so to anyone who has an interest in the production being made; accordingly the judge ought to decide on a general view of the facts whether the party applying has an interest, not whether the thing is his property, and thereupon either order production or else decline to make the order because the applicant has no interest. 10. Julianus goes further; even, he says, if I have no right to sue to recover a thing as owner, I may have an immediate right to production because I have an interest in such production being made; suppose, for instance, a bequest is made to me of a slave to be chosen by Titius, this is a case where I should have a good right of action *ad exhibendum*, because I have an interest in production being made in order that Titius may choose and I may thereupon have my action to recover, although I have no right myself to choose a slave who is produced. 11. If an action *ad exhibendum* is brought against me, I have no right to bring a similar action on the mere ground that I have been sued in the action in question; though it should be held that I have an interest in virtue of the fact that I am liable to have to hand over the slave. But this is not a sufficient ground; otherwise, even where a man fraudulently contrived to be out of possession, he might bring an action *ad exhibendum*, though he should not mean to bring a *vindicatio* or to apply for an interdict; indeed a thief or a robber might do the same thing; but this is far from being the case. Accordingly, there is a sound discrimination in the rule laid down by Neratius, that the judge in a case of production must carry his enquiry so far as to ascertain whether the party has a lawful and reasonable ground of action on the strength of which he asks to have production made. 12. Pomponius tells us that a number of different persons may very well have an action for production in respect of the same slave: suppose, for example, some slave should be the property of the first applicant, the second should have a usufruct in him, the third should maintain that he is in his possession and the fourth should declare that he was pledged to him as security for debt; in such a case all have good rights of action for production, because all are interested in the slave being produced. 13. The same writer proceeds to say that the judge, in pursuance of the judicial power with which he is entrusted through this action, is further bound to weigh any *exceptio* raised by the party in possession, and, if any one that is offered should be so clear as to be a plain bar to the plaintiff, that the party in possession should be dismissed from the action; but should it be somewhat doubtful or involve a larger question, the point must be reserved for the actual trial, production of the thing being in the meantime ordered: there are some pleas however which the *arbiter* who is judge in the action for production ought to deal with himself without more; for example, one founded on subsequent agreement, on malicious contrivance, on an oath, on a previous decision. 14. In some cases the justice of the claim for production is such that although a party cannot have any action *ad exhibendum*, an action is nevertheless allowed *in factum*. This point is discussed by Julianus. A slave, he says, who belonged to my wife kept my accounts, these accounts are in your possession and I desire to have them produced. According to Julianus, if the accounts are written on my paper, the action will lie, because then I have a right to proceed to recover them; if I own the paper, I must needs own what is written upon it; but, if the paper is not mine, then, inasmuch as I cannot sue to recover the paper, I cannot take proceedings for production either; consequently I have a good right of action *in factum*. 15. It should be borne in mind that in these proceedings the action may be brought not merely against a man who has civil possession, but equally well against one who occupies by way of natural possession. Lastly it is held that a creditor who has taken property by way of pledge for debt is compellable to make production:

4 POMPONIUS (*on Sabinus* 6) in fact, the action can be brought even where a thing is deposited with a man, or lent him or let to him.

5 ULPIANUS (*on the Edict* 24) Celsus has the following: if a man, after contracting to carry away goods, deposited them in a warehouse, an action for production can be brought against the party who so contracted; if he is dead, but has left an heir, it can

be brought against the heir, but, if there is no heir, it must be brought against the warehouseman; for (, Celsus proceeds to say,) if the goods are possessed by no one [else], then it is a plain fact that either the warehouseman possesses them or else, at any rate, he is the person who is able to produce them. The same writer asks:—how can a man, however, be said to possess goods which he contracted to carry? is it because he has a lien on them? The whole case shows that the mere fact that a man has it in his power to produce goods makes him liable to an action to produce them. 1. Julianus however tells us that on this principle a man is liable to an action to produce when he is in possession in order to preserve property or legacies, and equally so when he has something in his hands in virtue of a usufruct, though in this case too he certainly does not possess. Here Julianus asks the question what the production amounts to which these persons are respectively bound to make; to which he says that the former must make it in such wise that the plaintiff will have the possession, but the party against whom the action is brought will be in possession for the purpose of preserving the property; whilst the person who has the usufruct should make it so that the plaintiff should possess the property, but the party against whom the action is brought should use and enjoy. 2. Again, Julianus tells us that a purchaser who fails to give back loose timber and minerals (*ruta cæsa*) is liable to an action to produce, the damages being measured by my (*i.e.* the applicant's) oath as to the value at stake; but he immediately goes on to say "if the purchaser possesses or has used fraudulent means to avoid possessing." 3. Celsus says further that if you have heaped up dung on vacant ground of mine, you can by an action for production get an order to allow you to take it away, on condition however that you take away the whole; but you cannot get it on any other terms. 4. Again, if a boat should be carried by the force of a stream on to the field of a stranger, then, so Neratius tells us, the stranger can be sued for production. Hereupon Neratius asks the question whether the plaintiff must give the owner of the field an undertaking in respect of future damage only or of past damage as well, and he says it ought to be given for past damage as well. 5. Again, if, on a building falling down, something is thrown on your ground or into your house, you will be compellable to produce it, though you do not possess it. 6. Moreover, where the party has not got it in his power to hand a thing over, then, though he should possess it, still he will not be liable to an action for production; suppose, for example, a slave should have taken to flight; no doubt his liability will go as far as this, but no further, that he must give an undertaking to produce the slave, if he should ever come to be in his power. Even if your slave has not taken to flight, but you have given him leave to live where he likes, or you have sent him on a journey, or he is employed on your estates, you will only be compellable to give the undertaking.

6 PAULUS (*on Sabinus* 14) A jewel which is inserted in the gold of a different owner or a statuette attached to another person's candlestick cannot be claimed in an action on the ground of ownership, but an action for production can be brought to have them detached. The case of material built into a house is different, as to this, there is not even a right of action for production, because the Twelve Tables forbid the material being detached, but, by the same statute, there can be an action brought *de tigno juncto* (for the act of affixing material) for double the amount.

7 ULPIANUS (*on the Edict* 24) By the word *tignum* is understood in the Twelve Tables every kind of material, as some hold, and this opinion is correct. 1. But if you affix my wheel to your carriage, you will be compellable to produce it, (and this we are told by Pomponius,) even though in that case you should not in strict law possess it. 2. The same holds where you attach my plank to your chest or to your ship, so as to make it part thereof, or attach my handle to your bowl, or my inlaid work to your cup, or work my purple into your garment, or join to your statue an arm which belongs to me. 3. Again, a municipal body (*municipes*) can be sued for production, as it is in its power to hand the thing over; it is recognized law that it can possess and can acquire by user. The same rule must equally be applied to guilds (*collegia*) and other corporate bodies. 4. If the defendant does not possess at the time of joinder of issue, but comes to possess subsequently before the decision, it is held that the proper rule is that judgment should be given against him, unless he hands over the property. 5. Should the defendant possess at the time of joinder of issue and afterwards cease to possess, but without fraudulent intent on his part, the action ought to be dismissed; although, as Pomponius remarks, he is to some extent chargeable for not handing the thing over at once instead of allowing issue to be joined against him. 6. The same writer says that where a defendant possesses at the time of joinder of issue, but subsequently ceases to possess, and then comes into possession once more, whether it be in virtue of

his old title or a new one, the order ought to be made on him, unless he hands the thing over. 7. In the same place Pomponius adds reasonably enough that the person who sues for production ought to have an interest at both times in the property being handed over to him, that is, both when issue is joined and when the order is made; and Labeo takes the same view.

8 JULIANUS (*Digest* 9) Where an action for production is brought against a man who neither possesses nor has used fraudulent means to avoid possessing, after which he dies and his heir possesses the property, the heir can be compelled to produce it. We know that if I sue to recover a plot of land or a slave and the heir of the defendant comes into possession of the property in virtue of his predecessor's title, he will be compelled to hand it over.

9 ULPIANUS (*on the Edict* 24) Julianus has this:—if a man should kill a slave who was in his possession or should transfer the possession to someone else, or should spoil property to such an extent that it could not be kept, he will be liable to the action for production, because he used malicious means to avoid possessing. On the same principle, if he should spill or destroy wine or anything else, he will be liable to the action for production. 1. Mast falls from your tree on my ground and I turn on my cattle and let them feed upon the mast; to what action am I liable? Pomponius says that there is a good right of action for production against me if I turned the cattle on maliciously for them to eat the mast; as, in fact, even if the mast were still there, and I[1] refused to let you[2] take it, I[1] should be liable to the action, just as if I[3] were to prevent someone[4] from taking away materials belonging to him which had been laid on my ground; and Pomponius's opinion meets with general approval, whether the mast is still on the ground or has been consumed. We may add that, if it is there still, I [being owner of the tree] can have an interdict *de glande legenda* (for gathering mast), so as to enable me to collect the mast every third day, giving the undertaking against any damage to ensue. 2. Where a man has caused the property to come to the hands of another he may be held to have taken fraudulent means to avoid possessing, provided, that is, he really acted with craft. 3. Where a man produces the property in a worse condition than it was in before, he still remains liable to

[1] In text "you." [2] In text "me." [3] In text "someone." [4] In text "me."

the action for production, according to Sabinus. This is, no doubt, true where the thing is transformed maliciously into a different kind of object, for instance, where a bowl is reduced to a rude mass of metal; here, even if the defendant produces the mass, he is liable to the action for production, as, by changing the form of the thing, he almost destroys the actual substance. 4. Marcellus has the following:—ten pieces of money are bequeathed to you on a condition, and the usufruct of [the same] ten to me in absolute terms; whereupon the heir, while the condition is still pending, pays me, the usufructuary, the aforesaid ten pieces, without calling upon me to give the [regular] undertaking; in this case the heir is liable to an action for production, on the ground that he took fraudulent means to avoid possessing, the fraud consisting in the fact that he omitted to call for the undertaking on the part of the usufructuary, with the result that your legacy was lost, as you were no longer able to bring a *vindicatio* for the pieces of money. Of course the action for production will only lie in case the condition of the legacy comes to pass. You might however have taken measures to protect yourself by stipulating for payment of the legacies, and, if you have done that, you will not require the action for production. But if the heir failed to make the usufructuary give the undertaking, because he did not know of your legacy, then, according to Marcellus, the action for production cannot be brought, on the ground that there was no fraud on the part of the heir; but the legatee will, he says, get relief by an action *in factum* against the usufructuary. 5. To produce, as far as the action for production is concerned, is to present a thing in the same legal plight as it was in when issue was joined, so that the party, having full access to the thing, can proceed with the action[1] which he desired to bring, *without his case*[1] *being made at all the worse after he brought it to an issue*, although the object of the action was not to have the thing handed over, but to have it produced. 6. Accordingly, if, when the defendant produces the thing, it has become his property by user since joinder of issue, he cannot be held to have produced it at all, as the plaintiff has made nothing of his action, consequently the defendant cannot be discharged, unless he is prepared to meet the demand as referred back to the original day, mesne profits to be thereupon valued

[1] Read *actionem* for *actione* and *causa postquam* for *casu quam*. Cf. M. The text translated by the words in italics is "*in nullo casu quam intendit læsa*," which is plainly corrupt. The general sense is clear, but the words in which it was expressed cannot be recovered.

according to the statute. 7. As however in this action the plaintiff gets the benefit of legal accessions, Sabinus held that the child of a female slave should be handed over too, and that, whether the mother had been with child at the time [of joinder of issue] or had conceived afterwards; and with this view Pomponius agrees. 8. Besides this, the judge ought in his estimate to take account of any dependent advantage that may have been lost owing to the thing not being produced or being produced too late; accordingly Neratius holds that the subject-matter of the valuation is the use which the thing would have been of to the plaintiff, not its actual value, and that use, he adds, will sometimes be of less value than that which the thing itself bears.

10 PAULUS (*on the Edict* 26) Where a person has been given a right of option to be exercised by a given day, and the trial has dragged on for so long a time that production is of no use, the plaintiff's interest must not be lost sight of[1]; but, if it was not the heir's fault that he did not produce the thing at the time when he joined issue, he must be dismissed from the action.

11 ULPIANUS (*on the Edict* 11) We may add that if, owing to a slave not being produced, an inheritance should be lost, it is thoroughly fair that, in exercise of the judge's powers, the injury so done (*damnum hereditatis*) should be taken into account in assessing damages. 1. We may next consider in what place the production should be made and at whose expense. According to Labeo it ought to be the place where the property was when issue was joined, but the property should be brought or conducted to the place where the proceedings were had, at the risk and expense of the plaintiff. A slave must, he says, no doubt be provided with food and clothing and taken care of by the person who possesses him. My own opinion however is that in some cases the plaintiff ought to undertake this too, as, for instance, where the slave usually maintained himself by means of his services or by a handicraft, but is at present compelled to be idle. Similarly if the slave is lodged with the officers of the Court (*apud officium*) with a view to his production, the person who applied for production will have to answer for his board, assuming that the one who possessed him was not in the habit of finding him food, but, if he was, then, as he

[1] *utilitas petitoris conservetur.* These words are no doubt corrupt. The real text must have told the reader that the plaintiff would get damages corresponding to the loss he suffered, and M. accordingly suggests a reading which would convey that meaning.

finds him food, he may as well make no difficulty about paying for his board. In some cases the party in possession is bound to make production on the spot at his own expense; for example, it may be a case where he had deliberately put things away in some secret place so as to make it all the more troublesome for the plaintiff to procure production; in such a case as this he will be bound to produce at his own risk and expense at the place where the proceedings are had, so that he may derive no benefit from his own underhand dealing. 2. Where a man is sued in respect of a number of different things, and, at the time of joinder of issue, he was in possession of all of them, then, even if he should subsequently, without any fraudulent contrivance, cease to possess some of them, judgment must be given against him, unless he produces all that he can.

12 PAULUS (*on the Edict* 26) This action may well lie where the object is to procure the production of a man whom the plaintiff desires to have judicially declared free (*in libertatem vindicare*). 1. A son under *potestas* is liable to this action, so long as he has it in his power to produce the thing. 2. If a man brings several actions for production [of the same thing], then, where a later action is brought on the same ground as an earlier one, according to Julianus, there will be a good *exceptio*; but where a man brings a *vindicatio*, and, after joinder of issue, he takes a transfer of the thing[1] from some person, this constitutes a fresh ground of action, and consequently the *exceptio* is no bar. A similar rule holds where a man intends to sue for theft and, with a view thereto, applies for production, and the property is stolen again. Lastly, if a man applies for production for the purpose of exercising an option, and, after joinder of issue, an option is given him by the testament of some other person, he can have another action for production. 3. If a man makes must from my grapes or oil from my olives or garments from my wool, knowing that these materials are the property of another, he will be liable to an action for production in respect of both [the things used and the resulting product], as the sound view is that whatever is made out of a person's property belongs to that person. 4. If, after joinder of issue, the slave dies, though it should be without any malice or negligence on the part of the possessor, still he must sometimes be ordered to pay a sum of money equivalent to the advantage which it would have been to the plaintiff that nothing should be done by

[1] Read *rem* after or for *eam*. Cf. M.

the defendant to prevent the slave being produced at the time when issue was joined; especially if it should appear that he died owing to some circumstance which would not have taken place if he had been then produced. 5. If, on some reasonable ground, it is impossible for the property to be produced at once, the defendant will have, on the judge's command, to give an undertaking that he will produce on a day named. 6. The heir is able to make use of the action in question not as heir but on his own personal account; and similarly the heir of the possessor is liable on his own personal account; consequently it is beside the question to inquire whether the right of action is allowed to the heir or against the heir. It is true that, in the case of malice on the defendant's part, the action must be allowed against the heir [as such], in case the inheritance has become the richer through it, for example, where the heir has received the price paid for the property.

13 GAIUS (*on the Edict of the Prætor Urbanus:* Tit. "On liberty cases") Where it is alleged that someone is detaining a free man in confinement, an interdict can be had against the man who is alleged to detain to make him produce the other; the action for production in such a case is held to be useless, as such an action is treated as only open to one who has a pecuniary interest.

14 POMPONIUS (*on Sabinus* 14) Where a husband has received a gift of money from his wife, and, knowing that the property in the money did not pass, he gives it away in payment for something that he has bought, he maliciously contrives not to possess it, and is consequently liable to an action *ad exhibendum.*

15 THE SAME (*on Sabinus* 18) Treasure belonging to me is buried in your land and you decline to allow me to dig it up. So long as you leave it where it is, I cannot properly, according to Labeo, have an action for theft or for production in respect of it, because you neither possess it nor have used fraudulent means to avoid possessing it, as it is in fact possible that you do not know that the treasure is within your land at all. There is however, he says, no injustice, if I swear that I do not make the demand with a vexatious intent, in my being allowed either an interdict or an action to procure that you shall not use force against me to prevent my digging up, taking up and carrying away the treasure in question, provided there is nothing done on my part to prevent the proper security being given you in connexion with my operations against apprehended damage. But if the treasure in question is so much actual stolen goods, I can have an action for theft.

16 PAULUS (*on Sabinus* 10) If a slave has anything in his hands, his owner is liable to a direct action for production, but if the slave, without the knowledge of his owner, has used fraudulent means to avoid having the thing, a noxal action ought to be allowed, either for theft or for malicious fraud in respect of the slave, but no *utilis actio* for production can be put in force.

17 ULPIANUS (*on all the Courts* 9) If a man produces a slave crippled or blinded, as far as the action for production goes, he ought to be discharged; he has produced the slave and there is nothing in a production such as described to prevent the main action; still the applicant can bring an action under the *lex Aquilia* for the damage in question.

18 THE SAME (*Opinions* 6) When a note of hand is made of no account by payment and pledges given are released, there is still nothing to prevent the creditor suing for production of the documents connected with the debt by some other person than the debtor.

19 PAULUS (*Epitomes of Alfenus* 4) An action for production can be brought by anyone who has an interest in bringing it. A man however asked for an opinion as to whether this action would enable him to procure the production of his opponent's accounts, which he said he had a great interest in having produced. The answer was that the law of the land ought not to be used vexatiously and words ought not to be captiously interpreted; the proper course being to consider the intention of anything that was said. Indeed, on the principle contended for, a man who was anxious to study some branch of learning might say that he had an interest in the production of such and such books, because, if they were produced, he might become a more learned and a better man by reading them.

20 ULPIANUS (*Rules* 2) In cases of delicts committed by slaves, an action for production can be had with a view to examination by torture to compel the disclosure[1] of their accomplices.

[1] Read *indicandos* for *vindicandos*. Cf. M.

ELEVENTH BOOK.

I.

On administering Interrogatories before the Magistrate and on Interrogatory Actions.

1 Callistratus (*Monitorian Edict* 2) The heir should always be interrogated before the magistrate (*in jure*) as to what fraction of the estate it is for which he is heir, whenever legal proceedings are being taken against him and the plaintiff is uncertain what the fraction is for which the person whom he proposes to sue is heir. The case in which an interrogatory is necessary is where the action is *in personam* and [even then] only where the subject of the suit is a liquidated demand, as otherwise the plaintiff, not being aware what the fraction is for which the opposite party is heir to the deceased, may on some occasion make a demand in excess and so suffer some loss. 1. At the present day however interrogatory actions are not employed, as no one is compellable to answer any questions before the trial as to his legal position, and consequently people have less recourse to such actions and they have fallen into disuse. Only statements which are made by the other side in the course of a trial are available as evidence on behalf of those engaged in litigation, whether it be in cases of succession or of other matters which come in question in legal proceedings.

2 Ulpianus (*on the Edict* 22) The reason why the Prætor propounded his Edict on the subject of interrogatories was that he knew that it is difficult for a person who sues an heir or *bonorum possessor* to prove anyone to be heir or *bonorum possessor*;

3 Paulus (*on the Edict* 17) as it is often hard to show that entry has been made on the inheritance.

4 ULPIANUS (*on the Edict* 22) The Prætor desired to bind the person who is being sued by his own answer as given at the trial, so that, whether he confesses the truth or tells a lie, he may take the consequences on his own shoulders, and at the same time that he may be informed[1] by means of the interrogatory what is the fraction of the estate in respect of which any given person is heir. 1. With regard to the words in the Edict:—"A man who answers an interrogatory '*in jure*,'" this must be understood to mean answers before a magistrate of the Roman people or a governor of a province or any other judge; *jus*, he says, meaning simply the place where the judge has placed himself for the purpose of exercising jurisdiction or giving judgment, including the case of his doing so at his own home or while on his way.

5 GAIUS (*on the Provincial Edict* 3) When a man is interrogated as to whether he is heir or in respect of what fraction of the estate he is so, or whether he exercises *potestas* over someone on whose account a noxal action is brought, he ought to procure an order for further time to consider his answer, because, if he should make a wrong declaration, he is put at a disadvantage;

6 ULPIANUS (*on the Edict* 22) besides which, as it is in the interest of deceased persons (*sic*) that they should have someone to succeed them, so also is it in the interest of those who are living that they should not be hurried, so long as they are reasonably considering the question [of taking up the succession]. 1. Sometimes a man who is asked whether he is heir is not compelled to answer, for instance, where he is made defendant to an action in which his heirship is the matter in dispute; this was laid down by the Divine Hadrian; because otherwise, if the defendant denied that he was heir, he might be prejudicing his own case, or, if he said that he was heir, he might find himself entangled even if he should lose the inheritance.

7 THE SAME (*on the Edict* 18) If a man, on being interrogated before the magistrate as to whether a four-footed animal which has done *pauperies* is his, should reply [in the affirmative[2]], he is liable.

8 PAULUS (*on the Edict* 22) If a man, on being interrogated as to a slave who has done damage, replies that the slave is his, he

[1] M. would like to read *certioremur* for *certioretur*, on the ground, no doubt, that the person to be informed must be the plaintiff.

[2] M.

will be liable under the *lex Aquilia* as owner, and, if the action is brought against the man so answering, the real owner is freed from liability to the action.

9 ULPIANUS (*on the Edict* 22) If a man declares that he is heir, without any interrogation being addressed to him, he is treated as though he had been interrogated. 1. When we speak of a man being interrogated, we must understand this to mean not only by the Prætor but by the other party equally well. 2. But if a slave is interrogated, this is no interrogatory at all, any more than if a slave should interrogate. 3. One person must not be compelled to answer for another to the question whether the latter is heir; a man ought in a trial to be examined about his own case, that is, if he is defendant in the action. 4. Celsus tells us (*Dig.* 5) that if a person who defends an action on behalf of another, on being interrogated in the trial as to whether the person whose defence he is carrying on is heir, or for what fraction he is so, makes an untrue answer, he, such volunteer defendant, will be responsible to the plaintiff, but this will not prejudice the case of the person whose defence he has undertaken; nor is there any doubt that Celsus's opinion is sound. This being the case, it is worth considering, if he declines to answer, whether he is defending the action; and it certainly is only consistent to say that he is not, as he is not defending it fully. 5. When a man, in answer to an interrogation, replies that he is heir, without adding in respect of what fraction, he must be taken to have replied that he is heir to the whole, unless the question asked was, for example, whether he was heir in respect of half the estate and he answered "I am heir"; as, in that case, I should rather hold that he answered in the sense of the question asked. 6. A point which is raised is this:—Is a man compellable to answer whether he is heir by testament [or *ab intestato*[1]], or whether the inheritance came to him directly or through persons who are subject to his *potestas*, or through some one to whom he is heir? As to all this, the Prætor must form a conclusion in a general way, when such a question is asked, as to whether the party is bound to answer in what right he is heir, so that, if he should find that it is of great importance to the plaintiff, he may order that a fuller answer be given. This will apply in the case not merely of heirs but of successors by Prætorian title. 7. Add to the above that we have it from Julianus that a man to whom an inheritance has been (? was to be) handed over [in pur-

[1] M.

suance of a testamentary trust] is bound to say, if interrogated before the magistrate, whether the inheritance has been so handed over. 8. In the case of an action *de peculio* [it is held that] the father or owner cannot be called upon to answer whether he has the son or the slave in his *potestas*, as the only question asked is whether the *peculium* is in the hands of the person against whom the action is brought.

10 PAULUS (*on the Edict* 48) It is not beside the purpose that, when people wish to make a stipulation with a man against *damnum infectum*, they should interrogate him before the magistrate as to whether the house or the place from which the mischief is apprehended belongs to him, and to what extent, so that, in case he should say that the tenement is not his and decline to give the undertaking, he may be compelled either to give it up, or, if[1] he chooses to resist, to hand it over on the ground that his behaviour is fraudulent.

11 ULPIANUS (*on the Edict* 22) Sometimes too a man will be compellable to answer an inquiry as to his age. 1. If a man, not being heir, should on being interrogated, answer that he is heir as to a part, he may thereupon be sued as if he were heir as to that part; in fact credit will be given him against himself. 2. Where a man who is heir as to a quarter, or, say, is not heir at all, answers that he is heir to the whole, he may be sued in an action framed on the view that he is heir to the whole. 3. Where a man who is heir as to half says that he is heir as to a quarter, the punishment to which he will have to submit for his untruth is that he will be sued in an action for the whole; he had no right to tell a lie by declaring himself to be heir for a smaller portion [of the estate than he really inherited]. It may happen however that he believes on reasonable grounds that he is heir for a smaller part than he really is; for example, what if he acquired a share by accrual without knowing it, or he was appointed heir for an uncertain portion? why should he in such a case suffer by his answer? 4. Again, where a man in the Prætor's Court gives no answer, what he incurs is that, if an action is set on foot, he can be sued for the whole, just as if he had declared that he was not heir; a man who declines to answer at all is contumacious, and the penalty which he will have to suffer for his contumacy is that of being sued for the whole, just as he would have been if he had declared that he was not heir; the fact is that he is treated as

[1] Ins. *si* before *resistendum*. M.

guilty of contempt of the Prætor. 5. With regard to the Prætor's expression—"declines to answer at all," later authorities took his words in the following sense,—a man, they said, is held to decline to answer at all who does not answer the precise question he is asked, that is word for word. 6. Where a man is interrogated as to whether he is sole heir and replies that he is heir in part, then, if he is really heir as to half, the law is that he shall not suffer by this answer; this is an indulgent rule to apply. 7. It makes no difference, when a man is interrogated, whether he gives a negative answer or no answer at all, or gives an obscure answer so as to leave the interrogator in doubt. 8. There is no question that when a man answers an interrogatory he will be relieved on express cause shown; thus, if a man is asked whether he is heir to his father and he answers that he is[1], and, after that, a testament is produced by which it turns out that he was disinherited, it is quite proper that he should be relieved. This indeed is maintained by Celsus, who puts it on a different principle, viz. that facts which were unknown at the time but are discovered afterwards afford good ground for relief; for instance, testamentary papers might be hidden or taken to a distance and be afterwards discovered; why should this prejudice a man who stated in his answer what appeared to him to be true at the time[2]? I should apply the same principle to a case where a man answers that he is heir, but subsequently the testament is pronounced to be a forgery or inofficious or void; in such a case the answer was given honestly, but the party answering was misled by the document. 9. When a man answers an interrogatory, it puts him on the same footing of liability as he would be on if he were bound by a contract on which he can be taken to task, assuming that he is interrogated by a litigating party; but even if it is the Prætor who interrogates him, nothing turns on the authority of the Prætor; what is to the point is the answer of the party, or, [let us say,] his untrue statement. 10. Where a man declares that he is not heir in consequence of a reasonable mistake which he fell under, allowance ought to be made for him. 11. Even where a man gives an untrue answer without any intention to deceive, but still through negligence, the proper rule is that he should not be held liable, unless the negligence comes very near malice. 12. Celsus tells us that a man is allowed to revoke his answer, if the revocation does not put the plaintiff at a disadvantage; and this I should say is perfectly sound, especially where

[1] Ins. *esse* before *responderit*.

[2] *præsentia verum* for *præsentiarum*.

a man does something of this kind in consequence of fuller information subsequently received, being, for example, better advised as to his legal position by means of documents or of letters written by his friends.

12 PAULUS (*on the Edict* 17) If a son declines his father's inheritance, and then, in answer to an interrogatory before the magistrate declares that he is heir, he will be held liable; the very answer is deemed equivalent to acting as heir. But if a son, after declining the inheritance, gives no answer at all to the interrogatory, he must be protected, as the Prætor does not treat as heir a person who has really declined the inheritance. 1. Any *exceptio* which can be used in bar of an action put in train before the *judex* against [ordinary] defendants can equally be used by a man who is sued on his answer to an interrogatory, *e.g.* the *exceptio* of [subsequent] informal agreement, previous decision, and so on.

13 THE SAME (*on Plautius* 2) Persons who confess falsely by way of answer are only bound thereupon in cases where there is a good right of action existing against someone or other in virtue of the matter about which they were interrogated, as the rule is that where some other person would be liable to the action, supposing he were owner, the parties who make the confession thereby take the liability upon themselves. Accordingly, if someone is under the *potestas* of his own father, and I [in answer to an interrogatory] declare that he is my son, [the law is] that I am only held liable where his age is such that he might possibly be my son; as false confessions[, to be taken into account,] must accord with the facts of nature. *A consequence of this would be that if I answer on behalf of the* paterfamilias, *I am not liable*[1]. 1. A man who answers that someone who is really a *paterfamilias* is his slave is not liable to a noxal action; and, even if I am having in good faith the services of a free man, no noxal action can be brought against me; moreover, if such an action should be brought, full right will still remain to proceed against the man who actually committed the offence.

14 JAVOLENUS (*Extracts from Cassius* 9) Where issue has been joined in a noxal action, and, while the case is proceeding, the man in respect of whose act it was brought is judicially declared to be a free man, the case must be dismissed, and the plaintiff will take

[1] In M.'s opinion this clause has got into the text by mistake, and was really an annotation relating to what follows.

no advantage by any interrogation before the magistrate that he may have made, because, [true as it is that,] when a man has a right of action against another in respect of some individual, he may be able to transfer the liability [arising from the act] of that individual to the person who confesses before the magistrate that the individual in question is his slave, for instance, who makes such a confession with reference to the slave of another man; still, there being no right of action at all against a third person in respect of a free man, it follows that no liability can be transferred to anyone by means of any interrogatory or confession. This being the case, the result will be that no action can ever have been rightly brought in respect of a free man against a person who made a confession [in virtue thereof]. 1. The general rule is that confessions are upheld only in cases in which the matter confessed is something consistent with law and nature.

15 POMPONIUS (*on Sabinus* 18) If, before some inheritance is entered upon, I declare on interrogation that a slave who is part of the estate belongs to me, I am liable, as an inheritance is treated as an owner. 1. If a person confesses on interrogation before the magistrate that some slave is his own, and then the slave dies, the person who so answered is not liable, just as, if the slave had really been his, he would not have been liable for him after his death.

16 ULPIANUS (*on the Edict* 37) If a slave is taken prisoner by the enemy, and some person on interrogation before the magistrate answers with reference to him that he is in his *potestas*, however much ground for hesitation there may be founded on the rules of law as to *postliminium*, still I do not think there is any room for a noxal action, as slaves in such a case are not in their old owners' *potestas*. 1. Although the law goes as far as this, that a man may become liable even by confessing another person's slave to be his own, nevertheless it is very properly held that a man is only liable in this way where it was possible that he should have been owner, but, if he was incapable of acquiring such ownership, he is not liable.

17 THE SAME (*on the Edict* 38) If the slave is not the property of one sole owner, but of several, and they all have declared falsely that he is not in their *potestas*, or some of them have done so, or they have used fraudulent means to avoid having him in their *potestas*, each of them will be liable for the whole damages, just as each would be liable, if they really had the slave in their

potestas; but a single owner who uses no fraudulent means to avoid having the slave in his *potestas*, or makes no false declaration, will not be liable.

18 JULIANUS (*on Urseius Ferox* 4) A man who was heir to the extent of half the estate of a deceased person desired to defend an action on behalf of his fellow-heir in his absence, and in order to be able to avoid the burden of giving security [for the other], declared that he was sole heir, and judgment was pronounced against him. The plaintiff asked whether, seeing that this person was insolvent, he could have an order rescinding the previous judgment and allowing him an action against the actual co-heir. Proculus replied that the judgment might be rescinded and the action brought, and this is correct.

19 PAPINIANUS (*Questions* 8) If a son who appears on behalf of his father declines to answer when interrogated, the case must proceed in all respects as if he had not been interrogated.

20 PAULUS (*Questions* 2) Where a man answers that a slave who belongs to another is his own, then, if he is sued in a noxal action, the real owner is thereby discharged. This case differs from that of a man who confesses that he killed a slave who was really killed by someone else, or who declares [falsely] that he is heir; in this case the man who did the deed—or the real heir—is not discharged. There is no inconsistency in the above; in the former case there are two persons liable through the act of the slave in the way in which there are two held to be liable in the case of a slave owned in common, in which, if one is sued, the other is discharged; but a man who confesses that he killed or wounded is liable on his own account, and yet the offence of the man who did the deed ought not to go unpunished because of the liability of the one who confessed, unless the latter was taking up the defence on behalf of the man who did the deed or his heir and met the action on that footing; in that case an *exceptio* is allowed and the action will be barred, because the defendant can get back whatever he paid by an action of *negotia gesta* or *mandatum*. The same rule applies to a man who declares himself heir at the request of the real heir or who for any other reason desires to defend the action on his behalf. 1. If a man is asked before the magistrate whether he possesses a given *fundus*, I wish to know whether he can be compelled to give in his answer the exact share in respect of which he is in possession. The answer was:—We

read in Javolenus that the possessor of an estate is compellable to declare the exact share for which he possesses it, so that, if he is in possession in respect of a small share, the plaintiff may be put in possession of the land for the remaining share in respect of which there is no defence offered. 2. A similar rule holds where people give an undertaking as to *damnum infectum*; this is another case in which the party ought to declare what is the extent of his share in the tenement, so as to enable the applicant to frame the stipulation accordingly; here the penalty for refusing to give the assurance is that the applicant assumes possession, so that this is a reason why it is requisite to know whether the other party is in possession.

21 ULPIANUS (*on the Edict* 22) Wherever equitable considerations move the judge to allow it, there can be no doubt that it is also right that an interrogatory should be had.

22 SCÆVOLA (*Digest* 4) In answer to the Imperial Procurator who was interrogating in a matter relating to a debt due to the *fiscus* from a person deceased, one of the sons, who had not got an order for *bonorum possessio* and was not heir, declared that he was heir; is he liable at the suit of other creditors as having answered to an interrogatory? The answer was that a man cannot be sued upon his answer by persons who had not interrogated him before the magistrate.

II.

WHEN VARIOUS MATTERS ARE HEARD BY THE SAME JUDGE.

1 POMPONIUS (*on Sabinus* 13) If an action *familiæ erciscundæ* is brought among several parties and an action *de communi dividundo* or *finium regundorum* among the same, they ought to choose the same judge [for both actions]; and besides that, in order that the co-heirs or co-owners may be the better able to meet, they ought all to attend at the same place.

2 PAPINIANUS (*Questions* 2) When one out of several tutors is sued because the others are not substantial persons, on the application of that one, they may all be ordered to appear before the same judge. This is laid down in Imperial rescripts.

III.

ON CORRUPTING A SLAVE.

1 ULPIANUS (*on the Edict* 23) The Prætor says:—"Where a man is alleged to have harboured a slave of either sex belonging to another or induced him or her maliciously to act in any way with intent to deteriorate his or her character, I will allow an action against him for twice what the matter comes to." 1. A man who is a *bona fide* purchaser of the slave will not be liable under this Edict, nor[1] can he himself bring an action for corrupting the slave, as he has no interest in the slave not being corrupted; in fact, it is clear that, if his right to sue were admitted, two persons would have a good right of action for corruption of the slave, which is absurd. It may be added that, according to the received opinion, the action cannot be brought by one who has *bona fide* the services of a free man. 2. With regard to the word "harboured" (*recepisse*), as used by the Prætor, what this is taken to refer to is the case of a man taking in another man's slave at his own place of abode; "harbouring" is, strictly speaking, affording a slave a refuge with a view to concealing him, whether it be on the party's own ground or in a place or building belonging to another. 3. To induce (*persuadere*) is *to compel and constrain a person to obey you*[2]; but "induce" is a kind of neutral term, as the incitement may be applied by giving good advice as well as bad; accordingly the Prætor adds the words "maliciously" and "with intent to deteriorate the slave's character." So that one who solicits a slave to do or to plan something objectionable must be the kind of person who is held up to observation in this Edict. 4. Is a man, however, liable only where he has driven a well-conducted slave to commit an offence, or is he equally so where he instigates a bad slave, or shows a bad slave the way to commit it? The truer view is that even where he shows a bad slave how to commit an offence he is liable. Indeed, if the slave had made up his mind independently to run away or to commit a theft, and the

[1] del. *quia*. M.

[2] The Latin text here is "persuadere autem est plus quam compelli atque cogi sibi parere." These words having no meaning, I have ventured to follow a note in the Basilica and substitute the clause I have given in italics; in other words to omit *plus quam* and turn the two passive infinitives into the active.

party in question is shown to have applauded his design, he is liable; the slave's bad disposition ought not to be made worse still by approbation. Accordingly, whether a man makes a good slave bad or makes a bad slave worse, he will be held to corrupt him. 5. A person too makes a slave worse who induces him to commit wrongful damage or theft or to run away or to instigate a slave belonging to some other person to commit such offences, or to make his *peculium* undistinguishable, or to go after girls, or to loiter about, or to give himself up to magical arts, or to spend too much time at public shows, or to engage in riots, or again who induces [a slave who is] a bailiff, either by words or bribes, to mutilate [or] falsify his master's accounts or even to confuse an account put in his hands,

2 PAULUS (*on the Edict* 19) or who encourages a slave to live expensively, or to be insubordinate, or induces him to submit to *stuprum*.

3 ULPIANUS (*on the Edict* 23) By adding the expression "maliciously" the Prætor stigmatizes craft on the part of the person who induces; whereas if a man deteriorates a slave's character without wrongful intention he incurs no stigma; and he is not liable where he does it for a practical joke. 1. Hence arises this question: suppose a man incites the slave of another to climb on a roof or to go down a well, and the slave accordingly climbs up or goes down, and so falls and breaks his leg or breaks any limb or is killed, will the party be liable? The answer is that, if he did it without malice, he is not liable, but, if it was done maliciously, he is;

4 PAULUS (*on the Edict* 19) but the more convenient plan is to hold him liable to an *utilis* [*actio* framed on the] *lex Aquilia*.

5 ULPIANUS (*on the Edict* 23) The word "maliciously" must be applied equally in the case of one who harbours a slave, so that a man is not liable unless he harbours maliciously; if he harboured the slave with a view to keeping him safely on his owner's behoof or from motives of humanity or out of pity or on some other approved and lawful ground, he is not liable. 1. If anyone maliciously induces a slave whom he took for a free man to do anything, I should say that he ought to be held liable, as one who corrupts a slave whom he believes to be free commits a still greater offence [than if he knew him to be a slave], consequently, if the man really is a slave, the party will be liable. 2. The action is for

twofold damages, even where the defendant admits his guilt, though the Aquilian action only inflicts that penalty on one who denies. 3. Where the offender is a slave of either sex, the action is allowed with the option of surrender for *noxa*. 4. The action relates to the date at which the slave was corrupted or harboured, and not the date of the application, so that if the slave should be dead or have been disposed of or manumitted, the action may none the less be brought, and, the right to bring it having once accrued, it is not lost by manumission,

6 PAULUS (*on the Edict* 19) as, for the purposes of this action, an estimate is made of elements of value existing in past time[1];

7 ULPIANUS (*on the Edict* 23) as, of course, bad slaves may chance to get their freedom, besides which very often something may occur afterwards which furnishes a good ground for manumission.

8 PAULUS (*on the Edict* 19) The heir of the party whose slave was corrupted has the same right to bring this action, and that not only where the slave is still included in the estate of the deceased, but even where he has been taken out of it, for example, where he was left by way of legacy.

9 ULPIANUS (*on the Edict* 23) Where a man corrupts a slave which he and I have in common, the question is raised in Julianus (*Dig.* 9) whether he can be held liable to this action; and that writer says that he is liable to the action at the hands of his co-owner, moreover he can be sued in an action *communi dividundo*, or *pro socio*, so Julianus holds, if the co-owners are partners. We may however ask why it is that Julianus puts a co-owner in a worse position when he sues another co-owner than he is in when he sues a stranger. In the case of an action against a stranger the right of action is equally good, whether the defendant harboured the slave or corrupted him, but, if it is against a co-owner, it is only good where the defendant corrupted the slave, the alternative ground [viz. that of harbouring] is not admitted. It may be however that Julianus thought that the other ground could not apply as against a fellow-owner, as no one can harbour his own slave; still, if he took him in in order to conceal him, it may be argued that he is liable. 1. If I have the usufruct in a slave and you have the bare property, then, if the slave is deteriorated

[1] Paulus's words are applicable only to the last remark but one preceding. Cf. M.

by me, you can take proceedings against me, if the deterioration is your doing, I can bring an *utilis actio*; as this action is available in all cases of corruption, and the usufructuary clearly has an interest in the slave in whom he has the usufruct being well conducted. An *utilis actio* is similarly open to the usufructuary if some other person than the bare proprietor harbours or corrupts the slave. 2. The action is allowed for double what the case amounts to; 3. but it is open to question whether, in determining the amount, an estimate should be made of such damage only as is done to the slave in body or character, in short, of the extent to which the value of the slave is diminished, or whether other things should be considered as well. Neratius holds that the person who corrupted should be ordered to pay damages equivalent to the extent to which the slave's value is diminished by the fact that he was corrupted[1].

10 PAULUS (*on the Edict* 19) The damages to be recovered include the value of things which the slave took away with him, as all loss is multiplied by two, and it makes no difference whether the things were brought to the defendant or to another or even consumed; as it is more in accordance with justice that the original author of the offence should be held liable than that inquiry should be made for the party to whom the things were brought.

11 ULPIANUS (*on the Edict* 23) Neratius holds that thefts committed subsequently form no item in the assessment. This view I believe to be sound; the very words of the Edict—"what *that* matter comes to"—comprise all the mischief done. 1. I induce a slave to deface notes of hand given by his master's debtors. No doubt I am liable to the action; but if, having got into the habit of committing such offences, he proceeds to purloin, falsify or efface accounts or other similar documents, the proper rule is that the party who corrupted him is not liable on the ground of these acts. 2. Although however there is a good right of action for corrupting a slave in respect of things which are purloined, still there is an action for theft allowed as well, as the things must be held to be taken away with the aid and encouragement of the party inciting; and the plaintiff does not exhaust his means of redress by bringing one of the two actions, as the one leaves the other still open. Julianus lays down a similar rule as to a man who harbours a slave

[1] I have substituted *corruptus* for *subpertus*. This last word is not Latin at all.

and so conceals him and deteriorates his character [besides inducing him to steal]; the offence of thieving is distinct from that of deteriorating the character of a slave; and, besides being exposed to an action on these two heads, he is also liable to be sued in a *condictio* (personal action to recover the stolen goods), as even though the party injured should have recovered the slave by a *condictio*, and penal damages by an action for theft, still he has a good right to indemnification by an action for corruption of a slave,

12 PAULUS (*on the Edict* 19) since the defendant is still subject to this obligation, even after the property is restored.

13 ULPIANUS (*on the Edict* 23) This action can be brought at any distance of time, there is no limitation, and it is open to the heir and to successors of every kind; but it will not be allowed against the heir of the offender, as it is a penal action. 1. A man is equally liable to the action if he corrupts a slave who is part of the unclaimed estate of a deceased person; and he can also be sued as a plunderer in a "petition to recover an inheritance,"

14 PAULUS (*on the Edict* 9) so that the petition for recovery of an inheritance may have as wide a scope as this action. 1. There is no provision under this Edict for the case of a son or a daughter under *potestas* being corrupted, as the action established is one for corrupting a slave who is part of a man's property, and for a case in which[1] the proprietor can show that his means are reduced, though the honour and good name of his family are unaffected; but there is a good right to an *utilis actio* for an amount which the judge can be called upon to determine, as everybody has an interest in the character of his children not being corrupted. 2. If a slave which you and I have in common corrupts a slave who belongs to me in severalty, Sabinus holds that there is no right of action against a co-owner, any more than if my own slave had corrupted a fellow-slave. Again, if a slave owned by two in common corrupts the slave of a third person, it is a fair question whether there has to be one action against both co-owners, or each may equally well be sued separately, as in the case of other offences committed by slaves; but the better opinion is that each owner is liable for the whole, but, if one pays, the other is discharged. 3. If a slave in whom I have a usufruct corrupts a slave who belongs to me, I have a right to sue the bare proprietor. 4. A person who has pledged a slave for debt can bring this action in respect of him. 5. In this

[1] Ins. *ubi* before *pauperiorem*.

action the twofold damages are not something over and above the recovery of property (*i.e.* of the slave); what is doubled is the amount of loss incurred. 6. This being the case, the rule follows thereupon that if you induce my slave to commit a theft on Titius, you not only are liable for the amount to which the slave's character is deteriorated, but also for whatever I shall have to give Titius. 7. Moreover you are liable to be sued by me not only if the slave does me a mischief at your instigation, but even if he does it to a stranger, on the ground, that is, that I have to answer for it under the *lex Aquilia*; or, again, if I am liable to an action on a contract of hiring at the hands of someone because I let out a slave to him and the slave was deteriorated by your act, you will be liable on this ground, and so with any similar cases. 8. The measure of damages in this action is the extent to which the slave's value is reduced, and that the judge may be called upon to determine. 9. Sometimes indeed the slave becomes[1] of no value at all, so that it is not worth while having such a slave. In such a case, then, does it follow that the instigator is compellable to pay the whole value the slave bore and the owner has the slave over and above; or ought the owner to be compelled to hand over the slave and accept what he is worth? The true rule is that the owner must be allowed to elect whether he would like best to retain the slave and to accept damages equivalent to double the extent to which the slave is deteriorated, or to hand over the slave, if he is in a position to do so, and take his value, and, if he is not in a position to do so, still to take his value, and to assign to the instigator his rights of action for recovery of the slave, so that the latter can sue at his own risk. Of course what is said as to handing over the slave only applies where the slave is alive when the proceedings are brought. Suppose however the slave was manumitted before the proceedings were brought. It will not lie in the defendant's mouth to say in open court that the reason why he manumitted the slave was that he did not wish to have him in his house, his object being to get the money and to have a freedman too.

15 GAIUS (*provincial Edict* 6) It is a complete case of corrupting a slave's character if he is induced to treat his owner with contempt.

16 ALFENUS VARUS (*Digest* 2) The owner of a slave who had used the slave as steward manumitted him; after this he made

[1] Read *fit* for *sit*. Cf. M.

him produce his accounts, which the man was not able to make good, and his patron found that he had spent the money in the company of some woman of no character; the question was asked whether the patron could sue this woman for corrupting a slave, the slave being by this time free. The answer was that he could, and that so he might for theft too in respect of any money which the slave had put in her hands.

17 MARCELLUS (*Rules* 4) A husband is allowed an action against his wife on the ground of corrupting a slave, even while the married state still lasts, but only for the simple value, in consideration of matrimony.

IV.

ON FUGITIVE SLAVES.

1 ULPIANUS (*on the Edict* 1) A man who has concealed a fugitive slave is a thief. 1. The Senate laid down that fugitive slaves are not to be admitted into parks nor to be sheltered by the overseers or agents of landowners, and it prescribed a fine; but if any persons should within twenty days have either restored such slaves to their owners or brought them up before the magistrates, it excused their previous behaviour; indeed, further on in the same enactment, impunity is promised to anyone who hands over fugitive slaves to their owners or to the magistrate within the prescribed time after finding any such on his ground. 2. The decree allowed both soldiers and civilians a right of entry on the estates of Senators or private persons for the purpose of following up a runaway slave, in fact the *lex Fabia* and a decree of the Senate passed in the consulship of Modestus were enacted with a similar object. It was further laid down that persons who wished to search for fugitive slaves should have letters given them addressed to the magistrates, a fine of a hundred solidi being prescribed at the same time to be payable by the latter, if, on receiving such letters they declined to assist the persons engaged in the search; and a similar penalty was imposed on anyone who refused to allow a search to be made on his ground. Moreover there is a rescript of the Divine Marcus and Commodus of general application by which it is expressly laid down that governors, magistrates and

police are bound to assist any owner in[1] seeking out runaway slaves and that they must give them up if they find them, also that persons on whose ground the slaves are in hiding are to be punished if any unlawful behaviour is brought home to them. 3. Every person whatever who apprehends a runaway slave is bound to bring him forward publicly, 4. and the magistrates are very properly enjoined to keep any such slaves carefully in custody, so as to prevent their escape. 5. Under the term "fugitive" must be included a slave who is given to roving. But, according to Labeo (*on the Edict* 1), the term does not comprise a slave who is simply born of a runaway mother. 6. A slave is deemed to be brought forward publicly if he is handed over to the municipal magistrates or government officers. 7. Careful custody will allow putting the slave in irons. 8. The custody is continued until the time when the slaves are brought before the Prefect of the Watch or the Governor. 8 *a*. The magistrates must be informed of the names and marks of the fugitive slaves and as to who it is to whom any one of them professes to belong, so that they may be the more easily identified and secured; and the term "mark" will include scars. This direction applies equally where the case is advertised by means of a written notice in a public place or in a consecrated temple[2].

2 CALLISTRATUS (*Hearings* 6) Slaves who are simply runaways should be restored to their owners; but, where they affect the station of free men, the practice is to inflict severe punishment.

3 ULPIANUS (*on the office of Proconsul* 7) The Divine Pius laid down by rescript that, where a man desires to search for a runaway slave in someone else's ground, he may apply to the Governor, who must give him a letter, and, if the case requires it, an officer, so that he can get permission to enter and make a search, and that the Governor can in addition inflict a penalty on anyone who should refuse to allow the search to be made. Moreover the Divine Marcus delivered an oration before the Senate by which he authorized those who desire to search for fugitives and to examine[3] the sleeping-places or any traces of those who concealed them to enter on land of the Emperor or of Senators or private persons.

4 PAULUS (*Sentences* 1) Harbour-masters and police-officers, if any fugitive slaves are apprehended, do well to keep them in

[1] Ins. *in* before *inquirendis*. Cf. M.
[2] For *ædes* read *æde sacra*. Cf. M.
[3] Read *scrutandi* for *scrutari*. Cf. M.

custody. Municipal magistrates, on arrest of such slaves, send them on securely to the office of the governor of the province or the proconsul.

5 TRYPHONINUS (*Disputations* 1) If a fugitive slave gives himself up to fight in the amphitheatre, he cannot, even by exposing himself to the risk thereby incurred, which only amounts to peril of death, escape from the legal control of his owner; there being a rescript of the Divine Pius enjoining that such slaves should without further consideration be restored to their owners, either before or after a combat with beasts; as very often they have either misappropriated money or committed some more serious offence, and they would rather give themselves up to fight in the arena, so as to avoid inquiry or lawful punishment; accordingly they must be surrendered.

V.

ON GAMBLERS.

1 ULPIANUS (*on the Edict* 23) The Prætor says:—if anyone beats a man in whose house it appears that a game with dice has been carried on or damages his property, or, on a similar occasion, something has been taken out of his house[1] by anyone, I will not allow an action. Where a man uses violence for the purpose of a game with dice I will punish the offender as the particular case may require. 1. If parties to the game rob one another, an action will not be refused for *vi bona rapta* (goods taken with violence), it is only the entertainer that the Prætor says shall not be protected, not the gamesters as well, though indeed these too may well be thought unworthy of consideration. 2. It should be observed further that if an entertainer has been beaten or has suffered damage, the Prætor refuses relief irrespective of the place or time at which it happened, but [the rule about] theft is [that it is] committed with impunity in the house where and at the time when the gambling was carried on, and that although the person who commits *any one of the offences named*[2] should himself not have been engaged in the game. There is no doubt that by the word "house" we must understand habitation and place of abode. 3. With regard to the

[1] Read *tempore e domo* for *tempore dolo*. Cf. M.

[2] *quid eorum*. The writer ought to have said *furtum*, the theft, and left the reader to infer the generalization, or else have recast the sentence altogether.

Prætor's refusal to allow an action for theft, we may consider whether this refers to the penal action only, or includes the case of the party wishing to sue for production, or to bring a *vindicatio* or *condictio*. It is maintained in Pomponius that it is the penal action alone that is refused, but with this I do not agree, the Prætor's words simply are "if anything is misappropriated I will not allow an action." 4. He proceeds "where a man uses violence for the purpose of a game with dice, I will punish the offender as the particular case may require." This clause refers to punishment to be inflicted on the person who compels anyone to play, and requires that the party should be ordered to pay a fine or should be sent to the Quarries or put in chains as a criminal,

2 PAULUS (*on the Edict* 19) as it is a well known occurrence for people to coerce others to play, sometimes doing so from the very first, and sometimes compelling the winner to continue playing, where they have themselves lost. 1. A decree of the Senate forbade playing for money, except where the contest is one of throwing javelins or pikes, or running, leaping, wrestling or fighting for the sake of winning distinction;

3 MARCIANUS (*Rules* 5) where this is being done, the Titian, Publician and Cornelian statutes in fact authorize wagering, but there are others which prohibit this practice, where the contest is not with a view to winning distinction.

4 PAULUS (*on the Edict* 19) Where eatables are put on the table at a feast, it is allowable to gamble for them with dice[1]. 1. If a slave or a *filiusfamilias* loses, the owner or father, as the case may be, can recover what is paid thereupon. Conversely, if money is paid to a slave, an action *de peculio* will be allowed against the owner, not a noxal action, because it is founded on *negotia gesta*; but the defendant is not to be compelled to hand over more than the amount which there is in the *peculium* in consequence of the payment. 2. There is an *utilis actio* founded on this Edict which is allowed against a *paterfamilias* or a patron to recover money paid on a loss in gaming.

[1] Read *alea* for *familia*. Cf. M.

VI.

WHERE A SURVEYOR MAKES A FALSE REPORT AS TO DIMENSIONS.

1 ULPIANUS (*on the Edict* 24) The Prætor offers an action *in factum* against a land surveyor. People must avoid being deceived by surveyors, every one has an interest in getting a true report of the dimensions of land, where, for instance, a dispute has arisen about boundaries, or a vendor or purchaser wishes to know the area of the land which is being sold. The ground on which the Prætor promises this action is that the old lawyers did not regard the agreement made with a person such as the one in question as a contract of *locatio* and *conductio*, but held rather that his services were given as a favour, for which the payment which he received was a recompense and, for that reason, was called honorary; indeed, if an action is brought as upon a contract of *locatio*, it must be held that the issue raised is beside the mark. 1. The only ground for the action is positive malice (*dolus malus*), a surveyor was deemed to be most amply kept in control, though he were liable to be sued on the mere ground of positive malice, being a person who came under no civil obligation. Accordingly, if he has acted with a want of skill, the person who employed him has himself to blame for it, indeed, if the surveyor was simply careless, he will still incur no liability; no doubt gross negligence will be held equivalent to malice. Even if he receives a remuneration, still the wording of the Edict is such that he is not answerable for every degree of negligence; of course the Prætor is aware that such persons sometimes give their services for pay. 2. It is only a surveyor who makes a report who is liable to this action; a man must however be understood to make a report where he makes it through another,

2 PAULUS (*on the Edict* 25) or makes it in writing. If however you are a surveyor, and I commission you to undertake the survey of my land, whereupon you hand the matter over to Titius, and he is guilty of some act of positive malice in carrying it out, you will be liable; as you acted with [what is equivalent to] positive malice in relying on such a person.

3 ULPIANUS (*on the Edict* 24) If I commission two persons and both are guilty of malice, each is liable to an action for the whole amount, but if one is sued and complies with the demand, leave to proceed against the other must be refused. 1. The person who has a right to bring the action is the one in whose interest it was that there should not be a false report made of the dimensions, in other words, the purchaser or the vendor, as the case may be, who is prejudiced by the actual report. 2. We are told however by Pomponius that if, in consequence of the report, the purchaser gives the vendor too much, there can be no action brought against the surveyor, because the party has an action to recover what he paid in excess, in short the purchaser has no interest, as he has the action just mentioned;—unless indeed the vendor is insolvent; in that case the surveyor is liable. 3. If on the other hand the vendor is deceived by the surveyor and so delivers a larger extent of land, Pomponius says, on the same principle, that he has no action against the surveyor because he has an action on the contract of sale against the purchaser, unless, again, the purchaser is insolvent. 4. According to the same writer, if a surveyor is employed for the purposes of a trial and he defrauds me in the report which he makes, he is liable to an action, if the consequence is that I take less by the judgment. It is true that where he is employed by the judge and makes a report to my disadvantage maliciously, Pomponius is doubtful whether I have a right to sue him, but on the whole he thinks I have. 5. This action Pomponius says ought to be allowed to the heir and successors generally; but, as against the heir and successors, it must be refused. 6. In respect of a slave the right of action is noxal, he holds, rather than *de peculio*, though a civil action given [in a similar case] is *de peculio*.

4 PAULUS (*on the Edict* 25) This right of action is perpetual, as the origin to which the matter is referred is not the fraud practised but the engagement to undertake the business.

5 ULPIANUS (*on the Edict* 24) If the surveyor does not report the dimensions falsely, but delays reporting at all, and the consequence is that the vendor is discharged after promising to assign the premises by a given day, this action is not admissible; and, according to Pomponius, there will be no *utilis actio* allowed either; consequently recourse must be had to an action *de dolo*. 1. If a false report is made, and thereupon the purchaser sues the vendor on his contract, he can sue the surveyor too, but if he has no

interest in doing so, no order will be made on the surveyor. If he does not sue the vendor for the whole deficiency, but only for something less, then, as Pomponius says, and quite consistently, there is a right of action against the surveyor for the residue. 2. The Prætor extended the application of these proceedings; there is the same right of action where an appraiser appears to have given a false report as to the dimensions of anything else; so that, where he deceived his employer in respect of the measurement of a building or as to the quantity of corn or wine,

6 PAULUS (*on the Edict* 24) or in a case where there is an inquiry as to the breadth of a footpath or as to the existence of a servitude of support or of an overhanging eave, or where he takes the dimensions of a courtyard or measures the amount of materials used in building or of a quantity of stone and makes a false report thereon,

7 ULPIANUS (*on the Edict* 24) or[1] he misstated the size of anything else, he will in all cases be liable. 1. The action is equally allowed where the deceit is on the part of one who measures with the use of mechanical appliances. 2. In addition to the above the remark is made by Pomponius that this action is open against a man who is not a surveyor but who has made deceitful statements as to dimensions. 3. On the same principle the action ought to be allowed equally against an architect who has been guilty of deceiving; in fact the Divine Severus himself laid down that actions should be allowed against an architect or a contractor. 4. I should say myself that an action must be allowed in the same way against an accountant who reports a calculation deceitfully.

VII.

ON THINGS RELIGIOUS AND FUNERAL EXPENSES AND ON THE RIGHT TO CONDUCT FUNERALS.

1 ULPIANUS (*on the Edict* 10) A man who spends anything on a funeral is held to contract with the deceased and not with the heir.

2 THE SAME (*on the Edict* 25)[2] Aristo says that a spot in which a slave has been buried is religious. 1. A man who has laid a

[1] This section seems to continue the sentence from s. 5.

[2] M. thinks that pr. and 1. once followed 6.

dead body or caused one to be laid in another man's ground is liable to an action *in factum*. By "another man's ground" we must understand fields and buildings to be meant equally; but these words give the right of action to the owner, not to the *bona fide* possessor; where our authority says "another man's ground," it is clear that he refers to the owner, that is the person to whom the ground belongs. Even if it is a usufructuary who buries a body, he may be sued by the owner of the bare property. Whether a part-owner is liable, if he does the same without the knowledge of his fellow-owner, is a point open to discussion; but the better opinion is that he can be sued in an action *familiæ erciscundæ* or *communi dividundo*. 2. The Prætor says:—"If a body or the bones of a dead man are averred to have been carried to ordinary ground or to a burial-place where the party had no right to bury" etc. Whoever acts in this way is liable to an action *in factum* and will have to pay a pecuniary penalty. 3. The carrying which the Prætor had in his mind was carrying such as is done for the purpose of burying. 4. A spot is called ordinary (*purus*) which is neither sacred nor under a sanction nor religious, being a spot to which all these descriptions are held to be inapplicable. 5. A burial-place (*sepulchrum*) is a place where human bodies or bones are put away. Celsus adds that a place which is set apart for burial does not become religious throughout, but only so far as it is occupied by the corpse. 6. A monument is anything that has been set up in order to preserve memory. 7. A person who has a usufruct cannot make the ground religious. On the other hand, if one has the bare property and another the usufruct, even the former cannot make the ground religious, unless indeed he should bury in it the very person who bequeathed the usufruct, it not being equally convenient that the body should be buried somewhere else: this is stated by Julianus. No doubt, the rule is that the place cannot be made religious without the consent of the usufructuary; but, if the latter do consent, the better opinion is that the place becomes religious. 8. No one can make religious a place which is subject to a servitude, except with the consent of the person who has a right to the servitude. At the same time, if the party can enjoy the servitude no less conveniently over some other part of the ground, the burial cannot be held to be made with a design to interfere with the servitude, and consequently the place becomes religious: which no doubt is not unreasonable. 9. A man who has pledged his land for debt will make the ground religious, if he buries in it one[1] of his own family; and, if he should be buried there himself, the same thing follows; but he cannot make over the power to another.

3 PAULUS (*on the Edict* 27) However, where all parties concerned agree, it is more in accordance with public policy to hold that the ground may be made religious; and such is the rule given by Pomponius.

4 ULPIANUS (*on the Edict* 25) Where one who is appointed heir carries in the body of the deceased owner before he has made entry on the inheritance, he thereby makes the ground religious; and it need not be held that by this very act he is behaving as heir; let us suppose that he is still in the course of making up his mind as to making such entry. I should say myself that even where it is not the heir that has carried in the body, but some other person, whoever it be, the [one who is appointed] heir either keeping aloof or being absent or being afraid lest he should be held to be behaving as heir, still this person makes the ground religious; as a matter of fact, it is very common for the deceased to be buried before anyone has become heir. The ground becomes religious only where it was the property of the deceased; as the place in which the dead man is laid may be held, as a matter of common sense, to appertain to him, especially where he is laid in a place which he had himself chosen for the purpose. So much is this the case that, even where the heir lays the body in a place which is bequeathed away as a legacy, nevertheless the burial of the testator makes the spot religious, assuming that the body could not as conveniently have been buried somewhere else.

5 GAIUS (*on the Provincial Edict* 19) "Household burial-place" is the expression used of a burial-place which a man appoints for himself and his household; a burial-place is called "hereditary" where he appoints it for himself and his heirs,

6 ULPIANUS (*on the Edict* 25) or where the testator (*paterfamilias*) had acquired it by right of hereditary succession. But in both alike heirs and other successors of whatever kind may lawfully be buried and may lawfully bury, even though they should be heirs, whether by testament or upon intestacy, to a very small extent, and their co-heirs should not consent. The same right is allowed to children and remoter descendants of either sex and of

[1] Ins. *quem* after *suorum*. M.

whatever degree[1], even when emancipated, whether they have become heirs or they decline the inheritance. As for disinherited persons, they may be buried themselves, simply as a matter of humanity, unless the testator has expressly forbidden it, moved thereto by some reasonable antipathy, but they are not at liberty to bury others, except their own issue. Freedmen cannot be buried, nor can they themselves bury [in ground that was their patron's], unless they are heirs to their patron; though there have been patrons who have recorded by inscription that they had set up monuments for themselves and their freedmen. This has been declared by Papinianus, and the law has been often laid down to the same effect. 1. So long as there is a mere (*purum*) monument, it may be sold or given away; if it becomes a *cenotaphium* (a monument in memory of one who is not to be buried on the spot), the proper rule is that it may be sold; as the Divine Brothers laid down by rescript that such a monument is not religious.

7 GAIUS (*on the Provincial Edict* 19) A man who buries a body on another man's ground can be compelled by an action *in factum* either to take away the body which he buried or to pay the price of the ground. The action can be brought by the heir, and also against the heir of the wrongdoer, and the right to bring it is not liable to be lost by lapse of time. 1. Where a man deposits a dead body in a stone chest, the property of another, in which there has been no body placed already, the proconsul allows an *utilis actio in factum*, as the party cannot exactly be said to have laid the body in a burial-place or on ground belonging to another.

8 ULPIANUS (*on the Edict* 25) Where some stranger has buried bones or a body, it is matter of question whether the owner of the ground can dig them up or throw them out without a decree of the *pontifices* or an order from the Emperor; and what Labeo says is that the permission of the *pontifices* or the Emperor's order is required, without which the person who cast the remains out will be liable to an action for *injuriæ*. 1. If ground that is religious is averred to have been sold as profane, the Prætor allows an action *in factum* to the person concerned in the matter against the vendor; the action is equally open against the [vendor's] heir, as it amounts virtually to an action on a contract of sale. 2. If a man buries a body in ground dedicated to public use, the Prætor allows an action against him, if the act was done deliberately (*dolo*), and the party must be punished by the summary powers of the

[1] del. *filiis familiæ et.* M.

Court, though the penalty to be inflicted is not excessive; if the act was not done deliberately, the application must be dismissed. 3. In connexion with this action, the expression "profane spot" (*locus purus*) will be allowed to comprise buildings. 4. The right of action is enjoyed not only by the owner, but by anyone who has a *usufruct* in the ground in question, or has a servitude over it, such persons having a right to forbid the act as well as the owner. 5. Where a man is prevented from burying in ground in which he has a right to bury, he has a good right of action *in factum* and [he can ask for] an interdict, even though the resistance be made not to himself personally but to his agent, as, in such a case, it is held to be, in a certain sense, to himself.

9 GAIUS (*on the Provincial Edict* 19) When a man is prevented from burying the body or bones of a deceased person, it is open to him either to have recourse at once to the interdict by which forcible resistance is prohibited, or to bury the remains somewhere else and then bring an action *in factum*; and by the latter he will get damages equivalent to the interest he would have had in meeting with no resistance; this estimate will include the price of ground which he buys or the rent of any that he hires, or the value of his own ground, [this being a spot] which a man would not have made religious without some constraining necessity. I wonder indeed, considering the above, why it should be held to be established law that the action mentioned should not continue to be open in favour of the heir, nor yet against the heir of the wrongdoer,—as the subject of it clearly is an account establishing a claim for so much money; in any case, as between the original parties, the right of action will not lapse.

10 ULPIANUS (*on the Edict* 25) Where a vendor of land reserves a burial-place with a view to the interment therein of himself and his descendants, then, if he is prevented from using a roadway for the purpose of burying one of his family, he can bring his action; it is in fact held that the bargain between the purchaser and the vendor included a reservation of a right of way over the land for the purpose of burial.

11 PAULUS (*on the Edict* 27) But if a site for a monument is sold on the understanding that there is to be no burial there of persons whom there was a right to bury, an informal agreement to this effect is not enough, there must be an undertaking given by stipulation.

12 ULPIANUS (*on the Edict* 25) If a man has a burial-place, but no right of way to the burial-place, and the neighbouring owner obstructs his access, then, according to a rescript of the Emperor Antoninus and his father, the practice is for a pathway up to the burial-place to be asked for as a concession and to be granted, so that, in cases where there is no legal easement, the right may be obtained by request from the owner of the adjacent land. Still this rescript, which affords the means of obtaining the right by request, does not authorize a civil action; an application will be made to the Governor in virtue of his summary powers of jurisdiction (*extra ordinem*), and he is at once bound to require that means of access should be conferred upon the party for a reasonable consideration, subject always to this, that the judge should consider the suitability of the site, so as to prevent any great detriment being occasioned to the neighbouring landowner. 1. It is provided by a decree of the Senate that the use of a burial-place is not to be profaned by causing it to be varied, in short, the burial-place is not to be made subservient to uses involving the resort of strangers. 2. The Prætor says:—"As for any expense incurred[1] for a funeral, I will allow an action to recover it against the person therein concerned." 3. This pronouncement is made on very good grounds, so as to enable a person who has conducted a funeral to sue for what he expended; as the result is to secure that bodies shall not lie unburied, and on the other hand that a person's funeral shall not be conducted at the cost of a stranger. 4. The person who is bound to conduct the funeral is the one chosen by the deceased; still, should he omit to conduct it, no penalty is provided for the case, unless some valuable consideration was left him for the purpose; if this should be the case, and he still declines to comply with the will of the deceased, he is debarred the legacy. But, if the deceased made no such provision, and the duty has not been transferred to anyone, the matter falls upon those appointed heirs, and, if there is no one appointed, on the statutable successors or the cognates, these to be taken in the order in which they would succeed. 5. The amount of the funeral expenses is determined according to the means or the rank in life of the deceased. 6. The Prætor or the municipal magistrate is bound to order the expense required for the funeral to be paid, if the assets include money, out of such money; but if not, he must order a sale of such things as would perish by lapse of time, which it would impoverish the inheritance to keep; failing these, he must

[1] Read *factum* for *factus*. Cf. M.

order a sale or a pledge of gold and silver, if there is any such, so as to raise the amount required,

13 GAIUS (*on the Provincial Edict* 19) or [he may get the money] from debtors to the estate, if this can be easily done;

14 ULPIANUS (*on the Edict* 25) and if anyone should obstruct the purchaser, so as to prevent any such property being delivered to him, the Prætor is bound to intervene and to uphold whichever of the above measures was employed[1]. 1. If the deceased was a tenant or a lodger and no source can be found from which to pay for the funeral, then, as Pomponius tells us, the expense must be defrayed from the things "borne in and brought in" (*invecta illata*), and if any portion of them remains over and above, it will be available for arrears of rent. Add[2] to this that if the testator whose funeral is in question left any property by way of legacy, and there is no fund from which to pay for his funeral, recourse must be had to this property too; it is of more importance that the testator's funeral should be paid for out of his own assets than that some particular legatees should receive their legacies. Should the inheritance however only be entered upon after [a sale has taken place], the property sold must not be taken away from the purchaser, as a man who has purchased under the authority of the court is a *bona fide* possessor *and has the ownership*[3]. Still a legatee ought not to go without his legacy, if he can be preserved from loss by the heir; but, if he cannot, it is better that the legatee should be disappointed of gain than that the purchaser should suffer loss. 2. It is said by Mela that if a testator commissions someone to see to his funeral, and this person receives money, but omits to conduct the funeral, an action for *dolus* must be allowed against him; I am of opinion however that the Prætor ought, in exercise of his summary powers, to compel him to conduct the funeral. 3. The only expense which can be held to be incurred on account of a funeral is expense[4] without which the funeral could not be had; for example, any cost incurred for carrying out the body of the deceased; besides this, however, if money was spent on [the preparation of] the place where the body was to be buried, this expenditure, so Labeo tells us, must be held to have been made on account of the funeral, as the spot must needs be made

1 del. *si quid impediat* etc.: the leading supposition is repeated by mistake. M.

2 After *sed* ins. *et*. M.

3 Four words doubtless interpolated. Cf. M. and D. 50. 17. 137.

4 del. *qui ideo fuit ut funus ducatur*. M.

ready in which the body is to be laid. 4. An outlay which has been made for the sake of bringing home the body of one who died abroad is included among funeral expenses, though, so far, no funeral should have taken place; and a similar remark may be made as to a case in which anything has been done as to keeping watch over a body, or even for cleansing it[1], or to provide marble [for a monument] or dispose vestments. 5. But it is not right that along with the bodies there should be any ornaments placed or anything else of that kind in the way practised by the simpler sort. 6. This action, which is called the *actio funeraria*, is founded on consideration of what is just and reasonable; and it deals only with outlay made about a funeral, it does not include other expenses. The word reasonable must be interpreted by reference to the position in life of the person whose funeral is in question, to the circumstances of the case, to the time of the funeral, to the question of good faith, so that there must not be more charged in the way of funeral expenses than was really spent, nor even as much as was spent, if the cost incurred was immoderate in amount; as account should be taken of the means of the person whose funeral was the subject of the outlay, and of the actual property [out of which the payment is to come], where there is an excessive consumption of it without sufficient grounds. It may be asked—How if the cost was incurred in accordance with the testator's own wish? The answer to this is that even his own wish ought not to be followed, if the result would be to go beyond the proper grounds of expenditure; the outlay, so the rule is, should be in proportion to the means of the deceased. 7. There are cases in which a man who has gone to expense on a funeral cannot recover the amount, as where he was moved by a feeling of duty towards the deceased, and did not act with the expectation of recovering what he expended. This was in fact laid down by rescript by the present Emperor. Accordingly an *arbiter* will have to take into account and weigh thoroughly the question what was the intent with which the expense was incurred; does the party volunteer to act on behalf of the deceased or his heir, or in discharge of the duty laid on him by principles of humanity, or is he deferring to a charitable motive or one of family duty or private affection? Moreover we may go on to distinguish the degree of charitable concern felt so as to treat the charity or feeling of duty on the part of the person who held the funeral as being such that he simply buried the deceased in order that he should not lie unburied, without

[1] I read *commundandum* for *commendandum*: but see Cujas, Obs. 2. 17.

intending to go so far as to do this at his own expense[1]; and, if the judge is convinced of this, he ought not to dismiss the defendant from the action; how can a man, indeed, ever bury the body of one with whom he had nothing to do, without being actuated by some feeling of duty? The proper course will therefore be for him to make a formal attestation stating who it is that buries and what is his motive, so as to avoid being afterwards examined on the subject. 8. When sons conduct the funeral of their father, or other persons act who could have been appointed heirs to the deceased, then, true as it is that this bare fact does not justify the assumption that they are acting as heirs or making entry on the inheritance, still, lest heirs by compulsion should be held to have intermeddled with the assets or other persons to have acted as heirs, it is the common practice for them to make an attestation that in holding the funeral they are moved by feelings of duty. Should this be done without occasion, their object will be held to be to protect themselves against being supposed to have intermeddled, but not to recover their outlay; their very assertion is to the effect that they held the funeral in virtue of a feeling of duty; accordingly, if, besides this, they wish to recover their outlay, they must make the attestation go into further detail. 9. Here someone may possibly say that there are cases in which a certain amount of the expense incurred can be recovered, and so the party incur the expense partly as a voluntary agent for another and partly in deference to a feeling of duty. This is, on the whole, true; and in such a case he will recover some part of an outlay which he did not intend to bestow gratuitously. 10. The judge who hears applications founded on equitable grounds of the above nature ought in some cases not to allow an expenditure made at a low figure, where, for instance, the deceased had been a man of ample means and the outlay on his funeral had been kept down to a small amount by way of casting a slur upon his memory; certainly the judge ought to take no such expenditure into account, the case, that is, being that, in giving the deceased such a funeral, the intention was to insult his memory. 11. If a man holds a funeral over a deceased proprietor whose heir he believes himself to be, he cannot bring the action for funeral expenses, because he did not intend to act as a voluntary agent for anyone else; such is the opinion of Trebatius and Proculus. Still, I should say myself that even so the action should be allowed him on sufficient cause shown. 12. Labeo says that, where a man has some other kind of action for recovering the

[1] For *fecerit* read *faceret*.

cost of a funeral, he cannot bring the *actio funeraria*, and that, consequently, if he has the *actio familiæ erciscundæ*, he cannot bring the *funeraria*, though, no doubt, if the proceedings by way of *familiæ erciscundæ* have already been taken, the other action can be brought. 13. Labeo says further that if you conduct the funeral of the testator in spite of the heir's prohibition, the *actio funeraria* is open to you on good cause shown ; for instance, the person whom the heir forbade to act might be the testator's son ; no doubt, in such a case, the plaintiff can be met with the reply—"then you must have held the funeral out of a feeling of filial duty" ;—suppose however you[1] made the attestation : you[1] will then, he says, have the right to bring the *actio funeraria*, as it is best, in fact, that funeral expenses should come out of the estate of the deceased. Again, how if the testator requested you[1] to hold the funeral, but the heir prohibits it, in spite of which you[1] hold it, must you[1] not, as a matter of fairness, have a good right to bring the action? I should say that, as a rule, a judge who does his duty does not simply follow the action of *negotia gesta*, but applies equitable principles more liberally, this being something which the very nature of the action allows him to do. 14. However the Divine Marcus declared by rescript that any heir who should prevent the funeral being held by the person chosen by the testator would indeed do ill, but that there is no penalty provided by law to meet the case. 15. Where a man held a funeral at some other person's request, he cannot bring the *actio funeraria*, this is open only to the one that made the request, whether he paid the expense to the person to whom he made such request or still owes it. If a ward made the request without the concurrence of his guardian, an *utilis actio funeraria* against the heir ought to be allowed the person who made the outlay, as it would be unfair that the heir should be saved the expense. Where however a ward on whom the duty of holding the funeral falls makes the request without the authority of his guardian, my opinion is that the action ought to be allowed against him, if he is himself fully heir to the person whose funeral was held and the estate is solvent. On the other hand, if a person holds the funeral at the heir's request, then, according to Labeo, he cannot bring the *actio funeraria*, because he has the action on *mandatum*. 16. If he held the funeral as a voluntary agent for the heir, then, even if the latter declines to ratify, still, so Labeo tells us, he can bring the *actio funeraria*. 17. The action is allowed against the person, whoever it is, on whom

[1] In text put in the first person.

the duty of holding the funeral falls, for example, the heir or the *bonorum possessor* or any other successor.

15 POMPONIUS (*on Sabinus* 5) A patron too is chargeable with the cost of a funeral, where he applies for *bonorum possessio contra tabulas*.

16 ULPIANUS (*on the Edict* 25) Where anything comes to a man under the head of *dos*, the Prætor allows an *actio funeraria* against him; as it was held by those of old time to be most agreeable to justice that the funeral expenses of women should be defrayed out of their dowers, as though such were their own property, and that the man who on the death of the woman is the richer by the *dos*, whether father or husband of the deceased, ought to contribute to the funeral expenses.

17 PAPINIANUS (*Responsa* 3) But if the father has not yet recovered the *dos*, the husband alone can be sued, and he can charge the father with whatever he pays under the head in question.

18 JULIANUS (*Digest* 10) In fact, funeral expenses are a debt incurred by the *dos*;

19 ULPIANUS (*on Sabinus* 15) consequently the *dos* itself has to bear this debt.

20 THE SAME (*on the Edict* 25) Neratius asks this question:—Where a man who gave a *dos* for a woman stipulated that two thirds of it should be returned to him, and the other third should remain with the husband, and[1] afterwards agreed that the husband should not have to contribute anything to the funeral expenses, will the husband be liable to the *actio funeraria*? To this he says that, if the stipulator himself conducted the woman's funeral, the agreement will take effect and he will get nothing by the *actio funeraria*; but, if someone else conducted it, that person can sue the husband, as the agreement in question must not bar the law of the land. Suppose however a person gives *dos* for a woman on the understanding that it is to revert to him if the woman should die while still under coverture, or the married life should come to an end in any other way,—would he not in this case have to contribute to the funeral expenses? As to this, seeing that the *dos* returns to him by the woman's death, it may be said that he must contribute.

[1] del. *est* after *stipulatus*. M.

1. If the husband is the richer by the amount of the *dos*, he will be liable to the *actio funeraria*, and not the father. Still, in regard to this case, I should say that, if the *dos* is a very small one and so will not bear the cost of the funeral, an action ought to be allowed against the father for the unpaid balance. 2. If a woman who is not under *potestas* dies and her estate is insolvent, her funeral expenses are chargeable on the *dos* alone. We find this in Celsus.

21 PAULUS (*on the Edict* 27) Where the person whose funeral has been held was subject to *potestas*, the right to bring an *actio funeraria* exists against the *paterfamilias*, according to his position and means.

22 ULPIANUS (*on the Edict* 25) We read in Celsus:—on the death of a married woman, the funeral expenses should always be a charge on the *dos* remaining in the hands of the husband and on the general property of the deceased, in proportion to their respective values.

23 PAULUS (*on the Edict* 27) For example, if the *dos* is worth a hundred and the estate of the deceased two hundred, the heir must contribute two thirds of the expense and the husband one third;

24 ULPIANUS (*on the Edict* 25) and this, according to Julianus, without deducting legacies,

25 PAULUS (*on the Edict* 27) or the value of slaves who are manumitted,

26 POMPONIUS (*on Sabinus* 15) or deducting debts.

27 ULPIANUS (*on the Edict* 25) In this way the husband and the heir have to contribute to the funeral in proportion [to the amounts they receive]. 1. There can be no *actio funeraria* against the husband, if he handed over the *dos* to his wife during the coverture, so Marcellus tells us, and this is a sound opinion,—that is to say, in those cases in which the statutes allow the husband to act in the way described. 2. I may add that in my opinion a husband can be compelled to pay by means of the *actio funeraria* only to the extent of his means; the fact is that he is the richer by the amount which he would have had to hand over to his wife if she had sued him.

28 POMPONIUS (*on Sabinus* 15) Should there be no *dos*, then, according to Atilicinus, the whole expense ought to be paid by the father; or else by the heirs of the woman, supposing, that is, she should be emancipated. Should the woman have left no heirs, and the father be insolvent, the husband, he says, can be sued to the extent of his means, with the object of preventing its being set down to his misconduct that his late wife was left unburied.

29 GAIUS (*on the Provincial Edict* 19) If a woman who is divorced marries another man and then dies, Fulcinius holds that the first husband is not chargeable with funeral expenses, although he is the richer by the amount of the *dos*. 1. A man who holds the funeral of a married woman who was under *potestas* has a good right to sue the husband, so long as the *dos* is not restored to the woman's father; if it has been restored, his claim will be against the father; but, in any case, where the husband has been sued, he need hand over the less to the woman's father by the amount [which he has paid the plaintiff in the action].

30 POMPONIUS (*on Sabinus* 15) Conversely, whatever the father disbursed for the funeral of his [married] daughter or hands over in consequence of an *actio funeraria* brought against him by another, he can recover from her husband in an action *de dote*. 1. But if a married woman who has been emancipated dies during coverture, her heirs or *bonorum possessores* will have to contribute, and so will the father in proportion to the amount of the *dos* which he has received, and the husband in proportion to the amount of it by which he is the richer.

31 ULPIANUS (*on the Edict* 25) Where a son under *potestas* is a soldier and possesses *castrense peculium*, I should say that the successors to his estate are liable in the first instance, and, after that, recourse must be had to the *paterfamilias*. 1. A man who buries a slave of either sex belonging to another can bring an *actio funeraria* against the owner. 2. This action is not barred by the lapse of a year, but is perpetual; it is allowed to the heirs and to successors in general, also against successors [of the deceased owner].

32 PAULUS (*on the Edict* 27) If one who is in possession of an inheritance holds the funeral, but, after that, being adjudged to be disentitled, omits, in handing over the estate, to deduct the amount of the expense which he incurred, he will have an *utilis actio funeraria*. 1. If husband and wife should both die at the

same moment of time, then, according to Labeo, this action ought to be allowed against the heir of the husband in proportion to the amount of the *dos* that comes to him, the fact being that this liability passed to him as bound up with the *dos*.

33 ULPIANUS (*on the Edict* 68) If a man was once heir, but was afterwards deprived of the inheritance as being unworthy, the better opinion is that his rights in connexion with burial (*jura sepulchrorum*) remain as they were.

34 PAULUS (*on the Edict* 64) Where a site is left by way of legacy on a condition, and the heir buries the deceased while the condition is pending, this does not make the spot religious.

35 MARCELLUS (*Digest* 5) Our forefathers held that a man who came forward to ruin his country and to slay his parents and children was by no means one whose death need be mourned; so that, if a son killed such a father or a father such a son, they all held that it were no wickedness; nay, that the doer should receive a reward.

36 POMPONIUS (*on Q. Mucius* 26) When a place is taken by the enemy, everything religious or sacred loses its character, just as free men pass into slavery. But when places so taken are released from this calamitous situation, they recover the condition which they had originally, reverting to it by something like a kind of *postliminium*.

37 MACER (*on the five per cent. succession duty Statute* 1) Under the expression "funeral expenses" we must understand anything that is spent on the body itself, for example, in the purchase of ointments, also the price of the ground in which the deceased is interred, or any rent that may have to be paid, and the price of the sarcophagus, also the hire of carriages; and, besides these, I should say that the cost of the funeral includes whatever is consumed in connexion with the dead body before it is buried. 1. A sepulchral monument (according to a rescript of the Divine Hadrian) is whatever is constructed by way of a muniment[1], in other words, in order to protect the spot where the body is laid; so that, if the testator ordered any extensive building to be made, as, for instance, a series of porticoes in a ring, such expense is not incurred for the funeral.

38 ULPIANUS (*on all the Courts* 9) It is the duty of the Governor of the province to see that the bodies and bones of the

[1] Read *munimenti* for *monumenti*.

dead are not detained or shaken about or so dealt with as to prevent their being conveyed on the public highway or buried.

39 MARCIANUS (*Institutes* 3) The Divine Brothers ordered that a body which was once disposed of in the way of lawful burial, that is to say, laid in the ground, should not be disturbed; and a body is deemed to be laid in the ground if it is laid in a chest with the intention that it shall not be taken out again and put somewhere else. But it is not open to dispute that the chest itself may be lawfully moved to some more convenient place, if circumstances require:

40 PAULUS (*Questions* 3) for if a person has carried in a body with the sole intention of afterwards removing it to some other place, and so wished merely to leave it deposited where it was for a time rather than to carry out the regular burial or provide, so to speak, a lasting resting-place, the spot will remain profane.

41 CALLISTRATUS (*Institutes* 2) If the place where a body is brought for burial belongs to several co-owners, all will have to consent to the burial, if the deceased was a stranger; as to such owners themselves, there is no doubt that any one of them may be properly buried there, even though the others should not agree, especially if there is no other place in which the body could be buried.

42 FLORENTINUS (*Institutes* 7) A monument is, speaking in general terms, a thing handed down to posterity as a memorial; and if a body or remains should be laid inside it, it becomes a sepulchre (*sepulchrum*), but if nothing of the kind is laid in it, it is simply a monument which is made by way of a memorial, such as the Greeks call a *κενοτάφιον*.

43 PAPINIANUS (*Questions* 8) Some persons there are who, although they cannot make a spot religious, can still sue to good purpose for an interdict *de mortuo inferendo*; for instance, a bare proprietor who buries a dead body in land in which someone has a *usufruct*, or who attempts to do so; as, if he buries the body, he will not make the spot a lawful sepulchre, but, if he is interfered with, he can very well apply for the interdict in pursuance of which[1] an inquiry is held as to the ownership. Similar rules apply to the case of a co-owner who attempts to bury a body without the consent of a fellow-owner in the common land. The reason of this

[1] Read *quo* for *qui*.

is that, in the public interest, in order to prevent human remains lying unburied, the strict principle is set aside, and, in fact, in practice it is occasionally disregarded in doubtful questions connected with 'religion'; the really highest principle of all being held to be the one which makes for religion.

44 PAULUS (*Questions* 3) Where burial has been made in [two] different places, the religious character does not attach to both, as there cannot be two sepulchres in consequence of the burial of one person; but, as I should say, the place that is religious is the one where the principal part of the body is laid, namely the head, the part of which a likeness is made, the part by which[1] people are recognized. But when leave is obtained for removal of the remains from one spot to another, the place ceases to be religious.

45 MARCIANUS (*Fideicommissa* 8) Funeral expenses are always debited to the deceased's estate, moreover the practice is that they rank before all other debts, if the estate is insolvent.

46 SCÆVOLA (*Questions* 2) If a man had a number of pieces of land and left the usufruct in every one of them separately by way of legacy, his body may be buried in one of them, the heir being at liberty to select the one and thus able to favour the other owners; however, the usufructuary fixed upon must be allowed an *utilis actio* against the heir to enable him to recover an amount representing the extent to which the usufruct is depreciated by the selection made. 1. If the heir of a woman buries the body of the deceased in land which is part of her estate, he can recover from her husband, where the latter is bound to contribute towards the cost of the funeral, an amount depending on the value of the ground used. 2. Where wearing apparel is left to a man, but he disposes of it with a view to the [testator's] funeral expenses, the present law is that he should be allowed an *utilis actio* against the heir, and that with the preferential claim.

[1] Read *unde* for *inde*. Cf. M.

VIII.

On Carrying in a Dead Body and Building a Sepulchral Monument.

1 Ulpianus (*on the Edict* 68) The Prætor says:—"Whither and wheresoever such a one has a right to carry in a dead body without your leave, I forbid the use of force to prevent him from being free to take the body thereto and there to bury it." 1. Where a man has a right to bury, he is not [to be] hindered from doing so, and it is held that he is so hindered when either he is prevented from taking the body on to the ground in question or his approach to it is obstructed. 2. The bare proprietor of the piece of ground can have recourse to the interdict as to carrying in a body; in fact it is equally available in respect of ordinary land. 3. Again, if I have a right of way to a plot of ground, and I wish to carry in a body to that plot, but my approach is hindered, the law is that I can take proceedings by way of this interdict, inasmuch as, being hindered from using the right of way, I am hindered from carrying in the body, and a similar rule must be held to apply where I have any other servitude. 4. That this is a prohibitory interdict is plain on the face of it. 5. The Prætor says:—"Wheresoever such a one has a right to carry in a body without your leave, I forbid force being used to prevent him from being free to erect on the spot a sepulchral monument, he doing the same without malicious intent." 6. The reason why this interdict is offered is that the construction and ornamentation of monuments is desirable in the interests of religion. 7. No one is to be hindered from making a tomb or a monument on a spot where he has a right to do so. 8. A man is held to hinder the making of a structure even where he prevents the materials being brought to the spot which are required for purposes of construction. On the same principle, if a man prevents the necessary workmen from coming to the spot, the interdict will apply, also if he hinders the fixing of apparatus, assuming that he does so on a spot which is subject to the servitude; but, of course, if you attempt to set up your appliances on my ground, I shall not be liable to the interdict, if, in exercise of my rights, I decline to allow you to proceed. 9. A man must be understood to construct not only when he undertakes some fresh work of his own, but equally so when his object is to execute

repairs. 10. A man who takes measures to make a sepulchral structure fall over is exposed to this interdict.

2 MARCELLUS (*Digest* 28) One of the "Royal Statutes" lays down that, on the death of a woman with child, she will not be buried until the unborn infant is extracted; anyone who transgresses this rule may be said to have taken away the prospect of the living child in disposing of the body of the pregnant woman.

3 POMPONIUS (*on Sabinus* 9) If a man is erecting a sepulchral monument close to your house, you can serve on him a "notification of novel structure," but, when the work is finished, the only right of action you will have is that for an interdict *quod vi aut clam*. 1. If a body is once carried in close to the house of a stranger, that is over the statutable limits, the owner of the house cannot after that prevent the person [who does it] from carrying in another body to the same place, or from constructing a monument, if the act was originally done with the knowledge of such owner.

4 ULPIANUS (*Responsa* 2) The right to a burial-place is not acquired by long possession by one to whom it does not legally belong.

5 THE SAME (*Opinions* 1) If human remains are laid within some structure which is averred to be incomplete, there is no reason, so far, why it should not be completed. 1. But, if the place is already made religious, the *pontifices* ought to decide how far it is possible to meet the need of putting the structure in proper condition with due regard to religion.

TWELFTH BOOK.

I.

ON THINGS GIVEN IN CREDIT WHERE A SPECIFIC DEMAND IS TO BE MADE AND ON THE *CONDICTIO*.

1 ULPIANUS (*on the Edict* 26) It will be to the purpose, before we come to explanation of the text, to say a few words as to the meaning of the above title itself. 1. The Prætor gives under this title a number of rules of law dealing with contracts of various kinds, and it is for that reason he begins with the title called that of "things given in credit," as this comprises[1] every kind of contract which people make in reliance on the good faith of others; in fact, as Celsus says (*Questions*, b. 1), the term *credere* (to give in credit) is of general application, so that under this head the edict of the Prætor deals with the subjects of loan for return and of pledge. As a matter of fact, whenever people agree to any arrangement in reliance on the good faith of others, and are thereafter to receive something, they are said, in virtue of the contract, to give credit. The word "thing" too (*res*) was chosen by the Prætor as being one of general application.

2 PAULUS (*on the Edict* 28) People give a *mutuum* when they are to receive in return not the identical thing which they gave—or else it would be a case of *commodatum* or *depositum*,—but something of the same kind; were it to be of a different kind, as where a man is to get back wine for corn, it would not be a *mutuum*. 1. A gift of *mutuum* deals with subject-matter determined by weight, tale or measure, as people can contract a credit by a gift of such things as[2] admit of the contract being performed by payment in kind instead of return in specie; you cannot contract the credit with respect to other things, because it is impossible to pay the creditor off by giving him one thing in exchange for

[1] Perhaps "he includes." [2] Read *quæ* for *quia*. Cf. M.

another of a different kind, without his consent. 2. A gift of *mutuum* is so termed because the thing becomes yours instead of mine (*ex meo tuum*); accordingly, if it should not become yours, the obligation does not arise. 3. It follows then that giving in credit differs from making a *mutuum* in the way in which a genus differs from an individual thing; there may be a good gift in credit quite apart from things which are determined by weight, tale and measure, so that, in fact, it is a case of a credit where a person is to have the identical object returned. Again, there can be no *mutuum* [of money] unless the money changes hands, but there may well be a case of credit, even where nothing changes hands, as, for example, where a *dos* is promised after marriage. 4. In a case of a gift of *mutuum* the giver ought to be owner, and it is not inconsistent with this that sons under *potestas* or slaves can impose a valid obligation by advancing money which is part of their *peculium*; it is the same thing as if you were to give money at my request, that being a case in which I get the right of action, though the money was not mine. 5. People can also give credit by spoken words, where some positive act is added in order to create an obligation, such as a stipulation[1].

3 POMPONIUS (*on Sabinus* 27) When people give a *mutuum*, even if they do not take any assurance to the effect that what is returned shall be equally good, still the debtor has no right to give in return a thing of the same kind but of inferior quality, as, for instance, new wine in return for old; in making a contract the intention of the parties is deemed equivalent to an express assurance, and here the intention is held to be that the loan should be discharged with something of the same kind and of the same degree of goodness as that with which it was made.

4 ULPIANUS (*on Sabinus* 34) In a case where there is some person who has no occasion for lending at interest nor intention to do so, but you, having on hand a purchase of landed estate, require to borrow money for the purpose, though you have no wish to take up money on loan until you actually make the purchase, whereupon the [aforesaid person who is the proposed] lender, having, let us say, some pressing occasion to go to a distance, deposits the precise sum required in your hands, on the understanding that, if you make the purchase, you shall be liable accordingly as on a credit, [in

[1] *Veluti stipulatione.* This last word is possibly in apposition to "words" in the preceding line, in which case the translation would be "*e.g.* by a stipulation." Contra Bas.

such circumstances] the deposit described will be at the risk of the party who undertook to hold it. We know that, where a man receives some article in order that he may sell it and use the purchase money for his own purposes, he will hold the article at his own risk. 1. If a thing is given in pledge, it can, on payment of the money advanced, be sued for by a *condictio*. Again, produce taken on a ground which gives no lawful title should be sued for by a *condictio*; even if a tenant gathers produce after his term of five years has expired, it can undoubtedly be recovered by a *condictio*, assuming always that it was not gathered with the landowner's consent; if it was with his consent, then beyond all question there is no *condictio*. 2. Things which have been carried on to the ground by the force of a stream can be recovered in the same way.

5 POMPONIUS (*on Sabinus* 22) If you are bound to hand over something to me, and the thing is lost subsequently to some act of yours which prevents you from handing it over, it is recognized law that the loss falls on you. But when the question arises whether the act was yours, it will have to be considered not only whether the transfer was in your power or not, or whether or not you took deliberate means to prevent its being in your power at the time or at any time afterwards, but also whether there was any sufficient ground existing in consequence of which you were bound to know that you had to make the transfer.

6 PAULUS (*on the Edict* 28) A thing is called specific (*certum*) when the object or the quantity which is the subject of an obligation is expressly pointed out, either by name or by some description which is equivalent to a name, and its nature or amount is thereby ascertained. Indeed Pedius himself says (*Stipulations*, b. 1) that it makes no difference whether a thing is mentioned by its exact name or pointed out with the finger or described in so many words, inasmuch as those methods are interchangeable one of which is as effectual as another.

7 ULPIANUS (*on the Edict* 26) Every term that can be inserted in a stipulation may be equally made part of [an agreement connected with] an advance of money, consequently so may conditions.

8 POMPONIUS (*Extracts from Plautius* 6) Thus a loan on *mutuum* is sometimes in suspense, so as to admit of being set up by some subsequent matter; for instance, suppose I give

you a sum of money on loan on the understanding that, if a given condition comes to pass, the money shall become yours and you shall be under an obligation to repay me. Similarly, suppose the heir lends money which has been bequeathed to a legatee, after which the legatee declines to have it; as it is held that, from the day of entry on the inheritance, the money was the property of the heir, so that he can sue to recover the amount which he lent. We are told by Julianus that, even where the heir has delivered property [which had been bequeathed], the delivery is referred to the time when entry was made on the inheritance, in case the legacy or the gift to a co-heir is declined[1].

9 ULPIANUS (*on the Edict* 26) A specific *condictio* (*condictio certi*) is open on every ground and in pursuance of every kind of obligation in virtue of which a specific demand can be made, whether the contract on which the demand arises is in its terms specific or not specific; as a man can lawfully bring a *condictio* for something specific in pursuance of any kind of contract, provided only there is an actual existing obligation; no doubt, if the obligation is only to be binding on a future day or on the occurrence of a given condition, no action can be brought before the day arrives or the conditional event occurs. 1. This action can be brought equally well in pursuance of a legacy or on the *lex Aquilia*; indeed the claim to recover can be raised by means of this action even on the ground of theft. Again, if proceedings are taken under a *senatusconsultum*, the action is still open; for example, where the person who desires to sue is one who has acquired an inheritance under a testamentary trust. 2. A man may be properly sued in an action of this kind, whether he contracted the obligation on his own account or as agent for someone else. 3. Seeing then that the specific *condictio* is admissible on every kind of contract, whether the contract was made by act, or set words, or both together, we may mention certain cases with reference to which it may be fitly considered whether this action is suitable for the respective demands involved. 4. I advanced you ten, and I stipulated for repayment to someone else: which stipulation is

[1] *Cum repudiatum sit legatum aut adpositum.* For the last word Cujas reads *adquisitum*, acquired, Baro *agnitum*, accepted, Mommsen is inclined to *amissum*, lost. Kellinghusen retains *adpositum*, as meaning a legacy to an heir, and refers to D. 28. 5. 17 pr. (Cf. Pothier.) It is impossible to feel confidence in any one of these conjectures, but I have followed the last. Of course the contrast is then between *legatum* and *adpositum*, not *repudiatum* and *adpositum*.

null and void. Can I ask for ten by way of *condictio* by the action under discussion, on the ground that there are two contracts in the case, one made by act, that is by the advance, and another by words, consequently to no purpose, since I could not stipulate for another person? My own opinion is that I can. 5. It is a similar case if I take a promise by stipulation from a ward without the concurrence of his guardian, having advanced him the money with such concurrence; in this case, too, I shall still have a *condictio* in virtue of the advance. 6. A similar[1] question may be asked if we suppose that I have advanced you money, and I stipulate for repayment of it on the occurrence of some impossible conditional event; as, while the stipulation is null and void, the *condictio* will remain open. 7. Again, if I advance money to a man who is afterwards put under an interdict as to his property, and then I make a stipulation with him, I should say that his case is like that of a ward, as in fact he can acquire [rights] by stipulation too. 8. If I advance my own money on your behalf, as if it were yours, you being at the time absent and unaware of the fact, Aristo tells us that the *condictio* can be brought by you; Julianus, too, being consulted on the point, says (b. 10) that Aristo's opinion is sound, and that there is no doubt that if I give my money on your behalf at your request, you acquire the obligational claim, in fact, it happens every day that a man who wishes to lend money requests someone else to be lender in his name and so advance it to the person who is to become his, the requesting party's, debtor. 9. I deposited with you the sum of ten, after which I allowed you to make use of the money; Nerva and Proculus hold that I can bring a *condictio* for it against you, as on a *mutuum*, even before you have taken it up, and this is perfectly sound, as Marcellus himself holds, in fact you have[2] become possessor in virtue of your intention[3]. It follows that the risk is transferred to the person who asked for the loan, and he can be sued in a *condictio*.

10 THE SAME (*on the Edict* 2) If, on the other hand, I gave you leave originally, on depositing the money with you, to make use of it, if you wished, [the same authorities hold] that there is no loan until you take up the money, as, before that, it is not certain that any debt will be contracted.

[1] For *item* read *idem*.

[2] In the text "he has." [3] In the text "his."

11 THE SAME (*on the Edict* 26) You request me to lend you a sum of money. Not having it by me, I give you a dish or a quantity of gold for you to sell it and make use of the money you receive. If you sell it, I should say that there is a good loan of the money. But if, before selling the dish or the gold, you lose it without any negligence of yours, the question may be asked whether the loss falls on you or on me. For my own part I think the distinction made by Nerva is a very sound one, who holds that it makes a great difference whether or not I had the dish or the gold for sale, and that, if I had, the loss falls on me, just as if I had put it in the hands of someone else for him to sell it; but that, if it was not my intention to sell it, and my only object with reference to the sale of it was to enable you to use [the purchase-money], the loss falls on you, more especially if I let you have it without charging you any interest. 1. If I give you ten on the understanding that you shall owe me nine, Proculus says, and very rightly, that in law you are my debtor for no more than nine. But if I give the ten for you to owe me eleven, Proculus holds that there can be no action to recover more than ten. 2. If a runaway slave lends you money, the question is asked—can his owner bring a *condictio* to recover it from you? As to this, if my slave, being one who is allowed free management of his *peculium*, lends the money to you, this is a good loan; but a runaway slave, or indeed any slave who lends money against the will of his owner, does not thereby pass the property in it. Then what is the upshot? The coins can be claimed at law, if they are to be found, on the other hand, if you part with the possession of them maliciously, there can be an action for production of them; but, if you have spent them without fraudulent intent, I can bring a *condictio* for them.

12 POMPONIUS (*Extracts from Plautius* 6) If you accept money by way of a loan from a person who is in fact a lunatic, but you suppose him to be of sound mind, and the money is bestowed in your interest, hereupon, according to Julianus, the lunatic acquires a right of *condictio*; the law being that everything which is a good ground of action for a man who is not aware of the facts is equally so for a lunatic. Again, if a man who made a loan to a slave [owned by another] becomes a lunatic, and the slave thereupon spends the money in the interest of his owner, there is a good right of *condictio* to recover it on behalf of the lunatic; and if anyone advances by way of loan money belonging to another, and after that he becomes a

lunatic, and the money is spent, a right to bring a *condictio* is acquired by the lunatic.

13 ULPIANUS (*on the Edict* 26) There is no doubt that, if a thief advances you money by way of a loan, he does not pass you the property in it; still, if the money is spent, a right of *condictio* arises. 1. Hence Papinianus says (*Questions*, b. 8), "if I lend you somebody else's money, you are not liable to any action at my hands until you spend the money." He then asks the question whether, if you spend the money portion by portion, I have a right to sue for it portion by portion, and his answer is that I have, if I have been informed that the money had not been mine and I sued for a portion only because I had not yet discovered that the whole was spent. 2. If a slave owned in common lends ten, I should say that, whether the slave has been given the free disposal of his *peculium* or not, if the money is spent, an action for five is open to each co-owner; we are told by Papinianus that, if I lend you a hundred pieces of money which I have in common with another, I have a good *condictio* for fifty, even where each separate coin was owned in common.

14 THE SAME (*on the Edict* 29) If a son under *potestas* borrows money in contravention of the *Senatusconsultum* [Macedonianum] and repays it, whereupon his *paterfamilias* brings a *vindicatio* to recover the pieces of money, no *exceptio* can be pleaded in bar of his claim; but, if the money has been spent by the lender, then, according to Marcellus, there is no right of *condictio*, as a *condictio* is only allowed where the money was advanced under circumstances such that there would have been a right of action, if the property [in the coins] had passed to the person who received them, but this is not the case in the present instance. We may add that where money is lent in contravention of the *Senatusconsultum* and is repaid by mistake, the better opinion is that there is no right of action to recover it.

15 THE SAME (*on the Edict* 31) There are a number of special rules of law observed as to loans of money. If I order my debtor to hand to you the money which he owes me, you become answerable to me, though the money you received was not mine. This being acknowledged law in the case of two persons, a similar rule must be applied where there is only one, so that, where you owe me money on the ground of a *mandate* and you and I agree that you shall keep it in your hands as upon a loan, the construction is

that the money was paid me and then passed from my hands to yours.

16 PAULUS (*on the Edict* 32) If a co-owner of money advanced money of his own by way of loan, there is no doubt that the loan is complete though his fellow-owners refused to give their consent; but if he advanced money that was owned in common, he does not effect a valid loan, unless the others give their consent too, as he had no right to dispose of more than his own share.

17 ULPIANUS (*Disputations* 1) Where a son under *potestas* who was living at Rome in order to pursue his studies lent money forming part of his travelling allowance, Scævola expressed the opinion that he could get relief by means of proceedings *extra ordinem*.

18 THE SAME (*Disputations* 7) If I hand you money by way of making you a gift, and you accept it by way of a loan, then, as we read in Julianus, there is no gift made; but the question whether there is a loan is a point to consider. My own opinion is that there is no loan either, and on the whole I should say the money does not become the property of the person who took it, as his view of the transaction, when he took it, was not the same as mine. Consequently, if he spends the money, however much he is liable on a *condictio*, still he may very well plead *dolus*, by way of *exceptio*, seeing that the money was spent in accordance with the will of the giver. 1. If I hand you the money by way of deposit and you take it by way of loan, there is neither a deposit nor a loan; and we may say the same where one[1] gives the money by way of a loan for consumption (*mutuum*) and the other[2] takes it as a loan for use, with the object of making a display with it; but in both cases alike, if the money is spent, there is good ground for a *condictio* without any *exceptio* founded on *dolus*.

19 JULIANUS (*Digest* 10) An advance of money does not, as a matter of course, bind the man who takes it, it only does so where the very object is that he should be bound at once. For instance, a man who gives money by way of a *donatio mortis causa* no doubt advances money, but this will not put the party receiving under liability, except in a case where an occurrence takes place on which such liability was made to depend, for example that of the donor recovering from his illness or the donee dying first. Again,

[1] In the text "you." [2] In the text "I."

if money is given in order that something or other should be done, then, as long as it is a matter of uncertainty whether it will be done or not, there will be no liability ; but, as soon as it becomes certain that it will not be done, the party who received the money will be liable ; thus, if I give Titius ten on the understanding that he will manumit Stichus by the first of the next month, then, before that day, I shall have no right of action, but when it has passed I can bring an action, provided always, that is, the slave has not been manumitted. 1. If a ward, without the concurrence of his guardian, lends money or hands it over in payment of a debt, then, if the money is spent, he has a right of *condictio*, or is discharged of the debt, [as the case may be,] and that on no other ground than this, that the money appears to have come to the hands of the person who received it by the act of the ward ; accordingly, if the person who received the money in question as a loan or as payment of a debt hands it on to someone else by way of loan or payment, then, if the latter spends the money, the person first mentioned is liable to repay the sum to the ward, or must hold the ward discharged of his debt, as the case may be, and he will have a good claim against the party to whom he gave the money, or will be discharged of his debt to him. In short, the rule is that a man who hands over the money of another by way of loan, will, if the recipient spends it, have a good claim against him, and it is equally true that one who gives money by way of paying a debt will be discharged from all claim by the party who receives it.

20 THE SAME (*Digest* 18) If I make a gift of money to you for you to lend me the same money, will this be a loan? My answer was that where a case is put in such language as this, people do not use their terms correctly, as a contract such as mentioned is neither a gift nor a loan of money ; it is not a gift, because the intention in giving the money is not that it shall remain in the hands of the party receiving it at all events ; and it is not a loan, because the money is handed over rather by way of getting rid of a debt than of subjecting another party to an obligation. Accordingly, if a person who received money [from me] on condition that he should lend me the same does hand me the money so received, this will not be a loan, as I ought rather to be held to have received what is my own. This is the construction to give if we are to maintain the strict meaning of the words used :—no doubt the more indulgent rule is that both transactions are valid.

21 THE SAME (*Digest* 48) Some have held the opinion that a

man who sues for ten cannot be compelled to take five and carry on his action for the balance, and, on the other hand, if he asserts that a given estate is his, that he can equally little be compelled to confine his demand to a part of it; still in both cases it is held that the Prætor will be acting more indulgently if he compels the plaintiff to accept what is offered him, seeing that it is part of his official duty to keep down litigation.

22 THE SAME (*Extracts from Minicius* 4) A loan of wine was made and legal proceedings were taken to recover it; and the question arose to what time the valuation to be made of the wine should refer, the time when it was handed over to the borrower, or when he joined issue, or when judgment was given. Sabinus gave the opinion that if it had been agreed at what time the wine should be restored, the value assessed should be that which the wine bore then; *if no such agreement had been made, it should be the value it bore when*[1] the action was brought. I asked to what locality the valuation should refer. He replied that if it had been agreed that restoration should be made at some particular place, the valuation should follow the price at that place; if this had not been settled, it should be according to the place where the action was brought.

23 AFRICANUS (*Questions* 2) If a slave is left by way of legacy to you, and I thereupon take possession of him and sell him as if he were left to me, then, according to Julianus, if he dies, you have a good right of *condictio* against me for the purchase money, on the ground that I have become the richer out of your property.

24 ULPIANUS (*Pandectæ*) If a man stipulates for a specific thing, he does not acquire thereby the action *ex stipulatu*, he must sue for it by the condictitious action by which a demand is made for a specific thing.

25 THE SAME (*on the Office of Consular Men*) A lender who advances money for the purpose of restoring buildings has a preferential demand for repayment of the money lent.

26 THE SAME (*Opinions* 5) If a man who is *procurator* for a soldier lends the soldier's money and takes a surety for repayment, the law is that a right of action is allowed to the soldier to whom the money belonged, by analogy with the case of the guardian of a boy or the curator of a young man who stipulates for repayment of a loan of the money of either of them.

[1] Supplied from Basilica. *v.* M.

27 THE SAME (*on the Edict* 10) A town corporation (*civitas*) can be bound in pursuance of a loan made to it, provided the money is employed for its benefit; otherwise the town will not be liable, but only the individuals who were parties to the contract.

28 GAIUS (*on the provincial Edict* 21) A lender who has taken insufficient security does not on that account lose the right to demand payment of so much of the debt as is in excess of the value of the security.

29 PAULUS (*on Plautius* 4) Where a man employs his slave as an agent in business (*institor*), it may be fairly maintained, according to Julianus, that the employer is liable accordingly to be sued in a *condictio*, the construction being that the slave's contracts are made by the order of the person who appointed him.

30 THE SAME (*on Plautius* 5) Where a man who intends to take up a loan of money makes a formal promise to the person who is to lend it that he will repay it, he has it in his power to avoid liability by declining to accept it.

31 THE SAME (*on Plautius* 17) Where a *condictio* has been brought to recover an estate or a slave, I believe the present law is that after joinder of issue all accessions (*causa*) must be handed over, that is to say, everything which the plaintiff would have had, if the property had been given up at the moment when issue was joined. 1. I made a *bona-fide* purchase of your slave from a man who had stolen him, I not knowing the facts; the slave himself bought a boy[1] with money which was part of the *peculium* which he had with you, and the boy was delivered to me. Sabinus and Cassius hold that you can sue me for the boy in a *condictio*; but that, if I am at all out of pocket by the transaction in which the slave engaged, I have a right of action in my turn against you. Which is quite correct; Julianus himself says that he is inclined to think that the owner [of the slave] has the whole right of action founded on the purchase [of the boy], but the vendor can sue the *bona-fide* purchaser in a *condictio* [to have the boy handed over]. With regard to the money which came out of the *peculium*, if the coins are to be found, the owner of the slave can have a *vindicatio* for them, though he is liable to an action *de peculio* at the hands of the vendor for payment of the price; but, if they are spent,

[1] hominem.

there is an end of the action *de peculio*. However Julianus should have added that the vendor is liable to the owner of the slave, in an action on the purchase [of the boy] only on the terms of such owner paying him the whole price, as well as whatever would have been owing to him, if he had made his bargain with a free man. The same rule holds where I pay [the purchase money] to a *bona-fide* possessor [instead of the thief], provided always I am ready to assign to the true owner any right of action which I have against such possessor.

32 CELSUS (*Digest* 5) If you ask Titius and me to lend you money, whereupon I order my debtor to promise you to advance it, and you then make the stipulation under the impression that he is debtor to Titius, are you bound to [repay] me? I hesitate to say so, if you contracted no bargain with me, still I almost think that you are bound; not because I lent you money, as this cannot be the case where there is no agreement between the parties, but because money of mine came into your hands, and accordingly it is right and just that you should restore it to me.

33 MODESTINUS (*Pandectæ* 10) It is provided by imperial constitutions that Governors of a province and members of their suites should not enter into business or lend money or practise usury.

34 PAULUS (*Sentences* 2) The officials who attend the Governor of a province, inasmuch as their office is permanent, are free to lend money and to practise usury. The Governor of a province is not forbidden to borrow money at interest.

35 MODESTINUS (*Responsa* 3) The risk in respect of demands on debtors falls on the person by whose negligence the risk itself can be shown to have been intensified.

36 JAVOLENUS (*Epistles* 1) You owed me a sum of money unconditionally, and you have promised Attius, at my request, to pay it to him, subject to a condition. So long as this condition is pending, your liability to me is exactly what it would have been if you had promised[1] me the money subject to the alternative condition; and, that being the case, my question is—will an action on my part while the condition is pending produce no result? The answer was[2]:—I have no doubt that the[3] money for which I

[1] For *spopondisti* read *spopondisses*. Cf. M.

[2] The answer is put in the mouth of the interrogator as if it were his own opinion.

[3] For *mea* read *ea*. Cf. M.

stipulated unconditionally will remain on loan to you, even if the condition has not come to pass in which Attius is concerned, Attius having, with my consent, stipulated for payment of the same sum, subject to a condition; as the case is the same as if no stipulation [on the part of Attius] had been made in the matter; at the same time, so long as the event of the condition is in suspense, I cannot sue for the money, because, it being uncertain whether it may not come to be owing in pursuance of the latter stipulation, my suit must be held to be premature.

37 PAPINIANUS (*Definitions* 1) Where a condition refers to the time at which the contract is made, the stipulation is not suspended, and, if the conditional event is an actual fact, the stipulation is binding, even though the parties to the contract should not be aware that it is binding. For example, suppose the stipulation should be—"do you promise to give me a hundred if the king of the Parthians is living?" The rule is the same even where the condition refers to past time.

38 SCÆVOLA (*Questions* 1) In short, regard must be had to the question whether, so far as human nature admits, it can be known[1] that the money will be owing:

39 PAPINIANUS (*Definitions* 1) accordingly, the proviso only acquires the force of a condition when it is referred to future time.

40 PAULUS (*Questions* 3) There was read in the court of Æmilius Papinianus, Prefect of the Prætorium and learned in the law, a written promise such as follows:—"I, Lucius Titius, have set down in writing that I have received from Publius Mævius fifteen [*aurei*] as a loan paid down to me at the house of the same, and Publius Mævius stipulated and I Lucius Titius promised that the said fifteen in good money should be duly paid on the first day of the next month (*Kalendis futuris*). If on the day above mentioned[2] the [said] sum of money shall not have been given and paid to Publius Mævius, or to whatever person shall have a right thereto, nor security have been given in that behalf, then, for such time thereafter as I am in arrears with the payment, Publius Mævius stipulated and I Lucius Titius promised that there shall be given by way of penalty for every thirty days and for every hundred *denarii* one *denarius*. And we have both agreed that *to Publius Mævius out*

[1] For *scire* read *sciri*.

[2] Ins. *supra scripta* after *die*. M.

of the sum above mentioned[1] I should be bound to repay every month three hundred *denarii* out of the whole sum to him or to his heir." A question was asked as to the obligation to pay interest, as the number of months which was allowed for payment had passed by. My answer was as follows:—As a supplementary agreement (*pactum*) which is made at once is regarded as part of the stipulation, it follows that the present case may be treated as though the promisee, after stipulating for a given sum of money to be paid every month, had then made an additional agreement for interest in proportion to the delay in paying the instalments; consequently, I said, at the end of the first month interest on the first instalment would be due, and, in the same way, after the second and third periods, the interest on the respective unpaid amounts due by way of instalment would begin to mount up, but interest could not be demanded on any unpaid principal before the time at which a demand could be made of such principal itself. Some however maintained that the added agreement referred only to the payment of principal, not of interest too, the latter having been made the subject of a stipulation in plain terms in the previous clause, and this agreement, they said, would only furnish ground for an *exceptio*, so that, if the money were not paid by the promised instalments, interest was due from the day of the stipulation, just as if this had been expressed in so many words. But the time to sue for the principal having been postponed, it follows that interest is due too as from the day when the debtor began to be in default, and assuming, in accordance with the last mentioned opinion, that the agreement would only lead to an *exceptio*,—though this was not the view finally adopted,—still, as a matter of strict law, the obligation to pay interest will not be enforceable, as a man is not in default where he has an *exceptio* which is a good bar to a demand for the debt. Of course, people do stipulate for some quantity to be furnished on the occurrence of a conditional event, but one which is got together in the meantime, as occurs in the case of the produce of land, [and] a similar provision may be expressly made as to interest too, so that, if the money is not paid by the day, what[2] is coming in the way of interest may be payable as from the day when the stipulation was made.

41 AFRICANUS (*Questions* 8) A person having employed in one of the provinces his slave Stichus as an accountant, his testament was read at Rome, by which the same Stichus was given his freedom

[1] For *pro* read *Publio* (cf. M.): but the words in italics are interpolated. M.
[2] For *quo* read *quod*. Cf. M.

and appointed heir in respect of a share of the testator's estate; but Stichus still collected debts due to the deceased and also lent money, therewith on various occasions making stipulations for repayment and taking security, without being aware of his change of status. An opinion was asked as to how the law stood in the matter. The view held was that any debtors who had paid him had a good discharge, wherever they had themselves been unaware of the decease of his [late] owner; but with regard to such sums of money as had come to Stichus's hands, his co-heirs had no right to ask for an action *familiæ erciscundæ*, but one of *negotia gesta* only ought to be allowed. As to money which he had himself lent, the property in this only passed to an extent proportional to the share which he had in the inheritance; seeing that, even if I hand money to you for you to lend it to Stichus, [*sic*: *quære Mævius*?] and you give it him after my death, of which you are unaware, you will not pass the property in it; as a matter of fact, however much it may accord with acknowledged law that debtors who pay Stichus get a good discharge, it is not established law that he can pass the property in monies which he lends. If therefore there were no stipulation for repayment in the case, the money could not be sued for in respect of the share of a co-heir as money lent, nor could the securities be retained. If however Stichus went on to make a stipulation for repayment, an important question would be in what form he made it; as, if, for example, he stipulated expressly in favour of his master Titius, then dead, the stipulation would beyond all doubt be inoperative, but if he stipulated for repayment to himself, the proper view was that he acquired the benefit of such stipulation for the inheritance; the rule being that just as where free men or slaves of strangers are held to service in good faith, any acquisition which they make through the property of their reputed owners goes to these latter, so too acquisitions made through anything which is part of the inheritance are made for the inheritance itself. But after entry on the part of the co-heirs on the inheritance, the above does not apply to its full extent, at any rate where they know that Stichus was made co-heir along with them, since in that case they cannot be regarded as *bona-fide* possessors, as they have not so much as any intention of possessing at all. If however the case put before us is that of the co-heirs being unaware of the facts, for instance because they were themselves in the position of heirs by compulsion, the above answer may still be given, in which case the matter will come to this, that, if the slave in question has co-heirs of his own class, they will all be held to service in good faith to one another reciprocally.

42 CELSUS (*Digest* 6) If I stipulate for ten from Titius and then go on to stipulate from Seius for the amount by which what I can get from Titius falls short of his debt, then, if I sue Titius for ten, this is no discharge to Seius, or else Seius's undertaking to me is of no use; but if Titius complies with the order of the Court, Seius's liability will be at an end. But if I sue Seius, then, whatever the amount is by which what I can get from Titius at the time when issue is joined between Seius and me falls short of his debt, so much the less can I sue Titius for afterwards. 1. Labeo says as follows:—if you stipulate that the promisor shall make sure that ten are given, you cannot put in your statement of claim that the promisor is bound to give ten, as he can still be discharged of his promise by providing a more substantial debtor; in short Labeo's meaning is that the promisor cannot be compelled to join issue if he offers to find a substantial debtor.

II.

ON SWEARING AN OATH, WHETHER VOLUNTARY, COMPULSORY OR JUDICIAL.

1 GAIUS (*on the Provincial Edict* 5) A very great resource has come into use, in order to the despatching of cases before the Courts, consisting of the religious feeling attached to an oath, by means of which disputes are decided either in pursuance of an agreement between the parties themselves or else on the authority of the judge.

2 PAULUS (*on the Edict* 18) The taking of an oath wears the appearance of a compromise, and there is more weight attached to it than to a judgment.

3 ULPIANUS (*on the Edict* 22) The Prætor's words are:—"Where the party against whom proceedings are had takes an oath, on such terms being offered" etc. By the party against whom proceedings are had we must understand the defendant himself. The additional words—"such terms being offered"—are not superfluous, as if the defendant should take the oath without anyone tendering it to him, the Prætor will pay no heed to the oath so

taken, the party swears to himself; were it otherwise, anybody who has no scruples about swearing[1] would betake himself to the expedient of swearing an oath, though no one tendered it, and so rid himself of the burden of meeting an action at law. 1. Whatever kind of action it is in which a man is sued, if he take the oath, he will get the benefit of it, whether the proceedings are *in personam* or *in rem* or *in factum* or taken by way of a penal or any other kind of action or for an interdict. 2. Add that if the subject of the oath is the status of anyone, the Prætor will uphold the oath: suppose, for instance, I tender the oath and you swear that you are not subject to my *potestas*,—your oath must be regarded. 3. Accordingly, Marcellus has it that an oath may even be sworn on such a point as whether such and such a woman is with child or not, and the parties must abide by the oath; lastly he says that, where the inquiry is as to possession, the oath must be decisive; where, for instance, a woman claims to take possession of property on the ground of pregnancy, and, the other party repudiating her claim, either she swears that she is pregnant, or the other side swears the contrary; in which case, if she herself swears, she can take possession without misgiving, and if the oath is in contradiction of her claim, she cannot do so, even though, as a matter of fact, she should be pregnant; and, so Marcellus tells us, the woman who takes the oath will get the full benefit of it, so as not to be subjected to proceedings on the ground that she had taken possession as on behalf of an unborn child on a false pretence, nor to be exposed to disturbance when in possession. As to whether the oath avails to such an extent as to preclude inquiry, after a child is born, into the question whether the person whose child it is said to be is the father or not, this is a point discussed by Marcellus; who holds that there ought to be an inquiry into the actual fact, because the oath does not benefit nor prejudice any third person; accordingly the oath of the mother will not benefit the child, nor will any prejudice be occasioned if the mother tenders the oath and it is thereupon asserted on oath that she is not pregnant by such and such a man. 4. The oath must be taken as tendered: there is no doubt that if I tender an oath for you to swear by God, and you swear by your own head

4 PAULUS (*on the Edict* 18) or the heads of your sons,

5 ULPIANUS (*on the Edict* 22) such an oath will not be held good; but if I required you to swear by your own salvation and

[1] After *quisque* ins. *ad jurandum.* M.

you swear accordingly, we must abide by it. Every kind of oath that is lawful at all which anyone desires to have taken for his behoof is to the purpose, and if it be taken accordingly, the Prætor will uphold it. 1. The Divine Pius laid down that if an oath were sworn in accordance with some private superstition the parties must abide by it. 2. The oath being once taken, no other question is asked than whether the party really swore, and the point whether anything is owing is disregarded, this being treated as sufficiently settled by the oath itself. 3. However, where a man tenders an unlawful oath, I mean an oath pertaining to a religion subject to State disapproval, it may fairly be asked whether the case should not be treated as though no oath had been taken:—which on the whole I should say is the right view. 4. If no oath is taken, and the oath is not waived, the case must be treated as though the matter had never been referred to decision by oath at all. Accordingly, if the party is willing to take the oath on a subsequent occasion, such an oath will not bestead him, as it is not taken in pursuance of the tender.

6 PAULUS (*on the Edict* 19) A man is said to waive an oath where he first tenders it, but, the other party being prepared to swear, he dispenses with the oath, being satisfied with the willingness which the other shows in accepting it; but if the party to whom it was tendered did not accept it, then, even if he should subsequently be prepared to swear, but the plaintiff should not choose to tender the oath, it will not be held to be waived; an oath can only be waived if it has been accepted.

7 ULPIANUS (*on the Edict* 22) The Prætor's words are:—"For a thing as to which an oath has been tendered I will allow no action either against the party himself or against the person to whom the thing now belongs." The word 'thing' must be understood to apply whether an oath has been taken as to the whole property at stake or only a portion of it; what the Prætor promises is that he will not allow an action about a matter as to which an oath has been sworn, either against the party who swore or against those who succeed to the position of the one to whom the oath was tendered,

8 PAULUS (*on the Edict* 18) even if they succeed to the property:

9 ULPIANUS (*on the Edict* 22) the rule being that, after the

oath is once sworn, leave to bring an action is refused; or, if there is any dispute, that is, if it is contested whether or not the oath was taken, the party has an *exceptio*. 1. The oath having been taken or waived, the defendant will have gained a right of *exceptio* available on his own behalf and on that of some others, and the plaintiff acquires a right of action in which the only point into which inquiry is made is whether he swore that such and such a thing ought in law to be given him or, whereas he was prepared to swear, the oath was waived. 2. If judgment is pronounced against a man after the oath is sworn, in a case involving infamy, the better opinion is that infamy is incurred. 3. Where a man who was under a liability to me exposing him to an action the right to which would expire by lapse of time tenders the oath for me to swear that he is bound to pay, and I swear that he is, he will not be discharged by expiration of the time, because, after joinder of issue in the action against him, his liability becomes perpetual. 4. If one under twenty-five tenders the oath, and declares that advantage has been taken of him in respect of this very fact, the *exceptio* founded on the oath ought to be met on his part with a *replicatio*; so Pomponius says. However I should say that such a *replicatio* ought not to be allowed as a matter of course; I think, in most cases, the Prætor ought himself to go into the question whether advantage was taken of the minor, and give [or withhold] restitution *in integrum* according to the result of his inquiry; it does not follow, when a party is a minor, that simply by showing this fact he proves that he has been over-reached. It should be added that the replication[1] or inquiry referred to ought not to go beyond the prescribed time after the minor's twenth-fifth year is ended. 5. Again, if a man tenders an oath to a debtor in fraud of his own creditors, and an *exceptio* founded on the oath is pleaded to actions brought by the creditors, the latter must be allowed a replication of fraud: moreover, if a man, with fraudulent intent, tenders the oath to a creditor for the latter to swear that he has a good demand for ten, and afterwards, when his goods have been sold for insolvency, he wishes to bring an action, either leave to bring the action must be refused or else he can be met with the *exceptio* of its being a fraud on his creditors. 6. We are told by Julianus that where the oath is taken by an agent for the defence, whether voluntary or appointed, the same being tendered by the plaintiff, such oath is a valid defence and will furnish a good *exceptio* to the principal. Accordingly a

[1] In text *exceptio*.

similar rule holds where I appoint an agent to sue, and, on the defendant tendering the oath, he swears that my demand is good, as this gives me a right of action. This is a reasonable view. 7. If the claimant (*petitor*) has sworn, on the oath being tendered by the possessor, that the property is his, as plaintiff (*actor*) he will be allowed to bring an action ; but this is only against the party who tendered the oath or those who have succeeded to his position ; should he, on the other hand, desire to enjoy in an action against anyone else the advantage acquired by swearing, his oath will be of no use to him ;

10 PAULUS (*on the Edict* 18) as a transaction had between two particular persons must not be allowed to prejudice a third party.

11 ULPIANUS (*on the Edict* 22) But if the oath is tendered to a possessor, and he swears that the property does not belong to the plaintiff, then, as long as he is in possession, he can, for the purpose of meeting any action brought by the party who tendered the oath, plead such oath by way of *exceptio* ; but, if he should lose the possession, he will have no right of action [on the same oath], not even if the party who tendered the oath to him is in possession : he never swore that the thing was his, but only that it did not belong to the other. 1. Accordingly, if, when he was in possession, the plaintiff tendered him the oath, and he swore that the thing *was* his, the rule is, in keeping with the above, that, even if he should lose possession, and thereupon the party who tendered the oath should acquire it, he [the one who swore] will have a right to an action *in factum*. Moreover it is held that the produce derived from a thing which I have sworn to be mine ought to be given up to me, and there is no doubt that children born from female slaves and the young of cattle ought to be given up, after the oath is tendered. 2. Similarly, if I take the oath to the effect either that the usufruct in anything belongs to me or that it ought to be conveyed to me, I continue to have a right of action for so long time as the usufruct itself would last, if I were actually enjoying it, but in those cases in which the usufruct would be lost, I have no right of action. Again, if the party swears that he has a usufruct or has a right to have one conveyed to him in things in which no usufruct can be constituted, because it would consume the whole substance, I hold the opinion that the legal operation of the oath must be maintained, so that I should say that even then he must be held to have taken a valid oath, and that, in virtue of the same, he can demand the usufruct on offering the [regular] undertaking. 3. If there is a dispute as to an inheritance between you and me, and I swear that the inheritance is mine, I have a right to whatever I should get if judgment had been given in my favour in an action for the inheritance ; so that you are bound to hand over not only the things which you had in your possession at the time, but besides them any that came into your possession afterwards, and as much account is to be made of the oath sworn by me as if my case had been proved ; accordingly, I have a right to an *utilis actio*. But if I were in possession in pursuance of a title to the inheritance, and you took proceedings to recover it from me, I ought, after taking the oath in answer to your claim, to be allowed to plead such oath by way of *exceptio*. Of course, if some third person takes proceedings against me to recover the inheritance, then there is no doubt, as Julianus himself tells us, that the oath will be of no use to me.

12 JULIANUS (*Digest* 9) A similar rule holds where I desire to sue anyone else who is in possession of things which are part of the inheritance, as, even if I had brought an action to recover the inheritance against you and had proved that it was mine, nevertheless, if I sued anyone else, I should be obliged to prove the same fact.

13 ULPIANUS (*on the Edict* 22) Two men being both patrons [of the same freedman], this latter, on one of the patrons tendering the oath, swears that he is not his freedman : will the other of the two have a right to the possession of the whole of the property to which patrons are entitled or only to half of such property ? The answer given is :—if the one to whom the oath was sworn was patron, the other has a right to the possession of his own share in the goods [and no more], and he can derive no [legal] advantage from the fact that the freedman took an oath against the claim of the one first mentioned : still the patron in question will derive a great deal of weight and authority, in any application to the Court for the purpose of showing that he is the sole patron, from the fact that the freedman swore that the other was not his patron. 1. According to Julianus, a man who swears that an estate is his will, after the time has elapsed for entitling him to a plea of "long time," have a right to an *utilis actio* as well. 2. Julianus further holds that a man who swears that he did not commit theft must be held to have sworn as to every ground of action [*in personam*], and consequently he is not liable to be sued

either in the action for theft or in a "condictitious" action; such an action, he says, is one to which none is liable but a thief. Must we say then that where a man swears that he committed no theft at all, he will simply on that ground have a good *exceptio*, if he is sued in a *condictio*? No doubt, if the party who brings the *condictio* maintains that the ground of his action against the present defendant is that he is heir to the thief, he cannot be refused a hearing, and he ought to be allowed, so to speak, a *condictio* with a special issue against the heir to the thief, in which the judge must not allow him to proceed, as soon as he attempts to show that the defendant is the actual thief. 3. Where a man swears that I sold him something for a hundred, he can sue on the contract of purchase for the performance of whatever follows thereupon, that is, he can ask that the thing sold may be delivered and an undertaking given warranting him against recovery on the ground of superior title; but it is a fair question whether he can be sued on the contract of sale for recovery of the purchase-money. However, as to this, if the oath comprehended this very fact that the money was paid, no right of action for the money remains; but if the oath did not comprehend this, it follows that he is liable for it still. 4. A similar rule holds where a man swears that he entered into partnership, as he can be sued in an action *pro socio*. 5. Marcellus proceeds to say that where a man swears that he pledged his land as security for ten, he cannot bring an action on the pledge without paying ten: he adds[1] however this, that perhaps he can be sued for ten on the ground of his oath, which view he on the whole approves of. Quintus Saturninus is of the same opinion, and relies on the case of a man swearing that his *quondam* wife gave him such and such property by way of *dos*, whereupon, so he holds, the lady has a right to an *utilis actio* for *dos*: and I cannot say that this goes beyond what justice requires. 6. If, in a pecuniary matter, a man swears by the genius of the Emperor that he is not bound to pay, or that he has a right to ask for payment, and he swears falsely, or, again, if he swears that he will pay within a given time, and he does not pay, here the present Emperor and his father laid down that he must be sent off to be beaten with rods, the following warning being addressed to him:—"Do not be in a hurry to swear."

14 PAULUS (*on the Edict* 3) Whenever the oath is to be taken in regard of a thing [and not of a person], it cannot be waived in

[1] Read *adicit* for *adici*. Cf. M.

favour of one who is a *paterfamilias* or patron [to the party tendering]; and an oath is said to be taken in regard of a thing in the case, for example, of a loan of money, where the plaintiff swears that he has a legal right to payment, [not saying from whom] or the defendant swears that he is not bound to pay; [not saying to whom;] the same rule applies where an oath is required as to money promised by *constitutum*.

15 THE SAME (*on the Edict* 6) In the case of persons of pre-eminent rank or such as are confined to the house by ill health, an agent must be sent to their place of abode to administer the oath.

16 ULPIANUS (*on the Edict* 10) If a patron marries his freedwoman, he cannot be compelled to swear in an action for "things removed" (theft from a wife). Furthermore, if he himself tenders the oath to his freedwoman, he will not be obliged to swear that his proceedings are not vexatious.

17 PAULUS (*on the Edict* 18) Where the oath is taken out of Court, but in pursuance of an agreement, it cannot be tendered back. 1. A ward ought to tender the oath with his guardian's concurrence; if he tender it without such concurrence, there will, no doubt, be a good *exceptio*, but it can be met with a *replicatio*, as he is not legally competent to manage his own affairs. 2. If the oath is tendered by a guardian who is acting as such or the curator of a lunatic or prodigal, it ought to be upheld, as they are[1] able to pass the property in goods or to give a receipt for money paid, and they can possess the Court of a case by taking proceedings. 3. A tender by a procurator must also be upheld, wherever, that is, he is entrusted with the management of all his principal's property, or he was expressly commissioned to act in the particular case or he is procurator on his own behalf:

18 ULPIANUS (*on the Edict* 26) but, as a rule, a procurator who desires to tender an oath ought not to be listened to, so Julianus tells us (*Dig.* b. 10), or else, at some later time, a defendant who has already sworn may be sued by the principal; and he is not much the better off for any understanding that may have been given him that the principal would ratify; because, if the principal should sue him, the defendant will have to show the truth of what he swore, assuming, that is, that he is met with a *replicatio*[2] [to the

[1] After *res* read or understand *possunt*.

[2] In the text *exceptio*. Cf. Pothier.

effect that the principal did not authorize the procurator to undertake that he would[ratify], but if he should [being unable to do this] sue [the procurator] on the undertaking that the principal would ratify, this may compel him to show that his oath was false.

19 THE SAME (*on the Edict* 26) Accordingly, if the prosecutor was commissioned to bring an action, and he tendered an oath, he has done something different from what he was commissioned to do.

20 PAULUS (*on the Edict* 18) When a slave tenders an oath or takes one, it will be upheld if the slave had been allowed the management of his *peculium* ;

21 GAIUS (*on the Provincial Edict* 5) as a slave in that position can give a good receipt for money paid him in discharge of a debt and he has been given the power to novate an obligation.

22 PAULUS (*on the Edict* 18) Some indeed hold that if the slave tenders an oath to a plaintiff, an action *de peculio* must be allowed against his owner. Similar rules apply to a son under *potestas*.

23 ULPIANUS (*on the Edict* 26) If the slave swears that his owner is not bound to pay, his owner can claim the benefit of an *exceptio* and the other party has only himself to blame for tendering the oath to the slave.

24 PAULUS (*on the Edict* 28) Much more is it the case that a father can derive advantage from the conscientiousness (*i.e.* oath) of his son, the latter being a person who might in fact be made defendant to an action. But if such persons tender the oath back, they do not expose those in whose *potestas* they are to any legal disadvantage.

25 ULPIANUS (*on the Edict* 26) Again, if an oath is tendered to my slave originally or tendered back to him, and he swears that some property belongs to his owner or ought to be given to him, I ought to be allowed an action or an *exceptio* on the ground of the sanctity of an oath and in pursuance of the agreement.

26 PAULUS (*on the Edict* 18) Whenever anyone is averred to have sworn, it is immaterial what the person's sex or age may be ; the oath ought to be upheld absolutely, as against a party who was willing to take the risk of it when he tendered it ; at the same time a ward is never deemed guilty of perjury, as it is not held that he

deceives knowingly. 1. If a father swears that his son is not bound to pay, Cassius gave the opinion that father and son both should be allowed to plead the oath by way of *exceptio*; if the father swears that there is nothing in the *peculium*, there can be an action brought against the son, but the father can be sued too, on the principle, that is, of taking into account *peculium* subsequently acquired. 2. Putting a man on the terms of taking an oath is perhaps a transaction of the same class as novating or transferring a contract, as it is founded on an agreement, though it is tantamount to a judgment too.

27 GAIUS (*on the Provincial Edict* 5) An oath in fact takes the place of payment of the debt.

28 PAULUS (*on the Edict* 18) In the case of two correal creditors by stipulation, if one tenders the oath, it can be pleaded to an action by the other also. 1. Where a principal debtor swears, the surety gets the benefit of it too; and where an oath has been obtained from a surety, according to Cassius and Julianus, this benefits the principal debtor as well; the oath operates in the same way as payment, and hence it must be treated as doing so in this case too, always provided that recourse was had to the oath in order to deal with the contract itself and the matter at stake, and not merely with the position of the party swearing. 2. If a man has promised to produce my debtor before the Court, and I tender him the oath, whereupon he swears that he never promised to produce the person in question at all, this will be no defence to my debtor; but if what he swears is that he is not himself under any liability to me, in that case a distinction must be[1] made, and the pleadings can be mended by a *replicatio*, [the question being] whether he swore as mentioned[2] on the ground that after his promise he had actually produced the person in question or because he had paid the debt; and a similar distinction can be made with reference to a surety for a debt. 3. Of two correal debtors of a sum of money one took the oath; this can be pleaded by the other as well. 4. An oath can be pleaded by way of *exceptio* not only where the plaintiff is suing in the action with reference to which he got the oath taken, but even in a different action, provided only the same matter of fact is material for the purposes of the later suit; as, for instance, where an oath has been called for in connexion with an action on a mandate or a case of

[1] For *sit* read *est*. Cf. M. [2] Omit the first *an*.

voluntary agency or a partnership or with any other similar action, and then a specific *condictio* is brought founded on the same facts; the truth is the one action disposes of the other. 5. If a man swears that he did not commit a robbery, he cannot derive any benefit from this oath in an action for theft or a *condictio* [*furtiva*], as theft is a distinct offence, being one which can in fact be committed secretly. 6. If an action is brought against a tenant on his contract (*ex locato*), on the ground, it may be, of his having cut down trees, and he swears that he did not cut any, then, if he is sued afterwards on the Law of the Twelve Tables under the head of trees cut down, or on the *Lex Aquilia* for wrongful damage, or by application for an interdict *quod vi et clam*, he can make a good defence by pleading his oath. 7. If a woman swears that she did not remove her husband's goods in contemplation of a divorce, this does not enable her to defend herself by the *exceptio* in case she is sued in an action to recover the goods, so that if she maintains that they are her own property, another oath is required; on the other hand, if what she swore [at the outset] was that the goods were her own, this affords a defence to an action for removal. In short, the general rule is that, even where it is a different action in which the same inquiry takes place, an *exceptio* founded on the oath will be to the purpose. 8. Accordingly, where a man swears that judgment was never given against him, even though he is sued on a judgment founded on a promise by stipulation that the order of the Court should be obeyed, he will have a good *exceptio*. If, on the other hand, he should be sued on the promise that the order should be obeyed, and he thereupon swears that he was not bound to pay, it does not follow that he has a good *exceptio*; as it is possible that there is nothing payable on the [original] stipulation, although judgment was pronounced [against him]: unless, indeed, what he meant to swear to was that he was not even ordered to pay. 9. Again, Pomponius says that where a plaintiff swears that a theft was committed of property of his, he does not thereupon acquire good ground for a *condictio* as well [as an action for theft]. 10. Add that seeing that, under this part [of the Edict], the oath furnishes matter both for an action and an *exceptio*, if the defendant takes an oath out of court, on tender by the plaintiff, that he is not bound to pay and then the plaintiff takes an oath, on tender by the defendant, that he has a right to demand payment, or the order is the inverse, the claim founded on the later oath will be held to have the greater weight: but this will not prejudge the question as to the other party having committed perjury; the subject of inquiry in the action not being whether the defendant was under an obligation to pay, but whether the plaintiff swore that he was.

29 TRYPHONINUS (*Disputations* 6) Again, if I swear, on your tendering the oath, that you did not swear that I was bound to pay you, then, in answer to an *utilis actio* on your part, in which the question at issue is whether you swore that you had a right to demand payment, I can plead by way of *exceptio* my own oath which puts an end to the question at issue in the action.

30 PAULUS (*on the Edict* 18) According to Pedius, where a man swears, in an action in which the amount claimable is increased by the defendant's denial of liability, that something is owed him, he acquires a right to ask for the simple amount only, and not for twofold; as it is amply sufficient for the plaintiff that he should be relieved from the necessity of proving his case, since, setting aside this part of the Edict, the right of action for twofold remains unimpaired; and it may very well be said that, in a case such as the above, it is not the main question that is put in issue, but simply the plaintiff's oath is allowed to take effect. 1. If I swear that you are bound to hand over to me Stichus, there being no such slave existing, you, the defendant, are not bound to give me even so much as the man's value, except it be on the ground of theft or in consequence of default on your part; in such cases the value has to be given, even if the slave is already dead. 2. If a woman swears that ten are owing to her for *dos*, that entire sum must be given; but, if she swears that she gave ten by way of *dos*, the inquiry will leave alone the one point whether the sum was given, but it will be treated as given, and such part of it as ought to be returned to her will have to be handed over. 3. In an *actio popularis* [where anyone who likes can sue] an oath which a party has been made to swear will be available against a third person only where it was called for in good faith, since, indeed, even where a man takes the regular proceedings, this does not preclude an *actio publica* [on behalf of the State], unless the proceedings were collusive. 4. If a freedman, on his patron tendering the oath, swears that he is not his freedman, the oath must be upheld, so that no demand for services can be entertained, nor any order made for *bonorum possessio contra tabulas*. 5. If I swear that I have a right to have a usufruct conveyed to me, it ought to be granted only on the terms of my giving an undertaking that I will

enjoy it in accordance with the judgment of an impartial arbitrator, and that, when the usufruct expires, I will make over the property.

31 GAIUS (*on the Provincial Edict* 30) We must bear in mind that sometimes, even after the oath has been imposed, it is still allowable, in pursuance of imperial enactments, to resort to the regular proceedings, if the applicant alleges that he has found fresh documentary evidence and intends to use this only. These enactments however are held to be applicable only to a case in which the defendant has had judgment given in his favour,—as a matter of fact, a common practice is, in doubtful cases, for the judge to require the oath to be taken and to pronounce in favour of the party who swears;—but, where the oath has been taken in pursuance of a private arrangement between the parties, no second hearing of the old cause is allowed.

32 MODESTINUS (*Differences*, book —) A ward cannot dispense with the oath.

33 ULPIANUS (*on Sabinus* 28) Where a man swears by his own salvation, then, true as it is that he is held to swear by God, seeing that this oath involves a reference to the Divinity, still, if the oath has not been tendered to him in these express terms, he is not held to have sworn at all; accordingly he will have to take a fresh oath in due form.

34 THE SAME (*on the Edict* 26) The oath may be used both in pecuniary cases and in matters of any other kind, an oath may be tendered even in an action for the render of services, and the adverse party has no wrong to complain of, as he can tender the oath back. How then, if the defendant should declare that he is discharged on the ground that, whereas he promised to deliver Stichus, that slave is, he believes, dead? In this case, he cannot get off by tendering back, and accordingly, for this reason, Marcellus holds, and very rightly, that either he should be excused the oath or else time should be allowed him so that he may inform himself on the matter and then take the oath. 1. A man who takes up the defence (*defensor*) of a municipality or of any corporate body can tender the oath, if he has a mandate to do so. 2. An oath cannot be tendered to a ward. 3. A *procurator* is not compelled to swear, nor is a *defensor*, hence we read in Julianus (*Dig.* b. 10) that a *defensor* is not compellable to swear and that he need do no more with a view to a complete defence than be ready to join issue in the action. 4. When a man tenders the oath, he ought

himself first to swear the oath as to vexatious proceedings, if called upon to do so, and, that being done, the oath to be sworn to him will be taken. The above oath as to vexatious proceedings is one which is dispensed with in favour of both patrons and parents. 5. If the parties are not satisfied as to the sort of statement which has to be sworn to, the terms of it are for the *arbiter* to direct who decides the case. 6. The Prætor's words are:—"the party who is called upon to swear I will compel either to pay or else to swear"; accordingly, the defendant must choose one of the two, he must either pay or swear; if he declines to swear, he must be compelled by the Prætor to pay. 7. However, there is another course open to the defendant, viz. that of tendering the oath back, if he prefers it; and if the plaintiff declines terms which involve his taking the oath, the Prætor will not allow the action to proceed; and such a refusal on the Prætor's part would be perfectly just, as one who tenders an oath has no right to object to terms which consist in a similar tender being made to himself. We may add that the plaintiff cannot tender the oath denying vexatious proceedings to the party who tenders the oath back, as it would be intolerable that a plaintiff should expect an oath to be sworn him as to the vexatious character of terms such as were tendered by himself. 8. It is however not invariably suitable that the oath tendered back should be exactly such as was first tendered, as the diversity of matters and persons may chance to be such that points present themselves which give occasion for a difference between the two; accordingly, if any such thing should happen, the precise form of an oath of this kind must be settled by the judge on motion. 9. When the matter is left to be decided by oath, the judge discharges a defendant who swears, he will listen to one who wishes to tender the oath back, and, if the plaintiff swears, he must give judgment against the defendant; if the defendant declines to swear, then, if he pays, he discharges him, and, if not, he gives judgment against him; if the plaintiff, on the oath being tendered back, declines to take it, he discharges the defendant.

35 PAULUS (*on the Edict* 28) If the guardian of a ward tenders the oath, in the absence of all other means of proof, his application must be heard, as cases may arise in which the ward will be refused an action. 1. If the oath is tendered by a prodigal, he will not be listened to, and the rule is the same in other cases resembling his: as, whether the oath takes the place of a [fresh] agreement or a performance of the obligation or a judgment, a tender of it will not be sanctioned except when made by one who is a fit person for those cases. 2. Those persons who are not compellable to join issue in an action in Rome are equally free to decline to take the oath there, for instance, provincial legates.

36 ULPIANUS (*on the Edict* 27) If the plaintiff tenders the oath with reference only to money assured by *constitutum*, and the defendant swears, the latter will have a good *exceptio*, if he is sued on the *constitutum*: but if he is sued for the principal, that is sued on the antecedent ground of claim, he cannot plead an *exceptio*, unless he swore as to that ground of claim too, on the plaintiff tendering the oath.

37 ULPIAN (*on the Edict* 33) If the oath has not been waived by the person who tendered it, but no oath is taken by him in disavowal of vexatious proceedings, it is a necessary result that his action should be disallowed; a man has only himself to blame, if he has gone so far as to tender the oath without first taking the oath in disavowal of vexatious proceedings, so that he is in the same position as if he had waived the oath which he tendered.

38 PAULUS (*on the Edict* 37) Where a man is not willing either to swear or to tender the oath back, it is a case of plain dishonesty and equivalent to an admission of liability.

39 JULIANUS (*Digest* 10) If a man agrees with his debtor that no action shall be brought for the money, if the latter will swear that he did not ascend the Capitol or that he did or did not do anything else, it matters not what, and the debtor swears accordingly, he must be allowed the *exceptio* founded on the oath, and, besides this, if he pays, he can sue to get it back; as where, in respect of any ground of action, the parties put themselves on the terms[1] of an oath being taken, this is a perfectly legal arrangement for them to make.

40 THE SAME (*Digest* 13) When an oath is taken from a debtor, the result is that any pledge is released; the case is like that of a formal release of the debt, and it certainly gives rise to a perpetual *exceptio*. Hence, if the creditor sues for a penalty, he can still be barred by an *exceptio*, and, if the money should be paid, there can be an action to recover it; the fact being that, when the oath is once taken, there is an end of all dispute.

41 POMPONIUS (*Rules*) Labeo expressed the opinion that the

[1] Read *condicionem* for *condicione*. Cf. M.

oath may be dispensed with in favour of one who is absent or not informed of the fact; indeed it may be dispensed with by letter.

42 THE SAME (*Epistles* 18) An oath being tendered by a creditor who was proceeding against a ward for money lent, the ward swore that he was not bound to pay; whereupon the creditor demanded the money from a surety of the ward's: will he be barred by an *exceptio* founded on the oath? Let me have your opinion in writing. Julianus goes into the question at some length. If, he says, the question at issue between the creditor and the ward was whether the ward ever received the loan at all, and they agreed that the whole dispute[1] should be at an end if the ward took the oath, whereupon he swore, [as above mentioned,] that he was not bound to pay, the result of the arrangement must be to get rid of the natural obligation, and [therefore] any money paid could be recovered. But if the creditor contended that he had advanced the loan, and the ward's only defence was that his guardian had not intervened, and thereupon the oath in question was taken, the Prætor can in that case give no aid to the surety. If, however, it cannot be conclusively proved what the understanding between the parties was, and it is unknown, as indeed is generally the case, whether the dispute between the creditor and the ward was on a question of fact or a question of law, [the only thing known being[2]] that the ward swore on the creditor tendering the oath, we ought to take it that their intention was that, if he swore that he was not bound to pay, they should abandon the whole dispute[1]; the result of which is that, in the opinion we have come to, any money paid can be recovered, and an *exceptio* ought to be allowed to sureties. 1. If a surety swears that he is not bound to pay, the promisor can protect himself by pleading the oath, but if, on the other hand, the surety swore in terms implying that he never was surety for that amount at all, the promisor cannot derive any benefit from this oath. 2. Again, if, on tender by the plaintiff, a voluntary agent on behalf of an absent or [indeed a] present defendant swears that the person whom he is defending is not bound to pay, the *exceptio* founded on the oath ought to be allowed the person on whose behalf such oath was taken[3]. This principle applies equally where the person who swears is one who volunteered to take up the defence of a surety, as the principal

[1] For *condicione* read *contentione*. Cf. M.
[2] Some such words required. M.
[3] For *jurandum* read *juratum*. Cf. M.

will be allowed the *exceptio*. 3. Similarly, if the principal swore, his surety is protected, as, indeed, an actual decision in favour of either of the two will avail the other as well.

III.

On Swearing to the Claim.

1 Ulpianus (*on Sabinus* 51) When anything has been made the subject of a lawsuit, we do not suppose its value to be the greater because, by means of the oath to the claim, the order made upon the defendant may come to be for a larger amount, owing to his contumacy in not handing over the property; as the thing does not through this order become of greater value, but rather, through the defendant's contumacy, it is valued above its real worth.

2 Paulus (*on Sabinus* 13) Whether a man sues to recover something which belongs to him or brings an action for production, in some cases the only valuation made is that of the interest which the plaintiff has in the suit, for example, where the object is to punish the negligence of a defendant who omits to hand over property or to produce it; but when what is punished is fraudulent intention or wilful nonfeasance in not handing over or producing, the valuation is according to the plaintiff's oath to the claim.

3 Ulpianus (*on the Edict* 30) In a case where pieces of money have been deposited, the judge ought not to tender the oath to the claim so as to let a person swear to the extent of his interest, seeing that the value to be put on coins is fixed:—unless, indeed, what the party swears to should be the amount of interest he had in having the money repaid him on the proper day; suppose, for instance, he had to pay a sum of money under a penalty, or money for which he had given a pledge where, owing to the refusal to pay the money deposited, the pledge was sold.

4 The same (*on the Edict* 36) Let us consider who it is that can take the oath in a case of proceedings against a guardian, and against whom he can take it. No doubt the ward himself cannot take it, if under age; this has been very often declared by rescript. But the Divine Brothers laid down that the guardian himself cannot be compelled to swear, or the mother of the ward be allowed to do so, even if she should be prepared to do it, as it was held to

be going too far to allow that guardians should, without knowledge of the facts and without their own consent, in a matter involving gain for the benefit of another, encounter over and above the risks of false swearing. It is also provided by rescripts of our Emperor and his Divine Father that curators of a ward or minor (*adolescens*) must not be compelled to swear to a claim. Still, if guardians or curators desire to show so much regard to the wards or minors under their care, the authority of the law need not stand in the way of a termination of this kind being put to a trial to which such parties are committed; seeing that the valuation made by oath must be considered from the point of view of the advantage not of the party himself who swears, but of his principal, on whose behalf an account of the guardianship is demanded. At the same time the minor can take the oath if he likes. 1. The person who should tender the oath is the judge; certainly, if anyone else tenders it or the oath is sworn without being tendered at all, the religious sanction will not exist and there will be no oath; this is laid down by enactments of the present Emperor and his Divine Father. 2. There is no restriction as to the amount which may be sworn to; still, it is a question whether the judge may not set a limit to the oath, so as to keep the terms of it within a certain figure, for fear lest the party should seize the occasion offered him and swear to a value beyond all bounds. It is certainly held to be within the judge's discretion to tender the oath or to refuse it; and it may well be asked whether one who has it in his power to decline to tender the oath is not equally free to set limitations to the terms of it; which, in fact, is within the discretion of a judge who acts in good faith. 3. Again, we may consider whether the judge is not able, after tendering the oath, to decline to follow it, and either to dismiss the case altogether or even to order the defendant to pay a smaller sum in the way of damages than was sworn to, and the better opinion is that, on very special grounds, and on the discovery of further evidence, this may be done. 4. Add that in a case of negligence it is settled that the oath is not to be tendered, but a valuation must be made by the judge.

5 MARCIANUS (*Rules* 4) An oath to the claim is taken in actions *in rem* or for production and in *bona fide* proceedings. 1. But the judge can lay down a fixed amount which is not to be exceeded in the oath, since it was open to him at the outset to decline to tender the oath at all. 2. Again, even if the oath is taken, it is open to him either to dismiss the case or to order the defendant to pay a smaller

sum. 3. But, in all these cases, the oath to the claim can be taken for deliberate wrong only and not for negligence as well, matters under the last head are estimated by the judge. 4. No doubt, a party sometimes swears to the claim even in an action of strict law, for instance, where one who promised to deliver Stichus makes default and then Stichus dies, as the judge cannot put a value on property which has ceased to exist without tendering[1] the oath ;

6 PAULUS (*on the Edict* 26) though if proceedings are taken on a stipulation or on a testament, it is not the practice to swear to the claim.

7 ULPIANUS (*on the Edict* 8) It is commonly held to be a matter of course that it is only one who has the command of the case (*dominus litis*) who can swear to the claim: in fact, Papinianus says that no one can swear other than a party who has joined issue in the case on his own behalf.

8 MARCELLUS (*Digest* 8) A guardian who is in possession of the property of one just come of age refuses to give it up to him: I wish to know whether judgment should be given against him for what the thing is worth or for the amount for which the plaintiff swears to the claim. I replied:—It is not just that the measure of damages should be the actual value, I mean the amount that is at stake, seeing that contumacy itself has to be punished, and the amount ought rather to be fixed at the discretion of the owner by the power of swearing to the claim being allowed to the plaintiff.

9 JAVOLENUS (*Extracts from Cassius* 15) In the case of an action for theft the terms of the oath to be taken are that the thing was worth so much when the theft was committed, without the additional words "or more," because, given that a thing is worth more, it is, at any rate, worth as much.

10 CALLISTRATUS (*Questions* 1) In a case where someone fails to produce documents, the plaintiff is allowed to swear to the claim, so as to procure that the defendant shall be ordered to pay damages equivalent to the interest the plaintiff has in the documents being produced; this was laid down by the Divine Commodus himself.

11 PAULUS (*Responsa* 3) The false swearing of one who swears to a claim under compulsion of law is a thing as to which inquiry is not lightly allowed.

[1] Read *delatione* for *relatione*. Cf. M.

IV.

ON THE *CONDICTIO* TO RECOVER A THING GIVEN FOR A CONSIDERATION WHERE THE CONSIDERATION FAILS[1].

1 ULPIANUS (*on the Edict* 26) If money is given with a view to some unobjectionable act, as that a son should be emancipated or a slave manumitted or an action at law abandoned, then, if the act is executed, there is no right of action for return of the money. 1. If I give you ten by way of complying with a condition, and then decline an inheritance or a legacy [given me subject to that condition], I can sue to have the money returned.

2 HERMOGENIANUS (*Epitomes of law* 2) But we may add that if the testament is pronounced to be forged or void for inofficiousness, without fraud on the part of whoever gave the money, the ten can be recovered by an action grounded on failure of object.

3 ULPIANUS (*on the Edict* 26) I gave you so much money on the understanding that we should not go to law; so I may be said to have settled with you. Can I bring a *condictio*, if no undertaking is given me that the case will not come into Court? The truth is that it makes a great deal of difference whether the only object that I had in view in giving the money was that we should not go to law, or it was this as well, that in return I should have an assurance given me that we should not do so; if it was the latter, viz. that there should be the actual promise, I can bring a *condictio* for the money, in case the promise is not made; but if the object was that we should not go to law, then there is no right to bring a *condictio* so long as no proceedings are taken. 1. A similar rule will hold if I give you money on the understanding that you do not manumit Stichus; as an action for the return of the money will be admissible or will have to be disallowed, as the case may be, in accordance with the distinction above mentioned. 2. But if I gave you the money on the understanding that you

[1] *Condictio causa data causa non secuta.* The words *causa data,* or at least, the word *data,* cannot pass unquestioned. The sense would be expressed by *ob causam dati* or perhaps *causa dati* and I have assumed that one of these two was really written. See Roby, *Rom. priv. law,* II. 77.

would manumit Stichus; then, if you omit to do it, I can bring a *condictio* for the money, or, if I change my mind, I can do the same thing. 3. Suppose however I gave it on the understanding that you would manumit by a given day? In that case, if the day has not yet arrived, an action on my part for return of the money must be disallowed, unless I have changed my mind; but if the time has passed, I can bring the *condictio* for it. If however Stichus is dead, can the money that was given be recovered? According to Proculus, if he died after the time arrived at which he could have been manumitted, the money can be recovered, if not, no action can be brought. 4. In fact, it goes as far as this, if I did not give you anything on the understanding that you should manumit, but we had agreed that I should give something, you are quite free to bring the action which results from such a contract, that is the *condictio* [to compel payment], even though the slave is dead. 5. If a free man who was serving me as a slave in good faith should give me money on the understanding that I should manumit him, and I do so, a question which is asked is whether, supposing, after that, he should be shown to be free, he can sue me to recover the money; and as to this Julianus tells us (*Dig.* b. 12) that the manumitted man has a good action to recover it. Neratius, in fact, in his "Book of Parchments" relates that one Paris, a player, who had given Domitia, the daughter of Nero, ten, as the price of his liberty, sued her at law for the money, and the question was never asked whether Domitia had received the money with the knowledge that he was a free man. 6. If a man gives me ten, on the assumed ground that he is a *statuliber*, without having been directed to give them, then, as Celsus has it, he can sue to get the ten back. 7. Suppose however a slave as to whom it was provided by testament that he should give the heir ten and thereupon have his liberty is set free by a codicil unconditionally, but, not being aware of this fact, he still gives the ten to the heir, can he sue to get the money back? As to this, he informs us that the opinion of Celsus, his own father, was that he could not; but he himself, Celsus [the son], in consideration of natural justice, holds that the action can be brought. And this is the sounder view to take, although there can be no doubt, as, in fact, he says himself, that a man who gave money because he thought that he would get some recompense from the person who received it, or that the latter would be more of a friend to him, will not be able to get it back on the ground that he was carried away by a false impression. 8. Besides the above he offers some nice considerations on another question, viz. whether one who thought he was a *statuliber* would fail even to pass the property in money which he paid, because he gave it to the heir treating it as the heir's money instead of his own, although, as a matter of fact, the coins were his own, seeing that he received them subsequently to his acquisition of liberty by testament. To this I should say that, if he paid the money under the above idea it did not become the heir's property; as even where, to take another case, I give you my money, regarding it as your own, I do not thereby make it yours. How then if the man in question should give it not to the heir but to some other person to whom he thought he was ordered to give it? In this case, if he gave money that was part of his *peculium*, he would not pass the property in it; but if someone else gave it on his behalf or he himself gave it after he had become free, the property in it would pass. 9. It is true indeed that a *statuliber* is at liberty even to give money which is part of his *peculium*, where his object is to fulfil some condition, but, if the heir wishes to make the money secure, he can forbid him to give it; as by these means it will come to pass that on the one hand the *statuliber* will get his freedom, on the ground that the condition with which he was forbidden to comply is however treated as fulfilled, and, on the other hand, the money will not be lost. Still the person whom the testator wished to get the money can bring an action *in factum* against the heir so as to procure that the testator's order shall be carried out.

4 THE SAME (*on the Edict* 39) Where a man gives a formal discharge to his debtor after an agreement being made that the latter should furnish someone else who should promise to pay in his place, but he fails to furnish him, we may say that the money can be recovered by a *condictio* from the party to whom the formal discharge was given.

5 THE SAME (*Disputations* 2) If money has been given to you on the understanding that you would go to Capua, and, just as you were ready to start, some accidental circumstance or your own state of health put an obstacle in the way of your going, let us see whether there is a right to bring a *condictio* for the money. The truth is that, if the obstacle was none of your making, we may say that the money cannot be recovered; but, as it is open to the person who gave it to change his mind, it is quite certain that the money given can be sued for again, unless indeed you would have been the better off for not receiving the money with the

object in question ; as, if the state of things is such that, although you have not yet started, still you have so arranged your plans that you are obliged to go, or you have already made the necessary outlay for going, so that it is clear, for example, that you have spent more than you received, no *condictio* can be brought ; but if you have spent less, the *condictio* will be open, subject to this, that you must be indemnified in respect of whatever you have expended. 1. If a man hands over a slave to another on the understanding that he shall within a given time be manumitted by him, then, if the one who handed over the slave should change his mind and should inform the other of the fact, but the slave is manumitted subsequently to this change of mind, still the person who gave the slave has a good right of action on the ground of change of mind. No doubt, if the other do not manumit, the Imperial enactment takes effect and makes the slave free, if the man who handed him over with a view to that result has not by that time changed his mind. 2. Again, if a man gives Titius ten for him to buy a slave with the money and manumit him, but then he changes his mind, [the rule is that] if the slave has not yet been bought, the party's change of mind will give him a right to a *condictio* for the money, provided he lets Titius clearly know it, lest he should buy the slave afterwards and so suffer a loss ; but, if the slave is already purchased, the change of mind will do no wrong to the one who bought him ; merely, instead of the ten which he received, he will give up the slave which he bought, or, if the supposition made is that by that time the slave is dead, he need give nothing at all, if he did not cause his death. If the slave has run away, and this took place without the fault of the person who bought him, he need not give anything : it is true that he will have to promise that, if he should get him into his power, he will be handed over. 3. Let us consider this point. Supposing Titius received money to manumit a slave and the slave runs away before he is manumitted, can the money received be asked back in a *condictio* ? As to this, if he had intended to sell the slave in question, but he omitted to sell him for the reason that he had received money to manumit him, he cannot be sued in a *condictio* ; of course he will have to give an undertaking that, if the slave gets into his hands, he will give back what he received, with a reservation representing the diminution in the slave's value consequent on his flight. No doubt, if the man who gave the money still wishes the slave to be manumitted, but the other desires not to do it, because he has conceived a spite against him owing to his taking to flight, the latter must restore the whole sum that he received; but if the one who gave the ten pieces elects to have the slave himself given him, in that case either the slave must be given him or else the money which he gave must be restored to him. But if, [to take the alternative case to the one mentioned above,] *Titius* had not intended to sell the slave, then the money which he received must be given back, unless it so happen that, if he had not received money to manumit him, he would have kept him more carefully; should that be the case, it would not be fair that he should lose the slave and the whole price too. 4. Supposing he took the money for the sake of the manumission, and then the slave died, in this case, if he made default as to manumitting, it follows that the proper thing to say is that he must repay what he received; but, if he was not in default, the fact being that he had set out for the [court of the] Governor of the province or whoever the magistrate was before whom the manumission could be executed, and the slave died on the way, the better opinion is that, if he had intended to sell the slave or to use him for some purpose of his own, we shall have to say that he need not repay anything; but, if he had had no intention such as mentioned, it must still be to his loss that the slave died, as he would equally have died if his master had never received the money to manumit him,—unless, indeed, the very journey which was undertaken for the purpose of manumission gave occasion to the slave's death, for example, he was killed, say, by robbers or he was crushed by a stable falling in or run over by a carriage or was killed by some similar accident which would not have happened to him had it not been for the journey which he made in order to be manumitted.

6 THE SAME (*Disputations* 3) If a stranger gives a *dos* for a woman and makes an agreement that, in whatever way the coverture comes to an end, the *dos* is to be restored to him, but, after all, no marriage takes place, then, seeing that the agreement made had reference only to events which occur subsequently to marriage, and no marriage ensued, the question may arise whether the *condictio* is open to the woman or to the party who gave the *dos*. However the probability is that the man who gave the *dos* had an eye to his own interest in view of this case too; as a matter of fact a man who gave in consideration of an expected marriage can, if the marriage was not carried out, bring a *condictio* as if on the ground that the consideration had failed, unless it should be

the case that the woman shows by the most conclusive proofs that his object in doing it was to benefit the woman rather than himself. But even if a father gives the *dos* for his daughter and the above agreement is made, then, unless the intention was clearly different, according to Marcellus, the father has a right to bring a *condictio*.

7 JULIANUS (*Digest* 16) A man who believed himself to owe a sum of money to a woman promised her intended husband at her request to pay it to him by way of *dos* and paid it accordingly; after which the marriage never took place: the question was asked whether the man who paid the money or the woman herself was the person entitled to bring an action for return of it. Nerva and Atilicinus held that since the man believed that he owed the money, but he could have protected himself [if he had been sued] by an *exceptio* of *dolus malus*, he could bring the action himself. Had he, they said, made the promise knowing that he owed the woman nothing, the right of action would have been the woman's, because she would have a right to the money: but if he had really been debtor and had paid by way of an antenuptial gift, and then no marriage had taken place, he would have been entitled to bring the *condictio* himself, and nothing would remain in regard of the woman's title to be paid the debt except this, that the man who owed it would simply have been compellable to assign to her his right to bring a *condictitious* action and would be under no further liability. 1. When land is delivered by way of *dos*, then, if the marriage does not take place, it can be demanded back by a *condictio*; produce too can be asked for in the same way. There is a similar rule as to a female slave and children of the same.

8 NERATIUS (*Parchments* 2) With regard to what we read in Servius's book on dowers, namely, that if a marriage has taken place between persons either of whom has not reached the proper age for marriage, anything that has been already given by way of *dos* can be recovered, we must understand this to mean that, if a divorce takes place before both persons have reached the proper age, the money can be recovered, but so long as the two parties continue to cohabit as husband and wife, the money can as little be demanded back as can property given by an unmarried woman to her intended husband by way of *dos*, so long as the tie of betrothal remains between them: the fact being that whenever anything is given with that object before the marriage takes place, then, seeing that it is given under such circumstances that it may

become a fully established *dos*, it cannot be asked back so long as the possibility remains of its being so fully established.

9 PAULUS (*on Plautius* 17) If I was going to give [money] to a woman [by way of *dos*], and, at her request, I paid it to her intended husband, but no marriage took place, the woman can have a *condictio* for the money. But if I contracted with the intended husband and gave him the money in order that, if the marriage ensued, the woman should get the *dos*, and, if it did not ensue, the money should be returned to me, it is, as it were, given for a purpose and, the purpose failing, I can have a *condictio* for it against the intended husband. 1. If a man should, in consequence of a mistake, promise a woman's intended husband, at her request, to pay him a sum of money which he did not really owe her, and the marriage should take place, he cannot meet an action by the husband with the plea of *dolus malus*; as the husband is acting on his own account, he is guilty of no fraud, and he ought not to be disappointed, as he would be if he were compelled to have a wife who had no *dos*. Consequently the promisor has a right to bring a *condictio* against the woman, by which he can either ask that she should make good what he gave the husband or else that he should be released, if he has not yet paid. Should the husband sue for the money on dissolution of the marriage, there ought to be a valid bar to the action in respect of so much only as would have come to the woman.

10 JAVOLENUS (*on Plautius* 1) If a woman, intending to give a *dos* to a man whom she was about to marry, gives him a formal discharge as to a sum of money which he owes her, but the marriage does not take place, she will have a good right of *condictio* against him for the money; as it makes no difference, where the money came to him without ground, whether it was by direct payment or by formal discharge.

11 JULIANUS (*Digest* 10) If an heir should be ordered in a decision expressed by a freedman to erect a monument at an ascertained cost and should give the sum in question to the freedman [himself], but the latter, having received the money, should omit to erect the monument, he is liable to a *condictio* for it.

12 PAULUS (*on the Lex Julia et Papia* 6) If a man brings a *condictio* for the return of a *donatio mortis causa* on the donee's recovery from his illness, he can ask at the same time for any

produce of the things given, as well as the children of female slaves and accessions in general.

13 MARCIANUS (*Rules* 3) Where a son [of one deceased] brings anything into account for the benefit of his brother, as though he were going to take up *bonorum possessio*, but he never takes it up, then, according to what Marcellus tells us (*Digest* 5), he can have an action to recover it.

14 PAULUS (*on Sabinus* 3) If a man pays to one who pretends falsely to be *procurator* for someone else money which he did not owe at all, the only case in which the money cannot be recovered from the [pretended] *procurator* is that of the [alleged] principal ratifying the agency, but [in this case], as Julianus tells us, such [alleged] principal himself is liable. But if the latter should not ratify, then, even if the money paid had been really owing, it can be recovered from the [pretended] *procurator* himself; the fact being that the action for return of the money is not put on the ground of its being paid where it was not due, but on that of its being paid for a purpose and the purpose failing in consequence of there being no ratification; or the action may be on the ground of a theft committed by the pretended *procurator*, who, he says, not only can be sued for theft but is liable to a *condictio*.

15 POMPONIUS (*on Sabinus* 22) A slave of yours being suspected by one Attius of having stolen his property, you handed him over to be put to the torture, with this understanding that, if he should not be found to have behaved in the way above mentioned, he should be returned to you; after which Attius sent him on to the Prefect of Police as one who was caught in the act, and the latter inflicted the extreme punishment. You have a good right of action against Attius in which your allegation will be that he is bound to transfer the slave, inasmuch as he was really bound to hand him over before his death. According to Labeo, you can in fact have an action for production, as Attius contrived to avoid producing him. Proculus however says that, for Attius to be bound to transfer the slave, it would be necessary that you should have passed the property in him, and that, in that case, you would not have a right of action for production; but that, if the slave had remained your property, you would in fact have had a right to sue Attius for theft, on the ground

that he used the property of another in a way such that he must have known that his use of it was contrary to the will of the owner, or that, if the owner had known of it, he would have forbidden it.

16 CELSUS (*Digest* 3) I gave you money on the understanding that you should give me Stichus. Is a contract of that kind to a certain extent [?] one of purchase and sale, or is there no obligation in the case beyond that arising from something being given for a purpose and the purpose failing? I am inclined on the whole to this last view; and it follows that, if Stichus has died, I can sue for the return of whatever I gave on the understanding that you should give me Stichus. Let us suppose that Stichus belonged to some third person, but that nevertheless you made delivery of him [to me]; I shall have a right to recover the money from you, on the ground that you did not pass the property in the slave to the person who received him; and, to come back, if Stichus belongs to you and you decline to guarantee the purchaser against his being recovered by superior title, you will not be secure against my bringing an action to have the money returned.

V.

ON THE *CONDICTIO* ON THE GROUND OF AN IMMORAL OR UNJUST CONSIDERATION.

1 PAULUS (*on Sabinus* 10) Everything given is given either with an object (*ob rem*) or for a consideration (*ob causam*), and the object may be either immoral or honourable; moreover, if it is immoral, the immorality may be on the part of the giver and not the receiver, or on the part of the receiver alone and not the giver, or on the part of both. 1. If the gift is made for an honourable object, there can be an action for the return of it only where the object for which it was made is not realized. 2. But if the position is immoral on the part of the receiver, there can be an action for return of the gift even where the object is realized.

2 ULPIANUS (*on the Edict* 26) Suppose, for instance, I gave you something on the understanding that you would not commit sacrilege or theft or not kill a man. As to this case, Julianus says that if I give you the thing on the understanding that you will not

kill a man, there can be a *condictio* for the return of it. 1. Also if I give it you on the understanding that you will restore to me something which I deposited in your hands, or restore papers. 2. But if I made the gift on the understanding that the judge should decide in my favour in a good case, it has, no doubt, been said that a *condictio* may be brought, but a man who does this himself commits a crime, as he is held to be corrupting the judge, and, not very long ago, the present Emperor enacted that he should lose his case.

3 PAULUS (*on Sabinus* 10) But where it is a case of corrupt behaviour on the part of both giver and receiver, the rule is that no action can be brought to have the gift returned ; take the case, for example, of money being given as an inducement to an unjust judgment being pronounced.

4 ULPIANUS (*on the Edict* 26) The same rule holds where money is given as the price of lewdness, or where a man who is detected in the act of adultery pays to be let go, as there is no right of action to recover the money ; this is laid down by Sabinus and Pegasus. 1. Again if a thief gives money to avoid being given up, inasmuch as it is a case of immoral behaviour on the part of both parties, there is no action to recover; 2. but, whenever the immoral behaviour occurs on the part of the receiver alone, according to Celsus, there may be an action for return of the money; for instance, where I give you money on the understanding that you will not do me wrong. 3. Still money given to a harlot cannot be recovered at law, so Labeo and Marcellus tell us; this however is on a different principle, as the point is not that there is immoral behaviour on both sides, but on the part of the giver only ; the woman acts immorally in being a harlot, but, being one, she does not act immorally in taking the money. 4. If I pay you something as the price of information, viz. for you to let me know where my runaway slave is, or some thief who stole my property, there can be no action brought for return of what I gave, as there was nothing immoral in your receiving it. But if you take money from my runaway slave which he gives to induce you not to give information about him, I can bring a *condictio* for it as though you were a thief; again, if the actual thief or the companion of a thief or of a runaway slave received money from me as the price of information, I should say that a *condictio* can be brought.

5 JULIANUS (*on Urseius Ferox* 3) If a man should receive money from my slave as an inducement not to give information as to a theft which the slave committed, then, whether he gives the information or not, according to the opinion given by Proculus, there is a good right of action for return of the money received.

6 ULPIANUS (*on Sabinus* 18) Sabinus invariably approved of the view of the old lawyers, who held that when a thing is in anyone's hands on grounds insufficient in law, a *condictio* can be brought for it; and of this opinion is Celsus too.

7 POMPONIUS (*on Sabinus* 22) If money has been taken in pursuance of a stipulation which was extorted by violence, there is no doubt that an action can be brought for a return of it.

8 PAULUS (*Questions* 3) If you promise Titius something for an immoral consideration, then, although, if he sues for it, you can bar his action with an *exceptio* either of *dolus malus* or *in factum*, still, if you pay it, you cannot after that sue to have it back again; because, if the immediate determining circumstance, viz. the stipulation, is taken away, as being made ineffectual by means of the *exceptio*, still the original circumstance, that is the immorality, remains, and, besides that, if the position of both giver and receiver is that their behaviour is immoral, the advantage is with the possessor, and consequently there is no action for return of the money, although it was paid in pursuance of the stipulation.

9 THE SAME (*on Plautius* 5) If I lend you garments to make use of, and after that I pay money to have them returned, it has been laid down that I can properly proceed by a *condictio*, because, true as it may be that the money was given for an object and the object was realized, still the payment was improper (*turpiter datum*). 1. If you receive money from me given as an inducement to you to give up to me something that was let to you [by me] or sold [to me] by you or entrusted to your care, I shall have a right of action founded on letting or sale or mandate; but if my object in giving the money was to induce you to make over to me something which you owed me in pursuance of a testament or a stipulation, there will simply be a right of *condictio* for return of the money which I gave with the object mentioned. We read this in fact in Pomponius.

VI.

ON THE *CONDICTIO* FOR MONEY [PAID] THAT WAS NOT DUE.

1 PAPINIANUS (*on the Edict* 26) We will now consider the case of the payment of money that was not due. 1. To begin with, where a man pays what he does not owe, in ignorance of the fact, he can sue to recover it by this action; but if he paid knowing that he did not owe it, there is no right of action for the return of it.

2 THE SAME (*on Sabinus* 16) If a man pays on the understanding that if it should prove not to be due, or it should turn out to be a case where the *lex Falcidia* applies, the money should be returned, an action for the return will be in place, as there is a contract concluded between the parties. 1. If anything should be paid in pursuance of a testament, but afterwards the testament proves to be forged or inofficious or void or to have been avoided, what was paid may be asked back, and [the same is the case] if, after a long time, some debt owing from the estate should come to light, or codicils which have been long undiscovered[1] in which there is a revocation of legacies which have been already paid, or the legacies are reduced in amount by the fact that there are other persons discovered to whom legacies were left. This results from the rescript of the Divine Hadrian concerning forged or inofficious testaments, to the effect that an action must be allowed to the person in whose favour judgment should be given as to the right to the inheritance.

3 PAPINIANUS (*Questions* 28) The case is the same if, after the legacies are paid, some fresh and unexpected circumstance takes away the inheritance, for instance, the birth of a postumous son, whom the heir did not know to exist *in venter sa mere*[2], or, again, the return of a son who was a captive in the hands of enemies, whom his father assumed erroneously to be dead; as the Emperor Titus Antoninus laid down by rescript that an *utilis actio* must be allowed to a postumous son or to one to whom the inheritance was adjudged against those persons who had received legacies, on the principle that a possessor in good faith is liable to the extent to which he is made the richer, and [thus] the risk attending claims of this kind will not affect a person who pays [the money away] without being guilty of negligence.

[1] del. *prolati.* M.

[2] This expression is one of English law.

4 PAULUS (*on Sabinus* 3) The Divine Hadrian laid down the same for a case in which another testament should be brought forward:

5 ULPIANUS (*on Sabinus* 16) nor is it an unheard-of thing that, where one man pays, another should have a right to ask for return of the money. Where, for instance, a person under twenty-five years of age makes entry on an inheritance without due reflection and gets an order replacing him in his original position (*restitutio in integrum*) after he has paid the legacies, then, according to the rescript given to Arrius Titianus, the right to sue to have the money returned does not pertain to him, but to the person to whom the estate belongs.

6 PAULUS (*on Sabinus* 3) If your *procurator* pays what was not due and you do not ratify the payment, then, according to Labeo, in his books called *Posteriores*, there can be an action for return of the money; but, if the money was due, according to Celsus, it cannot be recovered; and the reason is that, where a man appoints someone as *procurator* in his affairs, this may be held to imply that he commissions him to pay his creditor what he owes him, and we have not after that to wait for him to ratify what his agent does. 1. Labeo says further that, if money not due is paid to a *procurator*, and his principal does not ratify, there can be an action for the return of it. 2. Celsus says that one who pays a *procurator* a real debt is at once discharged and no ratification is thought of; but that, if the *procurator* is paid what is not due, ratification by the principal is required [to make this latter liable], for the reason that he would be held to have given no instructions as to the getting in of that particular claim, and consequently, if the receipt of it is not ratified, any proceedings for the return must be against the *procurator*. 3. Julianus says that neither a guardian nor a *procurator* can ask for return of the money if they have paid it, and that it makes no difference whether they paid away their own money or money belonging to the ward or the principal [as the case may be].

7 POMPONIUS (*on Sabinus* 9) When money which is not due is paid by mistake, the action may be for the return of either the very money paid or an equal amount.

8 PAULUS (*on Sabinus* 6) If any payment is made to a wife by a third person on account of a husband who is unable to

discharge his debts, the person so paying cannot sue to have it returned, as at all events it is[1] a debt due to the wife.

9 ULPIANUS (*on the Edict* 66) In fact, even the husband, if, when completely insolvent, he gives his wife the dower, is so placed that he cannot sue to have it back.

10 PAULUS (*on Sabinus* 7) A man who is bound to pay by a given day is so much a debtor that if he pays before the day he cannot sue to have the money returned.

11 ULPIANUS (*on Sabinus* 35) If a man against whom an action has been brought *de peculio* should inadvertently pay more than there is in the *peculium*, he cannot sue to recover it.

12 PAULUS (*on Sabinus* 7) If I give you a usufruct in my land under the false impression that I am legally bound to do so, but I die without suing for the return of it, the right to bring the *condictio* for it will pass to my heir.

13 THE SAME (*on Sabinus* 10) Even a slave may be under a natural obligation; consequently, if anyone should pay a debt on a slave's account, or the slave himself should pay on being manumitted, so Pomponius says, there will be no right of action for return of the money, [even[2]] out of a *peculium* of which he has the free management; and for this reason any surety who has been accepted for the slave will be held liable and a pledge given on his behalf will be retained; moreover, if the slave, having the management of his *peculium*, should give something by way of a pledge for his debt, he must be allowed an *utilis actio* to redeem. 1. Again, where a ward takes a loan without the concurrence of his guardian and has become the richer for it, should he pay it after reaching the age of puberty, he cannot sue for the return of it;

14 POMPONIUS (*on Sabinus* 21) as it is only right, as a matter of natural law, that no one should become richer to the injury of another.

15 PAULUS (*on Sabinus* 10) The right of *condictio* to recover what has been given without being due is a matter of natural law, and consequently the action will include any accession there may be to the thing, for example, a child born of a female slave or soil deposited by alluvion; nay, we may add that it includes produce which has been gathered in good faith by the person to whom the

[1] Read *est* for *esset*. Cf. M. [2] v. M.

property was given. 1. Besides the above, if what was given was money belonging to a third person, there will be a good *condictio* to have the bare possession given back; just as, if I should deliver to you the possession of something or other in the erroneous belief that I am legally bound to do so, I could bring a *condictio* for it. Again, if I should have made the possession yours in such sort that, if you raised the plea of long user, the thing could not be taken from you, even then I could lawfully take proceedings against you by way of a *condictio* for money paid that was not due[1]. 2. And even if a usufruct in the thing handed over should belong to a third person, I could sue you in a *condictio*, making allowance for the usufruct.

16 POMPONIUS (*on Sabinus* 15) If a thing which is owing subject to a condition is given through a mistake, then, so long as the condition is still pending, there can be an action brought for the return of it, but, if the condition has come to pass, it cannot be sued for. Add that a thing which had to be given on a day not yet ascertained cannot be recovered after the day has arrived;

17[2] ULPIANUS (*on the Edict* 2) thus, if I promise to give something at my death, and I discharge the debt in my lifetime, according to Celsus, I cannot sue to have it returned; and this opinion is sound.

18 THE SAME (*on Sabinus* 47) But if the thing had to be given on a condition which in any case must come to pass some time or other, then, if it is once given, it cannot be recovered at law, though, if the condition had been a different one, as to which it was uncertain whether it would occur or not, an action might be brought for the return of it, if it were handed over before the condition occurred.

19 THE SAME (*on Sabinus* 22) If a debtor is released from his debt by way of a penalty on the person to whom it is owing, the natural obligation remains and, consequently, there can be no action for return of the money if once paid. 1. Even where a man receives payment of a real debt, still, if the party who pays gives what he does not owe, there is a good right of action for the return of it; suppose, for instance, a man believes erroneously that he is heir or *bonorum possessor* to someone and pays a creditor of the

[1] For *indebitam* read *indebiti*. Cf. M.

[2] M. would inverse the order of 17 and 18.

estate, here the real heir will not be discharged, and the other can sue for the return of what he paid[1]. 2. If I believe erroneously that I owe a sum of money, and I thereupon pay it in pieces of which some belong to a stranger and the others to me, I can bring a *condictio* for half the amount and not for half shares in the separate pieces. 3. If I believe myself to be bound to give either Stichus or Pamphilus, [whichever I please,] whereas I am really bound to give Stichus, and I give Pamphilus, I can sue for the return of Pamphilus, as being property given without being due; since I cannot be held to have made the transfer by way of discharging my real debt. 4. If two debtors who owed ten should join in paying twenty, according to Celsus, each can sue for the return of five, because, whereas they owed ten, they paid twenty, and the amount which the two paid in excess the two can sue to have returned.

20 JULIANUS (*Digest* 10) If the debtor and the surety join in payment of the debt, their position so far does not differ from that of two promisors; hence all that we have said as to these latter may be applied to the others as well.

21 PAULUS (*Questions* 3) No doubt, if you suppose that there are two debtors in respect of an obligation, not to pay one sum of money, but to do something different, say to transfer Stichus or Pamphilus, and thereupon two slaves are given jointly or, it may be, a cloak or a thousand *denarii*, we cannot, as before, say, as to the action for return of the thing given, that they can sue for separate portions respectively, because they could not have paid in that fashion at the outset. Accordingly, in such a case it is for the creditor to choose to which of the two he will hand what he received, so as to prevent an action being brought by the other.

22 POMPONIUS (*on Sabinus* 22) Again, if I believe myself to have promised something to you or to Titius, whereas no [such] promise was made to either or Titius was not personally included in the stipulation, and I give it to Titius, I can sue Titius for the return of it. 1. I by mistake conveyed a piece of land as subject to no servitude where I ought to have reserved a right of way; I have a right to bring a *condictio* for an unascertained amount in order to procure that a right of way be given to me.

[1] Here follows "As even where a man" etc., *i.e.* the initial clause of the subsection is repeated word for word, by apparent inadvertency.

23 ULPIANUS (*on Sabinus* 43) Pomponius raises the following nice point. If a man suspects that a compromise has been made as to some dispute by one to whom he is heir or by one to whom he is *procurator*, and he hands over something in pursuance of the supposed compromise, whereas none such was made,—is this, he asks, a case for an action for repayment? To this he says that the action can be brought, as the payment was made on grounds falsely assumed to exist. The rule I should say is the same if some compromise fails to be concluded with a view to which payment was made; again, the same holds if the compromise was revoked. 1. If a man agrees to a compromise after a judgment is given and pays accordingly, he can sue for a return of the money, for the reason that by the present law such a compromise is of no force; this being what is laid down in a rescript of the Emperor Antoninus and his Divine Father. Still anything which has been paid in pursuance of such a compromise can be kept, and credit must be given for it if an action is brought on the judgment. How then if there is an appeal made, or if there should be an uncertainty on the very question whether a decision was given at all or the judgment has any force? In that case the better opinion is that the compromise takes effect; the proper view to take is that the above-mentioned rescripts apply only where the compromise refers to an undoubted decision which it is useless to attempt to have amended. 2. Again, if the payment was made in pursuance of a composition in the matter of an alimentary provision left by testament, it is clear that an action can be brought for the return of what was given, as the composition is avoided by a decree of the Senate. 3. If a man after agreeing to a compromise is nevertheless ordered judicially to pay the debt, this is a deliberate wrong (*dolus*), but still the judgment is valid. It was however in the party's power, if, that is, he agreed to the compromise before joinder of issue, in case the plaintiff desired to join issue, to meet this with an *exceptio* of *dolus*, and, if the compromise was made after joinder, even then he can use the *exceptio* of [for?] subsequent *dolus*, as, where a man proceeds in spite of a compromise, and still demands payment, his behaviour is of the nature of *dolus*, and, consequently, if the defendant is ordered to pay, he can sue for the return of whatever he gave in pursuance of the compromise[1]. It is true that he gave it for a consideration and when anything is given for a consideration there cannot be an action brought for the return of

[1] The reasoning in this sentence seems to be confused.

it, if the consideration is carried out; but in this case it cannot be said that the consideration is carried out, as the compromise is not acted upon. If then it comes to an action for the return of what was given, it is out of place to plead the compromise by way of *exceptio*; it is impossible for both to take effect, the action for return [of what was paid] and the *exceptio* [to the action for payment]. 4. If any statute lays down at the outset that there shall be a right of action for twofold or fourfold, the rule is that an action may be brought for the return of money paid in consequence of the statute being falsely supposed to apply.

24 THE SAME (*on Sabinus* 46) If a man who was able to protect himself by a perpetual *exceptio* should, with the knowledge that he had this *exceptio*, promise to give something with a view to getting a release from his obligation, he cannot bring a *condictio*.

25 THE SAME (*on Sabinus* 47) In a case where two persons had become sureties for a debtor for the sum of ten, after which the debtor paid three, and then the sureties paid each five, it was held that the one who paid last might sue to have three returned; and this is perfectly just, as, on the debtor paying three, only seven remained due, and, at the moment when those seven were paid, there were three paid which were not due.

26 THE SAME (*on the Edict* 26) Where a man pays not principal but interest which is not due, he cannot sue for the return of it, if the principal was due on which the interest was paid; should he however pay over the statutable rate, then, according to a rescript of the Divine Severus by which the present practice is regulated, there is no action allowed for the return of the money, but it will be held to be paid in discharge of the principal, and if after that the debtor pays the principal, there will be an action allowed for the return of such principal [to the proper amount], as not having been due. Similarly, if the principal should have been paid before, any interest paid over the statutable rate can be recovered as if it were undue principal. How then if the party pay both [principal and interest] at the same time? We may take it that in that case too an action for return will lie. 1. Interest however, whether simple or compound, cannot be made the subject of a stipulation nor be demanded to the extent of more than double [the original sum lent], and, if paid, it can be demanded back, just as can interest on future interest. 2. If a man, under the mistaken belief that he owes a principal sum, pays interest thereon, he can bring a *condictio* for the return of it, and he is not held to have

paid knowingly what he did not owe. 3. The payment of money is taken to be undue, not only where it is not owed at all, but also where no action can be brought for it in consequence of some perpetual *exceptio*; accordingly, in this case too, there can be an action for return of the money paid, unless, when the party paid, he knew that he was protected by an *exceptio*. 4. If I owe a hundred and, that being the case, I hand over an estate worth two hundred, as if two hundred were the amount of my debt, then, according to Marcellus (*Digest* b. 20), I have a right to ask for a return of the estate, and the stipulation by which I promised to pay a hundred remains in force; because, although the law is that, if a thing is handed over instead of a sum of money, this may be a good discharge to the debtor, still, if, in consequence of a mistake as to the amount of the debt, something is given of greater value, a clear distinction is maintained between a share in the thing and a sum of money, as no one is compelled to become a part-owner; but a right of *condictio* remains for recovery of the whole thing, and the obligation [as to the hundred] is unaffected. However the land will be retained [by the creditor] until the money due is paid. 5. Again, Marcellus says that if a man who owes money hands over oil worth more than the amount of the debt, as though he owed more than he really does, or, owing oil, he gives oil, but as if he owed a greater quantity than he does, he can have an action for the return of the excess, though not of the whole amount given, and, that being the case, his obligation is at an end. 6. The same writer adds, that if I have a right to ask for a share in a piece of land, and a valuation being made on the assumption that I have a right to the whole estate, payment is made to me of a sum representing the value of the whole, a return can be claimed at law, not of the whole value, but of the value of so much of the estate as I had no claim to. 7. So true is it that the existence of a perpetual *exceptio* in bar of a demand confers a right of *condictio* [for the return of money paid in satisfaction of the demand], as Julianus has it (b. 10), that if the purchaser of a piece of land orders his heir to release the vendor from the obligation incurred by the sale, but, after that, the vendor, being unaware of this fact, delivers the property, he can have a *condictio* for the return of the land; and it is a similar case, he says, if a man should order [his heir] to release a debtor, and the latter, in ignorance thereof, should pay the debt. 8. A man who is debtor to a *filius-familias* in respect of the latter's *peculium* and pays him the debt is discharged thereof, if he was unaware of the fact that the *peculium* had been taken away; but if he was aware of it and still paid, he has no right of *condictio*, because he paid what was not due with knowledge of the fact. 9. If a son under *potestas* borrows money in disregard of the Macedonian decree of the Senate, and pays it, but afterwards becomes heir to his *paterfamilias* and desires to sue to recover the pieces of money at law as owner, he can be debarred by an *exceptio* from prosecuting the suit. 10. If a man pays money under a mistake on the assumption of an award made against him on an arbitration, he can sue to have it returned. 11. If money which is not due is paid to one who is either heir or *bonorum possessor* to a deceased person, an action can be brought for the return of the money, if the person to whom it was paid maintains at law his right to the estate; but, if he does not maintain such right, an action can be brought even for the return of money paid that was due. 12. A freedman, believing that he was bound to perform services to his patron, performed them accordingly; here, as we read in Julianus (*Digest* b. 10), he has no *condictio*, although he discharged the services in the belief that he was under a legal obligation to do so; as the fact is that a freedman is bound by natural law to perform services for his patron. Even where no such services were performed for the patron, but on the latter calling upon the freedman to perform some duty, he settled with him for the payment of a sum of money and paid it accordingly, he cannot bring an action for the return of it. If the services which he rendered to his patron were not of the nature of personal duty, but industrial, for example in the way of painting and so on, it being his belief that he was bound to execute them, let us see whether he cannot have a *condictio*. However, as to this, Celsus gives it as his opinion (*Digest* b. 6) that the grounds on which services may be required are such that the services vary as to their nature, and as to the persons who can render them or to whom[1] they are rendered; very often the physical strength of the freedman[2] or the actual character of the occasion will alter the ground for demanding services, so that a man may be unable to render them even though he should wish to do so. However, this writer proceeds, the services admit of a valuation in money; and it may very well be that people furnish one thing and bring a *condictio* for another; for instance, suppose I have made over [to you] land which I was not bound to give,

[1] M. suggests *quæ* for *neque*. This would give us: "as to the persons who can render them, though they are rendered to the same person."

[2] del. *ætas temporis*. M.

and I bring a *condictio* for the produce; or a slave whom I was not bound to give, and you, without any fraud, have sold him for a small sum, in such a case all that you need return is so much of the purchase money as you still have got; or say I raised the value of some slave at my own expense; will not these be cases for a valuation? Similarly, he says, in the present case, there can be a *condictio* brought for the amount which it would have cost the patron[1] to hire the services. In Marcellus (*Digest* b. 20) the question is asked [how the law is] in a case where the claim on a freedman[2] for dutiful services has been assigned to a third person; and what that writer says is that the freedman is not bound to discharge it, unless the services are of the nature of a handicraft; such as these, no doubt, if the patron should so require, would have to be performed for another; but if the freedman, in the case of an assignment, should perform dutiful services, he has no right of *condictio*, he can neither sue the creditor for whom he performed them,—such performance having been made in discharge of a duty to another, and the creditor in question having received what he had a right to,—nor can he sue his patron, because they were owing to him by natural law. 13. If a man stipulates[3] with me for "ten or Stichus," and I give him five, the question may be asked whether I can bring a *condictio* [for return of the five]; what gives rise to this is the doubt whether I am not discharged of my debt to the extent of five; as, if I am, I have no right of *condictio*, but I have, if I am not discharged. However, the rule is, as Celsus says (*Digest* b. 6) and Marcellus (*Digest* b. 20), that an obligational claim cannot be taken away as to half, so that, if a man[4] [in my position] pays five, the question whether he is discharged of his debt must be kept in suspense, and an action may be brought against him for "the remaining five or Stichus," whereupon, if he pays the remaining five, it must be held that, even as to the first five, he paid a real debt, but, if he hands over Stichus, then he can sue to recover five as not having been owing. Accordingly, his subsequent transfer will determine whether, when the first five were paid, they were owing or not owing. But here Celsus asks this further question: Suppose that, after the five were paid, Stichus was handed over too, but I prefer to keep the five and return Stichus,

1 In the text "me."

2 After *operas* ins. *præstaturus* or some such word: cf. M.

3 I read *stipulato* for *stipulatus*: but *stipulari* does sometimes mean to promise. The sense is clear.

4 For *eum qui* M. would read *cum quis*.

shall I get a hearing? As to this, his own opinion is that by that time there is once for all a good right of *condictio* for five, although, if both payment and delivery of Stichus had been made at the same time, I should have been allowed to choose which of the two I should like to retain. 14. The same writer says further that if the promisee leaves two heirs, you cannot give five to one of them and give the other a share in Stichus, and a corresponding rule holds if the promisor leaves two heirs. According to this, the debt is not discharged unless either five or a share in Stichus is given to each of the two.

27 PAULUS (*on the Edict* 28) Where a man believes that he is bound to pay in some particular place and he pays [there] what is not due at all, he can sue for return of the money in any place that he likes; the belief of the party who paid will not give rise to any corresponding particularity in the action for return of the money.

28 THE SAME (*on the Edict* 32) If a judge dismisses an action wrongfully, but the defendant thereby discharged pays of his own accord, he cannot sue for return of the money.

29 ULPIANUS (*Disputations* 2) There are cases in which the personal status of the party who paid affords ground for an action for return of the money; for instance, where a ward has paid without his guardian's concurrence, or a lunatic, or one who was restrained by order from dealing with his property; for all such cases it is an undoubted general rule that there is ground for the action; accordingly, if the pieces of money are to be found, there can be a *vindicatio* brought to recover them, and, if they are spent, it is a case for a *condictio*.

30 THE SAME (*Disputations* 10) When a man is both creditor and debtor to the same person, and the case is one of those in which there is no set off, [the rule is that,] if he pays the debt, he has no right of *condictio* for the money on the ground that payment was not due, he simply has the right to sue for his own debt.

31 THE SAME (*Opinions* 1) A man who by a mistake undertakes to pay a creditor [of a deceased person] a larger sum than his own share in the inheritance admits of has a right of *condictio* to recall a promise to give what was not due.

32 JULIANUS (*Digest* 10) If a man who is bound to give Pamphilus or Stichus, [whichever he likes,] should hand over both

together and, after that, either both or one of the two should cease to exist, he cannot sue to have anything returned, as such property as still exists will remain as given in discharge of the debt. 1. If a surety makes an agreement that he shall not be sued for the money which is owing, but through inadvertence he pays it, he can bring a *condictio* against the promisee to get it back, the consequence of which is that the principal debtor remains liable, but the surety himself is protected by the *exceptio* founded on his agreement. Whether it is the surety who pays or his heir is immaterial; should however the principal debtor become heir to the surety in question and pay the debt, he cannot sue for the return of it, and he will be discharged of the obligation. 2. If a woman's idea of her position should be such that she conceives herself to be bound to make over property by way of *dos*, then, if she gives anything as *dos*, she will be unable to sue for the return of it, as, independently of the question of mistaken belief, there is still the fact of conjugal duty, and what is given in pursuance of that cannot be recovered at law. 3. A man who promises in general terms to give a slave is in a similar position to that of one who is bound to give a slave or ten [pieces], hence, if he hands over Stichus under the belief that he promised to give Stichus in particular, he can bring a *condictio* to have him returned, and he will be discharged of his debt by giving any other slave.

33 THE SAME (*Digest* 39) If I built on vacant ground of yours and after that you were in possession of the building so erected, I should have no right of *condictio* [for the expense incurred], as you and I would have had no dealings with one another; the fact is that a man who pays money which is not due does thereby in some sort deal with the other, but when the owner of a site takes possession of a building erected there by someone else, no dealings are had. Indeed, even if a party who built on another man's ground should actually deliver possession, he would have no right of *condictio*, since he would not have passed the property in anything;—simply the owner would have come into possession of what belonged to him. Hence it is well understood that if a man who believed himself to be heir should shore up a block of chambers which was part of the inheritance, the only way in which he could make sure of recouping the cost he incurred would be by keeping the property in his hands.

34 THE SAME (*Digest* 40) Where a whole inheritance has been left a person by *fidei-commissum* and, on condition that he gives

ten to the heir, a parcel of land over and above, then, if the heir avers that he entertains doubts of the inheritance, and he hands it over under the Trebellian Senatusconsultum, the person mentioned has no reason for giving the money, and consequently he can have a *condictio* to recover anything that he may have given in the matter by way of fulfilling the condition.

35 THE SAME (*Digest* 45) Where a man pays a sum demanded in consequence of there having been no defence made to the action for it, then, even if he should later on be ready to make a defence, he will not be allowed an action to recover what he paid.

36 PAULUS (*Epitomes of Alfenus's Digest* 5) The slave of a certain person lent a man a dish without his owner's knowledge, the one to whom it was lent pledged it for debt and absconded, and the person with whom it was pledged declared that he would not give it back, unless he got his money; but, the slave having paid him the money, he returned the dish. The question was asked whether there could be an action brought against him for return of the money. The answer was that if the person with whom the dish was pledged knew that a dish was being left in his hands as a pledge which did not belong to the pledgor, he had made himself liable for theft, and, that being the case, that, if he had taken money from the slave by way of letting the latter buy back the thing stolen, there could be an action for the return of it; should he however have been unaware that what was left in his hands was not the pledgor's own, he was not a thief, moreover, if the money had been paid him by the slave as on behalf of the person from whom he had received the pledge, he could not be sued for the return of it.

37 JULIANUS (*on Urseius Ferox* 3) I bought from you my own slave in ignorance of the fact, and I paid you the purchase money; I am thoroughly of opinion that I can sue you for return of the money, and that I am entitled to bring a *condictio* with that object, whether you were aware or not that the slave was mine.

38 AFRICANUS (*Questions* 9) Two brothers being in the *potestas* of the same person, one of them borrowed a sum of money from the other and, after the death of their *paterfamilias*, repaid it: the question was asked whether he had a right to sue for the return of it. The answer was that he certainly might sue for the return of [so much of it as corresponded with] the share in respect of which he himself was heir to his father; but that, as for the share which

was inherited by his brother, he could sue for the return [of the corresponding amount] only on the assumption that at least as much had come to the hands of that brother out of his [the borrower's] *peculium*, as the pre-existing natural obligation [which would nullify his claim to the return] must be held to have been taken away by the very fact that his brother had received part of his [the borrower's] *peculium*; so much so that, if the *peculium* had been bequeathed in advance to the son, I mean the son who owed the money to his brother, the brother could retain out of it the sum which was owed him. This, he proceeded to say, was quite in keeping with the view approved of by Julianus, that, if he [the borrower above mentioned] had owed something to a stranger, and, after the death of his father he had had to pay him the debt, he would have had a right to recover from his co-heirs in an action *familiæ erciscundæ* the amount which the creditor would have been able to get from them by an action *de peculio*. Consequently it was equally true that, if he began with the action *familiæ erciscundæ*, the proper course was that the *peculium* should be so divided as that, with regard to a particular portion of it, he should be guaranteed by his co-heir [against having to pay it away in discharge of the debt], and, as he went on to say, if he had a right to be protected as against a stranger, much more could he claim to be guaranteed against a debt which he owed to his brother. 1. The question has been asked, whether, if a father lends money to his son and the latter after being emancipated repays it, he can sue for the return of it. The answer was—that, if no portion of the *peculium* remains in the hands of the father, the son cannot sue; as one thing which tends to prove that the natural obligation [to repay the loan] still exists is the fact that if a stranger brought an action *de peculio* within the year, the father would retain [out of the *peculium*] what his son owed him. 2. Conversely, where a father owed money to his son and pays it to him after he is emancipated, he cannot ask for the return of it; as here again the same argument applies in favour of the natural obligation still existing, namely, that if a stranger should bring an action *de peculio* within the year, the *peculium* will be held to include the amount which the father owes. A similar rule will apply equally where a son is disinherited and a stranger, being heir, pays the son what the father owed him. 3. I was guaranteed the payment of a legacy, and, the surety having paid me the amount, it turned out that I had no right to the legacy: our authority held that the surety could sue to have the money returned.

39 MARCIANUS (*Institutes* 8) Should anyone, when he is able to have security given him by a fide-commissary, omit to do so, according to a rescript of the Divine Severus and Antoninus, he can bring an action to recover as undue any payment that has been made in excess of the amount owing.

40 THE SAME (*Rules* 3) When a man has a perpetual *exceptio* to a demand, he can bring an action to recover any payment made by mistake; still this does not hold in every case; as where the *exceptio* is allowed for the sake of the person against whom proceedings are taken, he can sue for a return of what he paid, for example, in cases under the Senatusconsultum [Velleianum] on the subject of guarantees; but where it is given to punish the one to whom the money is owing, money wrongly paid cannot be recovered by action; for instance, where a son under *potestas* takes a loan of money contrary to the Senatusconsultum Macedonianum and, after becoming an independent person, repays it, he cannot sue to recover it. 1. If a portion of a house is left by *fidei-commissum* from and after a particular day, and, before the *fidei-commissum* vests, it is burnt, but the heir has it rebuilt at his own expense, it is well recognized that the cost of doing so must come out of the property left, and, if the heir delivers over the house without deducting the amount, a *condictio* may be brought for an unascertained amount to recover such cost, on the ground that the heir gave more than what was owing. 2. If a patron makes an agreement with his freedman that the latter shall not be sued for services, and after that any payment should be made by the freedman, an action may be brought to recover it.

41 NERATIUS (*Parchments* 6) If a ward without the guardian's concurrence promises in a stipulation to make some payment and pays accordingly, he has a right of action to recover the money, as he was under no obligation to pay it, even by natural law.

42 ULPIANUS (*on the Edict* 68) Penal sums being once paid it is not in accordance with the practice that there should be an action to recover them.

43 PAULUS (*on Plautius* 3) When a man has sworn that he is not bound in law to make over property, there is an end of all contention, and hence the rule is that, if any money is paid under these circumstances, there can be an action brought for the return of it.

44 THE SAME (*on Plautius* 14) No action for return can be brought against a man who has received what he had a right to, even though payment was made by someone who was not the actual debtor.

45 JAVOLENUS (*Extracts from Plautius* 2) Where a man who has sold an inheritance and delivered it to the purchaser omitted to retain what the deceased owed him, he can sue to have it returned, as anything paid in excess of a debt can properly be recovered by a *condictio.*

46 THE SAME (*Extracts from Plautius* 4) A person who pays on behalf of the heir and with the heir's own money legacies which are not due cannot himself sue for the return of what he gave; but, if he paid the heir's money without the latter's knowledge, then the owner of the coins, so our authority tells us, will have a good *vindicatio* for them. The same legal implications attach to corporeal property in general.

47 CELSUS (*Digest* 6) You promised under a mistake to pay money which you did not owe, and it was paid by the person who was surety for you. My opinion is that, if the surety pays on your behalf, then you will be liable to the surety and the promisee will be liable to you, and it is not necessary that you should first ratify, as you may be held to have commissioned the surety to make this very payment on your behalf. Should the surety have paid [as] on his own behalf a sum which he did not owe, [I should say] that he can sue the promisee for the return, as he has paid money which was undue on principles of universal law; and, whatever the amount is by which the sum which he succeeds in recovering from the person to whom payment was made falls short [of what he paid], so much he can get from you by an *actio mandati,* if, that is, when the promisee sued the surety, it was owing to the latter not being acquainted with the facts that he omitted to plead his *exceptio* in bar of the action.

48 THE SAME (*Digest* 6) When a man promises that, if something or other should be done by him or when it should be done, he will pay ten, then, if he pays what he promised before the thing is done, he will not be held to have done what he promised to do, and he can consequently sue for a return of the money.

49 MODESTINUS (*Rules* 3) A *condictio* can be brought to recover money against those only to whom the money has been in some

form or other paid, not against those [as such] who are benefited by the payment.

50 POMPONIUS (*on Quintus Mucius* 5) Where a man deliberately pays what he does not owe with the very intention of afterwards suing to recover it, he cannot sue.

51 THE SAME (*on Quintus Mucius* 6) In those cases in which people have a right of retention of a thing but no right to sue for it, they cannot bring an action to have it returned, if they have handed it over.

52 THE SAME (*on Quintus Mucius* 27) People make payment either on a ground (*ob causam*) or for a purpose (*ob rem*): it may be on a past ground, for instance, if my inducement for paying is that I have acquired something from you or something has been done by you, so that, even if the ground [assumed] is imaginary, there can be no action for return of the money: payment is for a purpose [when it is made] with a view to something ulterior to be done, and, if it is not done, the right to an action for return of the money takes effect.

53 PROCULUS (*Epistles* 7) An owner gave his slave liberty by testament, on condition that he paid ten; the slave not being aware that the testament was void, the ten were paid to me; the question is asked who it is who can sue for the return of the money. Proculus's answer is as follows:—if the slave himself gave money which was part of his *peculium*, without having received from his owner any permission to make such a payment, then the coins remain the property of his owner, and he can sue me for them, not, that is, by a *condictio*, but by an action *in rem*. But if someone else at the slave's request paid me his own money, the coins paid became mine, and the person who owned the slave in whose behalf they were paid can sue for them by a *condictio*: but a more considerate as well as more practical plan is that the person who advanced the money should recover what he has a right to [from me] directly.

54 PAPINIANUS (*Questions* 2) Wherever, owing to a mistake, payment has been made upon grounds of any kind which in law were of no weight or failed of effect, a *condictio* will lie.

55 THE SAME (*Questions* 6) Where urban estates are leased by one who knowingly took wrongful possession (*prœdo*), what he receives under the head of rent cannot be recovered in an action

brought by the person who paid it, but he [the wrongful possessor] will be bound to pay it to the owner. The same rule will be applied as to passage money in the case of ships which such a possessor let or worked without title, or money which he receives for the use of slaves whose services he let out; in fact, if a slave who was not let out at all hands over the price of his services to such a wrongful possessor, as if he were his owner, he will not pass the property in the money. Should such a possessor receive money paid for the use of vessels which had been let out by the owner or rents for blocks of chambers, he can be sued, on the ground of undue payment received, by the person so paying, and the latter is not discharged of his debt; so that, with regard to the common rule that a wilfully wrongful holder is liable to a *condictio* for profits [which he has received], this applies only where such profits belonged to the owner of the property.

56 THE SAME (*Questions* 8) There is quite enough to make a case of money not being due where the defence to an action for it founded on a given *exceptio* is one as to which it is uncertain whether it is temporary or absolute. If, for example, a person[1] makes an agreement that he shall not be sued for a debt until Titius becomes consul, then, seeing that the death of Titius may render absolute an *exceptio* which, if Titius takes the consulship, is temporary, it is perfectly correct to say that, if anything is paid in the meantime, an action can be brought for the return of it. In fact, just as an agreement which appoints a particular day for payment can never lead to a *condictio* [if payment is made sooner] any more than there would be one if the debtor paid on the day named, so too it is plain that where there is a legal defence which is founded on an agreement of uncertain operation [in the above particular] the case is practically one of a conditional obligation[2].

57 THE SAME (*Responsa* 3) Where a guardian pays down on behalf of a boy under age money that is not due, the latter has a right of *condictio* for the return of it. 1. A creditor requests that the debt should be paid to his agent; in this case, if money is paid in excess of the debt, an action can be brought against the agent for undue payment; but if the creditor, in pointing out a person to receive payment, expressly named a larger sum to be paid him, the action for the return of money paid unduly will be against the party

[1] Read *quis* for *qui*.

[2] Read *condicionis* for *condictionis*. Cf. M.

who pointed the other out, and the right of action is not held to be taken away if proceedings should have been taken against the agent to no purpose.

58 THE SAME (*Responsa* 9) A testator left a *fidei-commissum* to a slave whom he manumitted, provided always that he acquired his liberty by the testament; the slave received the money without any application being made to the judge, and, after that, he was declared to be freeborn. Hereupon, the money left by *fidei-commissum* not having been due, there can be an action for the return of it.

59 THE SAME (*Definitions* 2) If a surety who is legally discharged pays the money under a mistake, there will be nothing, so far, to prevent his suing for a return of it; but if the principal debtor should afterwards himself pay under a mistake, he cannot sue; the first payment, which was void, does not dissolve a natural obligation, nor does it a civil one, if the principal debtor was really bound.

60 PAULUS (*Questions* 3) Julianus declared that a man who really owed money and who paid it after issue was joined in an action could not sue for the return of it, if the action were still pending, because he could not sue if the case against him were dismissed, nor could he if he were ordered to pay, as, even if it were dismissed, he would still continue to be debtor by natural law; he would, in fact, Julianus adds, be in the position of a man who promised in such terms as these,—that he would pay whether such and such a ship came from Asia or did not come, seeing that one ground or else the other[1] gives occasion for the payment. 1. But where a man who owes money absolutely promises to pay it on a condition, his object being to novate the contract, many hold that so long as the novation is in suspense, if he pays, he can sue for the return of the money,—because it is not yet clear which is the obligation in pursuance of which he paid; and it is, in their opinion, a similar case if we suppose that two different persons promise the same sum, the one in absolute terms and the other on a condition with the object of novating the contract. But here the circumstances are different; as in the case [first mentioned] of the absolute and conditional stipulations, it is certain that it is the same person who will be debtor in either case.

[1] For *alterius* read *alterave*. Cf. M.

61 SCÆVOLA (*Responsa* 5) [A ward having become heir to his father,] the guardians of the ward paid some of the creditors out of the father's assets, but after that, as the property was not sufficient, they made the ward decline the inheritance: the question is asked whether the creditors will have to return the amount paid them by the guardians in excess or the whole of what they received. My answer was that, if there had been no fraudulent dealing, nothing was owing to the guardians or to the ward, but they were liable to the other creditors for so much of their own debts as had been paid in excess.

62 MÆCIANUS (*Fidei-commissa* 4) If payment of a *fidei-commissum* has been made the subject of a stipulation, in spite of the fact that it was not due, still, inasmuch as it has been promised with a view to the discharge of a testamentary trust by one who was aware of the facts, it is a legal debt.

63 GAIUS (*on Cases*) Neratius mentions a case that might arise of a man being unable to sue for the return of what he handed over, on the ground that he owed what he gave, in which however he is not discharged of his obligation. An instance is where one who was bound to deliver a particular slave hands him over when a *statuliber*; he is not, he says, discharged, because he does not pass the absolute property in the man to the promisee; still, he cannot sue to have him returned, because he owed all he handed over.

64 TRYPHONINUS (*Disputations* 7) If a slaveowner owed money to his slave and paid it to him after his manumission, he cannot sue for the return of it, even though he paid under the impression that he was liable to some action to compel him to do so, as he paid in recognition of an obligation good in natural law. Liberty we know exists in virtue of natural law and command over men was introduced by the law of the world (*jus gentium*), and thus the question of debt or no debt in connexion with the right to bring a *condictio* [for money once paid] must be considered from the point of view of natural law.

65 PAULUS (*on Plautius* 17) In short, to exhibit in general terms the law as to actions for the return of things handed over, it should be understood that property is delivered either in pursuance of a compromise of claims, or on a foregoing ground (*causa*), or in order to fulfil some condition, or for something to be done, or without any obligation; and in all these cases the question as to an action for the return of the property presents itself. 1. Now,

with regard to delivery in pursuance of a compromise, even if there was no good reason for it (*res nulla media*), there can be no action for the return; as, if there was any contention at law, the very fact that the contention is given up is held to amount to a ground. If, on the other hand, a plain case of fraud should be brought to light and the compromise be invalid, the action will be allowed. 2. Again, if something is given on some foregoing ground, for instance, because I thought that I had been helped in my business by the other party, though this was not really the case, then, seeing that I desired to make him a present, however erroneous my impression may have been, the action for return of the gift cannot be brought. 3. I can however proceed by *condictio* as having fulfilled a condition attached to a legacy or to an inheritance [which I thought was given me] whether in reality no legacy was made me or a legacy [that was made] is taken away, and thus I can sue for the return of what I gave,—the fact being that I did not give with the idea that I was concluding a contract,—since the object with a view to which I gave was not realized. The same holds where I was unwilling or unable to take up the inheritance. The rule will not apply in a case where my slave was appointed heir subject to a condition and I thereupon give something [in pursuance of the condition], after which the man takes up the inheritance, being then manumitted; as in this case the object aimed at is realized. 4. What is given for something to be done may be the subject of an action for return on principles of justice and fairness; for example, where I give you something in order that you may do a particular thing and you do not do it. 5. Where a man sues for the return of what was not owing, proceeds and the children of female slaves that were given must be handed over as well, with a reservation of the cost. 6. In a case of corn being delivered without obligation, its quality is taken into account, and, if the defendant has consumed the corn, the action will be for the value. 7. Similarly if what I gave was a *habitatio*, I can sue for the money, I do not mean for the amount which it could have been let for, but the amount for which you [the defendant] would have hired it. 8. If I hand over to you a slave whom I was not bound to give, and you manumit him, then, if you did this with knowledge of the facts, you will be liable to pay his value, but if without such knowledge, you will not be under that liability, but you must pay the value of the services due from him as a freedman, and you will have to make over any inheritance acquired from him. 9. Payment is "undue," not merely when it is not owing at all, but equally so when it is owing to one man but made to another, or in a case where what one man owes another pays as if he owed it himself.

66 PAPINIANUS (*Questions* 8) This *condictio,* introduced as it has been on principles of justice and fairness, has become the customary means of procuring the return of such property of one man as is discovered to be in the possession of another without any title to it.

67 SCÆVOLA (*Digest* 5) Stichus, after receiving by the testament of a person whom he believed to be his owner a gift of his liberty, on condition that, for ten years from the testator's death, he paid ten every year to his heirs, in accordance therewith paid the sum so specified for eight years; after which he discovered that he was really freeborn, and he made no payment for the years remaining; moreover he was judicially declared to be freeborn. The question was asked whether he could sue for the return of the money which he had given the heirs as not having been due, and, if so, by what kind of action. The answer was that, if he had paid money which had not been procured either by his own services or through the property of the man whom he had served in good faith, there could be an action for the return of it. 1. A guardian paid money to a creditor of his ward in excess of what was owing to him, and, when the action on guardianship was brought, he did not credit himself with the amount: I wish to know whether he has a right to sue the creditor for return of the money. The answer was "Yes." 2. Titius, being in debt to a great many persons, one of whom was Seius, assigned his property to Mævius in pursuance of a secret sale, on the understanding that the latter would satisfy the creditors. Mævius, on this, paid to Seius, as if it were owing to him, money which had already been paid by Titius himself; and the question was asked, on certain receipts being found in the possession of Titius the debtor relating to debts partly paid, who it was that had a right to sue for the return of the money paid unduly, Titius the debtor or Mævius, the latter having been made "*procurator* on his own behalf." The answer was that, taking the facts as stated, it was the one who paid last. 3. The inquirer asked further whether the agreement which it is the practice to insert on settling accounts, namely such as follows,—that there shall be no further dispute between the parties in pursuance of the contract herein referred to,—would be a bar to the action. The answer was that there was nothing stated which would make it a bar. 4. Lucius Titius lent to Gaius Seius, who was under twenty-five years of age, a given sum

of money, and received a certain amount from him by way of interest. The heir of Gaius Seius the aforesaid minor got an order for a *restitutio in integrum* from the Governor of the province as against Publius Mævius [heir of Lucius Titius?], to enable him to avoid paying the debt which fell on the deceased's estate, but[1] with regard to the interest on the principal, which interest Seius the person under twenty-five had paid the creditor, nothing was said in the court of the Governor as to any action for the return of it nor was any judgment given about it. I wish to ask whether the heir of Gaius Seius the person under twenty-five years of age can sue for the return of the interest which the latter had paid to the creditor as long as he lived. The answer was that, taking the facts as stated, there could be no action for the return of what the deceased had paid by way of interest. I wish to ask further, assuming your opinion to be that there can be no such action, whether the heir has a right to retain the interest out of some other debt. The answer was :—"No, not even that."

VII.

ON *CONDICTIO* FOR WANT OF GROUND.

1 ULPIANUS (*on Sabinus* 43) Again, there is a right of *condictio* in the following case, viz. where a person makes a promise without ground or where he pays what was not owing. Where however he has promised without ground, he cannot bring a *condictio* for values which he never gave but only for the *obligatio* itself; but we may add that if he promised on a foregoing ground, but the ground failed, the rule is that it will be a case for a *condictio*. 2. Whether the promise was made without ground at the outset, or there was a ground for the promise which is exhausted or has failed, the rule is that it is a case for a *condictio*. 3. It is acknowledged law that a *condictio* for anything can be brought against a man only where it has come to his hands either on no just ground or under circumstances which come to the same thing.

2 THE SAME (*on the Edict* 32) A fuller having engaged to wash some clothes, the clothes are lost, whereupon, being sued on his

[1] del. *et*. M.

contract, he pays their value to the owner, after which the latter finds them. What action must the fuller bring to recover the value which he gave? To this Cassius says that he not only can sue on the contract, but he can bring a *condictio* against the owner. My own opinion is that he has at any rate a right of action on the contract; but as to the right to bring a *condictio*, this has been questioned, as he did not pay anything which he did not owe; unless indeed we like to say that the money can be recovered by a *condictio* for the reason that it was given without ground, as, no doubt, when the clothes are found, the money may be held to have been given without ground.

3 JULIANUS (*Digest* 8) People who are under an obligation without ground can get discharged of the obligation by a *condictio* for want of ground brought for an unascertained amount; and it is immaterial whether the plaintiff contracted the whole obligation without ground or a more extensive obligation than he need have contracted, except indeed that proceedings taken in order to be freed from all obligation whatever differ from those taken in order to be relieved to some extent: for instance, a man who promised to give ten, if[1] he had no ground for making the promise, can, by a *condictio* for an unascertained amount, procure that he shall be formally released from the whole stipulation, but, if he promised ten where he need only have promised five, he can procure by a similar *condictio* that he shall be discharged of five.

4 AFRICANUS (*Questions* 8) It is immaterial whether a thing was given at the outset without ground, or the ground on which it was given failed.

5 PAPINIANUS (*Questions* 11) A woman in view of a marriage with her maternal uncle gave a sum of money by way of *dos*, but did not marry him. The question has been asked whether she can sue to have the money returned. To this I said that, when money is paid on a ground which is immoral on the part of both giver and receiver, there is no right of *condictio*, and, where both are equally guilty, the person in possession has the better right; adding that I supposed that anyone who followed that line of argument was likely to give the opinion that the woman could not bring a *condictio*; but that nevertheless it could be properly said on the other side that in the instance before us it was not so much a case of an immoral ground as of no ground at all, it being in fact

[1] del. *nam.*

impossible that the money which was given should be turned into a *dos,* as the object in view of which it was given was not illicit intercourse but marriage. 1. A stepmother gave money by way of *dos* for a marriage with her stepson, similarly a daughter-in-law for marriage with her father-in-law, but no marriage took place. At the first glance it looks as if there were no right of *condictio* to recover the money, because it is a case of incest by universal law; nevertheless, in these cases it is still clearer that there was no ground at all for the giving of *dos*; consequently there is a right of *condictio.*

THIRTEENTH BOOK.

I.

ON THE *CONDICTIO FURTIVA*.

1 ULPIANUS (*on Sabinus* 18) In the case of a thing stolen the *condictio* can be brought by the owner alone.

2 POMPONIUS (*on Sabinus* 16) Both lunatics and infants are amenable to a *condictio furtiva* (founded on theft), where they have become compulsory heirs, though they cannot be sued [in the action for theft].

3 PAULUS (*on Sabinus* 9) If a *condictio* founded on a case of theft is brought for a slave, there is no doubt that damages are demandable to the extent of the plaintiff's interest; say, for example, that the slave was appointed heir to someone and his owner is in danger of losing the inheritance. Julianus himself says this. Again, if the *condictio* is for a slave now dead, the plaintiff, he tells us, will get the value of the inheritance.

4 ULPIANUS (*on Sabinus* 41) If a slave or a son under *potestas* commits a theft, there is a right of *condictio* against the owner of the slave for whatever came to his hands; as for the balance, the owner can surrender the slave for *noxa*.

5 PAULUS (*on Sabinus* 9) A *condictio* founded on a case of theft can be brought against a son under *potestas*, as the only person who is ever liable to such a *condictio* is the one who committed the theft or his heir.

6 ULPIANUS (*on the Edict* 38) Accordingly, even where a theft is committed with the aid and advice of another, the latter will not be liable to the *condictio*, though he is to an action for theft.

7 THE SAME (*on Sabinus* 42) Where a man has settled for the loss as a thief, it is quite certain that this is no bar to a *condictio*; by settling for the loss the right of action for theft is taken away, but not the right of *condictio*. 1. The action for theft is brought for the statutable damages, the *condictio* for the actual goods; the result of which is that the right to an action for theft is not taken away by the *condictio* nor the right to a *condictio* by the action for theft. Accordingly, a man whose property has been stolen has a right of action for theft and a right of *condictio* and a right of *vindicatio* (action to recover as owner), he can also have an action *ad exhibendum* (for production). 2. The *condictio* for stolen goods, inasmuch as it is an action for a thing, is good against the heir of the thief too, and that not only while a slave [for example] who was stolen is living, but even after his death; in fact, where the stolen slave met with his death while in the possession of the heir of the thief, or even not in his possession, the rule still is that, after the slave's death, the right of *condictio* will run on against the heir. What we have just said of the heir applies equally to any kind of successor.

8 THE SAME (*on the Edict* 27) Where goods are stolen the *condictio* may be brought for the actual goods; but is this only so long as they are still in existence, or does it hold equally where they are no more to be found in the world? As to this, if the thief has delivered them up, then beyond doubt no *condictio* can be brought; but, so long as he does not do so, there remains a good right of *condictio* for the value put upon them, as it is impossible for the things themselves to be handed over. 1. Where a *condictio* is brought for stolen goods, the question arises what the time is to which the estimate of their value applies. As to this, the rule is that we must look at the time at which the thing bore the utmost value it ever had, especially considering that a thief will not get off by handing over property the value of which has been reduced; a thief is held to be always in default. 2. Lastly it should be observed that mesne profits are included in this action.

9 THE SAME (*on the Edict* 30) In a *condictio* on the ground of theft the defendant is liable not merely for the amount which has come to his hands, but for the whole, assuming that he is sole heir; but a man who is heir for a share is liable to the extent of such share in the thing stolen as he has in the inheritance.

10 THE SAME (*on the Edict* 38) A thief is liable to the *condictio*

whether he is "manifest" or "not manifest." But a thief manifest will only be liable to the *condictio* so long as the owner has not taken possession of the thing[1] stolen; it is clear that no thief is liable to a *condictio* after the owner has once taken possession. Hence Julianus, in order to be able to proceed with the discussion of the *condictio* in the case of a thief manifest, takes the case of the detected thief having killed or broken up or poured out what he had misappropriated. 1. A man who is liable for *vi bona rapta* (robbery) can be sued in a *condictio*, so Julianus informs us (*Digest* b. 22). 2. The *condictio* will be admissible only so long as the ownership in the thing has not passed away from the owner by his own act; so that, if he should transfer it to another, he loses the right of *condictio*. 3. Hence Celsus says (*Digest* b. 12) that if the owner bequeaths the stolen goods to the thief unconditionally, his heir cannot bring a *condictio* for them against him, and, even if the bequest is not to the thief himself but to someone else, the same rule holds and the *condictio* is lost, as the ownership is gone by the act of the testator, that is of the owner.

11 PAULUS (*on the Edict* 39) Even the legatee himself cannot bring the *condictio*; the *condictio* is open only to the person from whom the thing was stolen or to his heir; but the legatee has a good right of *vindicatio* for a thing which the owner bequeathed to him.

12 ULPIANUS (*on the Edict* 38) Accordingly Marcellus (b. 7) lays down the law in very apt language; what he says is:—If what was stolen is still your property[2], you can condict it; but it is equally true that, if you lose the position of owner otherwise than by your own act, you can still condict it. 1. Hence, where the thing was common property, it makes a difference, as he well says, whether you challenged your co-owner to *communi dividundo* proceedings or he challenged you; as if it was you who challenged, you lost the right to bring the *condictio*, but, if it was your fellow-owner, you have it still. 2. Neratius (*Parchment books*) mentions that it was held by Aristo that, where a thing has been given in pledge, the pledgee can, if it is stolen, bring a *condictio* for an unascertained amount.

[1] After *ejus* read *rei*. Cf. M.

[2] *Si res* mihi *subrepta tua remaneat, condices*. The word *mihi* is puzzling. M. suggests reading it before *condices*. I have left it out, which is practically the same thing. The above reading is impossible, but the sense is clear.

13 PAULUS (*on the Edict* 39) If cups have been made out of silver that was stolen, according to Fulcinius, they can be condicted; accordingly in a *condictio* for the cups, a value will be put upon any device engraved which was made at the expense of the thief; just as, where a [slave] child is stolen and grows to be a man, the valuation will be of his worth as full-grown, although he grow to manhood under the care and at the expense of the thief.

14 JULIANUS (*Digest* 22) If a stolen slave has been bequeathed subject to a condition, then, as long as the condition is in suspense, the heir can bring a *condictio*, but should the condition be fulfilled after joinder of issue, the action must thereupon be dismissed, just as if the same slave had been ordered by testament to be free subject to a condition, and the condition were fulfilled after joinder of issue: the fact being that the plaintiff himself has now no interest in getting hold of the man and the property has ceased to be his through no ill practice on the part of the thief. If judgment were given while the condition was still pending, the judge must form an estimate as to what price the slave would fetch in the market. 1. But in this action the plaintiff will not have to give security to the person against whom proceedings are taken. 2. If an ox is stolen and then killed, the owner has a good *condictio* for the ox and the hide and the flesh, where, that is, hide and flesh have been handled [so as to constitute theft], and the horns can be condicted too. But if the owner, by means of the *condictio*, gets the value of the ox, and afterwards brings a similar action for any other of the things above mentioned, he can beyond question be barred by an *exceptio*. Should he on the other hand condict the hide and get the value of it, and thereupon proceed to condict the ox, then, if the thief offers the value of the ox less the value of the hide, the plaintiff will be barred by an *exceptio* of *dolus malus*. 3. The rule is similar on a theft of grapes; there is a good right of *condictio* in law for the *mustum* and the grape-stones.

15 CELSUS (*Digest* 12) Where a slave steals from anyone, he will be liable to an action for theft on account of his act on becoming free; but no *condictio* can be brought against him, unless he handled the goods after he became free.

16 POMPONIUS (*on Quintus Mucius* 38) Where a man commits theft by making use of something which was lent him or deposited with him, he can be called to account by a *condictio* on the ground

of theft as well [as by the ordinary actions]. A difference between this and the *actio commodati* is that, if the thing is destroyed, even without any malice or negligence on the part of the defendant, he is still liable to the *condictio*; whereas, in the *actio commodati*, the defendant is rarely held liable except so far as he was guilty of negligence, and, in the *actio depositi*, only for deliberate malice[1].

17 PAPINIANUS (*Questions* 10) It is a matter of small account, as bearing on the extinction of the right of *condictio*, whether, when a slave has been stolen, there is an offer to restore him or the matter is brought under a different head of debt and a different kind of obligation; nor do I concern myself with the question whether the slave is on the spot or not, as the default which was involved in the fact of theft is got rid of by a sort of shifting of the claim (*veluti quadam delegatione*).

18 SCÆVOLA (*Questions* 4) Seeing that, if a man receives money which is not due with knowledge of the fact, this amounts to theft, we may consider the question whether, where a *procurator* pays with his own money, this does not amount to a theft on the *procurator* himself. Pomponius says (*Epistles* 8) that the *procurator* does have a right of *condictio* founded on theft; but that I myself [the principal] have a similar right, if I ratify such a payment of something that was not owed. However, if one action is brought, this puts an end to the right to bring the other.

19 PAULUS (*on Neratius* 3) Julianus gave it as his opinion that, where a daughter removed [her husband's] goods, a *condictio* must be allowed against her father, *in peculium* (to the extent of what her father allows her).

20 TRYPHONINUS (*Disputations* 15) Where the thief is ready to defend a *condictio*, and, as long as the thing stolen is in existence, it is within my power to bring the action, but after a while the thing is destroyed, the old lawyers were still of opinion that the right to a *condictio* would remain, as it is clear that where a man at the outset handled anything against the will of the owner, he is always in default in the matter of restoring it, it being a thing which he never ought to have taken away at all.

[1] Omit *depositi* before *agetur*. Cf. M.

II.

ON *CONDICTIO* UNDER THE STATUTE.

1 PAULUS (*on Plautius* 2) If an obligation is introduced by a new statute, and no provision is made in the statute itself as to what kind of action it is by which to proceed, the action must be "under the statute."

III.

ON A TRITICARIAN *CONDICTIO*.

1 ULPIANUS (*on the Edict* 27) A man who sues for a definite sum of money which he has advanced must employ the action referred to in the words "Where a definite demand is made," but one who sues for anything of a different kind must do so by a "triticarian" *condictio*. To state the law in general terms, the things which are sued for in this action are any which there may happen to be which differ from money advanced, whether they are determined by weight or by measure, and whether they are movable or consist of land. Accordingly, one may sue in this way for a piece of land, including the case of land let on perpetual lease, or one in which the plaintiff stipulated for the conveyance of a mere right, such as a usufruct, or a servitude to be attached to either kind of estate [urban or rustic]. 1. No one can sue in this action for his own property, except in those special cases in which this is allowed, for example, in a case founded on theft, or one in which a movable object[1] has been forcibly carried off.

2 THE SAME (*on Sabinus* 18) Sabinus goes further and says that, where a man has turned anyone by force out of his land, he is liable to a *condictio* for it, and Celsus too says the same thing, but this is only in case the person who was ejected and brings the action is the owner; and, if he is not owner, still, according to Celsus, he can bring a *condictio* for the possession.

[1] Read *re* after *vi*. M.

3 THE SAME (*on the Edict* 27) In this action, if the question is asked to what time the valuation of the thing sued for is to refer, the better opinion is, and this is held by Servius, that we must consider the time when judgment is pronounced against the defendant, and if, by that time, the thing [say any animal] should have ceased to exist, the time of death; but this, as Celsus says, must be taken with some allowance; we must not look at the closing moments of life, lest the valuation be brought down to a very small sum; for example, suppose a slave is mortally wounded. But whichever of the above times is taken, so Marcellus tells us (b. 20), if the object sued for lost value at a time when the defendant was already in default, an estimate must be made of the depreciation; consequently, if the defendant hands over a slave who, after he had come to be in default, was deprived of the sight of one eye, he is not really discharged; so that, in a case of that nature, the valuation must refer back to the moment when the defendant began to be in default.

4 GAIUS (*on the provincial Edict*) If the subject of the suit should be goods of any kind which ought to have been handed over on a given day, for example, wine, oil or corn, then, according to Cassius, the damages ought to be determined by the value which they would have borne on the day when the goods were to be handed over; or, if no agreement was made as to the day, then the value which they bore when issue was joined; and a similar rule applies as to place; so that an estimate should first be made with reference to the place where the goods were to be handed over, but, if there was no agreement as to place, then the place to be considered must be the one where the action was brought. In fact this principle is applied as to every kind of case.

IV.

ON THINGS WHICH ARE TO BE RENDERED AT A SPECIFIED PLACE.

1 GAIUS (*on the provincial Edict* 9) It used to be held that it was not open to any one to bring an action at a different place from that in which, according to the terms of his stipulation, the thing sued for would have to be rendered. As, however, it was unjust, supposing the promisor never came to the place where,

according to his promise, the thing would have to be handed over, whether because he purposely avoided the place or because he was unavoidably detained elsewhere, that the promisee should be unable to come by what he had a right to, it was therefore thought proper to provide an *utilis actio* to meet the case.

2 ULPIANUS (*on the Edict* 27) An arbitrarian action may be advantageous either to the plaintiff or to the defendant; where the advantage is on the side of the defendant, the judgment is for a smaller sum of money than is claimed, and, where it is on the side of the plaintiff, for a greater sum[1]. 1. The action in question may be founded on a stipulation such as the following: I stipulate with you that ten shall be paid me at Ephesus. 2. If a man sues on a stipulation that there shall be given him either ten at Ephesus or a slave at Capua, he cannot lay one of the two places out of the case when he brings his action, lest he should be depriving the defendant of the advantage given by locality. 3. According to Scævola (*Questions* b. 15), it is by no means the fact that what is implied tacitly in a stipulation is, as a matter of course, in the defendant's power; what he is [to be] bound to do he can, he says, determine, but not whether or not he is [to be] bound at all. Accordingly, where a man promises to give either Stichus or Pamphilus, he can choose what his delivery shall be of, so long as both are alive; but, as soon as one of the two dies, there is an end, he says, of his power of selection, or else it would be open to him to determine whether he is bound at all, assuming that he were unwilling to hand over the living slave whom alone he would be bound to give. Hence, in the case before us, if a man promised to give something at either Ephesus or Capua, he could not be sued at all, if it depended on his choice where the action should be brought, as he would as a matter of course choose a different place [from that in which the plaintiff was], and the result of this would be to put in his power to determine whether he should be bound at all; accordingly Scævola holds that the action can be brought against him in either of the two, and that without further mention of place, so that the plaintiff is allowed to select the place where to sue. In fact he lays it down in general terms that the plaintiff can choose where to sue and the defendant where to hand over, that is until the action is brought. Hence, he proceeds to say, if there is an alternative as to subject joined to an alternative as to place, the necessary result is to give the plaintiff the choice as to

[1] Del. *pecunia fiat.*

subject through his right of choice as to place; indeed the truth is you put it out of the plaintiff's power to bring an action by your wish to keep the choice [of subject] in the hands of the defendant. 4. If a man stipulates with the words "at Ephesus *and* Capua," what our authority says is that he must sue for part at Ephesus and part at Capua. 5. If he stipulates for a set of flats to be built, without adding the place where, the stipulation is void. 6. If a man's stipulation is for ten to be paid at Ephesus, then, if he sues before the day on which he can reach Ephesus, he sues to no purpose; [there is no doubt indeed that a suit is brought to no purpose[1]] before the time, as Julianus himself says that a particular day is tacitly implied in such a stipulation as the above. Consequently I believe that what Julianus holds is sound, that where a man stipulates at Rome for something to be given at Carthage on the same day, the stipulation is inoperative. 7. Again, Julianus discusses the following point, namely, where a man has stipulated that something should be given at Ephesus to either himself or Titius, whether, if payment should be made to Titius at some other place, the promisee can in spite of this last fact, claim by action that payment should be made to himself: as to which what Julianus tells us is that there is no discharge of the debt, so that an action can be brought for the amount of the promisee's loss. But Marcellus says, both in an independent discussion and in a note to Julianus, that it may be held that there is a good discharge even if payment is made to me in some other place, although I cannot be compelled to accept it against my will; and, if there is no discharge, the proper thing to say certainly is, in his opinion, that the promisee has still a right to ask for the whole sum: the case being like that of a man building a block of chambers on a different spot from that specified in his promise, who would not be discharged of any part of his obligation. However, my own view is that the case of paying a sum of money differs from that of building a set of flats, and consequently that the action can only be brought for the loss incurred. 8. We may proceed now to discuss the duty of the judge who hears such a case and consider whether he must follow scrupulously the amount named in the contract or either go beyond or fall short of such amount, so that if the defendant has an interest in making payment at Ephesus rather than at the particular place where the action is brought, this fact may be taken into account. Julianus, following in this

[1] Cf. M.

the opinion of Labeo, took into account also the position of the plaintiff, who sometimes might have some interest in getting payment at Ephesus; accordingly account must be taken of what is advantageous to the plaintiff. For example, what is to be said if he advanced money on a contract of bottomry and is to be repaid it at Ephesus, at which place he owed a sum of money under a penalty or on security, and the consequence of your [the defendant's] default is that the property which he pledged is sold or the penalty incurred? Or say he owed money to the treasury, and [his] your promisee's property has been sold for much less than its value; the amount of difference it made to him will have to be taken into account in the arbitrarian action, and that on a scale which may go beyond the statutable limits for interest on money lent. Suppose, again, he was in the practice of buying goods for sale; ought not the profit [which he missed the opportunity of making] to be taken into account and not simply the actual loss he incurred? My opinion is that the profit that he misses should be taken into account too.

3 GAIUS (*on the provincial Edict* 9) The reason why this action is submitted to the judge's decision is that we all know how much the prices of things vary from one city or region to another, especially in the case of wine, oil and corn; and, as for money, though it may be thought that its power is one and the same everywhere, still, in some places it is procurable easily and at a moderate rate of interest and in others with greater difficulty and only at a heavy rate of interest.

4 ULPIANUS (*on the Edict* 27) If, on the other hand, the action is brought at Ephesus, only the actual amount can be asked for, and nothing further, unless the plaintiff had made some stipulation for it, or unless the advantage of despatch comes in in the case [in some other way]. 1. Sometimes the judge before whom the action is brought, seeing that the case is arbitrarian, will be bound to discharge the defendant after first requiring him to undertake to pay the money at the place where the promise was made. For instance, how if it is alleged that the money was offered to the plaintiff at that place, or deposited there, or that it could easily be paid there: ought not the judge in some such cases to discharge the defendant? To state the matter briefly,—the judge who is appointed to hear such a case ought to keep equitable principles in view as well [as strict law].

5 PAULUS (*on the Edict* 28) If an heir is ordered by the testator to give something at a specified place, there is ground for an arbitrarian action;

6 POMPONIUS (*on Sabinus* 22) or money was lent on the understanding that it should be repaid at a specified place.

7 PAULUS (*on the Edict* 28) In *bona fide* cases, even though it was a term in the contract that a thing should be handed over at a specified place, the action allowed is that on purchase or on sale or on deposit, and not the *actio arbitraria*. 1. But if a man promised in a stipulation[1] that he would make delivery at a specified place, this last is the action to which to have recourse.

8 AFRICANUS (*Questions* 3) Having stipulated for the payment to you of a hundred at Capua, you took a surety; any action for the money brought against the surety will have to be on the same terms as if it were against the promisor himself; that is to say, if it is brought in any other place than Capua, it must be an arbitrarian action, and the damages must be laid at an amount representing the interest which either the defendant or the plaintiff, [as the case may be], would have in the money in question being paid at Capua rather than anywhere else. Should it moreover happen that it was owing to the default of the principal debtor that the whole hundred were not paid at Capua, the burden on the surety must not be any the greater, as this case cannot properly be compared with that of an obligation to pay interest; in such a case as that, there are two stipulations, but here there is only one, that is, a stipulation for repayment of money lent, in connexion with the performance of which the question of the measure of damages is entrusted to the equitable discretion (*arbitrium*) of the judge: and one thing which in my judgment exhibits very plainly the difference between the two cases is that, if, after the defendant has begun to be in default, part of the money owing is paid and an action is brought for the rest, the prescribed function of the judge is such that he must make an estimate of the interest which the plaintiff has in payment being made at Capua with reference to the reduced amount only which is the subject of the action.

9 ULPIANUS (*on Sabinus* 47) When a person promises to pay at a specified place, he is not at liberty to pay in any other place than the one for which he promised, without the consent of the promisee.

[1] *Stipulatus sit*: an unusual use of the word. Cf. D. 12. 6. 13.

10 PAULUS (*Questions* 4) If, after default of the promisor as to payment in Capua, the promisee should be about to bring an arbitrarian action, but he should first take a surety with reference to such action, let us consider whether it is not the case that any amount that might have to be added to the original debt by the judgment of the Court will not be owing [from the surety] and does not form part of his obligation; so that, in fact, even now, if the principal sum should be paid, or the action should be brought at Capua, the special power of the judge [*arbitrium*] is at an end; unless, indeed, it should be said, supposing, for instance, the judge would have to order payment of the sum of a hundred and twenty, that thereupon, if payment were made of a hundred, that sum must be held to be paid on the whole amount, that is out of [the amount due for] both the original debt and the penalty, so as to leave it still open to the plaintiff to sue for so much more as is still due of the original debt[1], with a penalty in addition for non-payment of that amount. But this view of the matter is in my opinion inadmissible, especially as, in accepting the payment the creditor may be held to have remitted the penalty.

V.

ON A *CONSTITUTUM* OF MONEY.

1 ULPIANUS (*on the Edict* 27) In this Edict the Prætor favours natural justice, as he maintains assurances by *constitutum* made in pursuance of agreement, seeing that to disappoint credit given is a serious matter. 1. The Prætor says:—"Where a man makes a *constitutum* of money owed" [etc.]. The word "man" must be taken to mean man or woman, as women too are bound by a *constitutum* of money, provided they are not guaranteeing a debt. 2. Nothing is said in the Edict as to the case of a boy under age; however, the boy is not bound by a *constitutum* without the concurrence of his guardian. 3. It has been asked whether a son under *potestas* is bound, if he makes a *constitutum*. In my opinion the truth is that he is bound by his *constitutum* and his father is bound *de peculio*. 4. If a person has made a stipulation which was inoperative, but his real wish was to make a stipulation

[1] Read *ex sorte* for *sortem*. Cf. M.

and not to have a *constitutum* given him, the proper view is that he cannot bring an action on *constitutum*, because what was done was not with the intention of making a *constitutum*, but of giving a promise. 5. The question has been asked whether the *constitutum* can be for anything other than what is due. Since however it is now good law that one thing can be given in discharge of a contract, in the place of another, there can be nothing to prevent a *constitutum* being made of something other than what is due; for instance, where a person owes a hundred and makes a *constitutum* of corn of that value, I should say the *constitutum* is valid. 6. A *constitutum* of a debt can be made, on whatever ground it is owing, that is to say on whatever kind of contract, whether it be one to give a specific sum or an unliquidated amount, and whether it is of purchase money owed in pursuance of a sale or money payable by way of *dos* or on the ground of guardianship or of any contract whatever. 7. Even a debt owing in natural law will be enough. 8. Add that a man who is liable to an "honorary" action and not by civil law will be bound by a *constitutum*; a debt owing in honorary law is held to be a debt. Hence too, if a *constitutum* is made by a *paterfamilias* or by the owner of a slave of a debt for which he can be sued in an action *de peculio*, the liability will extend to the amount which there was in the *peculium* when the *constitutum* was made; and, in fact, if he made it for anything over and above that amount on his own account, he will not be liable in respect of the excess.

2 JULIANUS (*Digest* 11) But if he engages by *constitutum* on his son's account that he will pay ten, then, although there should be [only] five in the *peculium*, he will be liable on *constitutum* to pay ten.

3 ULPIANUS (*on the Edict* 27) If a husband engages by *constitutum* for a larger amount of *dos* than his means admit of, then, seeing that he makes a *constitutum* of a debt, he is liable for all that he engages for, but the judgment given at the suit of the wife will be for payment to the extent of his means. 1. If a man engages by *constitutum* for a sum which he owes by civil law but does not owe by prætorian law, because, that is, he has an *exceptio*, the question is asked whether he is bound by the *constitutum*; to which the true answer is, as indeed Pomponius himself says, that he is not bound, as the money engaged for by *constitutum* is not owing by the principles of law in force. 2. Where a man who is debtor both by civil and prætorian law is under an obligation which

takes effect at a future day, we may ask whether he can bind himself by a *constitutum*. To this Labeo says that he can[1], and Pedius confirms this opinion. Labeo himself adds that the *constitutum* was introduced chiefly on account of the very case of such pecuniary debts as could not yet be sued for; with which opinion I am much disposed to agree: there is a plain advantage in a rule to the effect that a person who is bound from and after a given day and who gives a *constitutum* to the effect that he will pay on that day will be liable accordingly.

4 PAULUS (*on the Edict* 29) But if he engages by *constitutum* to pay on an earlier day, he is equally liable.

5 ULPIANUS (*on the Edict* 27) If a man promised to pay at Ephesus, and he engages by *constitutum* that he will pay at some other place, there is no doubt that he is liable. 1. Julianus says that a legate who engages by *constitutum* at Rome to repay something which he borrowed in the province cannot[2] be sued thereon, and this is perfectly true; indeed if he gave a *constitutum* not during his stay at Rome but while he was still in the province, to the effect that he would pay at Rome, no action on *constitutum* will be allowed against him. 2. The rule above laid down that what is assured by *constitutum* must be the payment of an existing debt, is one which regards the subject-matter; it does not go as far as this, that the person to whom the assurance is given must be already a creditor [of the person who gives it], as, if you engage by *constitutum* to pay [my creditor] what I owe [him], you will be liable accordingly, and, if an engagement is made to me by *constitutum* to pay [me] what is owing to you, the payment must be made. 3. Moreover, in Julianus (b. 11) we read the following:—"Titius sent me a letter in these words: 'I have given a written assurance at the request of Seius that, if he owes you anything, I[3] would, on the same being proved[4], give you an undertaking for payment thereof, and would discharge the debt without any dispute.'" Titius is hereupon liable on a *constitutum* of money. 4. Still, if one man gives a *constitutum* for payment by another, and not for payment by himself in the place of another, he is not liable. Pomponius tells us this (b. 8). 5. Again, if you give me

[1] Del. *constitutum*. M.

[2] Ins. *non* before *debere*. Cf. D. 5. 1. 8. and M.

[3] In the text, *Scripsi me secundum mandatum* etc. *me tibi cauturum*. Some would omit the second *me*, cf. M.: I would rather omit the first.

[4] For *debitum* read *debet cum*. Cf. M.

a *constitutum* to the effect that you will pay me, you will be liable, but, if you give me a *constitutum* that you will pay Sempronius, you will not be liable. 6. Julianus (*Digest* b. 11) says that a *constitutum* can be given to a procurator; which Pomponius explains to mean that you may engage by *constitutum* to pay the procurator himself, but not the principal. 7. Again, a *constitutum* can be given to the guardian of a ward or the *actor* (agent) of a municipality or the *curator* of a lunatic [or a minor[1]]. 8. But these persons will themselves be liable on their own *constitutum*. 9. If a *constitutum* is given to the *actor* of a municipality or the guardian of a ward or the curator of a lunatic or a minor, engaging that payment shall be made to the municipality or the ward or the lunatic or the minor, there will, I should say, have to be an *utilis actio* allowed, as a matter of equitable dealing (*utilitatis gratia*), to such municipality or ward or lunatic or minor. 10. It is settled that a *constitutum* can be given even to a slave, and also,—if it be given to a slave to the effect that payment will be made either to the owner of the slave or to the slave himself,—that the slave will acquire for his master an obligational demand, irrespective of the quality of such slave himself.

6 PAULUS (*Sentences* 2) This principle applies equally where a *constitutum* is given to one who serves me as a slave in good faith.

7 ULPIANUS (*on the Edict* 27) Indeed the *constitutum* is valid even where it is made to a son under *potestas*. 1. If I stipulate for payment to be made to me or Titius, then, according to Julianus, no *constitutum* can be given to Titius on his own account, since he has no right to sue for the money, though valid payment can be made to him.

8 PAULUS (*on the Edict* 29) But if you give a *constitutum* that you will pay either me or Titius, I have a good right of action; though if, after you have given a *constitutum* that you will pay me simply, you pay Titius, you will none the less be liable to me.

9 PAPINIANUS (*Questions* 8) However Titius will be liable to be sued in *condictio indebiti*, in order that money wrongly paid to him may be restored to the person who paid it.

10 PAULUS (*on the Edict* 29) The rule is the same where there are two promisees by stipulation, and thereupon a *constitutum*

[1] M. would insert this, not without reason.

is given to one of them and, after that, payment is made to the other; the truth being that the person to whom the *constitutum* is given ought to be regarded as in the position of one to whom payment has already been made.

11 ULPIANUS (*on the Edict* 27) Accordingly the *constitutum* will always be valid, so long as what is so engaged for is some real debt, even though no person should be forthcoming who is at the moment debtor; suppose, for instance, before entry is made on the debtor's inheritance, or at a time when he is in captivity in the hands of an enemy, some person should give a *constitutum* that he will pay the debt; Pomponius himself tells us that such a *constitutum* is good, as the money which is the subject of it is really owing. 1. If a man owes a hundred *aurei* and engages by *constitutum* to pay two hundred, he is liable to the extent of a hundred only, because that is the amount owing; accordingly, a man who gives a *constitutum* for principal and with it for interest which is not owing will be liable to pay the principal only.

12 PAULUS (*on the Edict* 13) Again, if the amount owed is ten, and the party engages by *constitutum* to give both ten and Stichus, it may be laid down that he is liable in respect of ten only.

13 THE SAME (*on the Edict* 29) But if a man who owes twenty engages by *constitutum* to pay ten, he is liable accordingly.

14 ULPIANUS (*on the Edict* 27) Any man who engages by *constitutum* that he will pay is liable, whether he goes on to name a particular amount or not. 1. If a man engages by *constitutum* that he will furnish security, then, if occasion for security arises, even a *constitutum* such as mentioned must be allowed. 2. Add that, if a man engages by *constitutum* that some particular person will guarantee his debt, the engagement, as Pomponius tells us, is equally binding. How then if that person refuses to be guarantor? I should say that the man who gave the *constitutum* is bound [thereby], unless something different was intended. Suppose however he (the proposed guarantor) dies before the time. If default has been made, a fair rule would be that the party who gave the *constitutum* should be liable either to pay damages representing the creditor's interest in the matter or else to offer some other person as guarantor who is equally substantial: but, if there has been no default, I should be inclined to say that the debtor is not liable [under the *constitutum*]. 3. People can

give a *constitutum* both when present and when absent, just as they can make an informal agreement by a messenger or in person, and they can use any phraseology they please.

15 PAULUS (*on the Edict* 29) Moreover, even if, when I give you a *constitutum*, the person through whom I give it is a free man, there will be no difficulty caused by the fact that this would be a case of an acquisition being made[1] through free persons, because in the present case the agent is held to be simply vouchsafing his services.

16 ULPIANUS (*on the Edict* 27) If two persons [say you and I,] give a *constitutum* as co-debtors, either one of us may be sued for the whole amount. 1. Moreover a man may engage by *constitutum* [to pay] at some particular place or time, and the creditor not only may sue[2] at the place pointed out by the *constitutum*, but can do so anywhere, as in the case of an *actio arbitraria*. 2. The Prætor says:—"Should it appear that the party who gave the *constitutum* neither discharges the original debt nor performs his engagement and there was nothing on the part of the plaintiff to prevent the performance of what was promised by *constitutum*" [etc.]. 3. It appears then that if there was nothing to prevent it on the part of the plaintiff, there is a good right of action, even though there was something to prevent it in the natural course of things; but the better rule is that the defendant should get relief. 4. There is some room for doubt, where the Prætor speaks of the party not performing his *constitutum*, whether his words relate to the time expressed in the *constitutum* itself or we have to carry them on to the time of joinder of issue, and I should take it to be the time expressed in the *constitutum*.

17 PAULUS (*on the Edict* 29) However, even if he offers to pay the debt on some other day, but the plaintiff declines to receive it, though he has no sufficient reason for so declining, it is only just that the defendant should be relieved, either by means of an *exceptio* or by a construction being put on the Prætor's words which meets the justice of the case, so that, down to the time of trial, if the plaintiff acts in the way mentioned, he will himself

1 There is a temptation to insert *non* before *adquirimus*: "the fact that people do not make acquisitions" etc. Cf. Pothier.

2 For *posse eum* we must read *potest is*, but the pronoun cannot refer to the debtor.

suffer by it; the result being that the above words, viz. "nor performs his contract" express the supposition that he does not perform it up to the day for which he made the *constitutum*, nor at any time afterwards.

18 ULPIANUS (*on the Edict* 27) We may add that the words of the Prætor which come after the above, "there was nothing on the part of the plaintiff" etc., give rise to a similar question. Here Pomponius is in doubt, where it so happens that there was nothing on the part of the plaintiff to prevent performance, on the day when the *constitutum* was to be carried out, but there was earlier or later. My own opinion is that these words also must be referred to the day fixed by the *constitutum*. Hence, if the plaintiff fails to attend, being prevented by bad health or by force or by bad weather, it is, as Pomponius says, at his own peril. 1. With regard to the words which follow "and [it appears] that the money at the time when it was promised by *constitutum* was owing," they require more detailed explanation. In the first place, one thing which they import is this, that if some debt was owing when the *constitutum* was made, but now it is not owing, the *constitutum* is nevertheless valid, because the right of action relates back. Consequently, as Celsus and Julianus tell us, if a man is bound by an obligation on which he can be sued only during a limited period, and he makes a *constitutum*, he ought to be liable, even though, after the *constitutum* is given the period in question should have expired. Hence, even if he gives a *constitutum* that he will pay at a time when he will have ceased to be bound, Julianus still is of the same opinion, seeing that he gave the *constitutum* at a time when there was an obligation, though he made it refer to a time when his liability under it would have ceased. 2. It is worth while to add here something on the question whether this action is penal or aims at an indemnity, and the better opinion is, as Marcellus himself holds, that it is for an indemnity. 3. It was long ago a question whether a man who had brought this action would have thereby extinguished his right under the original claim. As to this, the safest view is that it is when payment is made in consequence of these proceedings that the [original] debt will be discharged rather than when issue is joined, seeing that the payment will avail for both obligations.

19 PAULUS (*on the Edict* 29) Where anything is due subject to a condition and a *constitutum* is given which makes it payable

either absolutely or on a given day, it will be due subject to the same condition, so that, if the condition is fulfilled, [the party] is bound, but, if it fail, both rights of action are lost. 1. But if a man owes a debt absolutely and gives a *constitutum* subject to a condition, Pomponius says that he may be sued in an *utilis actio* [on the *constitutum*]. 2. If a *paterfamilias* or the owner of a slave has given a *constitutum* that he would pay the amount which there was in the *peculium*, the *peculium* itself will not be reduced by the fact that he thereupon came to be bound accordingly; and even if the *peculium* should be exhausted, still he is not released;

20 THE SAME (*on Plautius* 4) as the fact of the *peculium* becoming more or less extensive will not affect the right of action on *constitutum*.

21 THE SAME (*on the Edict* 29) If a man promises to hand over Stichus, and Stichus dies at a time when the promisor has let himself be in default, then, if he gives a *constitutum* that he will pay the value, he is liable accordingly. 1. If you give a *constitutum* without mentioning a day, it may be said that you are not liable, although the Edict is drawn in comprehensive terms; otherwise proceedings may be taken against you at once, unless you are ready to pay the moment you have given the *constitutum*; however, a short delay must be observed, that is, not less than ten days, before the demand is put in force. 2. A man who gives a *constitutum* that he will make a payment does not adequately discharge his engagement if he [only] offers security; but if a man [who] makes a *constitutum* to the effect that he will give security offers a surety or a pledge, his liability is at an end, as it makes no difference what kind of security he gives.

22 THE SAME (*Short Notes* 7) If a sum of money has been promised you by *constitutum*, [founded on a debt owing to you as an heir,] and after that you hand over the inheritance under the *Senatusconsultum Trebellianum*, then, as you have transferred to another the right to demand the original debt, you will not be allowed to sue for the money as owing by *constitutum*. The same principle will apply to one who had been in possession of the estate of a deceased person, if the inheritance has since been adjudged to another in virtue of superior title: but the better opinion is that leave to bring the action [on *constitutum*] ought to be granted

to the fideicommissary or to the person who succeeded in the action [for the inheritance].

23 JULIANUS (*Digest* 11) If a person promises to give a slave and the slave dies at a time when it was the promisor's fault that he had not been delivered, then, though what he engaged by *constitutum* was that he would hand over a slave, still he will be liable as for a *constitutum* of money and so have to pay the man's value.

24 MARCELLUS (*Responsa*) Titius sent a letter to Seius in the following words:—"I have in my hands a balance of fifty on your loan as the result of a contract made by my wards, which sum I shall be bound to repay you in good money on the Ides of May; and, if I do not pay it by the aforesaid day, I shall be bound to pay by way of interest" so much. I wish to ask whether Lucius Titius has by this undertaking put himself in the place of his wards as debtor. Marcellus's answer was that, if a stipulation had been made, he had taken their place. I also wish to ask, supposing he did not take their place, whether he is liable on *constitutum*. Marcellus replied that he was liable for the principal: that being the more indulgent and more beneficial construction.

25 PAPINIANUS (*Questions* 8) A man owed one or other of two things, [whichever he pleased,] and he made a *constitutum* of one of them: the question has been asked whether he can still give that one of the two which was not the subject of the *constitutum*. I replied that he must not be listened to if he wanted now to break faith as to the thing which he secured by *constitutum*: 1. If, on the oath being tendered to you, you swear that money is owed you, having already a right of action in regard of it, you have a right to take proceedings on a *constitutum* of money: indeed, if I do not tender the oath of my own accord, but do so only on being driven to it by the necessity I am under of tendering it back to you, as, in fact, it is generally admitted that a man acts more reasonably in tendering the oath back, than in taking an oath himself, there is no practical difference; even though it was owing to your assurance and my modesty that I came to feel compelled to tender it back.

26 SCÆVOLA (*Responsa* 1) A man wrote to his creditor in the following terms:—"Sir, the ten [pieces] which Lucius Titius received as a loan from your chest are at your disposition in my

hands, irrespective of what may appear due for interest." The opinion given was that, taking the facts as stated, the party was liable to an action for money secured by *constitutum*.

27 ULPIANUS (*on the Edict* 14) It matters little whether a *constitutum* is made in the presence or the absence of the debtor. Pomponius goes further and tells us (b. 34) that a man can give a *constitutum* even without the debtor's consent, and, accordingly, he regards the opinion of Labeo as false, who holds that if, after a person has given a *constitutum* on somebody else's behalf, the principal should enjoin him not to pay, he must be allowed an *exceptio in factum*; and Pomponius's opinion is very reasonable, as when the person who made the *constitutum* has once incurred the obligation, he cannot be allowed to escape liability by the act of the [principal] debtor.

28 GAIUS (*on the provincial Edict* 5) Where a man has given an assurance by *constitutum* that he will pay on another's behalf, the person for whom he gave such *constitutum* still remains bound.

29 PAULUS (*on the Edict* 24) A man who is liable to an action for *injuria* or theft or robbery will be bound by a *constitutum*.

30 THE SAME (*Sentences* 2) If a man engages by *constitutum* to pay money to [one or other of] two persons, [say] to you or Titius, then, although in strict law he remains liable by the appropriate action for the money promised by *constitutum*, even if he pays Titius, still he will have the benefit of an *exceptio*.

31 SCÆVOLA (*Digest* 5) Lucius Titius died owing money to the Seii; whereupon these latter assured Publius Mævius that the inheritance belonged to him and induced him to write them a letter in which he declared that he was their debtor, in terms implying that he admitted that he was the heir of his uncle [Lucius Titius], to which he added that he had debited himself with the money in his accounts. The question was asked whether, the fact being that nothing whatever came to Publius Mævius from Lucius Titius's estate, he could, in virtue of the above mentioned letter be sued on a *constitutum* of money, and, if so, whether he could avail himself of an *exceptio* of *dolus*. The answer was that no civil action could be brought on the ground in question, but that an action on *constitutum* was equally inadmissible, taking the facts as stated. The inquirer asked further whether there could be an action brought for the return of what had been paid by way of

interest in virtue of the circumstances above mentioned. The answer was that, taking the facts as stated, there could.

VI.

THE ACTION ON LOAN FOR USE OR THE COUNTER ACTION.

1 ULPIANUS (*on the Edict* 28) The Prætor's words are:—"Whatever any person shall be asserted to have lent, I will allow an action for the same." 1. The interpretation of this edict is not difficult; there is only one thing to be remarked, viz. that the magistrate who drew the edict mentioned loans where Paconius spoke of making use of a thing. Now between making a loan and giving a thing to be used there is, according to Labeo, the same difference as between genus and species; a movable thing may be lent, but not what consists in land, though even what consists in land may be given to be used. However, as we know, land too may be said with correctness to be lent; Cassius himself agrees with this. Vivianus goes so far as to hold that a *habitatio* can be lent. 2. Children under the age of puberty are not liable to be sued on a loan for use, as no such loan can so much as exist to which a boy under age is a party without the concurrence of his guardian, in fact, it goes as far as this, that even if, after attaining the age of puberty, the boy should be guilty of fraud or negligence, he is not liable to this action, as the loan had no force from the first.

2 PAULUS (*on the Edict* 29) Neither can an action on a loan for use be allowed to be brought against a lunatic. But actions for production will be allowed against both, so that, when the thing is produced, it may be made the subject of a *vindicatio*.

3 ULPIANUS (*on the Edict* 28) However my opinion is that, if the ward is enriched [by the loan], an *utilis actio* on the loan must be allowed against him in accordance with the rescript of the Divine Pius. 1. Should the thing lent be restored, but restored in a worse condition, it will not be held to be restored at all, being restored after having got into a worse condition,—unless the loss is made good,—as a thing may be said correctly not to be restored when it is restored in a worse condition[1]. 2. In this action there will be the same oath to the claim allowed as in *bona fide* cases in

[1] Sic!

general, and, in connexion with the question what is the value of the thing lent, the time taken into account is that at which the case is decided, although, for actions in strict law[1], what is considered is the time when issue is joined. 3. An heir of the person who received the loan will be sued in respect of the same share as that which he takes in the inheritance, unless it so chance that he has it in his power to restore the whole thing, but he does not do so; should that be the case, there will be judgment against him for the whole, that being held to be in accordance with the mind (*arbitrium*) of an impartial judge. 4. If the loan is made to a son under *potestas* or to a slave, the action must be only *de peculio*, but the lender can have a direct action too against the son himself. We may add that if the plaintiff lent to a slave woman or a daughter under *potestas*, the action can only be *de peculio*. 5. The *paterfamilias* or the owner, as the case may be, will not suffer judgment on the ground exclusively of wilful wrong done by the son or slave; as fraud too, though fraud only, on the part of the father or owner himself will be taken into account; this distinction is pointed out by Julianus (on the *actio pignoraticia* 11). 6. There can be no loan of an object which is consumed in the use, unless the borrower took it for purposes of ostentation or display.

4 GAIUS (*on verbal obligations* 28) Loans of money are often made with the object of letting the money serve for form's sake in the place of an actual payment.

5 ULPIANUS (*on the Edict* 28) If it is agreed that the thing lent shall be restored at some particular place or time, it is part of the judge's duty to take such place or time into account. 1. If a person brings this action and accepts an offer of the damages assessed, he thereby passes the property in the thing to the party so offering. 2. We have now to consider what it is that is taken into account in an action on a loan; is it only wilful wrong or negligence too, or again, every risk? As a matter of fact, in contracts people are sometimes answerable for wilful wrong alone, and sometimes for negligence as well; in a case of deposit, for wilful wrong; because, there being no question of advantage to accrue to the person with whom the deposit is made, it is quite right that wilful wrong only should be answered for: except, that is, in cases where there is the additional fact of a payment to be made [to the defendant],—as then negligence comes in as

[1] For *stricti* read *strictis iudiciis*. Cf. M.

well, as indeed has been enacted,—or cases in which it was agreed at the outset that the person in whose hands the thing was deposited should answer both for negligence and accident (*periculum*). But where the advantage of both parties is at stake, as in a case of purchase or hire or *dos* or pledge or partnership, the party answers for both wilful wrong and negligence. 3. In loan, for the most part the whole advantage accruing is that of the person to whom the loan is made, so that the opinion held by Quintus Mucius is really the more correct one, namely, that the party must be responsible for negligence, and answer for employing diligence, and, in case the thing has been handed over with a valuation, the whole risk must be borne by the one who engaged that he would make good the valuation. 4. But where mischief happens through old age or illness, or something has been forcibly taken by robbers, or[1] any similar misfortune occurs, the rule is that no loss which arises is to be laid to the charge of the person who took the loan, unless there was in the case some negligence on his part. On the same principle if any mischief happened through a fire or the fall of a building, or any other[2] unavoidable loss occurred, the borrower will not be held liable, unless, having it in his power to preserve the property lent him, he preferred preserving his own. 5. He is certainly bound to keep a watch on the things lent him and that a diligent one. 6. Still, whether such watch need be kept as to a slave who is lent him is a point on which the old lawyers were in doubt. There is no doubt that it is sometimes required even as to a slave, for instance where the slave is fettered when lent, or where he is of such an age as to require to be watched; in any case if the understanding was that the party who asked for the loan should keep watch the rule is that he must do so. 7. Sometimes even in case of death [of the slave or animal lent] the loss falls on the person who asked for the loan; thus, if I lend you a horse for you to take it to your country house and you go into battle with it, you will be liable to an action on the loan, and the same principle applies to a slave. No doubt, if I lent the horse with the understanding that you might take it into battle, I must bear the risk; as Namusa has it, if I lend you a bricklayer and he falls down from a scaffolding, the risk is mine. However this last, I should say, is true only if, when I lent the man, the very understanding was that he was to work on a scaffolding; but if it was that he was to carry on his work on the ground, but you made him get on a scaffolding, or the mischief happened in

[1] After *aut* ins. *si*. M. [2] For *aliquid* read *aliud*. Cf. M.

consequence of some fault in the scaffolding, which was fastened without sufficient care, though not by the man himself, or it was in consequence of the ropes or poles being too old, then I should say that the risk, happening as it did through the fault of the person who asked for the loan, must be borne by that person himself. We learn from Mela himself that if a slave who is lent to a stone-cutter is crushed to death by the scaffolding, the artisan is liable to an action on the loan, because he put the thing together without sufficient care. 8. Moreover, besides this, when a man makes use of what was lent him in some way other [than was intended], he is liable not only on loan but to an action for theft, so Julianus informs us (*Digest* b. 11). He goes on to say:—If I lend you a blank paper and you get your debtor to write on it a note of hand as an assurance to you, which I obliterate, then, if I lent you the paper with a view to the assurance being made on it for you, I am liable to be sued by you in a counter action; but, if this was not the case, and you did not let me know that the note of hand was written, you are in fact, he says, liable to an action on loan, indeed, he continues, even to an action for theft, because you make use of the thing lent in a different way [from that understood in the agreement], just as a man is liable for theft if he uses a horse or a garment in a different way from that with a view to which it was lent. 9. So far is the borrower bound to answer for diligence in the matter of a loan that he is answerable for it even in connexion with such objects as go with the thing lent; for instance, suppose I lent you a mare and the mare was accompanied by a foal; in this case the old lawyers held that you were bound to see to the safety of the foal too. 10. There are cases, no doubt, in which a person who asks for a loan will be answerable only for wilful wrong, as for example if he made express agreement to that effect, or where the lender made the loan entirely in his own interest, say he made it to his own *fiancée* or his wife, in order that she might be the better dressed when she was brought to his house, or the Prætor was exhibiting sports and lent [materials of some kind] to the players, or someone else volunteered to lend them to the Prætor. 11. We may now consider in what particular cases an action on loan will lie: as a matter of fact, the old lawyers were in a state of uncertainty about these cases. 12. I gave you a thing for you to pledge it with your creditor, and you so pledged it: but you do not redeem it in order to restore it to me. Here, Labeo says, an action on loan will lie, and this I should say is the case, unless there is some consideration in money given me; should that be the case, I should have to sue *in factum* or on a contract of letting and hiring. Of course if I give something by way of pledge on your behalf at your request, I shall have a right of action on *mandatum*. Labeo says further and very properly that if I am guilty of no negligence in the matter of redeeming the pledge, but the creditor declines to restore it, then you have a right of action on loan so far as this only, that you can call on me to assign to you my own rights of action against him. It will moreover be held that I am not guilty of negligence if either I have paid the money already or I am ready to pay it. No doubt the cost of the judicial proceedings and others connected with the case must in fairness be defrayed by the party who received the loan. 13. If you request me to lend you a slave with a dish, and the slave loses the dish, according to Cartilius, the risk is borne by you, as the dish itself is held to be lent, consequently you must answer for negligence in respect of it too. There is no doubt that, if the slave runs away and takes it with him, the party who received the loan is not liable, unless he was guilty of negligence in respect of the flight of the slave. 14. If you ask me to lay out a dining table for you and to furnish plate in discharge of that service, which I do, whereupon you request me to do the same thing on the day following, and, as I cannot conveniently take the plate back again home, I leave it where it is, and it is lost,—what is the proper action to bring and on whom will the loss fall? Labeo tells us that, as to the matter of risk, it makes a great deal of difference whether I set someone to watch or not; if I did, the risk is mine, but if not, it must be borne by the person in whose hands the plate was left. I should say myself that the proper action is one on loan, but that the person in whose hands the things were left must provide for their safe keeping, unless some other agreement was made expressly. 15. If a waggon is lent or let to two persons jointly, then, as we read in Celsus the son (*Digest* b. 6), the question may arise whether each of them is bound for the whole sum engaged for or only for a portion of it. What he says is that both of two people cannot have the ownership or possession of the whole of a thing, nor can anyone be the owner of a portion of an object, he can only have part ownership of the whole object for an undivided share. The use, no doubt, of a bath or a porch or a field may belong to each person as to the whole of it, as I do not have the use of a thing any the less for the fact that someone else has it too; but, in the case of a waggon which is lent or let, I do practically have the use of it in respect of a particular part, because I do not occupy the whole space of the waggon; still it is, he says, the better opinion that I must answer for *dolus* and negligence and diligence and provide for safe keeping in respect of the whole; and consequently the two persons will be treated very much as if they were correal debtors, and if one is sued and pays the damages this will be a discharge to the other, and they both have rights of action for theft:

6 POMPONIUS (*on Sabinus* 5) so that, if either of the two brings such an action, the other's right of action against the thief is taken away.

7 ULPIANUS (*on the Edict* 28) Hence the question arises whether, if one of the two brings the action for theft, it is he only who can be sued for the loan. What Celsus says is that if the other should be sued, the one, that is, who did not bring the action for theft, but he is willing that the first should be sued at his risk, namely the one who, in consequence of his bringing the action for theft, made gain out of the thing lent, he can claim to be heard, and the decision must be in his favour. 1. Should the lender have a right to sue the other of the co-debtors on the *Lex Aquilia*, we may consider whether he (the lender) will not have to assign his right of action [to the defendant in the action on the loan], assuming that the other did some damage which the one who is being sued on the loan will be compelled to make good; as, even if the lender had a right of action on the *Lex Aquilia* against the present defendant himself, the really just course is that when he sues on the loan he should release the other right of action: unless indeed it should be said that if he sues on the *Lex Aquilia* the damages he recovers will be the less by the amount which he recovered in pursuance of his claim on the loan; which, no doubt, is not an unreasonable view to take.

8 POMPONIUS (*on Sabinus* 5) People retain both the possession and the ownership of things which they lend;

9 ULPIANUS (*on the Edict* 2) as no one who lends anything thereby passes the property in it to the person to whom he lends it.

10 THE SAME (*on Sabinus* 29) When a man has received anything by way of loan, it is certain that, if he puts it only to the use

for which he borrowed it, he will have nothing to pay, if he has not made it in any respect the worse by his own negligence; no doubt, if he has made it the worse by negligence[1], he will be liable. 1. If I put a thing in the hands of a person, that he may look at it, the question arises whether he is in the same position with one to whom something is lent. As to this, if I put the thing in his hands on my own account, because I desired to find out what it was worth, he will be answerable to me for wilful mischief only, if it was on his own account, he must answer for the custody of it as well, and consequently he will have a right of action for theft. We may add that, if it should be lost on the way, when it is being brought back, then, if I had instructed him as to the person by whom he should send it, the risk will fall on me, but if he entrusted it to a person of his own choosing, he will have to answer to me for negligence as well [as wilful mischief], assuming that he received it on his own account,

11 PAULUS (*on Sabinus* 5) on the ground that he did not choose a sufficiently trustworthy person for it to be carried safely;

12 ULPIANUS (*on Sabinus* 29) but, if he received it on my account, he will answer for wilful mischief only. A slave who was sent to ask back a thing which had been lent, on receiving it ran off. If his owner had requested that it should be given to the slave, the owner bears the loss, but if he sent him in order to remind the other, so that the thing lent might be sent back, the loss falls on the person to whom it was lent[2].

13 POMPONIUS (*on Sabinus* 11) If a man who has received a loan should have judgment given against him in an action on loan on the ground that the thing is not to be found, an undertaking must be given him that if the owner finds it he will hand it over to him. 1. If a man takes a thing for the purpose of trying it, and makes some gain by it, suppose, for example, he takes horses, and they are hired out [by him], he will have to hand over the exact gain he makes to the person[3] who let him have them on trial; no one ought to be at liberty to make gain of anything until the thing is held at his risk. 2. If a free man has been serving me in good faith as a slave, and I lend him something, treating him as my slave,

[1] Omit *eius*. M.
[2] For *qui commodatus* read *cui commodatum*. Cf. M.
[3] After *præstabit* ins. *ei*. M.

let us consider whether I can sue him in an action on loan [on discovering him to be a free man]. Celsus the son used to say that, if I had ordered such a man to do anything, I could take proceedings against him either on *mandatum* or *præscriptis verbis* ; from which it would follow that there is a similar rule in a case of loan. It makes no difference that people who contract with a free man, who serves them in good faith as a slave, do not do so with the idea of putting him under a legal obligation, as, in fact, it very often happens that over and above the intention at the moment there arises a tacit obligation ; an example of this is a case in which money which is not owing is given by mistake with the intention of discharging a debt.

14 ULPIANUS (*on Sabinus* 48) If my slave lends you something belonging to me as to which you know that I object to its being lent you, this gives me a right of action on loan and of action for theft and also a right of *condictio* for the return of it on the ground of theft.

15 PAULUS (*on the Edict* 29) People can lend even the property of other persons which they have in their possession, and that although they possess it with the knowledge that it belongs to someone else,

16 MARCELLUS (*Digest* 5) so that even a thief or a plunderer who lends anything will have an action on loan.

17 PAULUS (*on the Edict* 29) In a case of loan an agreement that a person shall not be answerable for wilful wrong is not enforceable. 1. The counter action on *commodatum* can be brought even without the direct action, just as what are called counter actions can in general. 2. Where the action on loan is brought in consequence of something done by an heir of the borrower, judgment will be given against him for the whole damages, even though he is heir in respect of a share only. 3. Just as it is an act of free bounty and good feeling rather than compulsory to make a loan to anyone, so too it is for the person who confers the benefit to lay down terms and limits with reference to it. But when this has once been done, when, that is, the party has made the loan, then such an act as that of laying down limits and going back on the terms and depriving the other, at a wrong time, of the use of the thing lent, is forbidden not only by good feeling, but also by the obligation created by the handing over on one hand and the

receiving on the other. Each party does something for the other and consequently rights of action are allowed on both sides, so as to leave no doubt that what was at first a matter of favour and mere bounty takes the form of an interchange of performances and of civil rights of action on both sides. We see something of the same kind in the case of a man who has taken some steps in the way of looking after the affairs of an absent man; such a one cannot divest himself of all concern for things which are liable to be lost, without being obliged to answer for it, as, if he had left the business alone in the first instance, perhaps someone else would have taken it up; taking up a *mandatum* is a matter of free choice, but to carry it through is a necessity. It is on this principle that if you lend me tablets for my debtor to use to give me an undertaking, you have no right to ask for them back before the proper time, as, if you had refused to lend them, I should either have bought others or else procured witnesses. It is the same thing if you lend timber to shore up a set of flats, and then carry them away again, or perhaps even lend me some which you know to be rotten; when something is done as a favour, a man ought to be the better for it, not to be taken in. In such cases the rule is that the counter action is available as well [as the direct one]. 4. If two things have been lent, Vivianus sets down that the action for loan can properly be brought for one of them by itself; what Pomponius says is that this may be held to be true if they are quite distinct things, but that a man who has lent a chariot or a litter cannot properly bring an action about separate parts of it. 5. I lost a thing which you lent me and I gave you its value instead, after which the thing came into your hands; Labeo holds that, if I bring a counter action, you will have either to hand me over the thing or else give me back what you received from me.

18 GAIUS (*on the provincial Edict* 9) In a case of anything being lent, the sort of diligence to be exercised is such as any thoroughly diligent owner bestows on his own things, so that the only mishaps for which he is not responsible are those which cannot be resisted, for example, deaths of slaves which happen without any *dolus* or negligence on his own part, attacks by robbers or enemies, the machinations of pirates, shipwrecks, fires, the flight of slaves such as it is not the ordinary rule to keep watch over. With regard to what has just been said as to robbers, pirates and shipwrecks, we must always understand this to apply where something has been lent a man on terms which allow him to take it with him abroad;

of course if I lend a man silver because he told me he was going to ask some friends to dinner, and he takes it abroad with him, then, beyond all doubt, he must answer for anything that happens through pirates or robbers or shipwreck. All this is as I say if the property was lent for the sake of the recipient only; if it was for the sake of both parties, for instance, where you and I have invited a common friend to dinner, and you undertake to arrange the whole affair, but I lend you the plate, I know some writers hold that you need only answer for *dolus*; but it is worth considering whether it is not the fact that you are liable for negligence too, the decision as to what amounts to negligence being made on the same principles as in the case of things given in pledge or by way of *dos*. 1. Wherever a thing given in pledge, or property that is lent or deposited, has its value reduced by the act of the person who receives it, the other party has the right to bring not only the actions we have mentioned, but that on the *Lex Aquilia* too: but if any of those first mentioned is brought, the right to the others is taken away. 2. There may be sufficient grounds in the case to make it the proper course for an action to be brought against the lender, suppose, for example, the action is for expenses incurred in respect of the slave's health, or, in case he should take to flight, for the purpose of seeking him out and bringing him back; as for the expense of his keep, that, you may say, will on natural principles fall on the person who received him in order to make use of him. It may be remarked that what is above said as to expense incurred for the slave's health or in consequence of his flight must be taken to apply to outlay that is considerable in amount; as for the expenditure of small sums, the rule on the whole is that it falls on the person last mentioned, as does the cost of the slave's keep. 3. Again, where a man lends defective vessels, then if the wine or oil put into them should be spoilt or spilt, he must be ordered to pay for it. 4. Moreover, wherever a man could recover anything by means of a counter action, he can keep it in his hands even in the direct action which is brought against him, that is, by exercising the right of set off. It is however possible that what the borrower would have a right to recover on his side is more [than what the lender sues for], or the judge declines to take the set off into account, or no proceedings are taken against him for the restoration of the thing lent for the reason that the thing itself was accidentally destroyed, or it has been already restored without application being made to the judge: so we shall have to say that the counter action is necessary.

19 JULIANUS (*Digest* 1) The rule that people who engage to keep something or receive it to use are not answerable for wrongful damage done by another is beyond all doubt: how can people secure by any care or diligence that somebody shall not do them wrongful damage?

20 THE SAME (*on Urseius Ferox* 3) If I give silver lent by you to me to a slave of mine to bring to you, who is such a trustworthy man that no one need imagine that some set of rascals would get round him, then, if such persons get hold of it, the loss will be yours and not mine.

21 AFRICANUS (*Questions* 8) You lent me a thing, and then you carried it off: after this, you brought an action on loan and I was unaware that you had taken the thing, whereupon the judge ordered me to pay and I did so; but I subsequently found out that the thing had been carried off by you. The question was asked what sort of action I could bring against you. The answer given was that there could be no action for theft, but that I could have a counter *utilis actio* on the loan. 1. I, on a campaign, handed to my comrades some vessels to be used at our common risk, and my slave stole them and ran off with them to the enemy, but later on the slave was captured without the vessels. It is clear that I have a right of action against my comrades according to their respective shares; but they themselves can proceed against me for theft on account of the act of my slave, as the *noxa* follows the delinquent subject. And if I lend you a thing for you to use at your own risk, and it is carried off by my slave, you can bring an action for theft against me on account of the act of my slave.

22 PAULUS (*on the Edict* 22) If a slave whom I lent you commits a theft [against you], the question arises whether all you have a right to is the counter action on loan, just as that is the action which you could bring where you had laid out money in the way of medical expenses on the slave's behalf, or you can bring an action for theft. As to this, without any manner of doubt the party who asked for the loan has a right to a noxal action for theft, and the one who lent[1] is liable to a counter action on loan, if he lent the slave with knowledge that such was his character but the borrower was unaware of it.

1. After *teneri* ins. *qui commodavit.* M.

23 POMPONIUS (*on Quintus Mucius* 22) If I lend you a horse for you to use on the road to a particular spot, then, if the horse is reduced in value by means of the journey without there being any negligence of yours in the matter, you are not liable to an action on loan: the fact is the negligence is mine, because I lent, for such a long journey, a horse which was not able to stand the exertion.

VII.

ON THE ACTION ON PLEDGE OR THE COUNTER ACTION.

1 ULPIANUS (*on Sabinus* 40) A pledge can be contracted not by delivery only, but even by bare agreement, though nothing should be delivered. 1. We may consider then, in case a pledge has been contracted by bare agreement, whether it is not the fact that, supposing a man shows anyone some gold with the intimation that he will hand it over by way of pledge, but he thereupon hands over brass, he thereby makes a binding pledge of the gold, and it is in keeping with the above that it is a pledge of the gold and not of the brass, because to this last they did not agree. 2. Should a man, however, in making a pledge of brass declare that it is gold and hand it over by way of pledge accordingly, we may consider whether he does not thereby make a binding pledge of the brass, in short whether the true view is not that inasmuch as the parties are agreed as to the individual article to be given, it is pledged accordingly: and in fact this is the better opinion. At the same time the party who gave it is liable to a counter action on pledge, not to speak of the swindle (*stellionatus*) which he commits.

2 POMPONIUS (*on Sabinus* 6) If a debtor has sold and delivered an article which he pledged, and you have lent him money which he paid to the creditor to whom he gave the pledge, moreover you have made an agreement with him that the thing which he has already sold should be pledged with you, there is no doubt that your agreement is inoperative, as you have accepted for a pledge a thing which belonged to a third person; and in fact it follows from the above circumstances that the purchaser has come to have in his hands an article which is released from the pledge, and the fact that the article was released by means of money of yours is beside the question.

3 THE SAME (*on Sabinus* 18) If, in pursuance of an agreement with your debtor that he will pay the money owing at once you have given him back the article pledged, whereupon he has handed it through the window to a person whom he has specially placed there to receive it, then, according to Labeo, you can bring against your debtor an action for theft and also an action for production; should you moreover bring the counter action on pledge, and the debtor plead by way of *exceptio* that the thing pledged had been given back to him, you can by way of *replicatio* allege *dolus* and fraud, as in virtue of the fraud it will be held that the thing was not given back at all but abstracted by a dishonest manœuvre.

4 ULPIANUS (*on Sabinus* 41) If the parties have come to an agreement as to the sale of the thing pledged, either at the first or subsequently, then not only is a sale valid, but the purchaser at once becomes owner of the thing. However, even where there has been no agreement made about the sale of what is pledged, still the law in force is that a sale is allowable, provided there is no agreement that it should not be allowable; but, if it was agreed that there should be no sale, then, if the creditor sells, he is liable to an action for theft, unless the debtor was three times called upon to pay, and he did not do it.

5 POMPONIUS (*on Sabinus* 19) This is the rule, whether the agreement was that there should be no sale at all or something has been done in breach of the terms agreed to, either in reference to the amount or a condition or the place of sale.

6 THE SAME (*on Sabinus* 35) Should it be agreed that you are to be at liberty to sell the land which is pledged with you, still it does not at all follow that you can be compelled to sell, even though the person who gave you the pledge is insolvent, because the assurance in question was given you for your own sake. However, Atilicinus holds that on special cause shown the creditor can be compelled to sell; suppose, he says, the amount owed is much less than the value of the thing pledged, and the latter can be sold just now for more than it would fetch later on. Still, the better rule would be that the person who gave the pledge should be able to sell it, and pay the debt when he has received the purchase money, it being understood that the creditor is compellable to allow the property pledged to be inspected, if it is movable, provided the debtor gives him a sufficient undertaking to save him harmless;

the fact is that it would amount to cruelty that a creditor should be compelled to sell against his will. 1. If the creditor sells the land pledged with him for more than the amount of the debt, and he lends the surplus at interest, he must pay over the interest thereon to the person who gave him the pledge; moreover, if he uses the surplus himself, interest must equally be paid; but if he has been keeping it in his hands by way of deposit, he need not pay any interest.

7 PAULUS (*Sentences* 2) Should the creditor have allowed some time to elapse before handing over the surplus which he was allowed to keep on deposit, then, in consideration of his default, he must be compelled to give the debtor interest too, such as the case requires.

8 POMPONIUS (*on Sabinus* 35) If I incur some unavoidable expense in the matter of a slave or a piece of land which I took by way of security, I not only shall have a lien but even a right to the counter action on pledge: suppose, for instance, on some occasion the slave was ill, and I paid money to medical men, but he died, or, again, say that I shored up or repaired a set of chambers and after that it was burnt to the ground and I had nothing in my hands on which I could exercise a lien. 1. If several slaves are given in pledge, some of which the creditor sells for so much money, on the understanding that he assures the purchaser against their being recovered in virtue of superior title, and he thereupon pays himself his debt, he can keep the remaining slaves until an undertaking is given him that he shall be saved harmless in respect of whatever it was that he promised with reference to the event of the other slaves being recovered. 2. If one of the heirs of the debtor pays his share of the debt, still the whole thing given by way of pledge can lawfully be sold, just as it might be if the debtor himself had paid a portion of the debt. 3. If I stipulate for money to be paid me at the end of one, two and three years, and receive a pledge by way of security, and I agree that unless on each day assigned for payment the money is paid I shall be at liberty to sell the thing pledged[1], what is held is that I cannot sell the thing until all the sums have become payable, for the reason that by the above words all three payments are pointed out, and it is not a fact that on each day assigned for payment the money is not paid until all three days have arrived. But when all three times for payment have passed, then, if even one portion only should be unpaid, the pledge may be

[1] See D. 13. 7. 34, and Gradenwitz, *Interpolationen*, 37.

sold. Had the words been these:—"if any one payment should fail to be made on the day assigned for it" [etc.] then the promisee[1] would have a right to sue on the agreement at once[2]. 4. An agreement as to the right to sell a pledge should be framed generally so that everyone may be covered by it: but, even if it extends only to the creditor himself, his heir also may lawfully sell, if there has been no agreement contrary to this. 5. Where a pledge may be sold by virtue of an agreement, it may be sold on account not only of unpaid principal but also of other matters such as interest and expenses incurred in respect of the property.

9 ULPIANUS (*on the Edict* 28) If a debtor has given me by way of pledge the property of a third person, or has behaved in bad faith in relation to the pledge, the rule is that the counter action is available. 1. A pledge may be given not only for money but also on other accounts, for instance, where a man gives a pledge to someone in order that he may become surety for him. 2. Strictly speaking a thing is said to be pledged when it is handed over to the creditor: where even possession does not pass to the creditor we speak of hypothec. 3. For the action on pledge to be available all the money must have been paid, or satisfaction given in respect of it. By satisfaction given we mean satisfaction in such form as approved itself to the creditor, though there was no payment: whether he desired that security should be given to him by other pledges in order that he should renounce this one, or by sureties, or by the provision of another debtor, or by the payment of a money consideration or by mere agreement, the action on pledge is available. And the general rule may be laid down that in all cases in which the creditor has consented to release the pledge, satisfaction is held to have been given to him if he has received the form of security he desired, even though he committed an error of judgment in the matter. 4. One who has given a third person's property by way of pledge may bring the action on pledge if he has paid the debt. 5. Though one who has brought the action on pledge before payment has not brought it in the proper way, nevertheless, if he offers the money at the hearing, he is entitled to recover the pledged property and the amount of his interest.

[1] In text *ei*, not *mihi*.

[2] This section is somewhat puzzling. The writer seems to think that the sentences "on each day the money is paid" and "on each day the money is not paid" express an exhaustive alternative.

10 GAIUS (*on the provincial Edict* 9) But if he is prepared not to pay but to give satisfaction in some other way, say, for instance he is willing to give an *expromissor*, this is of no service to him.

11 ULPIANUS (*on the Edict* 28) If issue is joined with a debtor in respect of the debt, or a guarantor is sued, this is not regarded as amounting to payment. 1. If the obligation on which the debt rests is superseded (*novata*) this destroys the pledge, unless there has been an agreement that the pledge shall be renewed. 2. If I take a pledge from you on the understanding that I am going to hand over some money to you, and I do not hand it over, I shall be liable to the action on pledge though there has been no actual discharge by payment: the same rule applies if a formal receipt has been given for the money lent, or the condition on which the pledge was to depend has failed or a valid agreement has been come to that no claim for the money shall be made. 3. If the property was pledged in respect of the principal alone, or of the interest, the action on pledge is available when that money has been paid in respect of which the property was bound. But whether the interest was expressly contracted for or not, in any case if the property was pledged in respect of it also, the action on pledge will not be available so long as any of it is unpaid. The case is different with interest that a man has promised beyond the statutory limit, for this is entirely unlawful. 4. If there are several heirs to the creditor, and to one of these his share is paid, the other heirs of the creditor ought not to suffer any injury, [on account of this payment,] but having tendered to the debtor what he has paid to their co-heir they may sell the whole property. This opinion is not without foundation. 5. The money is regarded as having been paid not only if the payment was made to the man to whom the property was pledged, but also if it was made at his wish to a third person, or to one whose heir he is, or to his *procurator*, or to a slave appointed to collect debts. Accordingly if you rent a house and let part of it to me, and I pay the rent to your lessor, I can bring the action on pledge against you (for Julian lays it down that payment may be made to him). Of course the goods brought into the house by me will be liable only for the amount at which I hired my room, for it is incredible that the agreement can have been that my paltry things should be liable for the whole of the rent. There is considered to have been a tacit agreement with the owner of the house that he should have the benefit not of the agreement of the lodging-house keeper but

of his own. 6. We do not acquire an obligation by pledge by means of a free person: so fully is this the rule that in general we cannot acquire it through a *procurator* or a *tutor* and thus they themselves may be sued by the action on pledge. Nor is this affected by the rule, enacted by our Emperor, that possession can be acquired by means of a free person, for that rule operates to the effect that we can obtain, through a *procurator* or a *tutor*, the actual possession of a thing subjected to a pledge to us, but a free person will not always acquire the obligation itself for us. 7. But if my *procurator* or *tutor* gives a thing in pledge he himself can bring the action on pledge: this applies in the case of a *procurator* provided he had authority to give a pledge,

12 GAIUS (*on the provincial Edict* 9) or had been entrusted with the general administration of the property of one who was in the habit of borrowing money on the security of pledges.

13 ULPIANUS (*on the Edict* 28)[1] If, when the creditor is selling the pledge, an agreement is come to between him and the buyer that if the debtor pays the price to the buyer he shall be entitled to get his property back, Julianus holds, and there is a rescript to the same effect, that as a result of this agreement the creditor is compellable by the action on pledge to transfer to the debtor his action on sale against the buyer. Moreover the debtor himself can sue for recovery of the property, or bring an action *in factum* against the buyer. 1. In this action there is a liability both for wilful wrongdoing and for negligence, as in the case of loan for use; also, safe custody is required but there is no liability for *vis maior*.

14 PAULUS (*on the Edict* 29) Thus the same degree of care is required of the creditor as a diligent owner commonly bestows on his own affairs.

15 ULPIANUS (*on the Edict* 28) Upon returning the pledge the creditor should give the debtor security by way of personal undertaking against *dolus*, and if the property pledged was land, he must also give him an undertaking as to [the completeness of] his right, in case servitudes should have been lost, through failure of the creditor to exercise them.

[1] For *trigensimo* read *vicensimo*. Cf. M. and Lenel, Ed. Perp. (2) 246, n. 4.

16 PAULUS (*on the Edict* 29) If a tutor pledges the property of his ward in conditions which do not conflict with statutory rules, the pledge is valid, assuming that he receives the money for the purposes of the ward. The rule is the same in the case of the *curator* of a minor or lunatic. 1. It is clear that the creditor has a counter action on pledge. Accordingly if [the debtor] gives property which belongs to a third person, or is pledged to a third person or to the State, he is liable to this action though he is also liable to prosecution for swindling (*stellionatus*). But is this so only if he was aware of the facts or also if he acted in ignorance? So far as concerns the prosecution ignorance is a defence: in the case of the counter action, ignorance is, as Marcellus tells us (*Digest* b. 6), no excuse. But if the creditor takes the thing knowing that it is the property of a third person, or pledged, or unsound, the counter action is not available to him. 2. Even land held on perpetual lease (*vectigale prædium*) may be pledged, as may also a surface right (*superficiarium*), since nowadays *actiones utiles* are given to holders of these surface rights.

17 MARCIANUS (*on the hypothecary formula*) However, the Divine Severus and Antoninus have provided by rescript that the pledge will be without prejudice to the chief-rent.

18 PAULUS (*on the Edict* 29) If we have agreed that a claim against a debtor of mine shall be pledged to you, this agreement is to be maintained by the Prætor, so that he will protect both you in suing for the money and the debtor if I sue him. Accordingly if it was a money debt, you will set off against your claim the money you recover: if it was any specific thing, you will hold what you recover by way of pledge. 1. If the bare ownership is pledged a usufruct which afterwards falls in will be included in the pledge: the rule is the same in the case of alluvion. 2. If pledged land is sold the pledge still subsists, since the land passes subject to its incidents as in the case of a child born to a slave woman after sale. 3. If a person has made an agreement that a wood shall be pledged to him, Cassius holds that a ship built of this material is not subject to the pledge, for the material is one thing, the ship another, and therefore it is proper to add expressly in giving the pledge: "Whatever is made or grows out of this[1] wood." 4. If a slave pledges a thing belonging to the *peculium*, this is to be upheld if he had the right of free administration of the *peculium*. For he can also alienate these things.

[1] After *ex* insert *ea*. M.

19 MARCIANUS (*on the hypothecary formula*) We must understand the same rules to be laid down in the case also of a *filiusfamilias*.

20 PAULUS (*on the Edict* 29) A third person's property may be given in pledge with the consent of the owner: and, further, if it is given without his knowledge, and he ratifies the transaction, the pledge will be valid. 1. If a thing is pledged to several persons at the same time, the legal position of them all is the same. 2. If it is the creditor's fault that the money is not paid to him, the action on pledge may rightly be brought. 3. In some cases, even though the money has been paid, the action on pledge should be refused: for instance, if the creditor has bought his pledge from the debtor.

21 THE SAME (*Short notes* 6) Where a house is given in pledge the site also is subject to the pledge, for it is a part of the house. And, conversely, a building erected is subject to the rights over the soil.

22 ULPIANUS (*on the Edict* 30) If a pledge has been stolen and the creditor brings the action for *furtum*, Papinianus holds that he must set off against the debt whatever he recovers, and this is true even though the *furtum* was committed as a consequence of negligence on the part of the creditor. This is to be laid down still more strongly in relation to what he has recovered by the *condictio*. We must however consider whether what the debtor himself has paid under an action for *furtum* or the *condictio* is to be set off against the debt: and it is uniformly laid down, both by textbooks and in practice, that there is no obligation to restore to him what he himself has paid under an action for *furtum*. So says Papinianus (*Questions* b. 9). 1. Papinianus lays down the same rule for the case in which the creditor, under the influence of fear, has handed back to the debtor a pledged slave whom he had received in good faith as security, for if he brings the action founded on putting in fear and recovers fourfold, he will neither give back anything out of what he has received nor set it off against the debt. 2. If a thief gives property in pledge, the action on pledge is open to him in respect of produce also, although he himself will not acquire produce (for there is a right to bring against a thief both a vindication for existing produce and a *condictio* for that which has been consumed): he will therefore derive advantage from the fact that the creditor was a *bona fide*

possessor. 3. If, when the pledged property has been sold, the debtor, who has obtained permissive occupancy of the property, or has hired it, fails to give it up, he is liable under the counter action. 4. Where the creditor on the sale of the pledge gave a promise of double damages (this having been the ordinary practice and he having been sued on account of a claim of superior title (*evictio*) and condemned), can he avail himself of the counter action on pledge? It may be said that he has this resource provided that he sold in this way without *dolus* or carelessness, and conducted the affair like a careful owner. But if such a sale brought no advantage with it, but he was selling for what he could have got for the property even if he had not made this promise, then he cannot fall back [on this action],

23 TRYPHONINUS (*Disputations* 8) and thus he will not be able to recover from the debtor more than the amount[1] of the debt. But if there had been a stipulation for interest, and, five years, let us say, after having received[2] the price of the pledged property, being defeated [in an action for the double damages], he pays them to the buyer, he can recover from the debtor the interest for the intervening time, since it has become clear that nothing has been paid him in such a manner that it cannot be taken away. But if he has paid merely the single price he will be barred by an *exceptio*, on the ground of *dolus*, from a claim of interest, since he has had the use of the price which he had received from the buyer.

24 ULPIANUS (*on the Edict* 30) The point has been acutely put to me: if the creditor has obtained from Cæsar a decree that he shall possess the pledge [as his own] and it has been recovered from him by superior title, has he the counter action on pledge? As to this it seems to me that the obligation of pledge is at an end and that there has been an abandonment of the contract. On the other hand, the *utilis actio* on purchase is at his disposal, as if the property had been given to him by way of payment, so as to give him satisfaction up to the amount of the debt, or of his interest, and the creditor may have a right of set off, if, as it happens, an action is brought against him on pledge or on any other ground. 1. The question is asked, whether one who has paid the creditor with bad money has the action on pledge, as having paid the money

[1] For *summa* read *summam*. Cf. M.

[2] After *obligata* read *consecutus est*. Cf. M.

due. And it is settled law that he is neither entitled to bring the action on pledge nor released from the debt, for bad money does not release one who pays it: the coins ought in fact to be returned to him. 2. If the creditor has actually sold the pledge for more than was due, but has not yet recovered the price from the buyer, can he be sued by the action on pledge for payment of the excess, or, rather, ought the debtor[1] either to wait till the buyer pays, or to take transfer of actions against him? I hold that the creditor is not to be forced to make payment, but that either the debtor should wait, or, if he does not wait, the actions against the buyer should be assigned to him, at the risk, nevertheless, of the vendor. If however he has already received the money, he must hand over the excess. 3. If the creditor has misused pledged property, or has injured the health of slaves, account is taken of this in the action on pledge. Of course if, on account of their misconduct, the creditor has punished them, or put them in irons, or sent them before the *præfectus* or *præses* it must be said that he is not liable to the action on pledge. Consequently if he has prostituted a female slave, or compelled her to do any other discreditable act, the pledge of the woman is at once discharged.

25 THE SAME (*on the Edict* 31) If the creditor has given the pledged slaves instruction in handicrafts, there will be the counter action if they had already learnt something of them, or it was with the debtor's consent. If indeed neither of these was the case, but it was in necessary handicrafts, there will be the counter action, but not so that the debtor will be compelled to go without the slaves by reason of the magnitude of the charges. For just as his liability for *dolus* and carelessness does not permit him to neglect the thing[2], so also he must not put the pledged property into such a condition that the recovery of it is burdensome to the debtor: suppose for instance a large tract of land is pledged by a man who is hardly able to redeem it, much less to cultivate it, and you, having taken it as a pledge, put it into such a state of cultivation as to make it of great value: indeed, the truth is that it is not fair that I should be forced to seek other creditors, or to sell what I wished to get back, or to abandon it to you under pressure of poverty. These points should therefore be considered by the judge, taking a middle line, so that he should pay attention neither to a debtor making much of trifles, nor to a creditor inclined to overburden the debtor.

[1] After *debeat* ins. *debitor*. M. [2] After *creditorem* ins. *rem*. M.

26 THE SAME (*Disputations* 3) There is nothing surprising in the fact that a pledge is created where a magistrate for any reason puts a person into possession of property, since our Emperor, with his father, has frequently laid it down by rescript that a pledge can be created also by will. 1. It should be noted that where a pledge is created by a magistrate's order, it is not established until actual possession is taken.

27 THE SAME (*Opinions* 6) A debtor who had not the money at hand gave his creditor, who was asking for the return of a loan, certain articles in gold, that he might give them in pledge to another creditor. If the person who received them from the debtor holds them freed by payment and recovered [from the man to whom he pledged them] he is compellable to produce them. But if they are still in the hands of the creditor's creditor, they are considered as bound with the consent of the owner. But the appropriate action is available to the owner of them against his creditor to compel delivery of them when they are released.

28 JULIANUS (*Digest* 11) If a creditor who has taken a thing in pledge, having lost possession of it, brings the Servian action and recovers damages, the debtor afterwards suing for the same thing will be repelled by an *exceptio*, unless he offers to him [who holds it] what was paid for it. 1. If a slave takes a pledge on account of the *peculium*, the action on pledge is available to the debtor against the master.

29 THE SAME (*Digest* 44) If you buy a third person's property in good faith, and pledge it to me, and take it back in permissive occupancy (*precario*), and thereafter the owner makes me his heir, the pledge ceases and only the permissive occupancy will survive: for this reason your *usucapio* will be interrupted.

30 PAULUS (*Epitomes of the Digest of Alfenus Varus* 5) One who had lent money, to a man who traded with a lighter, detained the lighter in the river on his own authority, as the money was not paid on the agreed day. Then the river rose and carried away the lighter. The answer was that if he had detained it without the consent of the lighterman, the lighter was at his risk, but that if the debtor had allowed it to be detained, by his consent, negligence alone must be made good to him, not *vis maior*.

31 AFRICANUS (*Questions* 8) If a slave given in pledge commits *furtum* against the creditor, it is open to the debtor to abandon the slave by way of surrender for *noxa*. But if he gave him to me in pledge knowing that he was a thief, though he is ready to leave him with me, as surrendered for *noxa*, nevertheless I shall have the action on pledge, for an indemnity. Julianus says that the same rules are to be observed also if a slave deposited or lent commits *furtum*.

32 MARCIANUS (*Rules* 4) A creditor can bring the counter action on pledge against a debtor who has given a third person's property as a pledge, even though the debtor is solvent.

33 THE SAME (*on the hypothecary formula*) If the debtor has paid the money he can bring the action on pledge to recover property given in *antichresis*, for since there is a pledge he can use this word [in his claim].

34 MARCELLUS (*Responsa*) Where Titius had lent money to Sempronius, and taken a pledge for it, and because the money was not paid the creditor was about to sell the pledge[1], [the debtor] asked the creditor to buy the land at a certain price, and at the time of his request wrote a letter by which he declared that he had sold the land to the creditor. I ask whether the debtor can revoke this sale on offering the principal and interest which are due. Marcellus answered that on the facts stated he cannot revoke it.

35 FLORENTINUS (*Institutes* 8) When something is due on account of both principal and interest from one who owes money secured by pledges, whatever is received from the sale of pledges is to be credited in the first instance to interest which is admittedly due at that time, and then, if there is anything over, to the principal. In fact a debtor is not to be listened to, who when he knows that he is not solvent expresses a choice as to the obligation from which he prefers his pledge to be freed. 1. Pledge transfers only possession to the creditor, the ownership of the debtor being unaffected : he may however enjoy his property both by permissive occupancy and by hiring.

36 ULPIANUS (*on the Edict* 11) The question has been raised in what way a person is liable who in a case of pledge gives the creditor brass in substitution for gold. Sabinus observes most

[1] M. would insert *rem* after *eam*. See *h. t.* 8. 3 and Gradenwitz, *Interpolationen*, 37.

correctly on this case, that if, when gold has in fact been given, he substitutes brass, he is liable for theft, but that if he substitutes brass at the time of delivery he has behaved in a rascally way, but is not a thief. However, in this case also I think the action on pledge will apply, and so Pomponius holds. Moreover, as has been repeatedly laid down by rescript, he will be punished under the extraordinary procedure (*extra ordinem*) on the ground of swindling (*stellionatus*). 1. Add that if anyone knowingly and deliberately gives me the property of a third person in pledge, or pledges to me what is already charged to someone else, and does not tell me of this, he will be punished under the same charge. Of course if the thing is of great value and is pledged for a small amount of money, it should be said that not only is the accusation of swindling inapplicable, but so also are the actions on pledge and on *dolus*, the fact being that the person who took the second pledge was in no way defrauded.

37 PAULUS (*on Plautius* 5) If I let on hire to the owner a pledge which has been delivered to me I retain possession by the letting, for before the debtor hired the thing he had not the possession of it, while I have the intention of retaining possession, and, again, the hirer has no intention of acquiring it.

38 MODESTINUS (*Differences* 1) On account of the risk of the action on pledge, the sanction of a *tutor* is necessary to a *pupillus* who takes a pledge.

39 THE SAME (*Responsa* 4) Gaius Seius gave his land to Lucius Titius in pledge, on account of money lent. Later, an agreement was made between them that the creditor should possess the pledge for a certain time, as a set off against his money. However, before this time had expired, the creditor, in declaring his last wishes, provided by his will that one of his sons should have this land, and added "which I bought from Lucius Titius[1]," whereas he had not bought it. Gaius Seius, who was the debtor, also amongst others signed this will. I ask whether by the fact that he signed it he prejudiced himself in any way, since no instrument of sale is produced, but only the agreement that the creditor should take the produce for a certain time. Herennius Modestinus answered that the contract of pledge was not affected by the fact that the debtor had signed the will of the creditor in which he declared that he had bought the pledge.

[1] Probably this should be Gaius Seius.

40 PAPINIANUS (*Responsa* 3) A debtor cannot validly buy from the creditor a pledge he has given, since a purchase of one's own property is void, nor, if he buys it for less than the debt, and claims the pledge, or vindicates the ownership, is the creditor bound to restore possession to him, unless he offers the whole of the debt. 1. The debtor's son who is still in the *potestas* of his father cannot effectively acquire the pledge from his father's creditor with money of his *peculium*, and thus, if the patron of the debtor has obtained *bonorum possessio* in opposition to the provisions of the will he will acquire the ownership of a half[1]. For the pledge is released by the money which the son paid by way of price out of what belonged to his father. 2. When the money is paid the creditor ought to restore the possession of the pledge which was actually with him, and the debtor[2] is not required to pay any more. Accordingly if the creditor has meanwhile himself given the pledge as security, when the debtor has paid the money which he owed, no action will be given in respect of the second pledge, nor will any right of retention remain.

41 PAULUS (*Questions* 3) You gave a third person's property in pledge and thereafter you became owner of the property: an *actio utilis* on the pledge is given to the creditor. The same rule is not to be laid down if I become heir to Titius who has given my property as security without my consent, for in a case of this kind the right to recover the pledge is not to be granted to the creditor: it does not necessarily suffice in order to make the *actio utilis* on pledge available that the owner is the same person as he who owes the money. But if he had agreed to the pledge, so that a point can be made of his trickery, he cannot fairly oppose the bringing of the *actio utilis* against him.

42 PAPINIANUS (*Responsa* 3) In the action which lies on account of the giving of a pledge, the creditor is compelled by law to give back with interest the excess of the price [over the debt] and he is not to be heard if he seeks to substitute the buyer as defendant (*delegare*), since in the sale, which takes place under a pact[3], the creditor is carrying out a transaction of his own.

43 SCÆVOLA (*Digest* 5) A man gave a vacant plot of land as security to a creditor, and handed over the instrument of purchase. When he wanted to build on the land, a dispute having been raised

[1] See Inst. III. vii. 2. [2] After *cogitur* add *debitor*. M.
[3] For *facto* read *pacto*. Cf. M.

with him by the adjoining owner as to the width of the land, which he could not otherwise prove, he asked the creditor to produce the document of title handed over by him. As the creditor did not produce it he erected a smaller building and thus suffered damage. It was asked whether if the creditor claims the money or vindicates the pledge, supposing an *exceptio doli* is set up, the judge ought to take account of this damage. The answer was that if there was no intent that the debtor should be wronged by being deprived of the use of the instrument, he can bring the action on pledge when he has paid the money, but if the refusal was with that intent then there will also be an action for the amount of his interest against the creditor even before the money is paid. 1. Titius[1] borrowed money from Gaius Seius under a pledge of leather sacks. At a time when Seius had these sacks in his granary, a centurion sent from the office of food supply carried them off for commissariat purposes. They were afterwards recovered on the application of Gaius Seius the creditor. I ask whether Titius the debtor, or Seius the creditor, ought to bear the damage caused by this use of them. The answer was that on the facts stated [Seius][2] was not liable for the damage due to this cause.

[1] Omit *cum*. M. [2] M.

FOURTEENTH BOOK.

I.

On the Exercitorian Action.

1 Ulpianus (*on the Edict* 28) The usefulness of this Edict is known by all to be indisputable. People every now and then enter into contractual relations with masters of vessels, to meet the necessities incurred on a voyage, without knowing what is their class or character, and it was therefore right that the person who appointed the master for the ship should be bound by the contract just as is a person who has placed an *institor* (commercial agent) at the head of a shop or a business, it being in fact more necessary to make an agreement with the master of a ship than with a commercial agent; as the circumstances of the case make it easy for the party to form an opinion as to what the class of persons is to which the *institor* belongs and make a contract accordingly, but with the master of a ship the case is different, since, not uncommonly, place and time do not admit of a fuller judgment being arrived at. 1. By "master of a ship" we must understand the person who is entrusted with the care of the whole ship: 2. but should the agreement be made with one of the seamen, no action is allowed to be brought against the *exercitor*, although an action is allowed against him founded on a delict on the part of any one of those who are on board the vessel to aid in the navigation. The reason for this is that the ground of action in the case of the contract is a very different thing from the ground in the case of the delict, seeing that a man who appoints a master to a ship allows contracts to be made with him, but a man who engages seamen does not authorize contracts being made with them, though he is bound to see that they behave with no negligence or *dolus*. 3. Masters are appointed for the business of letting vessels for the purpose of cargo or for passengers[1] or to buy gear, but if a master

[1] Omit *conducendis*. Cf. M.

is appointed for the purchase or sale of wares, his act will bind the *exercitor* in these cases too. 4. It is of no consequence what is the rank of such a master, whether, for example, he is free or a slave, and, [if a slave,] whether he belongs to the *exercitor* or to someone else, nor will it matter what his age is; as the party appointing has only himself to blame [if he made a bad appointment]. 5. The law recognizes as master not only one who was appointed as such by the *exercitor*, but one who was appointed by a master; this is in fact an opinion given by Julianus as to a case on which he was consulted where the *exercitor* was not aware [of the appointment]; where, however, he is aware and he has allowed the person so appointed to discharge the office in question on the vessel, he is regarded as having put the person there himself. This appears to me to be a reasonable view; if I appointed a master, I am bound to make good whatever he does, otherwise those who contract with him will be disappointed, and the rule ought to be applied in the case of a master still more readily than in that of an *institor*, on grounds of public utility. What are we to say then if the *exercitor*, in appointing a master, laid down that the man appointed was not to be at liberty to appoint someone else? It is a point to be considered whether the opinion of Julianus is still to be followed. Suppose, indeed, he forbad the appointee in express terms such as these, "You are not to employ Titius as master." However, we shall have to say that the principle of consulting the interest of marine commerce requires us to go even to this length. 6. The word ship (*navis*) must be applied to seafaring vessels or to those used in rivers or in the course of navigating in lakes, or to rafts. 7. The Prætor does not allow a right of action against an *exercitor* on every kind of ground, but only in connexion with the particular kind of case for which [the master] was appointed, I mean where he was appointed to deal with cases of that kind; the ship may, for example, have been let out for the carriage of goods, or [the master] may have bought things which are useful to one who is navigating a ship or he may have engaged to pay or may have paid money with a view to repairs of the ship, or the crew may sue for their wages. 8. Suppose the master borrowed a sum of money, will this be held to be done on account of the matter in hand? As to this, Pegasus is of opinion that if he borrowed money in furtherance of the business for which he was appointed, an action ought to be allowed, and with this opinion I agree; how if he borrowed it in order to fit out or equip the ship or to provide sailors? 9. Here Ofilius raises the question,—supposing the master borrows money for the purpose of repairs to the ship and converts them to his own use, will an action be allowed against the *exercitor*? To which his own answer is that if the master received the money with the express agreement that he would spend it on the ship, but after that he changed his mind, the *exercitor* was bound and had himself to blame for appointing such a man master; but if from the very first he entertained the idea of defrauding the person who lent the money, and particularly avoided saying that he took the money for purposes connected with the ship, the conclusion must be different, and this distinction is approved by Pedius. 10. On the other hand, if the master practises deceit as to the prices of things which are sold to him, the loss must fall on the *exercitor* and not on the person to whom money is owing. 11. Again, if the master borrows money from a third person and pays off the one who lent money for repairs of the ship, I should say that such a lender must be allowed to bring an action, just as if he had lent for the purposes of the ship. 12. The fact is, it is the appointment which lays down the terms binding on the contracting parties; so that, if the master was appointed for the ship on the understanding only that he was to collect freight, but not that he was to let out [spaces on the vessel], the *exercitor* having, it may be, let out [such spaces] himself, the *exercitor* will not be liable, if the master lets; or, if the understanding was that he might let but not that he might demand freight, a similar rule will apply; or if it was that he should contract with passengers but not offer the use of the ship for carrying cargo, or the converse, then, if he transgress the restrictions laid down for him, he will not thereby put the *exercitor* under any liability. We may add that if the master was appointed in order that he should hire out the ship for the carriage of goods of a specified kind, say vegetables or hemp, and he should agree to carry marble or other materials[1] of any kind, the rule is that the *exercitor* is not bound. The truth is that some ships are transport vessels and some, to use the common word (*ut ipsi dicunt*), are passenger vessels (ἐπιβατηγοὶ), and there are, to my knowledge, a great many shipowners who tell the masters that they must not carry passengers, moreover, that business is to be done only in some particular parts and particular seas, for instance, there are ships which carry passengers to Brundisium from Cassiopa or Dyrrhachium but are not fit to take cargo, again, some are suitable for river navigation but are not fitted for sea voyages. 13. Should there be several masters

[1] For *alia materia* read *aliæ materiæ*. Cf. M.

appointed without the duties being distributed amongst them, a contract made with any one of them will be binding on the *exercitor*, but if their respective duties are assigned, so that one may let out [space in the vessel] and another take freight, then the *exercitor* will be bound by any one who acts within his duty. 14. Should however the terms of the appointment be, as they often are, that no person appointed is to make any contract apart from the others or other, anybody who contracts with one only will have himself to blame for it. 15. The term *exercitor* is understood to mean the person by whom all proceeds and payments are received, whether he is the owner of the vessel or he hired the vessel at a lump sum either for temporary use or altogether. 16. Whether the person who acts as *exercitor* is a man or a woman, *sui iuris* or under *potestas* or is a slave, is a matter of small account; but for a person *sui iuris* under age to be *exercitor*, the law requires the concurrence of his guardian. 17. People are allowed to choose whether they would like to sue the *exercitor* or the master. 18. On the other hand, [the Prætor] does not hold out a right of action[1] to the *exercitor* against persons who contracted with the master, because he did not require to be aided in the same way; but he can sue the master *ex locato*, if he is furnishing his services for a pecuniary payment, or, if he serves gratuitously, he can sue him *ex mandato*. Of course the *præfecti*, on account of the service of the food supply, and, in the provinces, the *præsides* of the provinces are in the habit of coming to their assistance by the extraordinary procedure (*extra ordinem*) in the matter of contract by masters of vessels. 19. If the *exercitor* of a ship is in the *potestas* of another person, and carries on the business with his approval, an action lies, on account of transactions with the shipmaster, against the person in whose *potestas* the *exercitor* is. 20. But though an action lies against him in whose *potestas* the *exercitor* is, still, it is available only if he carries on the business with his consent. The reason why the person who has the *exercitor* in his *potestas* is liable in full by reason of consent is that shipowning is of the highest public importance. But the employment of *institores* is not equally beneficial: for that reason those who have contracted with one who is, to the knowledge of his master, carrying on a business with property of the *peculium* are entitled only to take their share in the distribution [of the *peculium*]. But if the transaction with the shipmaster was merely with the master's knowledge and not also with his assent, are we to allow a claim

[1] For *actio non* read *actionem non*. Cf. M.

in full as in the case of an assenting master, or shall we give an action on the lines of the *actio tributoria*? In these doubtful conditions it is better to follow strictly the words of the edict and not to penalise the mere bare knowledge of the father or master in the case of ships, or, in the case of trading with property of the *peculium*, to give such an extended meaning to consent as to create an obligation for the full amount of the claim. In accordance with this Pomponius also seems so to lay it down for the case of one who is in the *potestas* of another: if he conducts the business with assent the master is liable in full, in cases short of this only to the extent of the *peculium*. 21. We must understand the expression "in *potestas*" to cover those of both sexes, sons and daughters, male and female slaves. 22. If a slave forming part of a *peculium* acts as *exercitor* with consent of the son in whose *peculium* he is, or an underslave does so with that of the slave, the father or master who has not lent his approval will be liable only to the extent of the *peculium*, but the son himself will be liable in full. Of course if they carry on the business with the consent of the father or master these will be liable for the whole claim, and, in addition, the son if he himself also assented, will be liable in full. 23. However, although the Prætor promises the action only if the transaction is with his shipmaster, yet, as Julian has also observed, the father or master will be liable in full even though the contract is with the *exercitor* himself. 24. This action against the *exercitor* lies in respect of the shipmaster, and thus if either of them has been sued, there can be no action against the other. Supposing some part of the money is paid, if this is by the shipmaster the obligation is reduced by direct operation of law (*ipso iure*); if it is by the *exercitor*, then, whether he pays on his own account, that is in view of the "honorary" obligation, or on behalf of the shipmaster, the obligation is reduced, since a third person also, who pays for me, frees me from the debt. 25. If several persons are jointly *exercitores* in respect of a ship, the claim for the full amount can be brought against any one of them,

2 GAIUS (*on the provincial Edict* 9) in order that a person who contracted with one may not be compelled to split up his claim amongst several opponents,

3 PAULUS (*on the Edict* 9) and it does not matter in the least what share each of them has in the ship: the one who has paid will recover from the others in the action on partnership.

4 ULPIANUS (*on the Edict* 29[1]) If, however, several *exercitores* manage the ship themselves, they are to be sued each to the extent of his share in the business; for they are not to be considered as acting as shipmasters for each other. 1. But where several *exercitores* have appointed one of their number to be shipmaster any of them will be liable to be sued on his account for the whole claim. 2. If a slave belonging to more than one person acts as *exercitor* with their assent, the law is the same as in the case of a plurality of *exercitores*. Evidently if he did it with the assent of one of them that one will be liable for the whole claim, and, accordingly, I consider that, in the case before mentioned, each of them is liable in full. 3. If it is a slave who was *exercitor* of a ship with the assent of his owner and he is alienated, the man who has alienated him is, none the less, liable in full. In the same way he will be liable though the slave dies, for the principal is also liable after the death of the shipmaster. 4. These actions will be available without limitation of time and both to and against heirs; accordingly if a slave dies, who was *exercitor* with his master's consent, the action will be available after a year has expired, though the action on *peculium* is not available after the year.

5 PAULUS (*on the Edict* 29) If you employ as shipmaster one who is in my *potestas* I also shall have an action against you if I make any contract with him: the same rule applies if he is owned in common by us. You will however have an action against me on the contract of letting, because you hired the services of my slave, since even if he had contracted with a third person you could sue me for a transfer of the rights of action which I held on account of him, just as you could have proceeded against a freeman if you had in fact hired one: if however the services were gratuitous you can bring an action on *mandatum*. 1. In the same way if my slave is *exercitor* of a ship and I contract with his shipmaster, there will be nothing to bar me from bringing against the shipmaster any action to which I am entitled by either civil or "honorary" law: this edict does not in fact bar any other person at all from proceeding against the shipmaster, for no transfer of any action is effected by this edict, but one is added. 2. If one of these *exercitores* contracts with the shipmaster, he will be able to sue the others.

6 PAULUS (*Short notes* 6) Where a slave is *exercitor* of a ship without his master's assent, if it is with his knowledge there

[1] The reference should be to b. 28. Cf. M. and Lenel, Ed. Perp. (2) 248.

is an action on the lines of the *actio tributoria*; if he does not know of it there will be an action on the *peculium*. 1. If a common slave is *exercitor* of a ship, with the consent of his masters, an action for the full amount due should be given against any of them singly.

7 AFRICANUS (*Questions* 8) Lucius Titius appointed Stichus as master of a ship[1]: he, having borrowed money, gave an acknowledgment that he had received it for the purpose of repair of the ship. The question was raised whether Titius was liable to the exercitorian action only if the creditor proved that the money had been spent in repairs to the vessel. The answer was that the creditor could effectively sue if at the time when the money was lent, the ship was in such a condition that it needed to be repaired: for while it is not reasonable that the creditor should be driven to this, that he should himself undertake the repair of the ship, and attend to the owner's business (which would certainly be the result if he had to show that the money had been spent in repairs), yet this may be required, that he shall know that he is lending for the purpose for which the appointment as shipmaster was made. And this certainly cannot be the case unless he knows this also, that the money is needed for repairs. From this it follows that even if the ship was in need of repair, yet, if much more money was lent than was wanted for the purpose, an action for the full amount ought not to be allowed against the owner of the ship. 1. Sometimes the question must also be taken into account whether the money was lent at a place in which the things on account of which it was lent could be acquired: what, in fact, are we to say, our authority asks, in a case in which money is lent for the purchase of a sail at an island such that a sail is absolutely not to be had there? To put it shortly, the creditor is bound to show some care in the matter[2]. 2. Our authority remarks that practically the same rules are to be laid down also if the institorian action is under discussion, for in that case also the creditor is required to know that this was a necessary acquisition of the goods for the purchase of which the slave was appointed, and that the fact that he lent it for this purpose suffices: it is not also to be required that he should himself undertake the burden of seeing to the application of the money to that purpose[3].

[1] For *navis* read *navi*. Cf. M.
[2] After *ea* ins. *re*. M.
[3] Text corrupt, but this seems to be the meaning. Cf. M.

II.

ON THE RHODIAN LAW OF JETTISON.

1 PAULUS (*Sentences* 2) It is provided by the Rhodian Law that if merchandise is thrown overboard to lighten the ship, the loss occasioned for the benefit of all must be made good by the contribution of all.

2 THE SAME (*on the Edict* 34) When jettison has been made on account of the labouring of the ship, the owners of the lost goods ought to sue the master of the ship *ex locato*, that is, if they had handed over their goods for carriage under a contract of *locatio*: he can then proceed *ex conducto* against the others, whose goods have been preserved, so that the loss may be distributed, in proportion. Servius, in fact, gave a *responsum* to the effect that they ought to sue the shipmaster *ex locato* requiring him to hold the goods of the other passengers till they make good their share of the loss. In any case, even though he does not[1] retain possession of the goods he will have independently an action *ex locato* against the passengers. For what are we to say if there are passengers who have no packages[2]? Clearly the more convenient plan is to hold the merchandise if there is any. But if one has not hired the whole of the ship he can proceed *ex conducto* like passengers who have hired accommodation on her, for it is eminently just that the burden should be shared by those who have secured, by the loss of others' goods, the advantage that their own goods are preserved. 1. If there is no loss of merchandise, but the ship is damaged or loses some of her rigging, there will be no general contribution, for those things which are provided for the purposes of the ship are in a different position from those on account of which one has received freight money: to take a similar case, if a smith breaks an anvil or a hammer this will not be charged against the person who employed him to do the work. But if this damage was done at the wish of the passengers[3], under the influence of fear, it must be made good. 2. In a case in which a number of traders had brought together on the ship various kinds

[1] After *etsi* ins. *non*. M.

[2] *i.e.* have only valuables about their persons. Pothier.

[3] After *vectorum*, omit *vel*. M.

of merchandise, and, in addition, many passengers, free and slave, had taken passage in her, upon the arising of a great storm, goods had been of necessity thrown overboard. Thereupon these points arose for discussion: whether all must contribute for the jettison, even those, if any, who had brought on board only goods which did not burden the ship, such as precious stones and pearls, and what proportion was to be paid, and whether anything was to be paid in respect of freemen, and by what action the matter could be adjusted. The rule laid down was that all to whom it was advantageous that the jettison should be made must share the loss, for they owed the tribute on account of the preservation of their goods[1], and, as a consequence, even the owner of the ship was liable in proportion. The amount of the loss must be divided in proportion to the value of the goods. No valuation can be made of free persons. The owners of the lost goods will sue the sailor, that is the shipmaster, *ex conducto*. In the same way it was discussed whether a valuation was to be made of each man's clothing and of rings, and the view held was that everything must be taken into account except what might have been brought on board for consumption, which would include food-stuffs, there being the stronger reason in this case that, if at any time there was a shortage of these on the voyage[2], each one would bring what he had into the common stock. 3. If the ship has been ransomed from pirates, Servius, Ofilius and Labeo hold that all must contribute, but as for what is taken away by the plunderers, the loss must fall on him to whom it belonged[3], and no contribution is to be made to one who has ransomed his goods. 4. The share [of the loss] is ordinarily contributed according to the value of the goods which are preserved, and of those which are lost, and it is in no way material that those which are lost might have been sold at a higher price[4], for what is made good is loss not profit. But with regard to those things in respect of which contribution has to be made, the valuation should be not according to the price at which they were bought, but to that for which they will sell. 5. Of slaves who are lost at sea no valuation is to be made, any more than if any sick slaves have died on the ship, or any have thrown themselves overboard. 6. If any of the passengers is insolvent the loss will not fall on the shipmaster, for the seaman is not required to investigate everyone's financial position. 7. If goods which have been thrown overboard are recovered, the

[1] Read *quia tributum ob id servatæ res deberent.* Cf. M.
[2] *navigatione.* Cf. M. [3] *fuerit.* Cf. M. [4] *potuerunt.* Cf. M.

obligation to contribute is discharged: in the event of the contribution having already been made, those who have paid can sue the shipmaster *ex locato*, so that he may proceed *ex conducto* and pay back what he recovers. 8. What is thrown overboard [to save the ship] remains however the property of the owner, and does not vest in anyone who gets possession of it, for it is not considered to have been abandoned.

3 PAPINIANUS (*Responsa* 19) If a mast or other gear of the ship is cast overboard in order to avoid a peril to all, contribution is due.

4 CALLISTRATUS (*Questions* 2) If in order to lighten the burdened ship because, with her cargo, she could not enter a river or harbour, certain goods are put over the side into a boat, lest the ship should be endangered outside the river or in the entrance itself or in the harbour, and the boat is sunk, an account must be taken between those who have their goods saved on the ship and those who lost theirs in the boat, exactly as if these goods had been thrown overboard. It may be added that Sabinus also approves this opinion (*Responsa* b. 2). On the other hand if the boat is saved with some of the goods, but the ship is lost, no account is to be taken in respect of those who lost their goods in the ship, because jettison leads to contribution only if the ship is saved. 1. But there is also a *responsum* of Sabinus to the effect that if a ship which has been lightened in a storm, by jettison of the goods of a merchant, is lost elsewhere, and the goods of some merchants are recovered by divers, for pay, an account must be taken as between him whose goods were thrown overboard during the voyage, to lighten the ship, and those who afterwards recovered their goods by means of divers. But [he says that] he whose goods were thrown overboard has, if some of them are recovered by divers, no account to render to those whose goods were not[1] thus saved, for their goods cannot be said to have been thrown overboard to save the ship, which was in fact lost. 2. But when jettison has been made from the ship, and the goods of someone, which remained on the ship, have been damaged, we must consider whether he should make contribution, since he ought not to be burdened with the double loss of both contribution and deterioration of his goods. But the view may be defended that he must contribute on the basis of the present value of his goods. Thus, for example, if the goods of two persons were

[1] Ins. *non*.

worth twenty each and those of one of them came to be worth only ten, owing to damage by water, the one whose goods are not affected will contribute on a basis of twenty, the other on a basis of ten. It is possible however to hold an opinion on the point, turning on our making a distinction as to the cause by which the goods came to be damaged, that is, whether it was due to their becoming exposed owing to the throwing overboard of merchandise, or to some other cause, say, for instance the goods lay somewhere in a corner and a wave reached them. In this case the owner will have to contribute, but ought he not to be free from contribution in the first case, since the jettison injured him too? Or ought he [to be liable] even in this case, where his goods have been damaged by water, owing to the jettison having been made? But we must apply a more subtle distinction, as to whether the greater burden is involved in the damage or in the contribution: if, for example, the goods were worth twenty and the contribution amounts to ten, but the damage is two, then, the damage being deducted, he must contribute for the rest. How then if the damage involves a greater loss than the contribution? Say, for instance, the goods are damaged to the extent of ten *aurei* while the contribution amounts to two: certainly he ought not to bear both charges. But here let us consider whether a contribution ought not to be made to his loss. For what difference does it make whether I lose my goods by jettison, or now have them in a damaged state by reason of their having been exposed? In fact, just as relief is given to one who has lost his goods, so there should be relief to him who now holds his goods in a damaged condition by reason of the jettison. Papirius Fronto laid down these rules in this way in a *responsum.*

5 HERMOGENIANUS (*Epitomes of Law* 2) The loss of the ship is not made good by contribution from those who saved their goods in the wreck, for the accepted view is that the justice of this contribution is admitted only when, by the remedy of jettison, the interest of other owners has been looked after and the ship is safe. 1. If the mast has been cut away to save the ship with her cargo there will be a just claim to contribution.

6 JULIANUS (*Digest* 86) A ship caught[1] by a storm, her rigging, mast and yards burnt by lightning, was driven into Hippo. Being there provided with a hasty emergency rig she sailed for Ostia and safely delivered her cargo. The question was raised

[1] For *depressa* read *deprensa.* Cf. M.

whether those to whom the cargo belonged were bound to pay a contribution to the shipmaster towards the expense. The answer was that they need not do so, for this expenditure was incurred rather to fit out the ship than to save the cargo.

7 PAULUS (*Epitomes of Alfenus's Digest* 3) The jurist gave a *responsum* to the effect that if a ship was wrecked or stranded, what each man saved of his own property he kept for himself, as [in case of goods saved] from a fire.

8 JULIANUS (*Extracts from Minicius* 2) Those who throw any goods overboard to lighten the ship have no intention to treat them as abandoned. Indeed if they find them anywhere they may carry them off, and if they form an idea as to the place at which they were cast ashore, they may make a demand for them: so that they are in just the same position as one who, overloaded by his burden, drops something on the road intending to return shortly with others and carry it off.

9 VOLUSIUS MÆCIANUS (*on the Rhodian Law*) A petition of Eudaimon of Nicomedia to the Emperor Antoninus. Lord Emperor Antoninus: Being shipwrecked in Icaria[1], we have been plundered by the taxfarmers[2] who live in the Cyclades Islands. Antoninus said to Eudaimon: I am indeed lord of the world, but the Law is lord of the sea. This matter must be decided by the maritime law of the Rhodians, provided that no law of ours is opposed to it. The most divine Augustus also laid down the same rule.

10 LABEO (*Probabilities, epitomised by Paulus,* 3) If you have taken a contract to carry slaves no freight is due to you in respect of a slave who died on the ship. Paulus: Say rather that the question is, what were the terms of the contract, whether freight was to be due in respect of those put on board or of those landed? As to the case in which this cannot be made out, here it will suffice for the shipmaster to prove that the man was put on board. 1. If you hired a ship on the terms that your goods were to be carried in her, and the shipmaster, knowing that you did not wish it, and not under any pressure of necessity, transferred your goods to a worse ship, and your goods were lost with the ship in which they were last carried, you have an action *ex conducto locato* against the master of the first ship. Paulus: This is by no means

[1] For Ἰταλίᾳ read Ἰκαρίᾳ. Cf. M.

[2] For δημόσιων read δημοσιωνῶν. Cf. M.

the case supposing both ships were lost on the voyage, since the event was not a consequence of *dolus* or negligence of the sailors. The rule will be the same if the first shipmaster, detained by the public authority, was prevented from sailing with your goods. The same rule will apply if he took the contract from you on the condition that he should pay you a certain penalty unless by an agreed day he had landed your goods in the place for carriage to which you had handed over the goods[1] and it was through no fault of his that he did not wait[2], though the penalty was [in fact] remitted to him. We shall have to lay down the same rule in the same kind of hypothesis, if it is proved that the shipmaster, prevented by illness, was incapable of making the voyage, or again if the ship became unseaworthy without *dolus malus* or negligence on his part. 2. If you have hired a ship of the capacity of two thousand *amphoræ* and have put *amphoræ* on board you owe the freight for two thousand *amphoræ.* Paulus: Naturally if the ship was hired as a whole (*per aversionem*) you owe for two thousand *amphoræ,* but if the freight was fixed according to the number of *amphoræ* put on board, the rule is the contrary one; for you owe the freight for as many *amphoræ* as you shipped.

III.

ON THE INSTITORIAN ACTION.

1 ULPIANUS (*on the Edict* 28) The Prætor has thought it fair that, just as we derive profits from the administration of *institores,* so also we should be bound by, and liable to be sued on, their contracts. But he does not make the same provision with regard to the person who has appointed an *institor,* that he also may sue. If indeed he had his own slave as *institor,* he may rest secure, as the rights of action are acquired to him. If however [he has appointed] either another man's slave, or even a freeman, he will not be able to sue, but he will nevertheless be able to sue the *institor* himself or his master, either on *mandatum* or on voluntary agency (*negotiorum gestorum*). But Marcellus holds that an action should be given to the person who appointed the *institor* against those who have contracted with him,

[1] *locasses.* Cf. M. [2] For *spectaret* read *exspectaret.* Cf. M.

2 GAIUS (*on the provincial Edict* 9) in the form applicable to the mode in which the *institor* contracted, provided that he cannot protect his interests in any other way.

3 ULPIANUS (*on the Edict* 28) An *institor* is so called because he intervenes (*instet*) in conducting a transaction, and it is of no great importance whether it is a shop that he is appointed to manage or any other sort of business,

4 PAULUS (*on the Edict* 30) for they sometimes take goods to the [houses of] people of good position and sell them there. The place at which the selling and buying occurs does not affect the basis of the action, since in each case it is true that the *institor* has bought or sold.

5 ULPIANUS (*on the Edict* 28) Thus, to whatsoever business he has been appointed, he will be rightly called an *institor.* 1. For Servius, also (*on Brutus* b. 1), says that if any business is done with the manager of a set of flats, or with a man whom you have appointed to look after a building, or to buy corn, you will be liable in full. 2. Labeo has also said that one who has appointed [a man] to lend money at interest, to cultivate lands, or to carry on commercial dealings, or to undertake public contracts, is liable in full. 3. So also if a man has put a slave in charge of a money-changer's table, he will be liable on his account. 4. And it is also established that those to whom clothiers and linen weavers give clothing to be hawked and sold, whom we commonly call *circitores*, are properly described as *institores.* 5. So too we may rightly call mule drivers *institores*, 6. and the managers appointed[1] by fullers and tailors. Stablekeepers also are to be considered as holding the position of *institores.* 7. Further, Labeo tells us that if a shopkeeper sends his slave about the country to buy merchandise, and send it to him, he is to be considered as in the position of an *institor*. 8. The same writer says that if an undertaker has a slave employed to prepare corpses for burial, and he robs a corpse, an action on the lines of the institorian action should be given against him, although the action on *furtum* and that on *injuria* are both available. 9. Labeo says further that if a baker was in the habit of sending his slave to a certain place to sell bread, and then he (the slave), having taken money in advance from some people[2] to deliver bread to them every day, failed to do so,

[1] For *præpositus* read *præpositos*. Cf. M.

[2] After *præsenti* ins. *a quibusdam*. M.

there is no reason to doubt that [the baker] will be liable if he authorized the giving of money to him in this way. 10. And further where a fuller, setting out on a journey had requested that orders should be given[1] to his apprentices, to whom he had handed over the shop fully equipped, after whose departure an apprentice had received clothing and run away, the fuller is not liable if the apprentice was left as *procurator*, but if it was as *institor*, he is liable. Of course if he told me I might safely trust his workmen, he will be liable not to the institorian action, but to that on *locatio*. 11. It is not however every transaction with the *institor* which binds the person who appointed him, but only cases in which the contract was made with reference to the matter to which he was appointed, that is to say only to that[2] to which he appointed him. 12. Accordingly if I have appointed a man to sell goods I shall be liable on his account to the action on purchase, and again, if, as it may be, I have appointed him to buy, I shall be liable only to the action on sale, but (and Cassius also adopts this view) one will not be bound if he was appointed to buy and he sells, or he was appointed to sell and he buys. 13. However if a person lends money to an *institor* appointed to buy there is ground for the institorian action, and similarly if he was appointed to pay the rent for the shop; this I believe to be true, supposing he was not forbidden to borrow. 14. If a loan of oil is made to a person whom I have appointed to buy and sell oil, the rule will be that the institorian action is available. 15. So also, if an *institor*, when he had sold some oil, took a ring by way of earnest, and does not return it, his master is liable to the institorian action, for the contract had reference to the business to which he was appointed, unless, indeed, he was instructed to sell for cash. It follows that if the *institor* happened to take a pledge for the price, the institorian action will be available. 16. Again, the institorian action is available to a guarantor who intervened on behalf of the *institor*, for this is a consequence of his transaction. 17. If an *institor* has been appointed by someone, but the person who appointed him is dead, and there is an heir to him, who employs the same *institor*, there can be no doubt that he will be liable. Moreover if a contract was made with him before the inheritance was entered on, it is fair that the institorian action should be given to one not aware of the facts. 18. Again, if my *procurator*, *tutor* or *curator* has appointed an *institor*, it

[1] For *imperaret* read *imperaretur*. Cf. M.

[2] For *ad id* read *id ad*. Cf. M.

must be said that the institorian action should be given as if he had been appointed by me.

6 PAULUS (*on the Edict* 30) But the institorian action will also be available against the *procurator* himself, if he was a general *procurator*.

7 ULPIANUS (*on the Edict* 28) And further, if anyone, voluntarily acting in my affairs, appoints [an *institor*], and I ratify the act, the same rule must be laid down. 1. It matters little who is the *institor*, male or female, free or your own slave or the slave of someone else. Also [it is indifferent] who the person appointing[1] is: for if a woman has appointed, the institorian action will be available, as the exercitorian is, and if a woman is appointed she herself will also be liable. Moreover if a woman under *potestas*, or a female slave, is appointed, the institorian action is available. 2. A child who is *institor* binds the person who appointed him by the institorian action, since he has himself to blame for appointing him,

8 GAIUS (*on the provincial Edict* 9) for, again, many people appoint boys and girls to manage shops.

9 ULPIANUS (*on the Edict* 28) However, if the person who appoints is himself a child under guardianship, he will be bound if the appointment was with the sanction of the *tutor*, but not otherwise.

10 GAIUS (*on the provincial Edict* 9) But an action will nevertheless lie against him so far as he is enriched by the transaction.

11 ULPIANUS (*on the Edict* 28) But if a child under guardianship becomes heir to the person who appointed, it is perfectly just that the child should be liable so long as he remains in charge, for he should have been removed by the *tutores* if they did not wish to avail themselves of his assistance. 1. Further, if the person who appointed was a minor under 25, he will not be relieved on account of non-age without enquiry into the matter. 2. A man is not considered to hold the position of one in charge of a business if a notice is publicly set up that there is to be no contracting with him: the rule is not indeed that there may be dealing with an *institor* only if it is permitted, but that one who wishes to prevent contract with him must prohibit it: apart from this the person who appointed

[1] For *quisquis præposuit* read *quis sit qui præposuit*. M.

him will be bound by the appointment itself. 3. Publicly set up is understood as meaning, in plain letters, so that the notice can be easily read from the ground, that is, in the front of the shop or place where the business is carried on, not in an obscure place but in the open. May it be in Greek or must it be in Latin? I think this is according to the character of the place, so that there may be no ground for a plea of inability to understand the writing. Assuredly if anyone pleads that he cannot read writing or had not observed what was set up, while in fact many people read it and it was openly posted up, he will not be listened to. 4. It is necessary that the notice be permanently set up, otherwise if the contract was made at a time when there was no notice posted up, or it was hidden, the institorian action will lie. In like manner if the owner of the merchandise put up a notice but someone else took it away, or by the effect of time, or of rains or anything of that sort, the result produced was[1] that there was no notice or none was apparent, it must be held that the person who appointed is liable. So if the *institor* himself, with the intention of deceiving me, took it down, his *dolus* ought to affect the person who appointed him, unless the other contracting party was privy to the *dolus*. 5. A condition on the appointment must be taken into account, for what are we to say if the employer wished dealings with him to be made under a certain condition, or with the cooperation of a certain person, or with security, or in a certain matter? It is eminently just that the purpose of his appointment should be regarded. So too if he had several *institores* and wished contracts to be made with all together, or only with a particular one. And again if he gives notice to anyone not to contract with him he is not liable to the institorian action: for we can prohibit both a certain person and a certain class of persons or traders from contracting, or we may permit it to certain persons. But if he has forbidden contract now with this man and now with that, with continual changes, all of them are entitled to the institorian action against him, for persons making contracts ought not to be misled. 6. If however the employer absolutely prohibited any contract with him, then he is not considered to be in the position of one put in charge of the business, since he is rather in the position of a caretaker than in that of *institor*: he will not therefore be able to sell anything, not the merest trifle, out of the shop. 7. If the institorian action has been rightly brought the tributorian action is excluded by direct operation of law, for there can be no tributorian action in relation to the

[1] *contigit.* Cf. M.

master's goods [as opposed to the *peculium*]. But if he was not an *institor* of his master's goods the tributorian action survives. 8. If I hire from your slave the services of his underslave, and make him *institor* of my goods, and he sells an article to you, this is a purchase, for when a master buys from his slave, though he is not legally bound, there is a purchase, even to this extent that the master may possess and acquire by long possession, as a buyer,

12 JULIANUS (*Digest* 11) and accordingly you will have an *actio utilis institoria* against me, while I, on the other hand, shall have against you either an action on the *peculium* of the managing slave (*dispensator*), if I choose to proceed *ex conducto*, or on the *peculium* of the underslave on the ground of having given him a *mandatum* to sell, and the price at which you bought may be considered as applied to your concerns (*in rem tuam versum*) on the ground that you became a debtor to your own slave.

13 ULPIANUS (*on the Edict* 28) A man had appointed a slave to manage an oil business at Arles, and the same slave to borrow money: he had borrowed money: the creditor, thinking the money had been received for the oil business, brought the action in question but could not prove that the slave had received it for the purpose of the business. Although the right of action is consumed, and he can take no further proceedings on the ground that he was also appointed to receive loans of money, yet Julianus holds that an *actio utilis* is available to him. 1. But it must be borne in mind that the master is liable to the institorian action only if there has been no supersession (*novatio*) of the obligation, either by the *institor* or by some third person who makes a stipulation with the intention of superseding it. 2. If two or more persons are carrying on a shop and they appoint as *institor* a slave whom they held in unequal shares, Julianus asks whether they are liable in proportion to their shares in him, or equally, or in proportion to their shares in the business, or for the whole debt. And he says that the better view is that, as in the case of *exercitores* and of the action on the *peculium*, any one of them can be sued for the whole debt, and whatever he who was sued has paid he will recover by the action on partnership or by that for the division of common property. This opinion we have also approved above.

14 PAULUS (*on Plautius* 4) It will be the same if a third person's slave has been appointed to a business owned in common, for an action for the whole debt ought to be given against either

owner, and of whatever either of them has paid he will recover a share by the action on partnership or by that for the division of common property. Certainly in any case in which the action on partnership or that for division of common property is not available it is clear law that each is liable to condemnation only for his part, as, for instance, if he to whose slave money was lent, having instituted two heirs, freed the slave, for each heir is to be sued only in respect of his part, because the action for division is not available between them.

15 ULPIANUS (*on the Edict* 28) Finally it should be noted that these actions are available without limitation of time and both to and against heirs.

16 PAULUS (*on the Edict* 29) If a contract is made with anyone's bailiff (*vilicus*) no action lies against the employer, for a bailiff is appointed to collect produce, not to trade. If however I have a bailiff who is also appointed to sell goods it is not unfair that an action on the model of the institorian action should lie against me.

17 THE SAME (*on the Edict* 30) If a man is appointed to buy and sell slaves or beasts of burden or stock, not only is the institorian action available against the employer, but also the redhibitorian and that on the stipulation for double or single value are available against him for the whole claim. 1. If you have the slave of Titius as *institor* I can proceed either against you under this edict or against Titius under the edicts considered below. But if you forbade dealing with him there can be an action only against Titius. 2. If a child under fourteen becomes heir to a father who had *institores*, and thereupon there is dealing with them it must be said that an action lies against the child, on the ground of advantage to the common course of trade, as in the case in which, after the death of a *tutor* with whose sanction an *institor* was appointed, there is dealing with him. 3. Pomponius also has laid it down that an action should certainly be given on account of a contract which came into existence before the inheritance was entered on, even though the person who becomes heir is insane; for no blame attaches to one who, knowing that the employer has died, contracts with the *institor* carrying on the business. 4. Proculus says that if I give you notice not to lend to a slave appointed by me there is ground for the *exceptio*: "if he (defendant) did not notify him (plaintiff) not to lend to that slave." But if he has *peculium*

or proceeds of that contract have been applied to my affairs[1], and I am not willing to pay to the extent of my enrichment, a *replicatio* on the ground of *dolus malus* should be used, for I must be considered to have committed *dolus malus* in seeking to profit by another's loss. 5. It is true that a *condictio* will also lie in this case.

18 THE SAME (*Various Passages*) An *institor* is one who is appointed to a shop or place to buy or sell, or is appointed to such a function with no specification of place.

19 PAPINIANUS (*Responsa* 3) An *actio utilis* on the model of the institorian action will be given against one who appointed a *procurator* to borrow money, and this will be equally true where the *procurator* who has promised money, in answer to a person stipulating, is solvent. 1. If a master who had a slave *institor* at a table for receiving deposits of money, also, after he has freed the slave, carries on the same business through the *libertus*, the conditions of liability will not be affected by the change of status. 2. A son appointed by his father, to manage a shop, borrowed money for purposes connected with his merchandise: his father became guarantor for him: proceedings by the institorian action will also lie against him, for by his guaranty he associated the case of borrowing money with the trade of the shop. 3. A slave appointed solely for the purpose of lending money at interest does not as *institor*[2] make his owner liable in full, under prætorian law, by taking a debt on himself by way of surety, but with regard to money which he promised to a third person by way of substituted liability (*delegatio*) on behalf of one to whom[3] he lent at interest, an action will rightly lie against the owner, who has acquired a claim for money lent against the person who offered the substitute.

20 SCÆVOLA (*Digest* 5) Lucius Titius had a *libertus*, appointed to manage a money-changer's table which he was conducting: this man gave an undertaking to Gaius Seius in these words: "Octavius Terminalis, managing the affairs of Octavius Felix, to Domitius Felix greeting. You have 1000 *denarii* in the bank of my patron, and I shall be bound to pay over these *denarii* to you on the last day of April." It was asked whether, Lucius Titius having died without an heir, and his goods having been sold, Terminalis could be sued at law on this letter. The answer was that neither was he

[1] The words *ex eo contractu* are to be placed after *aut*. Cf. M.

[2] For *institorem* read *institor*. Cf. M. [3] For *qui* read *cui*. Cf. M.

bound in law by these words, nor did there exist any equity to base a claim against him, since he wrote this in the course of his duty as *institor* in support of the credit of the business.

IV.

ON THE TRIBUTORIAN ACTION.

1 ULPIANUS (*on the Edict* 29) The utility of this edict also is not small, since a master, who, apart from it, has a privilege in cases of contract by a slave (inasmuch as he is liable only to the extent of the *peculium*, the assessment of which is made subject to the deduction of what is due to the master), is however required under this edict to rank for dividend like an outside creditor, if he knew that the slave was trading with property of the *peculium*. 1. Though the expression merchandise is rather narrow, so that it does not apply to slaves who are fullers or tailors or weavers or slavedealers, yet, according to Pedius (b. 15), the edict is to be extended to businesses of all kinds. 2. Merchandise of the *peculium* is not to be defined in the way in which *peculium* is, for *peculium* is understood subject to a deduction of what is due to the master, but merchandise of the *peculium* renders the master liable to the tributorian action, even though there is nothing in the *peculium* [beyond what is due to him], but[1] only if the business is carried on with his knowledge. 3. In this case the knowledge to be understood is that which includes assent, or rather, as I think, not assent but tolerance; the master need not desire it, but must not disapprove it. Thus if he knows the facts, and makes no protest and opposition, he will be liable to the tributorian action. 4. The word *potestas* is to be extended to both sexes; and also to all those who are under the domestic control of another. 5. The tributorian action will apply not only to slaves but also to those who are in apparent slavery to us in good faith, whether they are free or the slaves of someone else or slaves in whom we have a usufruct,

2 PAULUS (*on the Edict* 30) provided however that the wares traded with in connexion with the *peculium* belong to us.

[1] Ins. *at*. M.

3 ULPIANUS (*on the Edict* 29) If however it is a common slave and both owners know the facts, the action will lie against either of them, but if one knows and the other was ignorant, the action will lie against the one who knows; whatever is due to the one who was not informed will however be deducted in full. If action is brought against the one who was not privy, since he is sued on the *peculium*, what is due to the one who was, will also be deducted, and that in full, for, if he were sued by the action on the *peculium*, what was due to him would be deducted in full. And so Julianus has laid it down (*Digest* b. 12). 1. If the slave of a child under guardianship, or of a lunatic, trades with merchandise of the *peculium* to the knowledge of the *tutor* or *curator* it is my opinion that the *dolus* of the *tutor* or *curator* should not prejudice the ward or lunatic, or be, on the other hand, a source of profit to him, and consequently, that he should be liable to the tributorian action, by reason of *dolus* of the *tutor*, only to the extent of any profit that may have come to him: I think the same also in the case of a *lunatic*. Pomponius however holds (*Letters* b. 8) that if the *tutor* is solvent the ward is liable on account of his fraud, and it is clear that he will be liable to this extent, that he must assign the action he has against the *tutor*. Moreover if there was *dolus* on the part of the ward, he being of such an age as to be capable of *dolus*, this has the effect of making him liable, although knowledge on his part would not be enough, in respect of the trading. What then is the conclusion? It is that knowledge on the part of the *tutor* and *curator* ought to create liability to this action: to what extent *dolus* creates liability I have shown.

4 PAULUS (*on the Edict* 30) If the ward whose *tutor* was aware [of the trading] is guilty of *dolus* after reaching puberty, or the lunatic, when he is of sound mind, they are liable under this edict.

5 ULPIANUS (*on the Edict* 29) But Pomponius does not doubt, nor do we, that knowledge and *dolus* of a *procurator* create liability. 1. When an underslave of my slave carries on trade, if this is actually with my knowledge I shall be liable to the tributorian action: if I am not aware of it but the principal slave is, Pomponius tells us (b. 60) that an action on his *peculium* is available and that nothing is to be deducted from the *peculium* of the underslave in respect of what he owes to the principal slave, while what is due to me is deducted. If however we were both aware of the facts, the same authority holds that both the

tributorian action and that on the *peculium* are available, the tributorian on account of the underslave but that on the *peculium* in respect of the principal slave (the plaintiff however being required to elect under which action he prefers to proceed), but on the terms that both what is due to me and what is due to the principal slave will have to rank for dividend in the tributorian action, while, if the principal slave had not been privy, whatsoever was due to him from the underslave would have been deducted in full. 2. And, again, if a female slave carries on trade, it is held that the tributorian action is to be allowed. 3. So, too, it matters little whether the contract is with the slave himself or with his *institor*. 4. [The words] "in respect of the business" (*mercis nomine*) are very properly added, lest every kind of dealing carried on with him should give rise to the tributorian action. 5. The law is that under this action everything received from the stock in trade or in respect of it must be divided. 6. Those who hold the slave in *potestas* are summoned to rank for dividend with the creditors of the concern. 7. The question has however been raised whether the master shares in the division of the goods only in respect of what is due to him in connexion therewith, or also if in fact anything is due to him on another account. And Labeo lays it down that [the rule applies] on whatever account money is due to him, and that it matters little[1] whether the slave became indebted to him before the trading began or afterwards, for it is enough that he has lost the privilege of deduction. 8. What, however, is to be said, if those who made contracts with the slave have taken the goods in pledge? I think it must be held that they are to be preferred to the master, by right of pledge. 9. Whether the indebtedness is to the master or to those who are in his *potestas*, in any case it must rank for dividend. 10. If there are two or more masters, a dividend will certainly be payable to each of them in proportion to his debt. 11. It is not however the whole *peculium* which is available for division, but only that which is connected with the business, whether there is existing merchandise, or the value of it has been received and devoted to the *peculium*. 12. Moreover if money is still due on account of goods from persons to whom the slave was in the habit of selling, this also will be available for division, as it is received. 13. If this slave has in the shop, besides the stock, utensils of trade, are these also available for distribution? And Labeo lays it down that these too

[1] For *referret* read *referre*. Cf. M.

will be divided, and this is perfectly just; for this outfit is commonly, indeed always, provided out of the funds of the business. Things other than these however which he had in the *peculium* will not be distributed, say, for instance, he had gold or silver, except in the case in which he has acquired them with the capital of the business. 14. So too if he had in the business slaves acquired by means of the stock, these also will be part of the divisible fund. 15. If the slave had several creditors, but some of them were in respect of particular businesses, are they all to be grouped together and summoned to share in the distribution? Suppose he was carrying on two kinds of business, those, let us say, of mantle making and linen weaving, and had separate creditors. My view is that they must be summoned to distribution separately, for each of them gave credit to the concern rather than to the man. 16. Further[1], if he had two shops doing the same kind of trade, and I did business, say, with the shop in the Bucinum quarter and another dealt with that across the Tiber, I think it most fair that the distribution should be made separately, lest one set of creditors be paid out of the goods or property of the other[2]. 17. Clearly if goods were being offered for sale in the same shop, even though those now there were acquired with money of one creditor, they will all be available for distribution unless they were pledged to the creditor. 18. But if I have handed over my goods for sale, and they still exist, the question must be considered whether it is not unfair that I should be required to rank for dividend. If, indeed, my right has become a mere personal claim against you, it is a case for distribution; where however it has not done so, since sold property does not cease to be mine, even though I have sold it, unless the money is paid or a guarantor given, or satisfaction made in some other way, in that case the rule will be that I can bring a vindication. 19. The distribution is made in proportion to the amount due to each, and thus if one creditor appears, requesting a distribution, he will receive his portion in full, but since it may happen that there may be another creditor or other creditors of the business carried on with the *peculium*, this creditor must give security that he will refund proportionately if it happens that other creditors present themselves.

6 PAULUS (*on the Edict* 30) For this action does not, like that on the *peculium*, give a more advantageous position to the first claimant, but puts all in the same position, whenever claiming.

[1] For *sed* read *sed et*. Cf. M. [2] Omit *alii damnum sentiant*. M.

7 ULPIANUS (*on the Edict* 29) He ought also to give security that, if anything else should turn out to be due to the master, he will make a proportionate refund to him. For suppose a conditional debt is impending, or there is an undiscovered debt, this also must be allowed, since the master ought not to suffer injustice though he is called on to share in the distribution. 1. But how if the master will not distribute the goods or undertake this troublesome matter, but is ready to give up the *peculium* or the merchandise? Pedius puts it on record that he is to be listened to, which opinion has justice in it, and it will usually be the duty of the Prætor to appoint an arbitrator in this matter, by whose mediation the merchandise of the *peculium* may be distributed. 2. If, owing to the *dolus malus* of anyone, distribution in the proper way is prevented, the tributorian action lies against him to compel him to make good the amount by which what was distributed was less than what ought to have been distributed. By this action a check is placed on the *dolus malus* of the master. It is considered to be distributing too little if nothing at all is distributed. If, however, not knowing what the slave has in stock, he distributes too little, he is not considered to have done so with *dolus*, but if, on learning the facts, he fails to distribute it, he is not now free from *dolus*. In like manner if he procures payment to himself out of this merchandise he may be certainly said to have distributed less [than was due]. 3. Further if he has allowed the stock to go to waste, or has misapplied it or has intentionally sold it at too low a price, or has not made buyers pay the price, he must be held liable to the tributorian action, assuming that his action was wilful. 4. Again, if the master denies that anything is due to anyone at all, we must consider whether there is a case for the tributorian action. And the better opinion is that of Labeo, that the tributorian action is available: otherwise it will be to the advantage of the master to deny. 5. This action is available both without limit of time, and against the heir, to the extent only of what he has received,

8 JULIANUS (*Digest* 11) because the action is not one on *dolus* but involves a claim of property. For this reason even though the slave be dead, the master, and his heir also, should be held liable, without limitation of time, for the act of the deceased, although the action is available only if *dolus* has been committed.

9 ULPIANUS (*on the Edict* 29) What is laid down as to the heir will also apply to other successors. 1. A man must

choose by which action he will proceed, whether by that on the *peculium*, or by the tributorian action, since he knows that he will not be able to fall back on the other. Of course if a man desires to bring the tributorian action on one claim and that on the *peculium* on another, he should be listened to. 2. Labeo holds that, if the *peculium* is left to a slave freed by will, the heir ought not to be liable to the tributorian action, as neither having received anything nor committed *dolus*. But Pomponius (b. 60) has laid it down that the heir is liable to the tributorian action, unless he has taken care to get security from the slave or has deducted from the *peculium* what ought to have been distributed, a view which is not without reason, since he who has so acted as to prevent distribution is himself the promoter of *dolus*. For the action against the heir, limited to what he has received, lies when he is sued in respect of *dolus* of the deceased, not when he is sued on his own.

10 PAULUS (*on the Edict* 30) The action on the *peculium* can be brought against a buyer of the slave also: the tributorian action cannot.

11 GAIUS (*on the provincial Edict* 9) It is sometimes advantageous for plaintiffs to proceed by the action on the *peculium* rather than by the tributorian, for, in the action which we are discussing, only that comes in for division which is included in the merchandise with which the business is carried on, and whatever has been received in respect of it, but in the action on the *peculium* the whole amount of the *peculium* is taken into account, in which the merchandise also is included. And it may be that the business is being carried on with a half or a third or even a less part of the *peculium*: it may also be the case that he owes nothing to his father or owner.

12 JULIANUS (*Digest* 12) One man sues the master on account of the slave, by the action limited to the *peculium*; another sues by the tributorian action: the question was raised whether the master ought to deduct from the *peculium* what he will be paying to the plaintiff in the tributorian action. The answer was: proceedings can be brought by the tributorian action only in a case in which the master, in distributing the value of the merchandise, has not satisfied the terms of the Prætor's edict; that is, when he has deducted a greater part of his own debt than he has divided among the creditors, for instance, if, when the stock was worth 30 of which he

himself had advanced 15, but two outside creditors had advanced 30, he deducted the whole 15 and gave the creditors the remaining 15, when the right course was to deduct only 10 and to give the creditors 10 each. It follows that when he has acted in this way, he is not to be considered as having freed the slave from liability to him, because he has still to pay five on his account in the tributorian action. Accordingly if proceedings on the *peculium* are begun, there being, let us suppose, *peculium* other than this stock in trade, he will be entitled to deduct five as being still a creditor of the slave.

V.

DEALINGS ALLEGED TO HAVE BEEN HAD WITH A PERSON IN THE *POTESTAS* OF ANOTHER.

1 GAIUS (*on the provincial Edict* 9) The proconsul makes every provision that one who has contracted with a person in the *potestas* of another, even though the above-mentioned actions, that is to say, the exercitorian, the institorian or the tributorian, be not available, may yet come by his own, so far as the state of the case permits, having regard to considerations of equity and good conscience. For, if the transaction was entered on with the authorisation of the person in whose *potestas* he is, he promises an action for the full amount in respect of it: if on the other hand it was not with his authority, but proceeds have been devoted to his purposes, he creates an action to the extent of the application to his purposes: if again it was neither of these, he establishes an action to the extent of the *peculium*.

2 ULPIANUS (*on the Edict* 29) The Prætor says, "after enquiry I will give an action to the extent of what he is able to pay against a person who is emancipated or disinherited or has abstained from the inheritance of one in whose *potestas* at death he was, whether the business was done of his own motion or on the authorisation of the person in whose *potestas* he was, and whether the proceeds were applied to the purposes of the *peculium* or to the concerns of the person in whose *potestas* he was." 1. Moreover if he has become independent (*sui juris*) without emancipation or has been given in adoption and thereafter his natural father has died, and again, if such a person has been appointed heir for a

very small share, it is most just that this action should be given against him also, after enquiry into the facts, to the extent of his ability to pay.

3 THE SAME (*Disputations* 3) Whether in this case what is due to others should be deducted may afford matter for discussion. Certainly if they are creditors who contracted with him when he was in the *potestas* of another, the correct rule will be that the first claimant has the better position, except in the case in which a creditor with a special priority appears, for, not without reason, account will be taken of this prior claimant. But if there are creditors who contracted with him after he became independent, it is my opinion that they should be taken into account.

4 THE SAME (*on the Edict* 29) But if the son is appointed heir for a considerable share, it rests in the choice of the creditor whether he will sue him for the whole debt, or for the fraction of it due from him as heir. But here too it is the duty of the judge to determine whether on the facts he is to be sued only to the extent of his ability to pay[1]. 1. But sometimes, even if the son is disinherited or emancipated, an action will be given against him for the full amount due, as, for instance, if at the time when the contract was made with him he falsely declared himself to be a *paterfamilias*, for Marcellus has laid it down (*Digest* b. 2) that even if he has not the means to pay he is liable to be sued, by reason of his falsehood. 2. Though on his contracts an action lies against him [only] to the extent of his means, he is nevertheless liable in full on his delicts. 3. Relief is given to the son alone, not to his heir as well, for Pomponius, also, tells us (*Questions* b. 9) that an action for the whole debt lies against the son's heir. 4. But should not lapse of time be taken into account, so that if proceedings are actually brought against the son at once the action is given to the extent of his capacity to pay, but if it is after many years there should be no such indulgence? And it is my view that account should be taken [of this]: for the enquiry into the facts will go into this. 5. One who has sued on the *peculium* when he might have sued on the basis of authorisation is in the position of not being able afterwards to bring the action on an authorised contract, and so thinks Proculus. But if he sued on the *peculium* owing to his having been deceived as to the facts, Celsus holds that relief should be afforded to him. This opinion is sound.

[1] Text probably corrupt. Cf. M.

5 PAULUS (*on the Edict* 30) If a *filiusfamilias* has been sued and condemned during the life of his father, an action on the judgment should be given against him to the extent of his capacity to pay, if he has been emancipated or disinherited. 1. If the inheritance of the father is transferred under the *Senatusconsultum Trebellianum* to a son who was disinherited, he should be condemned to pay not to the extent of his means but the whole debt, since in effect he is in a sense heir. 2. But if he has intermeddled with the inheritance, under compulsion, with the intention of transferring it, the course followed should be exactly as if he had abstained.

6 ULPIANUS (*Disputations* 2) A man who has pretended to be a *paterfamilias* and has made a stipulation on the *mandatum* of someone is, according to Marcellus, liable to the action on *mandatum*, though he be not in a position to pay the amount due; and it is obviously true that he ought to be liable, since he has committed *dolus*. The same may also be said of all actions resting on good faith.

7 SCÆVOLA (*Responsa* 1) A father allowed a son to borrow money, and gave a *mandatum* by letter to the creditor to lend to him: the son became heir to the father for a very small share. I answered that it lay in the discretion of the creditor whether he would prefer to sue the son to whom he had lent the money for the whole amount, or the heirs, each in proportion to the share to which he succeeded. But the son is condemned to the extent of his ability to pay.

8 PAULUS (*Decrees* 1) Titianus Primus had appointed a slave to lend moneys and take pledges: this slave was also in the habit of undertaking, on behalf of dealers in barley, debts arising from purchase, and paying them. The slave having run away, and the person to whom he had been given as a substituted debtor (*delegatus*), to pay the price of the barley, having sued the master on account of the *institor*, he[1] denied that he could be sued on this account, for the man had not been appointed for this traffic. But as it was proved that the same slave had engaged in other transactions and had hired granaries and had paid money to many people, the prefect of the grain supply gave judgment against the master. We contended that this appeared to be a sort of guaranty, since he was paying money for another, for[2] he undertook debt for

[1] Ins. *is*. M. [2] For *non* read *nam*. Cf. M.

others, but that it was not the practice to give an action against the master on this ground, and that it did not seem[1] that the master had authorised this. But, as he appeared to have appointed the slave to act for him in all these matters, the emperor upheld the judgment.

VI.

ON THE *SENATUSCONSULTUM MACEDONIANUM*.

1 ULPIANUS (*on the Edict* 29) The terms of the *Senatusconsultum Macedonianum* are as follows: "Whereas Macedo, to the other causes of wickedness which nature bestowed on him, added also indebtedness, and (to say no more) one who lends money on dubious obligations often provides evil dispositions with means of ill-doing, it is enacted that to one who has lent money to a *filiusfamilias* no action or claim be given even after the death of his parent, so that those who, setting a most evil example, lend money at interest may know that no acknowledgment of a *filiusfamilias* can be made a good claim by waiting till the death of the father." 1. If the question whether the son is in *potestas* is in suspense, for instance because he has a father in the enemy's hands, the question whether there has been an infringement of the *senatusconsultum* is in suspense. For if he relapses into *potestas* the *senatusconsultum* operates; if he does not it has no application: therefore in the mean time an action should be refused. 2. Certainly, if a person who has been arrogated borrows money and afterwards gets an order of restitution, so that he is to be emancipated, the *senatusconsultum* will apply, for he was a *filiusfamilias*. 3. Official position in a *filiusfamilias* has no force to prevent the *Senatusconsultum Macedonianum* from applying; for though he be Consul or of what dignity you will, the *senatusconsultum* applies, unless indeed he has a military *peculium*, for in that case the *senatusconsultum* will not operate,

2 THE SAME (*on the Edict* 64) so far as the military *peculium* extends, since *filiifamilias* are in the position of independent citizens in respect of the military *peculium*.

[1] For *videtur* read *videri*. Cf. M.

3 THE SAME (*on the Edict* 29) If a person believed a man to be a *paterfamilias*, not being misled by mere foolishness or ignorance of law, but because he appeared as a *paterfamilias* publicly, to people generally, and was in the habit of acting, contracting, and executing the duties of offices, as such, the *senatusconsultum* will not apply. 1. Accordingly Julianus tells us (b. 12) that the *senatusconsultum* does not apply in the case of one who was in the habit of farming the public revenues, and there have been frequent imperial enactments to this effect. 2. So also in the case of one who could not know whether the man was a *filiusfamilias*, Julianus (b. 12) says that the *senatusconsultum* does not apply, for example, in the case of a child under guardianship or a person under twenty-five years of age. But in the case of the minor relief should also be given, by the Prætor, after enquiry: while in that of the ward he was justified also on another ground in saying that the *senatusconsultum* would not apply, since the money which the ward hands over without the sanction of his *tutor* does not become a loan, just as Julianus himself says (b. 12), that, if a *filiusfamilias* lends, the *senatusconsultum* does not apply, as the money does not become a loan even though he had the free administration of the *peculium*. For the father in giving the right of free administration of the *peculium* does not authorise the throwing of it away; and therefore, he says, the right of specific vindication of the money remains to the father. 3. It is only one who has lent money to a *filiusfamilias* who offends against the *senatusconsultum*, not one who has contracted otherwise, for instance one who has sold or let on hire, or contracted in some other way; for it was the giving of money which was considered dangerous to their parents. And therefore, although I have become a creditor of a *filiusfamilias* either on the ground of a purchase, or of some other contract in which I have paid no money, though I may have made a stipulation, notwithstanding that the matter has become a loan, nevertheless, since payment of money does not enter into it, the *senatusconsultum* does not apply. This will be the rule only if there was no scheme for a fraud on the *senatusconsultum*, so that one who could not lend money preferred to sell to him, so that the other party should have the value of the goods in place of a loan. 4. If I have made a stipulation [for payment] with a *filiusfamilias*, and lent him the money after he has become a *paterfamilias*, whether he has suffered *capitis deminutio*, or has become independent by the death of his father, or otherwise, without *capitis deminutio*, the rule to lay down is that the

senatusconsultum does not apply, as the loan was made to one who was already a *paterfamilias*;

4 SCÆVOLA (*Questions* 2) for the common saying that it is not allowed to lend to a *filiusfamilias* is to be referred not to the verbal transaction, but to the payment of the money.

5 PAULUS (*Questions* 3) Accordingly in this case he will also be condemned for the whole debt, not to the extent of his ability to pay.

6 SCÆVOLA (*Questions* 2) On the other hand, if you have made the stipulation with a *paterfamilias* and afterwards lend the money to him when he has become a *filiusfamilias*, it will be correctly laid down that the power of the Senate is to be applied, because the essential part of the obligation was perfected by the payment.

7 ULPIANUS (*on the Edict* 29) So if a *filiusfamilias* has given a guaranty, Neratius says (bb. 1 and 2) that the *senatusconsultum* does not apply. Celsus agrees (b. 4). But Julianus adds that if recourse was had to this as a pretext, so that a *filiusfamilias* who was going to receive a loan became a guarantor, some other person being made the principal debtor, the fraud effected on the *senatusconsultum* prejudices [the claim] and an *exceptio* should be given both to the *filiusfamilias* and to the principal debtor, since relief is given also to the guarantor of a *filiusfamilias*. 1. The same writer says that if, when the money was to go to a *filiusfamilias*, I accepted two debtors, Titius and the *filiusfamilias*, but I accepted Titius as a principal debtor, with the object that he should not avail himself of the help of the *senatusconsultum* as a guarantor of the *filiusfamilias*, an *exceptio utilis* should be given on account of the fraud. 2. But, further, if a *filiusfamilias*, at a time when his father was banished or was absent for a long time, promised a dowry for a daughter, and gave something of his father's as a pledge, the *senatusconsultum* will not apply; the father's property will not indeed be bound [by the pledge]: of course if the son becomes heir to the father and sues to recover the pledge he will be defeated by the *exceptio* on the ground of *dolus*. 3. It is a point to be considered whether we ought to regard as a loan not only one of money paid over, but, in fact one of any thing which can be lent for consumption. But the words appear to me to be meant to apply to money paid, for the *senatusconsultum* says "has lent money." But if there has been a fraud on the *senatusconsultum*,

grain, for instance, or wine or oil having been given so that, this produce having been sold, the price may be used, relief should be given to the *filiusfamilias*. 4. If the *filiusfamilias* was in the *potestas* of one person when the money was lent, but is now in that of another, the intention of the *senatusconsultum* is not inapplicable, and the *exceptio* will therefore be given. 5. Again if not death, but some other event has happened to the father, whereby he is removed from citizenship, the *senatusconsultum* must be held to be applicable. 6. The action is refused not only to him who lent the money, but also to his successors. 7. In like manner also, if one person handed over the money, and another made the stipulation [for repayment], the *exceptio* will be given against the latter, though he himself did not pay the money. But if one or the other of them did not know that he was in the *potestas* of this father, the somewhat severe rule is that both are affected by the knowledge. The same rule applies where there are two co-stipulators. 8. Again if I have accepted two *filiifamilias* as debtors, but supposed one of them to be a *paterfamilias*, it will be a material point to which of them the money went, so that, if I knew the one to whom it went to be a *filiusfamilias*, I am barred by the *exceptio*: if it went to the one as to whom I was in ignorance, I am not barred. 9. But whether the money was lent at interest or without interest the case is within the *senatusconsultum*. 10. Though the Senate does not explicitly say to whom it gives the *exceptio*, yet it must be understood that the heir of the *filiusfamilias*, if he dies a *paterfamilias*, and his father, if he dies a *filiusfamilias*, may avail themselves of the *exceptio*. 11. In some cases even though the *senatusconsultum* is available, nevertheless an action lies against a third person: suppose for instance a *filiusfamilias* who is an *institor* has borrowed money; for Julianus tells us (b. 12) that the *institor* himself will rely on the *senatusconsultum* if he is sued, but the institorian action lies against the person who appointed him. However, he says, if the father himself had appointed him to manage his business, or had allowed him to carry on one with the *peculium*, the *senatusconsultum* would not apply, for the contract may be considered to have been made with the father's assent, since if he knows that he is trading he may be supposed to have allowed this too, if he did not expressly prohibit it[1]. 12. In like manner, if he has received money and applied it to his father's concerns the *senatusconsultum* does not apply, for he received it on behalf of his father,

[1] Omit *merces accipere*. M.

not for himself. Moreover, if he did not in the first instance receive it with that purpose, but, later on, did in fact apply it to his father's concerns, Julianus tells us (*Digest* b. 12) that the *senatusconsultum* does not apply, and that he must be understood to have received it in the beginning with a view to its application to his father's purposes. But if he pays to his father, in discharge of his own debt, money which he has borrowed, he will not be considered to have expended it in his father's concerns, and thus, if the father did not know of it, the *senatusconsultum* will still apply. 13. The observation that the *senatusconsultum* would not apply in the case of one who, being away for the purpose of his studies, had borrowed money, holds good provided he has not exceeded a reasonable limit in his borrowing, at any rate the amount which his father was in the habit of allowing him. 14. If a son has borrowed money to pay off one who, if he sued, could not be met by the *exceptio*, the *exceptio* on the *senatusconsultum* does not apply. 15. Moreover the *senatusconsultum* will not apply if the father begins to pay what the son has borrowed, on the ground that he has ratified the transaction. 16. If after he has become a *paterfamilias* he pays part of the debt the *senatusconsultum* will not apply and he will not be able to recover what he has paid.

8 PAULUS (*on the Edict* 30) If, however, it has been paid by a *curator*, in ignorance, it should be recovered.

9 ULPIANUS (*on the Edict* 29) But if, when he has become a *paterfamilias*, he gives a thing by way of pledge, the rule to be laid down will be that the *exceptio* on the *senatusconsultum* is to be refused to him, to the amount of the value of the pledge. 1. If the son pays to the creditor money which a third person has given to him as a present, can the father bring a specific vindication for this or recover it [by *condictio*]? And Julianus says that if the money was actually given to him on the condition that he should pay it to the creditor, it is to be considered as having passed immediately from the donor to the creditor, and the moneys become the property of the receiver: if indeed it was simply given to him, the son had no power of alienation of the moneys, and therefore, if he pays, the *condictio* is available to the father in any case. 2. This *senatusconsultum* applies also to women in *potestas*, nor is it material if they are alleged to have acquired ornaments with the money; for by the decree of the most distinguished order an action is refused also to one who has lent money to a *filius-*

familias, and it does not matter whether the coins have been consumed or are extant in the *peculium*. Much more therefore will the contract of one who has lent money to a *filiafamilias* be disapproved by the rigour of the *senatusconsultum*. 3. Relief is given not only to the *filiusfamilias* and to his father, but also to his guarantor, and to his *mandator*, who also themselves have the resource of the action on *mandatum*, unless indeed they intervened with the intention of making a gift, for then as they have no right to fall back on him, the *senatusconsultum* will have no operation. But, further, if they did not intervene with the intent to make a donation, but at the wish of the father, the whole contract will be considered to have been approved by the father. 4. And yet those who have intervened on behalf of the *filiusfamilias* without the father's consent cannot recover on paying, for so the Divine Hadrian also enacted, and it may be said that they will not get their money back. And yet they are protected by a perpetual *exceptio*; but so also is the son himself, but nevertheless he does not recover, for only those cannot recover what they have paid who are freed from an action by way of penalty on the creditors, and not because a law aimed at absolutely destroying their liability[1]. But although they do not recover on paying,

10 PAULUS (*on the Edict* 30) because the natural obligation remains,

11 ULPIANUS (*on the Edict* 29) yet, nevertheless, if, not having pleaded the *exceptio*, they are condemned, they can avail themselves of the *exceptio* on the *senatusconsultum*. And so Julianus tells us in the case of the *filiusfamilias* himself, on the analogy of the woman who has become a guarantor.

12 PAULUS (*on the Edict* 30) If money is lent to a son with the bare knowledge of the father, it should be held that the *senatusconsultum* does not apply. But if the father has authorised lending to the son, and has afterwards changed his mind without the knowledge of the creditor, there will be no case for the *senatusconsultum*, as the beginning of the contract is what has to be considered.

13 GAIUS (*on the provincial Edict* 9) If, with the intent of superseding the old obligation, we stipulate with a *filiusfamilias* for payment of what we have lent to a third person, Julianus writes that the *senatusconsultum* is no obstacle.

[1] See however M.

14 JULIANUS (*Digest* 12) I have a son and by him a grandson: money was lent to my grandson with his father's assent: the question was raised whether this was done contrary to the *senatusconsultum*. I said that though in the language of the *senatusconsultum* sons are mentioned, yet the same rule ought to be observed in the case of a grandson too: the assent of this father will not prevent the money from being regarded as lent contrary to the *senatusconsultum*, since he himself is in the condition of not being able to borrow money against the will of his father.

15 MARCIANUS (*Institutes* 14) It matters nothing who has lent to a *filiusfamilias*, whether it is a private citizen or a city; for the Divine Severus and Antoninus have laid it down by rescript that the *senatusconsultum* applies to the case of a city also.

16 PAULUS (*Responsa* 4) If a *filiusfamilias*, in the absence of his father, has given an acknowledgment as having received money under a *mandatum* from his father, and has written to his father to pay the money in the province, the father, if he disapproves the action of his son, ought, without delay, to communicate an expression of his contrary wish.

17 THE SAME (*Sentences* 2) If a *filiusfamilias* borrows money for the purpose of giving it as a marriage portion on behalf of his sister, the father will be liable to the action for money applied to his concerns; for, if the girl dies married, a right to recover the marriage portion is given to him.

18 VENULEIUS (*Stipulations* 2) Julianus says that the creditor of a *filiusfamilias* cannot receive a guarantor after the latter's death, because there survives no obligation either civil or natural with which the guarantor can be connected: of course a guarantor can properly be received from the father on account of the action on the *peculium* which may lie against him.

19 POMPONIUS (*Various Passages* 7) Julianus says that the *exceptio* under the *Senatusconsultum Macedonianum* stands in the way of no one except one who knew or could have known that the person to whom he lent was a *filiusfamilias*.

20 THE SAME (*on Senatusconsulta* 5) If one to whom money had been lent while he was in his father's *potestas*, made, in ignorance of the facts, after he had become a *paterfamilias*, an independent promise of the money, in such a way as to supersede the old obligation, and a claim is brought on that stipulation, an *exceptio* based on the facts should be pleaded.

FIFTEENTH BOOK.

I.

On the Action on the *Peculium*.

1 Ulpianus (*on the Edict* 29) The Prætor thought it the orderly method to set forth first those contracts of persons who are subject to the *potestas* of another which give a right of action for the whole debt and then to proceed to the present case in which an action is given on the *peculium*. 1. This edict is, however, threefold, for there arises from it either an action on the *peculium*, or one based on the application of property to [the defendant's] concerns, or that based on authorisation. 2. The words of the edict are of this kind: "whatever transaction shall be gone through with him who is in the *potestas* of another." 3. It speaks of him, not of her, but an action is nevertheless given under this edict in respect of one who is of the female sex. 4. If a contract is made with a *filiusfamilias* or a slave, who is under the age of puberty, the action on the *peculium* is given against the father or master if the *peculium* of these persons has been enriched. 5. The word *potestas* is to be understood as applied in common both to the son and to the slave. 6. No greater attention is to be paid to the ownership of the slaves than to the fact of having them at disposal, for we may be sued on account not only of our own slaves, but also of common slaves, and indeed of those also who are, in good faith, in the relation of slaves to us, whether they be freemen or slaves of another person.

2 Pomponius (*on Sabinus* 5) The action limited to the *peculium* and the other "honorary" actions lie against the holder of usufruct or *usus* in a case in which the slaves held in usufruct or *usus* would ordinarily acquire [to the holder]: in other cases, against the owner.

3 ULPIANUS (*on the Edict* 29) Although the Prætor promises the action where[1] there has been a transaction with one who is in *potestas*, yet it must be understood that the action on the *peculium* is given though he is in the *potestas* of no one, for example, if a contract is made with a slave who forms part of an inheritance before the inheritance is entered on. 1. Hence Labeo says that if a slave is substituted in the second or third grade, and while the heirs in the first grade are deliberating, a contract is made with him, and he then, on their repudiating, becomes free and heir, it may be said that he is liable to be sued on the *peculium* and to the extent to which proceeds have been applied to his concerns (*de in rem verso*). 2. It is of little moment whether a slave belongs to a man or to a woman, for a woman also is liable to the action on the *peculium*. 3. Pedius says that even owners under puberty are liable on the *peculium*, for the contract is not made with the children themselves, that the sanction of a *tutor* should be looked for. The same writer adds that a ward cannot confer a *peculium* on a slave even with the sanction of a *tutor*. 4. We hold, further, that the action on the *peculium* should be given against the *curator* of a lunatic, for even the slave of such a person may have a *peculium*, not by reason of its having been granted to him that he should have it, but where there has been no prohibition of his having it. 5. The question has been discussed whether if a *filiusfamilias* or a slave becomes guarantor for anyone or accepts liability as surety in any other way, or gives a *mandatum* [for a loan of money], there is an action on the *peculium*. Here the better view is that in the case of the slave regard must be had to the reason for the guaranty or *mandatum*. And Celsus (b. 6) approves this opinion in the case of a slave guarantor. If therefore the slave undertakes the liability as a voluntary surety, not as doing a piece of business affecting the *peculium*, the master will not be liable on the *peculium*. 6. Julianus also writes (*Digest* b. 12) that if a slave gives a *mandatum* for a payment to my creditor it is a material point[2] what ground he had for giving the *mandatum*. If the *mandatum* was for payment to him, as a creditor of his own, the master has incurred liability on the *peculium*, but if he merely rendered a service as voluntary guarantor, the master does not incur the liability on the *peculium*. 7. With this agrees what the same Julianus says, that if I have taken a guarantor from my son, whatever I receive from the guarantor, I shall have to account for in an action on *mandatum*, not as for money applied to my concerns, but to the extent of the

[1] For *tamen* read *tum*. Cf. M. [2] Omit *ait*.

peculium. You may say the same in the case of a guarantor of a slave, and also if a third person makes a payment to me on behalf of my son who is indebted to me. He adds that if, however, my son was not indebted to me, the guarantor will be able to avail himself of an *exceptio doli,* and to bring a *condictio* if he has paid. 8. If a slave, while living as a free man, agrees to a reference to arbitration, the question is raised whether an action on the *peculium* should be given for the penalty agreed to be paid on disobedience to the award, the case being regarded as one of voluntary agency (*negotia gesta*), just as the action lies [for the penalty] in the case of maritime loan[1]. But to both Nerva *filius* and myself the better view appears to be that an action on the *peculium* ought not to be given on a reference by a slave, for neither is an action given against him (the master) if the slave is condemned in an action at law. 9. But if a son is accepted as a guarantor, or as any kind of surety, it is a question whether he binds the father to the extent of the *peculium.* The sound view is that of Sabinus and Cassius who hold that the father is always liable to the extent of the *peculium,* and that [a son] differs in this respect from a slave. 10. Accordingly the father will always be liable on a reference to arbitration. Papinian speaks in the same sense (*Questions* b. 9), and he says that it is immaterial on what matter the reference was agreed to, whether it was on one on which [the creditor] could have brought an action on the *peculium* against the father, or was, in fact, on one on which he could not have done so, since the father is sued on the stipulation. 11. The same authority says that the father is liable also to an action on a judgment to the extent of the *peculium,* and so Marcellus thinks, even under an action in respect of which the father could not have been liable to an action on the *peculium,* for, just as in a stipulation a contract is made with a *filiusfamilias,* so it is in an action at law. Thus not the origin of the action, but the actual liability on the judgment, is to be taken account of as the source of obligation: accordingly, he is of the same opinion where the son is condemned as voluntary defendant on behalf of another (*defensor*). 12. It is clear law that a *condictio* on the ground of theft lies against a *filiusfamilias.* There arises a question, however, whether the action on the *peculium* should be given against the father or the master: and the better view is, that the action on the *peculium* should be given to the extent to which the master has been enriched by the theft committed. Labeo approves this view, on the ground that it is

[1] Cf. D. 22. 2. 9.

most unjust that, by the slave's theft, the master should be enriched without incurring any liability. For the action on the *peculium* is also available in connexion with the action for things carried off, brought on account of a *filiafamilias*, to the extent of what has reached the father. 13. If a *filiusfamilias* who is a *duumvir* has not taken care that security is given [by a *tutor*] for the future safety of the ward's property, Papinianus says (*Questions* b. 9) that the action on the *peculium* is available. And I am of opinion that the question whether he became a *decurio* at the wish of his father changes nothing, for the father's obligation was to safeguard the public interests.

4 POMPONIUS (*on Sabinus* 7) Not that of which the slave keeps an account separately from his master forms part of the *peculium*, but that which the master has himself set apart, keeping his own account distinct from that of the slave. For since the master can take away the whole *peculium* of the slave or increase it or diminish it, what is to be considered is not what the slave, but what the master, has done with the view of creating a *peculium* for the slave. 1. This however I consider to be correct in the case in which the master wished to release the slave from a debt, so that if the master has remitted what the slave owed, by a mere expression of intent, the slave ceases to be a debtor, but if, on the other hand, the master makes statements of account so as to make himself out a debtor to the slave, when, in actual fact, he is not a debtor, I hold otherwise, for a *peculium* is to be increased not by mere words but by actual transactions. 2. From these rules it is apparent that not whatever a slave may hold without his master's knowledge is in the *peculium*, but whatever he holds with his consent, otherwise what a slave has stolen from his master will also be in the *peculium*, which is not the case. 3. But it often happens that a slave's *peculium* undergoes diminution without the master's knowledge, for instance when the slave does damage to the [property of] the master, or commits theft. 4. If you commit theft against me with the help of my slave, that must be deducted, from the *peculium*, by which what I can recover in respect of the stolen property falls short [of what is due]. 5. If the *peculium* is exhausted by debt due to the master, the assets nevertheless retain their character as *peculium*, for if the master should make a gift of the debt to the slave, or a third person should pay the master on behalf of the slave, the *peculium* is made up, and there is no need of a new grant by the master. 6. That is to be considered

in the *peculium* of underslaves of which they keep an account distinct not only[1] from the master, but also[2] from him in whose *peculium* they are.

5 ULPIANUS (*on the Edict* 29) The father or master is liable to be sued on account of a deposit only to the amount of the *peculium*, and so far as I may have been defrauded by any *dolus malus* on his part. 1. Further, if any property has been handed over to a *filiusfamilias* or slave on permissive occupancy (*precario*) the father or master is liable only to the extent of the *peculium*. 2. If a *filiusfamilias* has tendered an oath, and it has been sworn, an action on the *peculium* should be given, as if a contract had been made, but in the case of a slave the rule is different. 3. The *peculium* is so called as being a small sum of money or property (*pusilla pecunia vel patrimonium pusillum*). 4. Tubero however defines *peculium* thus, as Celsus reports (*Digest* b. 6): what the slave, by the master's permission, holds distinct from the master's accounts, that being deducted from it, if anything, which is due to the master.

6 CELSUS (*Digest* 6) According to Labeo the definition of *peculium* which Tubero expressed does not cover the *peculium* of underslaves, but this is incorrect, for by the very fact that a master has conferred a *peculium* on his slave, he must be understood to have authorised one for the underslave.

7 ULPIANUS (*on the Edict* 29) And Celsus also himself approves this opinion of Tubero. 1. And he adds that a ward or lunatic cannot, indeed, grant a *peculium* to a slave, but a *peculium* already created, that is before the lunacy supervened, or by the father of the ward, will not be taken away by these conditions. This opinion is sound and agrees with what Marcellus, commenting on Julianus, adds, "that it may happen that a slave has a *peculium* in respect of one of his masters, and not in respect of the other, for example if one of the masters is a lunatic or a ward, if (as, he says, some think) a slave cannot have a *peculium* except by the master's concession. But I think that, for him to have one, it is not essential that it be permitted by the master for the slave to have a *peculium*, but that it be not taken away." The case of free administration of the *peculium* is different, for this must be expressly granted. 2. Clearly, however, it is not necessary

[1] The words *non solum* appear to be misplaced. Cf. M.
[2] Omit *id cuius*. Cf. M.

for him to know all the individual things, but to have a more general knowledge, and Pomponius leans to this view. 3. A son, as well as a slave, under the age of puberty, can have a *peculium*, says Pedius (b. 25), since, he remarks, in this matter all depends on concession by the master. And thus if the son or slave becomes insane he will keep the *peculium*. 4. Things of all kinds may be in the *peculium*, both moveables and land: he may also have in his *peculium* underslaves and the *peculium* of underslaves, and, also, beyond this, claims against debtors. 5. Further, if anything should be due to the slave in an action of theft or in any other action, it will be reckoned in the *peculium*; also, as Labeo says, inheritance and legacy. 6. Moreover he will have in the *peculium* what his master owes him, if, let us suppose, he has spent money on the master's business and the master has been willing to remain a debtor to him, or if the master has sued a debtor of his. Thus, if, for instance, the master has recovered double damages for *evictio* under a purchase by the slave, this will be applied to the slave's *peculium*, unless, as it happened, the master had the intention not to allow it to be in the *peculium* of the slave. 7. So also if a fellow-slave owes him anything it will be in the *peculium*, if, in fact, he has a *peculium*, or comes to have one, as the case may be.

8 PAULUS (*on Sabinus* 4) Property of the master, as to which he has formed a wish that it shall be in the *peculium*, he has not then and there made *peculium*, but [only] if he has handed it over, or, as it was in the hands of the slave, has treated it as handed over: for the thing needs an actual transfer. But, on the other hand, so soon as he has formed a contrary desire, the *peculium* of the slave ceases to be *peculium*.

9 ULPIANUS (*on the Edict* 29) But if the master does damage to [property of] the slave this will not be credited to the *peculium*, any more than if he stole [from the slave]. 1. Certainly, if a fellow-slave has done damage, or stolen, this appears to be held to be in the *peculium*, and so says Pomponius (b. 11): for, again, if the master has recovered, or can recover anything from one who has stolen property from the *peculium*, this, says Neratius (*Responsa* b. 2), is to be credited to the *peculium*[1]. 2. The *peculium* is however to be estimated subject to a deduction of what is due to the master, for the master is considered to have stepped in first and proceeded against his slave. 3. To this limitation Servius added, further,

[1] Omit *ei*. M.

anything which may be due to those who are in his *potestas*, for no one doubts that this also is due to the master. 4. Moreover that also will be deducted which is due to those persons who are in the *tutela* or *cura* of the master or the father, or of whom he is managing the affairs, provided he is free from *dolus*, for, again, if he puts an end to, or lessens, the *peculium*, by *dolus*, he is liable. For if the master is held always to step in first and sue, why may he not be supposed to have proceeded against himself also in this case, in which he will be liable either in an action on *tutela*, or in one on voluntary agency (*negotia gesta*), or in an *actio utilis*? For, as Pedius accurately puts it, the reason why the *peculium* is less by what is due to the master or father is that it is not likely that the master would assent to the slave's having in the *peculium* what is due to him. Indeed since in other cases we hold one who is managing affairs for another or administering a *tutela*, to have recovered the money from himself, why should he not in this case, of *peculium* also, have exacted what ought to have been exacted? The view will therefore be maintainable that it is as if he had paid to himself, if anyone seeks to proceed on the *peculium*. 5. The slave's creditor who has become heir to his master also deducts from the *peculium* what is due to him, if he is sued, whether the slave has received a gift of liberty or not, and the same holds if the slave is given by way of unconditional legacy: for he will deduct what is due to him as if he had stepped in and proceeded against himself, though he at no time had the ownership of the man freed or left as an unconditional legacy. So says Julianus (b. 12). Of course if the slave has received a gift of liberty under a condition, Julianus says, less doubtfully, in the same passage, that the heir will deduct, for he has become the master. In support of his view Julianus also adduces the point, that if I become heir to one who, after the death of the slave or son, was liable to be sued within the year, on the *peculium*, I shall without doubt deduct what is due to me. 6. Whether he is in debt to the master on contract or for unpaid balances in account, the master will deduct. So too, if he is in debt to him on delict, for example, by reason of a theft which he has committed, there will equally be a deduction. But it is a debateable point whether [there will be deducted] the amount of the theft itself, that is, only the actual loss incurred by the master, or so much as he could have claimed if the slave of another person had committed the theft, that is, with the penalties for theft. But the view first expressed is the sounder, that only the amount of the theft itself may be deducted. 7. If the slave has wounded himself, [the master] ought not to deduct this damage, any more than if he killed himself or threw himself over a precipice, for even slaves are entitled to inflict personal injuries on themselves. But if the master has looked after the slave wounded by himself, I think he has become a debtor to the master in respect of the expenses, though, if he had attended to him in ill-health, he would have been rather looking after his own interests. 8. Also if the master has incurred an obligation on account of the slave or, having incurred an obligation, has satisfied it, this will be deducted from the *peculium*; so too, if money has been lent him with the master's sanction, for Julianus (*Digest* b. 12) lays it down that this should be deducted. But I consider that this is true only if what was received by him has not been applied to the purposes of the master or father, otherwise he will be bound to charge this against himself. Again, if he becomes guarantor for the slave, Julianus says (*Digest* b. 12) that this should be deducted. But Marcellus holds that, in both cases, if the master is not as yet out of pocket, it is better that the money should be paid to the creditor, on the terms that he gives security that he will refund, if the master, having been sued on account of the matter, pays something, than that there should be a deduction in the first instance, so that, preferably, the creditor should have the interest of the money in the meantime. If however the master, having been sued on the *peculium*, is condemned, it will be proper that there should be a deduction in a later action, for the master or father has become liable to an action on the judgment: for, again, if, not having suffered judgment, he had paid something to the creditor on account of the slave, he would deduct this also.

10 GAIUS (*on the provincial Edict* 9) If however the first action on the *peculium* is as yet in suspense, and judgment is given under the later action, no account of the first action ought to be taken in any way in the condemnation under the second, since, in the action on the *peculium*, the first comer has the better position; but he is held to be the first comer, not who first joined issue, but who first reached the stage of decision by the judge.

11 ULPIANUS (*on the Edict* 29) If a master, sued in a noxal action, has paid the damages, this must be deducted from the *peculium*, whereas if he has made noxal surrender nothing can be deducted. 1. Again, if the master has given a formal undertaking that he will pay something on behalf of the slave, it will be right that a deduction be made, just as if the slave had promised the

master to take over the obligation (*expromiserat*) of a debtor to him. It is the same also if he has taken over liability under a promise of payment to his master for his liberty, he having become a debtor to his master, but only if the action is brought after he is freed. 2. But if a slave has obtained payment from a debtor of the master, the question arises whether he has made himself a debtor to the master, and Julianus says (*Digest* b. 12) that the master will not be able to deduct, otherwise than if he has ratified the taking: the same things are to be said also in the case of a *filiusfamilias*. And I consider the view of Julianus to be correct; for we take into account natural debts in deduction from the *peculium*, and it is in accordance with nature that a son or slave should be free from liability, by reason of the fact that he has apparently exacted what was not due. 3. But it is a debateable point whether what the master has once deducted when he has been sued, he ought again to remove from the *peculium* if he is sued, or whether, in fact, a deduction having once been made, payment should be considered to have been made to him. Here Neratius and Nerva think, and Julianus also tells us (*Digest* b. 12), that if he actually took it away from the *peculium* it ought not to be deducted, but that if in fact he left the condition of the *peculium* unaffected he should deduct. 4. Then he says that if a slave had in the *peculium* an underslave worth 5, and owed the master 5, on account of which the master deducted the underslave, and, afterwards, the underslave having died, the slave acquires another of the same value, he does not cease to be a debtor to the master, as if the first underslave had died to the loss of the master, unless, as it might be, he died when [the master] had taken him away from the slave, and paid himself. 5. The same writer says, with truth, that if, when the underslave was worth 10, the master, sued on the *peculium*, paid 5 on account of the slave, because 5 were due to himself, and, thereafter the underslave died, the master will be able to deduct 10 as against another plaintiff on the *peculium*, because he had made the slave his debtor in respect also of the 5 he had paid for him. And this opinion is sound, unless he took the underslave from the slave in order to pay himself. 6. But what we have said, that what is due to him who is sued on the *peculium* ought to be deducted, is to be understood thus: provided he could not recover this in any other way. 7. Julianus goes on to say that if a vendor who has sold the slave, with the *peculium*, is sued on the *peculium*, he ought not to deduct what is due to him, for he could have deducted this from the balance sheet of the *peculium*, and can now bring a *condictio* for it as not having been due (for what is due to the master is not in the *peculium*)[1]. He can also, he says, bring an action on sale. This is to be approved, provided there was so much in the *peculium* when it was sold that the master could satisfy his claim; apart from this, if, later on, there was an addition to his claim, the condition of a debt which the master had not deducted[2] becoming satisfied, the contrary must be said. 8. The same writer says: if one has acquired a slave in respect of whom he had an action on the *peculium*, can he deduct what is due to him, since he has an action on the *peculium* against the vendor? And he rightly holds that he can: for so also any other person can choose whether he will proceed against the buyer or the seller: this man, therefore, chooses deduction instead of action. And I do not see what the creditors have to complain of, since they themselves can sue the vendor if they think that perhaps there is something in the *peculium*. 9. However not only what is due to him who is sued is to be deducted, but, indeed, anything which may be due to his partner, and so Julianus says (*Digest* b. 12), for by the same principle as that on which either may be sued for the whole debt, he is entitled to deduct what is due to the other. This opinion is the accepted one:

12 JULIANUS (*Digest* 12) for in this case action may be brought even against that owner in respect of whom there is no *peculium*.

13 ULPIANUS (*on the Edict* 29) But it is not correct in the case of buyer and seller, and in that of usufructuary and owner, and of others who are not partners, and of the owner and the *bona fide* buyer, for Julianus also says (b. 12) that neither of these can deduct what is due to the other.

14 JULIANUS (*Digest* b. 12) Again, where, by a will, it is directed that a slave shall be free at once, the action on the *peculium* should be brought against each of the heirs, and none of them will deduct more than is due to himself. 1. So, where the slave died during the master's life, and then the master, within the year, left several heirs, both the action on the *peculium* and the right of deduction are divided.

15 ULPIANUS (*on the Edict* 29) But if there are two *bona fide* possessors, it must still be said that neither will deduct more than is due to him, and the same is true if there are two usufructuaries,

[1] After *debetur* insert *potest*. Cf. M.

[2] For *distraxerat* read *detraxerat*. Cf. M.

since they have no partnership relation between them. The same rule will sometimes be laid down in the case of partners if, as it happens, they have separate *peculia* as between themselves, so that one cannot be sued in respect of the *peculium* of the other. Otherwise, if the *peculium* is common, they will be sued for the whole and, also, that will be deducted which is due to either of them.

16 JULIANUS (*Digest* 12) What case, then, is there in which the *peculium* of a common slave will belong to one alone of his masters? First, if one sells a half share in a slave and gives him no *peculium*: again, if one gives money or property of any kind to a common slave, with the intention to retain the ownership of the things, but to give the slave the administration of them. Marcellus adds the note: that also is a case, where one owner takes away the *peculium*, or where an owner has, in truth, certainly granted one, but the grant applies to debts due to the master.

17 ULPIANUS (*on the Edict* 29) If my ordinary slave has underslaves, can I deduct from the *peculium* of the ordinary slave what the underslaves owe me? And the first question is this: whether their *peculia* are reckoned in the *peculium* of the ordinary slave. Here Proculus and Atilicinus hold that just as these underslaves are in the *peculium*, so too are their *peculia*. And, in fact, what their master, that is the ordinary slave, owes me, can be deducted from their *peculium*, that however which the underslaves themselves owe, only from their own *peculium*. But, also, if they owe something, not to me but to the ordinary slave, it will be deducted from their *peculium* as being due to a fellow-slave. That however which the ordinary slave owes to them will not be deducted from the *peculium* of the ordinary slave, because their *peculium* is in his *peculium* (and Servius gave a *responsum* to this effect), but, as I think, their *peculium* will be increased, as in the case in which a master owes to his slave.

18 PAULUS (*Questions* 4) From which it follows that if his *peculium* is left to Stichus, and he sues under the will, he will not be compelled to give up what his underslave owes to the master, unless he, that is the underslave, has a *peculium*.

19 ULPIANUS (*on the Edict* 29) Hence the question arises whether, if an action on the *peculium* has been brought, in respect of the ordinary slave, action can still be brought in respect of the underslaves; and I think it cannot. But if an action has been brought on the *peculium* of the underslave, there may also be an

action on the *peculium* of the ordinary slave. 1. There may be, belonging to me, a *peculium* of a twofold legal nature: suppose there is a dotal slave: he may have a *peculium* which concerns me; he may also have one which concerns my wife. For what he has acquired in the husband's affairs or by his labour, this belongs to the husband, and accordingly if he has been appointed heir or a legacy has been given to him, in contemplation of the husband, Pomponius says that the latter is not under an obligation to hand this over. If, then, an action is brought against me on a contract which concerns me, can I deduct everything, whatever it may be, which is due to me, whether in an affair of mine or in one which concerns my wife? Or do we in fact distinguish the origins of the business, as referring to two *peculia*, in such a way that regard is had to the origin of the debt which is sued on, so that if the action is in fact brought on a contract which concerns the wife, I can deduct what is due from that *peculium*[1], if on a contract which concerns me I can deduct my own claim? And this question is more luminously treated in the case of a usufructuary, whether an action on the *peculium* can be brought against him only on that contract which[2] concerns him, or on any. Here Marcellus tells us that the usufructuary is also liable, and on any contract, for he who contracts contemplates the whole *peculium* of the slave as his property. Clearly, he says, this must be admitted, in any case, that, when the person whom the matter concerns has been first sued, the other, for whom there was no acquisition [under the contract], may be sued for the residue. And this is the more probable view and is approved by Papinianus. The same must be said in the case of two *bona fide* buyers. But in the case of the husband it is better to say, simply, that he is liable to the action on the *peculium*. But if the husband has paid something on account of a slave of this kind, can he deduct it as against the wife suing on account of *dos*? And he says that if what was paid to the creditor concerns the *peculium* of each kind, it ought to constitute a diminution of each, proportionately, and it can be gathered from this that if the contract refers to either one[3] of the *peculia*, there will be in the one case a deduction for the wife alone, in the other there will not, if the contract referred to that *peculium* which remained with the husband. 2. Sometimes an action on the *peculium* is given even to the usufructuary himself against the

[1] For *peculio* read *contractu* and for *contractu* read *peculio*. Cf. M.
[2] For *quod* read *qui*. Cf. M.
[3] For *alterum* read *alterutrum*. Cf. M.

master, for example, if he has a *peculium* in respect of the latter, but in respect of the former has either none or less than is due to the usufructuary. The same considerations may give a result in the contrary sense, although in the case of two owners the action on partnership or that for division of common property suffices:

20 PAULUS (*on the Edict* 30) for partners cannot bring the action on the *peculium* against each other.

21 ULPIANUS (*on the Edict* 29) The Prætor has also with excellent reason charged in the *peculium* whatever the master has done with *dolus malus* by which the *peculium* is lessened. But we must understand it to be *dolus malus* if he has taken away the *peculium* from him; and further, if he has allowed him to entangle the affairs of the *peculium* to the destruction of the creditors' interests, Mela writes that this is something done with *dolus malus*. So also if, when one has an idea that a third person is going to proceed against him [on the *peculium*], he hands the *peculium* over to someone else, he is not free from *dolus*. But if he pays a debt to a third person, I have no doubt about this, that he is not liable, for the payment is to a creditor, and it is lawful for a creditor to be active in recovering his own. 1. If the act is done with *dolus* of a *tutor*, or a *curator* of a lunatic, or a *procurator*, it is to be considered whether the ward or the lunatic or the employer can be sued on the *peculium*. Here I think that, if the tutor is solvent, the ward is liable to account for his *dolus*, especially if any proceeds have reached him, and so Pomponius tells us (*Letters* b. 8). The same must be said in the case of *curator* and *procurator*. 2. A buyer however will not be liable for the fraud of his vendor, nor will an heir or other successor, except so far as proceeds have reached him. But whether the act done with *dolus malus* is before joinder of issue or after, it comes within the official purview of the judge. 3. If the master or father declines the action on the *peculium* he is not to be listened to, but should be compelled to join issue, as in the case of any other personal action.

22 POMPONIUS (*on Sabinus* 7) If the master has given an undertaking as to apprehended damage (*damni infecti*) in respect of a house belonging to the *peculium*, account ought to be taken of this, and therefore security should be given by him who is suing on the *peculium*.

23 THE SAME (*on Sabinus* 9) The undertaking as to apprehended damage in respect of a house in the *peculium* must be

given in full, in the same way that a noxal action on account of an underslave must be submitted to in full, because the plaintiff, if the proper steps in defence are not taken, takes away the things, or possesses them, as a pledge.

24 ULPIANUS (*on Sabinus* 26) The *curator* of a lunatic can both give and deny the administration of the *peculium* to the slave, as well as to the son of the lunatic.

25 POMPONIUS (*on Sabinus* 23) Such clothing is included in the *peculium*, as the master has given with the intent that the slave is to have the use of it permanently and has handed over to him, on the terms that no other person is to use it, and that it may be kept by him with a view to that use. But clothing which the master has so given to the slave to use, not that he may always use it, but only for a certain purpose at stated times, for instance, when in attendance on him or waiting on him at table[1], this clothing does not form part of the *peculium*.

26 PAULUS (*on the Edict* 30) If the master has once, when sued on the *peculium*, made good what was due on this ground, that is, what he had done with *dolus*, he will not have to make anything good to others on the same facts. And, further, if the slave owes him as much as that by which he has, with *dolus*, diminished [the fund], he will not be liable to condemnation. It will follow from these propositions that also where the slave has been freed or alienated, he is liable on the ground of *dolus* too, within the year.

27 GAIUS (*on the provincial Edict* 9) The action on the *peculium* is given in respect both of female slaves and of *filiæ-familias*: especially is it available against such a person if she is a tailoress or weaver or carries on any common handicraft. Julianus says that the action on deposit, also, and on loan for use, should be given in respect of them, and that the tributorian action should be given if they have carried on business with merchandise of the *peculium* to the knowledge of the father or master. Much more undoubted also is it where there has been application to the concerns of the father or master, and where the contract was with his authorisation[2]. 1. It is settled law that the master's heir ought also to deduct such property of the inheritance as the slave, in respect of whom an action on the *peculium* is brought against him, had carried away, consumed or damaged, before the inheritance was entered on.

[1] Text corrupt. Cf. M. [2] For *est quod* read *exque*. Cf. M.

2. If a slave has been alienated, notwithstanding that the Prætor promises an action on the *peculium*, within one year, against the person who has alienated him, yet, nevertheless, an action is also given against the new master, and it is immaterial whether he has acquired another *peculium*, with him, or [the new owner] has granted to the same man that which he bought or received as a gift together with him. 3. The view has been generally accepted, and Julianus also approves it, that it is to be freely permitted to the creditors to sue heirs[1] singly for their proportions, or to proceed against any one for the whole. 4. But Julianus is of opinion that it is not to be allowed to the person who sold the slave to bring an action on the *peculium* against the buyer in respect of that which he had lent to the slave before the sale. 5. And, again, if I lend to a third person's slave, and buy him and then sell him, he holds, similarly, that no action should be given to me against the buyer. 6. He considers, however, that an action should be given to me against the vendor, but only within a year reckoned forward from the purchase, for what I lent while he was still the property of another person, with a deduction for what the slave has in the way of *peculium*, in relation to me. 7. But, just as Julianus thinks that when he has been alienated no action ought to be given to me against the buyer in respect of what I myself have lent to my slave, so also he denies that it should be permitted to me to proceed against the buyer in respect of what my own slave has lent to my own slave, if the one to whom the loan was made has been alienated. 8. If one has contracted with the slave of two or more persons, it should be permitted to him to sue for the whole debt any one of the owners he chooses, for it is unfair that he who contracted with one should be driven to a divided attack against several adversaries; and account should be taken, not merely of that *peculium* which the slave has in connexion with the one against whom action is brought, but also of that which he has in relation to the other. This, however, will not result in loss to the one who is condemned, since he himself can get back again from his partner or partners, by the action on partnership, or that for the division of common property, what he has paid above his proportion. Which view Julianus considers to hold good, provided there was also a *peculium* in respect of the other owner, for in that case each owner, in paying, may be regarded as freeing his partner from debt, but if there is no *peculium* in respect of the other owner, the contrary is the rule, for he is not considered to be freeing him from debt in any way.

[1] Read *heredibus singulis.*

28 JULIANUS (*Digest* 12) Accordingly if no one has become heir or Prætorian successor (*bonorum possessor*) to the partner, he against whom the action has been brought should be condemned to the extent of any *peculium* there is in respect of him and of so much as he is able to recover out of the estate [of the other partner].

29 GAIUS (*on the provincial Edict* 9) If a man has, by will, directed that a slave is to be free, having left as heirs those who have contracted with the slave, the co-heirs may even proceed against each other by the action on the *peculium*, for each is liable, at the suit of any other person, in respect of that *peculium* which has fallen to him. 1. Even though a master prohibits dealing with his slave an action on the *peculium* will lie against him.

30 ULPIANUS (*on the Edict* 29) It has been matter of dispute whether the action on the *peculium* lies even though there is nothing in the *peculium*, when the action is brought, provided only that there is at the time of judgment. Proculus and Pegasus say that it lies[1] nevertheless, for the obligation is rightly alleged, even though there is nothing in the *peculium*. The same has been laid down in respect of the action for production and the real action, and this opinion merits our approval. 1. If the action is brought against one who is part heir to the master or father, he is to be condemned to the extent of the *peculium* which falls to the heir who is sued. In the same way[2], the action for money applied to his concerns lies proportionately (unless he has applied something to the purposes of the heir himself), nor is the heir liable to be sued like one of common owners, but only for his share. 2. And, again[3], if the slave himself is made heir to a share, the action may be brought, in the same way, against him. 3. If however the son is appointed, even for a share, he will none the less be liable to an action for the whole. But if he wishes to acquire the proportionate obligation of his co-heir he is to be heard, for what if the property has been applied to the father's purposes? Why should the son not recover from his co-heir what is in the father's estate? So also if the *peculium* is rich. 4. He who has once brought the action on the *peculium* can sue again for the residue of the debt, when the *peculium* has been increased. 5. If a creditor has been defeated by the vendor by means of the *exceptio* based on the expiration of a year, relief should be given to him against the buyer, but if it is

[1] For *teneri* read *tenere*. Cf. M. [2] For *idem et* read *item de*. Cf. M.
[3] For *sed* read *sed et*. Cf. M.

by any other *exceptio,* he is to be relieved to this extent, that, deduction being made of the amount that he might have recovered from the vendor, he may recover the residue from the buyer. 6. In an allegation of *dolus* time is to be taken into account; for it may be that the Prætor will not allow the point of *dolus malus* to be taken after the limit of time for the action on *dolus,* since the action on *dolus* is itself not given after the established limit of time. 7. But in the case of the heir the clause as to *dolus* ought so to be framed as to extend[1] to what has reached him, not beyond this.

31 PAULUS (*on the Edict* 30) But if the heir himself has committed *dolus,* he makes it good in full.

32 ULPIANUS (*Disputations* 2) If one is sued, out of two or more heirs of a person who could have been sued within the year, the slave having been freed [*inter vivos*] or directed to be free [by will], or been alienated, or died, all the heirs will be released from liability, although he may not be condemned in a greater amount than[2] that of the *peculium* which he who is sued holds, and this Julianus so lays down. And it is the same also if the proceeds have been applied to the concerns of any one of them. Further if there are several usufructuaries, or *bona fide* possessors, one, being sued, releases the others, although he ought not to be condemned in a greater amount of *peculium* than he holds. But though this results from strict law, yet equity requires that an action should be given against those who are released by an accident of the law, so that recovery rather than the bringing of the action should free them; for he who contracts with the slave has in mind as his property, the whole of the *peculium* which exists anywhere. 1. But though in this action the previous one is restored, nevertheless account should be taken of both increase and decrease, and, therefore, whether there is now nothing in the *peculium* or something has been added to it, the present condition of the *peculium* is to be looked at. Consequently, in relation also to vendor and buyer, this appears to us to be the truer view, that we can recover from the buyer what has accrued to the *peculium,* and the claim from the buyer is not to be dated backwards, as in one and the same litigation, to the time at which the vendor was sued. 2. If the vendor of the slave has sold the slave with the *peculium,* and delivers the *peculium,* he will not be liable to action even within the year, for, as Neratius has said, this price of the slave is not *peculium.*

[1] For *fieri* read *finiri.* Cf. M. [2] After *maiorem* insert *quam.* M.

33 JAVOLENUS (*extracts from Cassius* 12) But if a person has sold a slave on the terms that he was to receive a price for the *peculium*, the *peculium* is looked on as being in the hands of him to whom the price of the *peculium* went,

34 POMPONIUS (*extracts from various passages* 12) not of him who holds the things in the *peculium*.

35 JAVOLENUS (*extracts from Cassius* 12) But where the *heres* has been directed to hand over the *peculium* on payment of a fixed sum, the *peculium* is not considered to be in the hands of the heir.

36 ULPIANUS (*Disputations* 2) It is a debateable point whether, in contracts resting on *bona fides*, the father or master should be liable on the *peculium* or for the full amount[1], just as it has been discussed in the action on *dos*, where a *dos* has been given to a son, whether the father is to be sued only to the extent of the *peculium*. However, I am of opinion that the action is available not only on the *peculium*, but also so far as, beyond this, the woman has been tricked and defrauded by the *dolus malus* of the father, for, if he holds the property and is not ready to give it up, it is fair that he should be condemned to the extent of its value. For Pomponius has said that what is expressly laid down in the case of a slave who has received a thing in pledge is to be held applicable also in the other *bonae fidei* actions. For, again, if a thing has been given in pledge to a slave the action is available not only on the *peculium* and for what has been applied to [the master's] concerns, but it has also this additional clause, "and so far as the plaintiff has been tricked and defrauded by *dolus malus* of the master." Now the master may be considered to be acting with *dolus* if he will not restore when he has the power of restoring.

37 JULIANUS (*Digest* 12) If a creditor of your son appoints you heir and you sell the inheritance, you will be liable on the *peculium* under the clause in the stipulation: "whatever amount of money shall come to you under the inheritance." 1. If you give your slave permission to buy an underslave for 8 *aurei*, he buys for 10 and writes you that he has bought for 8, and you authorise him to pay the 8 out of your money, and he pays 10, you will recover by real action only 2 *aurei* on account of this, but these will be made good to the vendor to the extent only of the *peculium* of the slave. 2. I sold to Sempronius a slave whom I owned in

[1] Omit the first *an*. M.

common with Titius: the question arose whether, if an action on the *peculium* is brought against Titius or Sempronius account ought to be taken of such *peculium* as is in my hands. I said that, if the action is brought against Sempronius, account ought in no case to be taken of the *peculium* which I hold, because he has no action against me by which he can recover what he has paid. Further, if action should be brought against Titius more than a year after I have sold, in the same way, the *peculium* which is with me is not to be reckoned, for an action on the *peculium* cannot now be brought against me. But if action should be brought within the year, then account must be taken of this *peculium* too, since the acceptance of the rule that where the man has been alienated, it is to be permitted to the creditor to sue both the seller and the buyer. 3. If an action on the *peculium* has been brought against one who has an usufruct in the slave, and the creditor has recovered less [than was due], it is not unfair that he should recover his own out of the whole of his *peculium*, whether it be in respect of the usufructuary or of the owner. It does not matter whether the slave has hired his own labour from the usufructuary or has borrowed money from him[1]. And thus it will be right to give him an action against the owner, that being deducted which the slave has by way of *peculium* in respect of the usufructuary.

38 AFRICANUS (*Questions* 8) I have deposited 10 with a *filiusfamilias* and I bring an action on deposit on the *peculium*. Although the son owes the father nothing and holds these 10, he held nevertheless that the father was none the more liable to be condemned, if there is no *peculium* beyond this, for this money, as it remains mine, does not form part of the *peculium*. He says, further, that if any other person whatsoever is suing on the *peculium*, there cannot be the least doubt that it is not to be reckoned. And thus I ought to bring an action for production, and, upon production, a *vindicatio*. 1. If his future wife has promised to a *filiusfamilias* a certain sum by way of *dos*, and, a divorce being effected, brings an action on the *dos* against the father, ought she to be released from the whole promise, or with a deduction of what the son owes the father? He answered that she was to be released from her whole promise, since even if an action was brought against her on the promise, she could certainly

[1] This sentence, which appears to refer to indebtedness to the usufructuary, seems quite irrelevant to the context. See however M.

defend herself by the *exceptio doli mali.* 2. Stichus has in his *peculium* Pamphilus who is worth 10, and this Pamphilus owes the master 5; if an action on the *peculium* is brought on account of Stichus, he held that the value of Pamphilus ought to be included, and, indeed, the whole value, with no deduction of what Pamphilus owes the master, for no one can be understood to be himself in his own *peculium*: thus in this case the master will suffer a loss, just as he would if he had lent to any other of his slaves who had no *peculium.* And he says that it will appear more clearly that this is so, if the case is put of the *peculium* being left to Stichus, who, if he sues under the will, is certainly not compellable to suffer a deduction for what his underslave owes, except out of the *peculium* of the latter; otherwise the result would follow, that if the underslave owes the master as much [as the *peculium*], the slave himself will be considered to have nothing in the *peculium,* which is plainly absurd. 3. I lent money to a slave whom I had sold to you: the question arose whether the action on the *peculium* against you should be given to me on the terms that there should be deducted whatever remained with me out of the *peculium.* But this is in fact not in the least true, and it will not be material whether I sue within a year from the time when I sold or afterwards, for, indeed, no action against me is given to other persons who contracted with him at that time. Moreover, on the other hand, if those who had previously contracted with this slave proceed against me, I may not deduct what he began to owe me after [the sale]. From which it is clear that the liability of that *peculium* which has remained with me should have no connexion with contracts of a later time.

39 FLORENTINUS (*Institutes* 11) The *peculium* consists also of what the man has put by through frugality, or what he has by some service earned as a gift to him, from any person, where that person's wish was that the slave should have this as his own, to be, as it were, his property.

40 MARCIANUS (*Rules* 5) The *peculium* comes into existence, grows, lessens and dies, and thus Papirius Fronto justly said that the *peculium* resembled a man. 1. It has been a topic of debate how a *peculium* comes into existence. And the ancient writers distinguish, in this way: if the slave has acquired what the master is not bound to provide, this is *peculium,* but if [he has acquired] tunics or anything of that sort which the master is bound to give him, this is not *peculium.* Thus, therefore, does the *peculium* come into

existence: it grows when it is added to, it lessens when underslaves die or things are destroyed: it dies when it is taken away.

41 ULPIANUS (*on Sabinus* 43) Neither can a slave owe anything, nor can anything be owed to a slave, but when we misapply this word we are rather pointing out a state of fact than connecting the obligation with the civil law. Accordingly the master will properly claim from third parties what is owed to a slave: as for what the slave himself owes, an action is given against the master in respect of that, on the *peculium*, and so far as anything from it has been applied to the master's concerns.

42 THE SAME (*on the Edict* 12) Some authorities rightly think that an action on the *peculium* should be given against an arrogator, though Sabinus and Cassius consider that an action on the *peculium* ought not to be given on account of earlier dealings.

43 PAULUS (*on the Edict* 30) If, after I have brought an action against you on the *peculium*, before the matter is adjudicated on, you have sold the slave, Labeo considers that you ought to be condemned in respect also of that *peculium* which he has acquired while with the buyer, and that no relief should be given to you, for it was the fault of yourself, who had sold the slave, that this came upon you.

44 ULPIANUS (*on the Edict* 63) If anyone has contracted with a *filiusfamilias* he has two debtors, the son for the whole debt, and the father to the extent of the *peculium*.

45 PAULUS (*on the Edict* 61) And therefore if the father has taken away the *peculium* from the son, the creditors can nevertheless proceed against the son.

46 THE SAME (*on the Edict* 60) One who grants administration of the *peculium* is understood to allow in general terms what he would be ready to allow specifically.

47 THE SAME (*on Plautius* 4) Whenever notice is written up in a shop to this effect: "I forbid business to be done with my slave Januarius," it is settled law that the master has secured only this, that he is free from liability to the institorian action, not also to that on the *peculium*. 1. Sabinus said, as a *responsum*, that where a slave had become a guarantor, the action on the *peculium* was not to be given against the master, unless the guaranty was given in the master's concerns or on a matter affecting the *peculium*. 2. If the action on the *peculium* has once been brought,

although when judgment is given there proves to be less in the *peculium* than he owes, yet it has been laid down that there is no ground for undertakings as to future additions to the *peculium*: for that this does exist in the action on partnership is due to the fact that the partner owes the whole amount. 3. If a creditor of the slave has recovered part from the buyer, Proculus says that a *iudicium utile* for the residue is available against the vendor, but that it is not to be permitted to the creditor to divide his action in the first instance, so as to proceed at the same time against the buyer and the vendor; for it is enough that this alone is granted to him, that, when, having chosen one defendant, he has recovered less [than was due], an action is given to him against the other, the previous action being rescinded. And this is the accepted law. 4. But not only any outside creditor can proceed against the vendor, in respect of previous dealings, but also the buyer himself, and this view approves itself to Julianus (although he himself can also deduct against another plaintiff), provided that he allows for what he has in his possession. 5. If a slave is sold with a reservation of the *peculium*, the outcome is that the vendor can avail himself of deduction [if the slave owed him anything before the sale][1], and that if the slave incurs any indebtedness to the vendor after the sale this does not diminish the *peculia*, because he does not owe it to his master. 6. The rules we have laid down as to the buyer and the seller are the same also if ownership is changed in any other way, as by legacy or by a gift of *dos*, for the *peculium* of a slave, wherever it may be, is looked on as resembling the property of a freeman.

48 THE SAME (*on Plautius* 17) The free administration of the *peculium* does not continue to exist in the case either of a *fugitivus* or of one who has been stolen, or of one as to whom one does not know whether he is alive or dead. 1. One to whom administration of his *peculium* has been given can agree with his creditor and a debtor of his own that the latter shall be accepted as a substituted debtor (*delegare debitorem*).

49 POMPONIUS (*on Quintus Mucius* 4) Not only that is *peculium* which the master has granted to the slave, but, in fact that also which has been acquired without his knowledge indeed, but which, nevertheless, if he had known of it, he would have allowed to be in the *peculium*. 1. If a slave, without my know-

[1] See M.

ledge, manages transactions of mine, he will be considered to be a debtor to me to the same extent as that to which he would have been liable if, as a freeman, he had administered my affairs. 2. For a slave to be regarded as a debtor to the master or the master to the slave, the matter must be looked at from the point of view of civil law: and therefore, if the master in his accounts has entered himself as a debtor to his slave, when, in absolute fact, neither had he borrowed money, nor had any other ground of liability previously existed, the mere entry does not make him a debtor.

50 PAPINIANUS (*Questions* 9) At a time when there is nothing in the *peculium*, the father goes into hiding: I, who am about to bring an action on the *peculium* against him, cannot be put into possession of his goods with a view to the protection of the estate, for he who would be entitled to absolution if he joined issue is not hiding with intent to defraud. Nor is it germane to the matter that it may happen that a condemnation follows, for also if money is due under a condition or at a future time, the debtor is not considered to be hiding with intent to defraud, although he may be condemned by a wrongful decision of the judge. But Julianus considers that a guarantor, given when there is nothing in the *peculium*, is liable, since a guarantor can be taken for a future right of action also, provided that he is expressly so taken. 1. If a creditor appoints as heir a father who was liable on the *peculium*, as the time of death is looked at for Falcidian purposes, the *peculium* at that date will be considered. 2. Even after the master has been sued on the *peculium*, a guarantor can be taken on behalf of the slave, and[1], for the same reason as that for which if a slave pays the money after issue has been joined in an action he cannot get it back any more than if issue had not been joined, a guarantor will be taken to have been validly accepted, because the natural obligation, which even a slave is understood to incur, has not been brought into issue. 3. A third person's slave, while he was acting as slave to me, with good faith[2] [on my part], gave to me, that I might free him, moneys borrowed from Titius, and I did manumit him: the creditor asked whom he should sue on the *peculium*. I said that although in other cases the creditor would have the choice, yet in that stated the owner was to be sued, and he would bring an action for production against me for the money, which had become vested in him and had not been alienated by reason of

[1] Omit *ideo*. M. [2] For *bonae fidei* read *bona fide*. Cf. M.

the transaction stated to have been gone through in relation to the civil status of the slave; nor was the distinction to be admitted of those who hold that, if I do not manumit, the money is the owner's, but that if a manumission does in fact follow, the money is considered to have been acquired for me, as in my affairs, for the money is given to me by reason of, rather than in, an affair of mine.

51 SCÆVOLA (*Questions* 2) In respect of what is owed to the slave by third persons the master is not as a matter of course to be adjudged liable, to a person suing on the *peculium*, to the full amount of the debt, since both the expenditure in recovering it and the result of execution of judgment may be uncertain, and account is to be taken of the delay of time allowed to those who have suffered judgment or that involved in sale of the goods, if that is the better course to take. Consequently, if he is prepared to assign his rights of action, he will be absolved. What is said[1] where action is brought against one of partners, namely, that the whole *peculium* is to be reckoned, as there is an action against the partner, will come to the same result in that case[2], if he is prepared to assign his rights of action: and in the case of all those whom we hold to be liable for this reason, that they have a right of action, the substitution (*delegatio*) has the force of lawful payment.

52 PAULUS (*Questions* 4) A question is asked on an actual case: a man who was administering a *tutela*, as a freeman, was adjudged a slave. If his master is sued on the *peculium* by the ward, whose claim has in fact been declared by rescript to be preferred to those of other creditors of the slave, is that which is due to the master deducted from the *peculium*, even here? And, if you think it can be deducted, does it matter whether he became a debtor to the master while he was still acting as a freeman, or afterwards? And is the action on the *peculium* available to the *impubes*? I answered that no privileged claim can have priority over the father or master when sued on the *peculium* in respect of the son or slave. Clearly in the case of other creditors account is to be taken of privileged claims, for what if a son has received a *dos*, or has administered a *tutela*? This has therefore been rightly laid down by rescript, in the case of a slave also who has acted as *tutor*, and since the position of the first claimant is ordinarily the better, action[3] on the part of others will be barred.

[1] Omit *enim*. M. [2] For *in eodem* read *in eo eodem*. Cf. M.
[3] Omit *quam*. M.

Certainly if he has made loans in the ward's business or has deposited moneys in a [banker's] chest, a real action is given to him (the ward) for the moneys and a *utilis actio* against the debtors, that is, if they have consumed the moneys; for he had no power to alienate them: and this is also to be laid down in the case of any *tutor*. Nor, however, do I think it material when he became indebted to the master, whether when he was in possession of liberty, or afterwards, for, so too, if I lend to the slave of Titius and come to be his master, I shall deduct what I have previously lent to him, if I am sued by the action on the *peculium*. How[1], then, does the matter stand? Since the action on the *peculium* is not available a *utilis actio* based on the action on *tutela* should be given against the master, so that what this man held as his property may be considered to be his *peculium*. 1. If a *dos* has been given to a *filiusfamilias*, or he has adminstered a *tutela*, account will have to be taken of the special priorities in the action on the *peculium*, a postponement being granted in the action of other creditors, or security taken if they who have no privilege sue first, that what they have received shall be refunded if action is afterwards brought against the father on the privileged claim.

53 THE SAME (*Questions* 11) If the *peculium* was not taken away from Stichus when he was freed, it is considered to have been granted: he cannot however sue debtors unless the rights of action have been transferred to him.

54 SCÆVOLA (*Responsa* 1) [A testator] gave to one amongst his heirs a *prælegatum* of lands as they were equipped, with the slaves: these slaves were debtors of the master. The question was asked, whether the action on the *peculium* is available to the other heirs against him. His *responsum* was that it was not available.

55 NERATIUS (*Responsa* 1) He whom I was suing on the *peculium* was forcibly carried off by you: what was in the *peculium* at the time when you forcibly carried him off is what must be taken into account.

56 PAULUS (*on Neratius* 2) What my slave has promised to me as a substituted debtor (*expromisit*) for a debtor to me should be deducted from the *peculium*, and is none the less due from the debtor. But let us consider whether the debt of him for whom

[1] Words appear to have been omitted here or earlier in the text, indicating that the owner has not granted a *peculium* to the slave in question.

the substituted promise was made should not be thought to become a claim of the *peculium*. Paulus: certainly if when any-one sues on the *peculium*, [the master] wishes to deduct this, he makes the claim part of the *peculium*.

57 TRYPHONINUS (*Disputations* 8) If a son or a slave, in respect of whom an action limited to the *peculium* has been brought, dies before the case is ended, that *peculium* will be taken into account which any one of them had when he died. 1. But Julianus writes that he who by his will directs that his slave is to be free, and leaves him the *peculium*, is understood to leave him the *peculium* as at the time at which the liberty attaches to him, and, therefore, all increases of the *peculium*, in whatever form, acquired before the inheritance is entered on, belong to the freedman. 2. But if one leaves the *peculium* of the slave to a third party, [he holds] that the question turns on a conjectural inference as to the wish of the testator, and that the more probable view is, that that is left which is in the *peculium* at the time of the death, in the sense that whatever accessions there are to things in the *peculium* before the inheritance is entered on, such as children of female slaves and young of stock, are due, but such things as are given to the slave, or as he acquires by his labour, do not belong to the legatee.

58 SCÆVOLA (*Digest* 5) [A testator] left to one amongst his heirs lands as they were equipped, with slaves and other things and whatever was there: these slaves were indebted to the master, as well in other matters as in respect of their periodical accounts. The question was asked whether the action on the *peculium* is available to the other heirs against him for the money owed by them. His *responsum* was that it was not available.

II.

WHEN THE ACTION ON THE *PECULIUM* IS LIMITED TO A YEAR.

1 ULPIANUS (*on the Edict* 29) The Prætor says: "After the death of him who was in the *potestas* of another, or after he has been emancipated, freed or alienated, I will give an action within one year from the time when action could first have been brought on the matter, to the extent of the *peculium* and so far as anything has been done by the *dolus malus* of him in whose *potestas* he

was[1] by which the *peculium* is lessened." 1. So long as the slave or son is in *potestas* the action on the *peculium* is without limit of time, but after his death, or after he has been emancipated, freed or alienated, it becomes limited in time, that is, to a year. 2. But the year will be reckoned so far as it is available (*utilis*), and therefore Julianus has said that if[2] the obligation is conditional, the year is to be reckoned[3], not from the time when he was emancipated, but from that at which, the condition being satisfied, action could be brought. 3. It is with reason that the Prætor has made the action temporary in this case, for since the *peculium* is extinguished by death or alienation, it sufficed that the obligation was prolonged to the extent of a year. 4. Alienation and manumission, however, apply to slaves, not to sons, but death applies to slaves as well as to sons, emancipation, indeed, only to a son. But, further, if he ceases to be in the *potestas* in some other way, without emancipation, the action will be limited to a year. Again, if the son becomes independent (*sui iuris*) by the death or deportation of the father, the heir of the father, or the *fiscus*, will be liable to the action on the *peculium* within the year. 5. In the case of alienation is certainly included a vendor, who is liable to an action on the *peculium* within the year: 6. but also if he has made a gift of the slave, or exchanged him, or given him as dowry, he is in the same position: 7. so too is the heir of one who has made a legacy of the slave, not with the *peculium*. For if he has either given him as a legacy or directed that he is to be free, with the *peculium*, this has been the subject of discussion: and it seems to me to be the truer view that the action on the *peculium* ought not to be given either against the freedman or against him to whom the *peculium* was left. Then, is the heir liable? And Cæcilius says he is liable, because the *peculium* is in the possession of him who has released himself from obligation by paying it over. But Pegasus holds that an undertaking should be given to the heir by him to whom the *peculium* has been left, because the creditors come to him: thus if he hands it over without an undertaking he will be liable to be sued. 8. Where the heir is directed to transfer the inheritance, the slave and *peculium* being retained, if he is sued on the *peculium*, he may not avail himself of the *exceptio* on the [*Senatusconsultum*] *Trebellianum*, as Marcellus, discussing the point, admits: but he to whom the inheritance is transferred is not liable, as Scævola says, since he has not the *peculium*, and has not done

[1] For *est* read *fuerit*. Cf. M. [2] Omit *et*. M. [3] Omit *ex eo*. M.

anything with *dolus* by which he is prevented from having it. 9. Pomponius (b. 61) has said that, also, if a usufruct has ceased, the action should be given against the usufructuary within the year. 10. In a book of Labeo's the question was discussed whether you should be allowed to sue again when the error was discovered, if, when the son was alive you, thinking him dead, sued by the action limited to a year and were defeated by the *exceptio*, because the year had elapsed. And he says it should be permitted to the extent of the *peculium*, but not also to what has been applied to [the defendant's] concerns, for, in the earlier proceeding the *actio de in rem verso* was rightly brought, since the *exceptio* based on the expiration of the year relates to the *peculium* and not to what has been applied to his concerns.

2 PAULUS (*on the Edict* 30) Since, after the death of the *filiusfamilias*, there is an action against the father, limited to a year, just as there was without any limit while the son was alive, therefore, if there was an action on the *peculium* in a case of *redhibitio*, it will be for six months after the death of the son, and the same is to be said in the case of all other actions subject to a limit of time. 1. If the slave to whom credit has been given is in the hands of the enemy, the action on the *peculium* against the master is not to be limited by the year, so long as it is possible for him to return, with *postliminium*.

3 POMPONIUS (*on Quintus Mucius* 4) The conception of *peculium* has sometimes to be employed also if the slave has ceased to exist, and the Prætor gives an action on the *peculium* within the year. For in that case too, both accession and diminution are to be admitted, as of a *peculium* (although by the death or manumission of the slave it has already ceased to be a *peculium*), so that there may be accession to it as to a *peculium*, by fruits or the young of stock, and by children of female slaves, and diminution, as where an animal has died, or has been lost in any other way.

III.

ON THE *ACTIO DE IN REM VERSO*.

1 ULPIANUS (*on the Edict* 29) If those who are in the *potestas* of another have nothing in the *peculium*, or have something, but not all that is due, those who hold them in *potestas* are liable if what was received has been applied to their concerns, the contract being considered to have been, as it were, made rather with them.

1. Nor does the action on application to his concerns (*actio de in rem verso*) appear to be promised without useful effect as that on the *peculium* would suffice, for Labeo very rightly says, that it may be the case that the property has been applied to [the master's] purposes and also the action on the *peculium* is not available. For what if the master has taken away the *peculium* without *dolus malus*? What if the *peculium* is determined by the death of the slave and the available year (*annus utilis*) is ended? For the *actio de in rem verso* is perpetual and is available whether he has taken away [the *peculium*] without *dolus malus*, or the action on the *peculium* is ended by the [lapse of a] year. 2. In the same way, if several are proceeding on the *peculium*, the facts ought to be to the advantage of him whose money has been applied to [the master's] concerns so that he should have the more productive action. Certainly, if someone has stepped in first and proceeded on the *peculium*, it must be considered whether the *actio de in rem verso* is barred. And Pomponius reports Julianus as holding that the *actio de in rem verso* is destroyed by the action on the *peculium* (because what has been applied to the master's concerns and paid on account of the slave has been embodied in the *peculium* just as if it had been paid to the slave himself by the master), but only in the case in which the master has paid over, under the action on the *peculium*, what the slave had applied to his concerns: otherwise, if he has not paid it over, the *actio de in rem verso* remains.

2 JAVOLENUS (*Extracts from Cassius* 12) The *actio de in rem verso* cannot be brought against one who has freed a slave for money received, because, owing to his giving the liberty, he is not enriched by the moneys.

3 ULPIANUS (*on the Edict* 29) However, if the slave gives to the master, that he may be freed, a sum of money that he has borrowed from me, this sum is not indeed to be reckoned in the *peculium*, but there is considered to have been applied to his concerns any sum by which what the slave paid exceeds the value of the slave. 1. There is considered to have been application to the concerns of the master, if the slave applies to the master's purposes the very thing which he has received (as where he has received wheat and has used it up as food for the master's slaves), or if he pays, to a creditor of the master, moneys he has received from a lender (and, also, if he made a mistake in paying, and thought a man to be a creditor who was not, Pomponius says (b. 61) that this amounts to application to the master's concerns, so far as the master has the right

to recover it as not being due), or when the slave has engaged in a transaction with the view of carrying on or administering any affair of the master's (if, for instance, he has borrowed money in order that he may buy grain to feed the slaves or in order to provide them with clothing), or when, having borrowed for the *peculium*, he afterwards applies [the money] to the master's uses: for the rule of law is that there may be an *actio de in rem verso* even though he applies it at first to the *peculium* and afterwards to his master's affairs. 2. And we lay it down generally that there is an *actio de in rem verso* in those cases in which a *procurator* would have an action on *mandatum*, or one who had attended to business without authority would have an action on *negotia gesta*, and wherever the slave has consumed anything in order to improve property of the master or to prevent its deterioration. 3. Thus, if a slave has procured money in order to supply himself with food and clothes, according to the practice of his master, that is, to the extent to which his master had been in the habit of providing for him, Labeo writes that he is considered to have applied it to his master's concerns. Therefore it will be the same also in the case of a son. 4. But if, having borrowed money, he has decorated his master's house with frescoes and various other things which contribute to luxury rather than utility, there is not considered to be [such] application, for a *procurator* could not have charged this, unless perhaps he had the *mandatum* or [express] wish of the master, nor ought the master to be burdened by reason of what he himself would not have done. What then is the result? The master ought to allow the creditor to take these things away, that is, without injury to the house, lest the owner be compelled to sell the house in order to make good the amount by which it has been increased in value. 5. The same Labeo says that if a slave, having borrowed moneys from me, lends them to another, the master is liable to the *actio de in rem verso*, since he has acquired an obligatory right: Pomponius approves this opinion, provided he did not make it a debt to the *peculium*, but dealt with it as on his master's account. 6. Labeo says that that also is applied to the master's concerns, which the slave, having borrowed money, buys for the master, with his assent, as a provision for luxury, such as unguents, or anything he may have procured for pleasures or discreditable outlay: for we do not enquire whether what was consumed went to the good of the master, but whether it was in the master's business. 7. Hence it is rightly said, also, that if a slave has acquired grain for feeding the master's slaves and has put it in the master's granary, and it has been destroyed or spoilt or burnt, it is considered to have been applied [to the master's concerns]. 8. And again, if he bought for his master a necessary slave, and he died, or put up supports to a block of buildings and it fell down, I should say that there was an *actio de in rem verso*. 9. But if he received it as intending to apply it to the master's concerns, but did not, and deceived the creditor, it is not considered [so] applied, nor is the master liable, lest the credulity of the creditor prejudice the master or the cunning of the slave injure him. What, however, if he was a slave who was in the habit of applying what he received [to the master's concerns]? Still I think this does not injure the master, if the slave received it with another intention, or if, having received it with this intention, he afterwards applied it in another way: the creditor ought, then, to take pains to see to what purpose it is applied. 10. If the slave has borrowed money to buy clothing, and the moneys are destroyed, which can bring the *actio de in rem verso*, the lender or the vendor? I think, however, that if the price has in fact been paid, the lender will have the *actio de in rem verso*, even where the clothing has been destroyed, but if the price was not paid, but the money was given for this purpose, that clothing should be bought, and the money is destroyed, but the clothing has been distributed to the slaves, the lender will certainly have the *actio de in rem verso*. But has not the vendor also [the action], since his goods have been applied to the master's affairs? Reason requires that he should be liable, from which it follows that the master becomes liable to two persons on one transaction. Thus, again, if both the money and the clothing have perished, it will have to be said that the master is liable to both, since both intended to apply [the subject-matter] to the master's concerns.

4 GAIUS (*on the provincial Edict* 9) But it should be laid down that the position of the first comer should be the better, for it is unfair that the master should be condemned to both on the ground of application to his affairs.

5 ULPIANUS (*on the Edict* 29) If the slave buys things not required by the master, as if they were necessary, such as slaves, Pomponius says there is an application to the master's concerns to the extent of the true value of the slaves, while, if he had bought things actually needed, the master would have been liable to the full amount at which they were sold. 1. The same writer says that whether the master ratifies the slave's contract or does not, the *actio de in rem verso* lies. 2. An *actio quod iussu* lies for what the

slave bought for the master if he bought it at the actual wish of the master, but if it was not at his wish, but the master in fact ratified it, or, apart from this, if he bought something necessary or advantageous to the master, there will be an *actio de in rem verso*; if, however, none of these was the case, there will be an action on the *peculium*. 3. It is held that not only that money is applied to the master's concerns which passes immediately from the lender to the master, but also that which was at first in the *peculium*: this, however, is true in all cases in which the slave, managing an affair of the master's, enriches him with money of the *peculium*. Otherwise, if the master takes away the *peculium* from the slave, or sells him with the *peculium*, or sells the things in the *peculium*, and receives the price, this is not regarded as applied in the master's concerns.

6 TRYPHONINUS (*Disputations* 1) For, if this were true, he would be liable to the *actio de in rem verso*, even before he sold the things in the *peculium*, because by the very fact that the slave had the things in the *peculium* he was enriched, which is obviously false.

7 ULPIANUS (*on the Edict* 29) And therefore, also, if the slave gives the master property of the *peculium*, the *actio de in rem verso* will not be available: and these propositions are correct. 1. Certainly, if the slave has borrowed money and pays it [to the master] with the intention of making a gift, where he does not wish to make him a debtor to the *peculium*, there is an *actio de in rem verso*. 2. That is not true which Mela says, that if you give silver to my slave, that he may make cups for you out of any silver he likes, and then, when the cups have been made, the slave dies, you have an *actio de in rem verso* against me, because I can bring a real action for the cups. 3. That is certainly true which Labeo says, that if the slave buys perfumes and unguents and devotes them to a funeral which concerned his master, there is considered to have been application to the master's concerns. 4. The same writer says that if I buy from your slave an inheritance which belonged to you, and I pay money to the creditors, and then you take this inheritance away from me, I shall recover it from you by an action on purchase, for there is considered to have been application to your concerns: for, again, if I buy an inheritance from a slave, with the view of setting off what was due to me from the same slave, though I have paid nothing, yet I shall recover by the action on purchase what has gone to the profit of the master. I, however, do not think that the

buyer has an *actio de in rem verso*, unless the slave acted with the intent of applying the proceeds to the master's concerns. 5. If a *filiusfamilias*, having borrowed money, gives it as dowry for his daughter, there is held to have been an application to [his] father's concerns to the extent to which the grandfather was going to give [dowry] for the granddaughter. This opinion appears to me to be true only if he gave the money with the idea of acting in his father's business.

8 PAULUS (*on the Edict* 30) And Pomponius says that it does not matter whether he gives it on behalf of his daughter or his sister or a granddaughter, issue of another son: We shall therefore say the same also if a slave has borrowed money, and given it by way of dowry, on account of his master's daughter.

9 JAVOLENUS (*Extracts from Cassius* 12) If indeed the father was not going to give a dowry, there is not considered to have been an application to the father's concerns.

10 ULPIANUS (*on the Edict* 29) If a son has become guarantor for the father and has paid the creditor, there is considered to have been application to the father's concerns, since he freed his father from obligation. 1. Similar to this is what Papinianus writes (*Questions* b. 9): if a son has undertaken litigation on behalf of his father as voluntary defendant (*defensor*), and has been condemned, the father is liable to the *actio de in rem verso*, for, indeed, the son has released him by undertaking the litigation. 2. Papinianus further deals with the case in which I have made a stipulation with the son for what the father owed, and then sued the son: for, here also, there will be an *actio de in rem verso*, unless the son, in binding himself, desired to make a gift to the father. 3. Accordingly it may be said, also, that if he undertakes litigation on the *peculium*, as voluntary defendant, on behalf of his father, the father will be liable to the *actio de in rem verso*, to the extent of the *peculium*, the advantage of which conclusion will be this, that if the action on the *peculium* is ended, he may be sued by the *actio de in rem verso*. I think that the father is liable to the *actio de in rem verso* even before condemnation, when issue has been joined in the action undertaken on the father's account. 4. But there is considered to be application to the father's concerns, so far as anything has been [so] applied, and therefore if part has been applied, the action will lie for that part. 5. But will the master be liable only for the principal, or also for interest? Here

if [the slave] promised interest, Marcellus says (*Digest* b. 5) that the master must make it good, but if it was not promised it will certainly not be due, because it was not included in the stipulation. Clearly, if I, having the master in mind, have given money to a slave who was not administering an affair of his master's, but being myself administering it, I shall be able to sue for interest too, by the action on voluntary agency (*negotia gesta*). 6. Applied [to the master's concerns] we must understand to mean, continuing to be [so] applied, and thus the *actio de in rem verso* lies only if the money has not been paid by the master to the slave or the son. If, however, it has been paid, to the destruction of the creditor's interests, that is, has been paid to the son or the slave who was likely to lose it, since[1] it has been paid, the application has ceased indeed, but it is most just that the action on *dolus malus* should be available against the father or master; for a debtor to the *peculium*, also, is not released if he pays to the slave, fraudulently, what he owed him. 7. If the slave is a debtor of the master, and, having borrowed from a third person, pays him, to the extent to which he is in debt to the master he is not applying it [to his concerns], but as to what is in excess, he is [so] applying it. Thus, if, when he owed the master 30, having borrowed 40, he paid it to his creditor, or expended it on the establishment, we shall have to say that the *actio de in rem verso* lies for 10, but[2] if he owes the same amount, then nothing is considered to have been [so] applied. For, as Pomponius says, the principle is that relief is given against profit to the master, and therefore, if he was a debtor to the master when he applied property to his concerns, it is considered that nothing has been applied; if, again, he became a debtor to the master afterwards, it ceases to be so applied, and the case will be the same, if [the master] pays it to him. He says, further, that if the master makes him a gift of an amount equal to what he paid the creditor for him, if this was by way of reward there is considered to have been no application to the master's concerns; if however he gave it to him in any other way, the application still exists. 8. The same writer discusses this point: if he applied 10 to his master's purposes, and afterwards borrowed the same sum from his master, and has a *peculium* of 10 besides this, we must consider, he says, has the application to the master's concerns ceased? Or are we, in truth, not to take away the *actio de in rem verso*, since there is *peculium* from which the debt can be taken? Or should we rather

[1] For *quamvis* read *quoniam*. Cf. M. [2] For *aut* read *at*. Cf. M.

deduct from each proportionately? I, however, think that the *actio de in rem verso* is destroyed, since he has become a debtor to the master. 9. The same writer also asks whether, if he has applied property to your concerns, and has become your debtor, and then your creditor, for the same amount as he owed you, the *actio de in rem verso* revives, or whether it cannot be rehabilitated through subsequent events. And this is the true view. 10. The same writer deals with the question whether a son can apply property to the father's concerns, according to the event, for instance, if the father and son are co-debtors, and the son, having borrowed money, pays it on his own account, or if you have lent money to the son with the authorisation of the father, and the son has paid you the debt. It appears to me that if the money had in fact come into the father's hands, there will be considered to have been application to his concerns: if, however, this was not so, and the son paid, as dealing with his own business, there is no *actio de in rem verso*.

11 PAULUS (*on the Edict* 30) What a slave has borrowed for this purpose, that he may pay it to his own creditor, will not be applied to the master's concerns, although the master is freed from an action on the *peculium*.

12 GAIUS (*on the provincial Edict* 9) If a *filiusfamilias* or slave buys land for the father or master, this is indeed considered to be application [to his concerns], but in the sense that, if it was worth less than what it was bought for, so much is considered to have been applied to [his] concerns as it is worth: if, however, it is worth more, only so much as it was bought for is considered to have been applied to [his] concerns.

13 ULPIANUS (*on the Edict* 29) If there has been application to the concerns of one of [two] masters, the question arises whether he alone, to whose concerns the thing was applied, can be sued, or also his partner. And Julianus says that he alone is to be sued to whose concerns it was applied, as in the case in which he alone authorised the contract: which opinion I think to be correct.

14 JULIANUS (*Digest* 11) Note by Marcellus: Sometimes, too, the *actio de in rem verso* may be brought against one co-owner, by reason of the fact that there has been application to the concerns of the other, and when he has been sued he can recover from his partner that in respect of which he has been condemned: for what shall we say if the *peculium* is taken away from the slave by

one owner? Paulus: accordingly this question is thus settled if there can be no action on the *peculium*.

15 ULPIANUS (*Disputations* 2) If a *filiusfamilias* has made a *constitutum* of what the father owed, it must be considered whether the *actio de in rem verso* ought to be given. He did not however release the father, for he who makes a *constitutum* binds himself indeed, but does not, in point of fact, free the father. Of course, if he pays after making the *constitutum*, though he may be considered to have paid on his own account, that is, by reason of his having made a *constitutum*, he will nevertheless be rightly said to have applied property to the father's concerns.

16 ALFENUS (*Digest* 2) A man let out a field, for cultivation, to his slave, and had given him oxen. As these oxen were unfit, he had given authority for these to be sold and others again provided with the money received: the slave had sold the oxen, had bought others, had not paid the moneys to the vendor, and had afterwards become insolvent. He who had sold the oxen claimed the money from the master, by an action on the *peculium* and for money applied to concerns of the master, as the oxen on account of which the money was claimed were in the master's hands. The *responsum* was, that there was not considered to be any *peculium*, except what might be left over after deduction of what the slave owed to the master, that it appeared to him that the oxen were indeed applied to the master's concerns, but that he had paid on that account what the first oxen had been sold for: to whatever extent the later oxen were worth more money, to this the master ought to be condemned.

17 AFRICANUS (*Questions* 8) A slave, having borrowed money for the master's purposes, lost it without negligence: the jurist held that notwithstanding this an *actio de in rem verso* could be brought against the master. For, so too, if my *procurator*, when about to expend money in my business, having borrowed money, lost it without negligence, he could properly proceed on account of it [against me], by the action on *mandatum* or that on *negotia gesta*. 1. I made a contract with Stichus, the underslave of your slave Pamphilus: the action on the *peculium* and for property applied to your concerns ought to be given in such a way as to cover whatever has been applied to your own affairs or to the *peculium* of Pamphilus, that is to say, even though the action is brought when Stichus has died or been alienated. If however I sue after the death of Pamphilus, the better view is that, though

Stichus is still alive, nevertheless, in respect of that which has been applied to the *peculium* of Pamphilus, the action ought not to be given except within one year from the time at which he died, for I may be considered to be then suing, in a sense, on the *peculium* of Pamphilus, as in the case in which I sue for what I lent with his authorisation. Nor ought the fact to affect us that Stichus, on whose *peculium* the action is brought, is alive, since this thing cannot be in his *peculium*, unless the *peculium* of Pamphilus still exists. The same principle will give the result, that we must say that what has been applied to the *peculium* of Pamphilus, must be made good, in the sense that a deduction is first made of what Pamphilus owes you, but what has been applied actually to your concerns will be made good even without any deduction for what Pamphilus owes you.

18 NERATIUS (*Membranes* 7) Although you have become guarantor for my slave in a matter which was undertaken with a view to application to my concerns[1] (for instance, if, where a slave had bought grain for the maintenance of the slaves, you gave a guaranty to the vendor of the grain), yet it is the more reasonable view that you may have an action on the *peculium* on that account, but not the *actio de in rem verso*, so that in any contract there shall be an *actio de in rem verso* only on the part of the one person who advanced the very thing which has been applied to the master's purposes.

19 PAULUS (*Questions* 4) A *filiusfamilias* bought a *toga*: afterwards, he having died, the father, in ignorance, and supposing it to be his own, applied it to the purposes of his funeral rites. Neratius says (*Responsa*) that this is considered to be application to the father's concerns, but that, in the action on the *peculium*, what is non-existent ought to be reckoned in one case, where this results from the *dolus malus* of the person against whom the action is brought. However, if the father was under an obligation to buy a *toga* for the son, it was applied to the father's concerns, not now, when it is used in the funeral, but then when he bought it (for the funeral of the son is a debt of the father, and Neratius, also, who thought the father liable to the *actio de in rem verso*, declared this transaction, that is the burial and funeral ceremonies of the son, to be a debt of the father, not of the son): he has therefore become a debtor to the *peculium*, though the thing does not exist, so that he can be sued

[1] For *versaretur* read *verteretur*. Cf. M.

on the *peculium*, in which action account is also taken of what has been applied to the master's concerns; which additional clause is however needed, when a year has elapsed since the death of the son.

20 SCÆVOLA (*Responsa* 1) A father promised a dowry for his daughter, and agreed that he would maintain the daughter: as the father did not make this good, the daughter borrowed money from her husband, and she died married. I gave the *responsum*: if what was lent was expended on things without which she could not take care of herself, or maintain the slaves of the father, an *actio utilis de in rem verso* ought to be given. 1. The slave of one who was absent on state service lent money to the slaves of a ward, the *tutor* endorsing the memorandum of stipulation, which stated the *tutor* as the contracting party: the question was asked whether an action was available against the ward. I gave the *responsum*: if, having been given for the purposes of the ward, it was applied to his purposes, although[1] for the better confirmation of the act of the slaves, the *tutor* promised, it may nevertheless be said that there will be an *actio de in rem verso* against the ward.

21 THE SAME (*Digest* 5) A man married a *filiafamilias*, the father promising a dowry, and it was agreed between all parties that either the father or she herself should bear the cost of her maintenance: the husband lent her money, reasonably thinking that the father would give an allowance equal to what he had arranged to give his daughter: she employed these moneys in necessary purposes for herself, and on the slaves she had with her, and (his domestic affairs being entrusted to her) she applied a certain amount of her husband's money to the same purposes: thereafter, before the father has paid all the allowance, the daughter dies; the father repudiates the expenditure: the husband keeps possession of the property of the wife. I ask whether the *actio de in rem verso* lies against the father. The *responsum* was: if what was lent was spent on things without which she could not take care of herself or maintain the slaves of the father, an *actio utilis de in rem verso* ought to be given.

[1] For *et* read *etsi*. M.

IV.

ON THE *ACTIO QUOD IUSSU.*

1 ULPIANUS (*on the Edict* 29) Upon authorisation by the master an action is very properly given against him in full, for, in a sense, the contract is made with him who authorises it. 1. Authorisation is however to be understood, whether one gives it with witness, or by letter, or by words, or by messenger, and whether it was specially for one contract or in general terms: and therefore also, if one has made a declaration, in such a form as this: "do what business you will with my slave Stichus at my risk," he is considered to have given sanction for everything, unless an express declaration prohibits something. 2. But I ask whether he can revoke this authorisation before the obligation is incurred, and I think he can, just as if he had given a *mandatum*, and afterwards, before the contract was made, had, changing his mind, revoked the *mandatum* and notified me. 3. So, too, if the father or master has given a *mandatum* he is considered to have authorised. 4. And, again, if the master has endorsed the slave's memorandum of agreement, he is liable to the *actio quod iussu.* 5. How then, if he becomes guarantor for the slave? Marcellus says that he is not liable to the *actio quod iussu*, for he intervened in the transaction as a third party; and he does not say this because the master is liable on the ground of guaranty, but because to authorise (*iubere*) is one thing, and to guarantee (*fideiubere*) is another: the same authority goes on to say that, even though his guaranty is invalid, yet he is not liable as having authorised, and this is the truer opinion. 6. If one has ratified what a slave of his or a son has done in the way of business, the *actio quod iussu* lies against him. 7. If a ward, who is owner, gives authorisation, he is certainly not liable unless he authorised with the sanction of the *tutor*. 8. If a contract with the slave is made with the authorisation of the usufructuary, or, again, with that of one to whom, in good faith, he is acting as slave, Marcellus thinks the *actio quod iussu* should be given against him, and I also approve this opinion. 9. If a contract with a slave is made with the authorisation of the *curator* of a minor, or of a lunatic, or of a spendthrift, Labeo thinks the *actio quod iussu* should be given against those whose slave he was: the same holds in the case of an actual *procurator*. But if he is not an actual *procurator*, the same Labeo says that an action should rather be given against him himself.

2 PAULUS (*on the Edict* 30) If a loan is made to the slave of a ward, with the authorisation of the *tutor*, I think that if the loan was to the advantage of the ward, an action should be given against the ward, "*quod iussit tutor*." 1. If a loan is made with the authorisation of the master of a female slave, or with that of the father of a girl, the *actio quod iussu* should be given against him. 2. If, with my authorisation, a contract is made with a third person's slave, and I afterwards buy him, I shall not be liable to the *actio quod iussu*, lest an action which was at the outset without effect, be validated by the course of circumstances.

3 ULPIANUS (*Responsa* 2) A master who has authorised the loan of money to his slave, at six per cent. interest, is liable to the extent to which he has authorised, and an obligation of pledge does not attach to those lands which a slave has bound without the consent of his master.

4 THE SAME (*on the Edict* 10) If a transaction is effected with the slave of a city, on the authorisation of the person appointed to the administration of the affairs of the city, Pomponius says that an *actio quod iussu* can be brought against him.

5 PAULUS (*on Plautius* 4) If a father, or master, being about to receive a loan of money, gives authorisation for it to be paid to a son or to a slave, there is no question but that the *condictio* can be brought against him himself: certainly in this case the *actio quod iussu* is not available. 1. If one of the masters of a slave authorised the making of a contract with him, he alone will be liable, but if two gave the authority, the action can be brought against either of them for the whole, because they are similar to two persons who have given a *mandatum*.

For EU product safety concerns, contact us at Calle de José Abascal, 56–1°,
28003 Madrid, Spain or eugpsr@cambridge.org.

www.ingramcontent.com/pod-product-compliance
Ingram Content Group UK Ltd.
Pitfield, Milton Keynes, MK11 3LW, UK
UKHW051448290926
15471UKWH00008B/1077

* 9 7 8 1 1 0 7 6 5 1 0 1 2 *